DAISY MARVEL JONES
Arizona State University

CURRICULUM TARGETS IN THE ELEMENTARY SCHOOL

PRENTICE-HALL, INC., Englewood Cliffs, New Jersey   07632

Library of Congress Cataloging in Publication Data

JONES, DAISY MARVEL (date)
   Curriculum targets in the elementary school.

   Includes bibliographies and index.
   1. Education, Elementary—Curricula.   I. Title.
LB1570.J63   372.1′9   76–26901
ISBN   0–13–196337–6

PRINTED IN THE UNITED STATES OF AMERICA

10 9 8 7 6 5 4 3 2 1

Prentice-Hall Curriculum and Teaching Series
Ronald T. Hyman, Editor

PRENTICE-HALL INTERNATIONAL, INC., *London*
PRENTICE-HALL OF AUSTRALIA PTY. LIMITED, *Sydney*
PRENTICE-HALL OF CANADA LTD., *Toronto*
PRENTICE-HALL OF INDIA PRIVATE LIMITED, *New Delhi*
PRENTICE-HALL OF JAPAN, INC., *Tokyo*
PRENTICE-HALL OF SOUTHEAST ASIA PTE. LTD., *Singapore*
WHITEHALL BOOKS LIMITED, *Wellington, New Zealand*

11-7-79 PP

CONTENTS

PREFACE

This book is designed to help you decide what to do about improving the curriculum and why. It suggests guidelines to effective action to meet situations, make decisions, and judge results in terms of the needs and abilities of the pupils. Thoughtful curriculum planning enables you to exert a direct and positive influence on what happens in the classroom. Theorists may produce outlines and office staff members may decree requirements, but only you can determine what experiences pupils will actually have as they pursue the *curriculum targets* under your guidance.

Part One is a guide to getting organized for teaching. It offers concrete suggestions on managing the classroom situation and working with others. It deals with scheduling, using materials, planning lessons, classroom management, discipline, and communication with others.

Part Two puts curriculum into action. It presents language as a learning tool, social studies as human behavior, science as a way of life, mathematics as a language as well as a tool, and the humanities as insight into human nature.

Part Three offers practical ways for judging the results, measuring attainments, keeping records, and reporting findings as a basis for planning next steps and showing evidences of accomplishment with the deviant child as well as the "average" child.

This book will help you see curriculum as more than a list in a notebook. It is made up of accounts of real and practical experiences that you will be able to apply each day with pupils. Here you will find concrete help in developing skills, imparting information, and creating attitudes.

Learning how to do things and mastering facts may produce scores on tests, but thinking and feeling add the human touch. You have it in your power to select the *targets* as you build curriculum with and for your students. You may help them master skills and lead them to gather information. You may influence what they think. What a responsibility! You need to establish specific objectives in order to achieve these vitally important goals. The suggestions in this book point the way.

Many of the ideas and examples presented in this book have been collected through actual experiences in the classroom with children, teaching preservice teachers, and helping in-service teachers. To acknowledge the contributions of a few individuals would be incomplete and unfair, and to name them all would be impossible. I do express my sincere appreciation for the ideas gathered from many different classrooms. They have had a part in forming the philosophy on which this message is based. No doubt many of my teacher acquaintances will recognize themselves in some of the examples.

Next I should like to express appreciation to the Arizona State University Photo Service for their help with the illustrations. Personal recognition is due David V. Poor, Supervisor of ASU Photo Service, and to Robert Drudge, the photographer. In addition I would like to recognize the administrators, teachers, and children in Skiff Elementary School, Wilson District in Phoenix, Arizona, and Lowell Elementary School in Mesa, Arizona.

Finally, I owe personal thanks to my husband, a former elementary principal, who not only supported my efforts while the writing was in progress, but also served as a helpful counselor and critic for both the content and the format of the manuscript.

DAISY MARVEL JONES
Arizona State University

part one

Setting Conditions for Learning

AN INTRODUCTION

Before you start out on a journey you should get ready. Even the shortest journey must start somewhere; and taking that first step calls for planning and organizing. If you enter the classroom on that first day with conditions set up to provide positive learning experiences for your pupils, you are making a good start for the day, the year, and your career.

Do you know where you are going and why? Have you already identified the *targets*? Are you aware of the influences that will be brought to bear on you and the school to alter curriculum content? You need to orient yourself in terms of the processes through which you are going as well as the product you are developing.

Do you know how to determine the goals? Subject matter, learning activities, and special problems all will have their influence on curriculum design. You will need to think about long-term goals in organizing your time, but eventually you will face the children and be forced to take into account what happens in the day-by-day program. This means you need a schedule. You need to know where your materials are and how to put your hands on what you need when you need it. You need a plan.

Planning is one of the most important parts of your work. When both you and your students know what you are going to do, why you are going to do it, and how, things run smoothly and goals are accomplished.

Managing the classroom means accepting, organizing, and working with the children. Signs along the way will tell you where the trouble spots are and how to proceed. There will be many issues to face. Being aware of the issues means that you can be prepared to meet them. If you do not know what to expect, you may find yourself constantly struggling with unanticipated problems. This is a negative approach. If you do know what to expect you will be able to meet daily occurrences positively and prevent many problems.

And remember, you are not acting alone. You will be working constantly with others. The children are only one part of your professional relations. You will work with their parents. You will have many contacts with other adults in the community. Some will be critical, and some will offer friendly help. Other members of the staff will contribute to your success, and you should never forget that you are also contributing to theirs. Administrators are there to assist you. Other teachers are your teammates. Still other people are working in the school to keep the records, maintain the physical plant, supply the materials, and help the children. Knowing who these people are and what they have to offer as well as how to use their services will add to your success in teaching.

It is the purpose of Part One to help you identify goals and get organized for teaching. This is basic to success in pursuing the targets in the various subject matter areas.

Learn.
    Think.
        Plan.
            Organize.
                Communicate.

IDENTIFYING THE TARGETS

Where Are You Going? And Why? And How?

Courtesy, Skiff School, Phoenix, Arizona

TARGETS

Whether you call them objectives, goals, aims, purposes, or *targets,* you are still talking about where you hope to go and what you hope to accomplish through teaching. Only when the learner learns has the teacher taught. To hit all around the target isn't good enough. You must learn to hit the bull's eye.

Then what are your TARGETS?

What do you want the learners to be able to do?

What do you want them to know?

How do you want them to feel?

Perhaps it might even be more appropriate to ask what the learners want to do, what they want to know, what goals or targets they see for themselves.

Are these the same as yours, and should they be?

If not, why not? And if so, why?

Who influences curriculum content? And why? And how?

What influences the goals? How and why?

Do you know what has happened in the past?

Are you ready to establish your own perspective?

Will you be concerned about the product, or the learning process, or both? And why?

Let's consider three facets of the curriculum one at a time—skills, knowledges, and attitudes.

Curriculum in the elementary school is one of those subjects that everybody has an opinion about. Most adults have attended school. Their experiences vary. They either liked school or they didn't like it. Few are indifferent. Consequently, they tend to have firm convictions about what schools ought to teach, what they ought to do, and what they ought to accomplish.

TARGETS

As teachers our responsibility to ourselves and to our pupils is to determine the targets. Unless we know where we are going, what we hope to accomplish, what factors we are allowing to influence us, and on what basis we are organizing our planning, we are likely to end up in the same situation as Alice in Wonderland, who, when she asked the way to go received the answer, "That depends on where you are going." When she replied that it didn't matter where she went the answer was, "Then it doesn't matter much which way you go." If our approach to curriculum content and organization is like Alice's approach to Wonderland, we may find ourselves confused about what to teach, what to do, and how to organize, not to mention unable to justify what we have done. Before we can make decisions about what, why, and how, we need to identify the targets, determine the factors influencing decisions, and establish a basis for organizing the content and the experiences we are planning for the learners. These include skills, knowledge, and attitudes. Each one has its place.

Skills

Learners learn how to do something. The target of someone who wants to become a swimmer is to learn how to swim, of someone who wants to become a typist to learn how to type, of someone who wants to become a reader to learn how to read, of someone who wants to become a speller to learn how to spell, and so on. Learning how to do something is one very legitimate objective of education. Some skills are physical and some are mental.

Physical Skills.   Some skills are performed by the physical body. They range from running, skipping, hopping, and jumping to more minute movements such as handwriting, typing, and even eye movements used in the reading process. Most of these skills can be learned, and many of them can be enhanced through planned teaching. It is the business of education to provide the know-how and to guide the learning. It is the business of curriculum to identify the appropriate skills and provide suitable experiences for learning and growth.

Mental Skills.   Skills that call for memory, reasoning, decision making, and application involve mental activity. These skills can be acquired and improved. Remembering events in history, characters in fiction, materials needed for an experiment, sequence of activities in a narrative, locations of geographical features, melodies in a song, principles of perspective, steps in a ballet dance, are all examples of mental skills that call for acquiring information, cataloging it for insight, and storing it for recall as needed. Deciding which elements are related as to cause and effect, major and subordinate, which are pertinent to an immediate problem, or are useful in planned activities—these are mental skills that call for reasoning. Activities which call for decision making go a step farther and include evaluation of alternatives, plans for action, and carrying out of plans. They also call for careful record keeping of accomplishments and willingness to abide by decisions, or alter plans as needed. Ultimately mental skills acquired through memory, reasoning, and decision making need to be reduced to generalizations and applied as principles to new situations. Remembering the relation of climate to crops and reasoning about the appropriateness of specific crops to specific regions lead to decision making about effective farming techniques. This kind of application of mental skills results in purposeful learning. The curriculum maker needs to provide the learner with these experiences.

Knowledge

Knowledge differs from skills in that skills involve knowing how to do something, whereas knowledge implies perceiving with the senses or the mind, that is, being aware that something is the case, being fixed in memory. Everybody seems to agree that children should learn something, but there is great lack of agreement about what should be learned. The secretary thinks students should all know the rules of spelling, grammar, punctuation, and syntax. The traveler thinks they should all know place geography. The politician thinks they should all know principles of government. The artist thinks they should all know line, color, and design. The musician thinks they should all know harmony. The mathematician thinks they should all know numerical relationships. While all these learnings and many others have considerable value, it is impractical if not impossible for any one learner to know everything.

The essential learnings are different for different people, depending on personal and professional plans. It involves perceptions or understandings gained through experience or study. It is influenced by instruction. Some information thus attained is worth knowing because of its high utility. Some of it is worth having because of its general interest. The question is, "How shall we determine what facts and what information will be learned by which children?"

Facts. Must every child learn that two plus two equals four, that Columbus discovered America in 1492, and that Albany is the capital of the state of New York? Must every child learn alphabetical sequence? To list all the facts available would be an endless task. To sort from that list those facts which are worth knowing would be not only endless but controversial. Given a list of 100 accepted facts, if ten persons were asked to identify the ten most important ones, there would be considerable disagreement. Is there a body of facts that all children should learn? Or should certain facts be prescribed for certain individuals depending on sex, nationality, or personal goals? And if so, who is going to determine what facts apply to which situations?

Information. Information might be defined as an accumulation of facts. Perhaps information can be distinguished from a mere listing of facts in that information involves seeing relationships among the facts and assembling them into a meaningful context. Persons who are informed have more than mere rote memory. They see how facts form a pattern and provide a basis for ideas and opinions. One of the targets of the curriculum is to develop well informed persons. But what shall they be informed about? History? Politics and government? Consumer economics? Industry? Grammar? Literature? Science?

Deciding what information to provide is not so simple as to take the opinion of an authority, write it into a book, and say to the child, "Learn it." While not all authorities will agree on what information is most relevant for the individual, it is even more significant that not all learners can agree on what information is relevant to their own goals and aspirations.

Attitudes

As children grow in awareness of self and the environment, perception of the significance of others also grows. The work of Combs (2:50–54) and Rogers (2:21–23) in the domain of self concept has revealed much about the significance of the children's feelings about themselves as persons of worth. The work of sociologists has revealed much about the learners' attitudes toward others and how they affect learning. The early work of Thorndike (26) and Dewey (8) has revealed much about motivation and how it affects learning. Attitudes toward self, toward others, and toward learning affect not only the curriculum but the targets set for curricular experiences in the classroom.

Attitudes Toward Self. Combs (7:15) has told us that children who see themselves as persons "who can't" and "who don't" cease to try and thus cease to learn. Those who see themselves as of little worth perform accordingly, accomplishing little or nothing. The learners who think of themselves as ones "who can't" see no point to trying. On the other hand, learners who see themselves as adequate personalities, and who see life in positive ways, tend to become responsible, effective persons, and to face new experiences with confidence. One of the major objectives of curriculum experiences must be to convince the learners that they have some ability, that "they can," and that "they must."

Attitudes Toward Others. If children see you, the teacher, as a threat to their personal security, they will avoid you. If they see you as a support for their growing experiences, they will respond positively to your help. If they see their peers as rivals and competitors, they will strive to win. And if competition results in failure, they will tend to quit. If competition results in success, they will tend to measure their own worth not in terms of accomplishments but in terms of "beating the other person." If they see law-enforcement officers as threats to their personal freedom, they will resist any help from them. If they see them as workers who make society safer, they will respond with cooperation. If they see their parents as suppressors of personal freedom, they will seek to escape. If they see them as supportive of growth and development, they will seek their advice and counsel. It is part of the goal of curriculum to guide and direct the learners' attitudes toward others.

Attitudes Toward Learning.   Learning is a challenge. Children are naturally curious about their environment. From the very day of birth they are exploring everything about them with all their senses. When these exploratory ventures result in satisfaction, they tend to expand. When they are curbed, the restrictions tend to inhibit learning. It is the goal of curriculum to help the learners expand their environment and their perception of learning. Perhaps the most valuable contribution the school can make to the pupils is to help them learn how to learn, and to direct them toward becoming lifetime learners.

INFLUENTIAL FACTORS

As new needs have developed, curriculum content has grown and expanded. When problems arise or knowledge expands, everybody—the layperson, the educator, the professional—turns to the schools to "do something about it." Curriculum content has been influenced by tradition, need, understanding of the nature of the learner, and the explosion of knowledge.

Suppose we had a bowl of marbles. Once the bowl is full, adding more marbles merely allows the excess to roll off the top. If a bit of pressure is applied, some of the marbles already in the bowl roll out to make room for the new ones being piled on. An alternative would be to provide a larger bowl.

The time factor might be compared to the size of the bowl. This could relate to the length of the school day, the length of the school year, or the numbers of years the learner spends in the school system. As we add new learnings and new experiences to the curriculum, something has to give. Either we let some of the old make way for the new, or we increase the time devoted to the learning. One possible alternative might be to provide for more efficient learning experiences in order to get more value from time expended. Some curriculum designers see still another alternative in the open school which permits more alternate choices on the part of the learner. It might give us more perspective to pause a moment to examine the answers to such questions as, "*Who* influences curriculum content?" and "*What* influences curriculum content?"

Who Influences Curriculum Content

Persons who influence what is taught and what experiences shall be provided as a basis for learning might be divided into three categories. There are those outside the school exerting pressures for change but doing nothing constructive to affect change, those outside the schools working as professionals but not in direct contact with the learners, and those within the schools who are making things happen.

Society Outside the School. The general public makes up society. Each person has a reason for wanting a say in what the schools teach and how they go about it. *Parents* are perhaps nearest to the school situation. Most of them view the school by comparison with what they remember from their own school days. Some want their nostalgic memories perpetuated. Others want unpleasant experiences eliminated. Most want their children to have a better education than they did. Their targets are indefinite. At one and the same time they resist eliminations in subject matter, encourage innovations, look with skepticism on experimentation, demand more learning, resist pressures, and want higher standards. *Lay persons* want a better society with less expense, view the unusual as typical, and express alarm at a situation which they have not actually experienced for many years. *Employers* make demands for spelling, English, mathematical proficiency, behavior, appearance, intelligence, and responsibility because they are helping pay the bill and are hiring the end products.

Professionals Outside the School. There are many professionals who are knowledgeable about school programs and curriculum practices but are not actually in the classroom where the teaching and learning are in progress. *Critics* are plentiful. We need to listen to them, but we also have a right to ask, "Have they done what they recommend? and can they do it? Are they willing to pay the price?" *Publishers* of instructional materials are sensitive to curriculum practices. Sometimes it is difficult to determine whether teachers teach what is published or publishers publish what is taught. Authors, editors, and sales people are conscientious about producing material that is educationally sound, research based, and useful, but their first aim is to produce products that will sell. When pressure groups make demands, publishers respond by adjusting their materials. *Designers* of instructional settings also influence activities in the schools. Architects plan buildings sometimes with, and often without, consultation with the users. Manufacturers of furniture and other equipment influence the instructional program. Sometimes it is hard to tell whether they manufacture what the schools want and need or whether schools buy what is available. It is our responsibility to influence production so that the setting will be conducive to the planned program.

Educators Within the School.   Instructional leaders, teachers, and pupils work in the school setting. The *leaders* include administrators, supervisors, curriculum specialists, research workers, and other non-teaching staff members. Theirs is an overall view. *Teachers* face the children daily and are probably the most influential members of the profession, for no matter what is in the texts, manuals, or guides, it is the teacher who determines what, if anything, happens. *Pupils* must not be forgotten because no matter what is presented it is still the learner who accepts or rejects what is being taught. Ragan (22:4) defines curriculum as "the sum total of the experiences of the child over which the school exerts any control." The implication is that it is the learners who must engage in the learning experiences. And unless they do so no learning is likely to take place. By passive resistance any child can reject the most carefully planned curriculum. By active participation any child can make any curriculum, even a mediocre one, a genuine learning situation. Perhaps it would be more accurate to extend Ragan's definition to include in curriculum the sum total of experiences which the child gleans through the influence of the school.

What Influences Curriculum Content

Persons involved in determining curriculum content find themselves influenced by external factors. Even when they have the best of intentions and the loftiest of ambitions, they often are deterred by tradition, immediate need, ability of the learner, or urgency of content.

Tradition.   In spite of research and innovation, tradition often exerts an undue influence on curriculum content and practice. Why do we teach American literature? We always have. Why do we ask children to learn the multiplication tables or to devote time to penmanship practice? These have long been considered necessary skills. We do not stop to reason that tables, computers, machines, and accountants have reduced the need. Tradition says that children should learn certain facts and skills at certain periods in their school life. Because it is traditional the writers of textbooks include these facts and skills on the theory that the books would not sell without them. The curriculum outlines continue to include such content because it is available in the adopted materials. The teachers continue to teach it because it is in the curriculum outlines and the texts. Anyone who varies from tradition is looked upon with skepticism if not with dismay. Seldom does anyone question the use of chalkboards, textbooks, individual seating, bells, clocks, written assignments, and tests. Even when a few are bold enough to question such things as workbooks, homework, letter grades, memory work, drill, and dozens of other well-rooted practices, they find themselves bearing the burden of the proof. Innovations do not come easily in the curriculum of the public schools. In spite of comments about change in the schools, there is good reason to believe that there is an element of truth in the saying that it takes at least fifty years for a new idea to permeate the schools. Perhaps we should add that it takes another fifty years for an outworn and useless idea to be weeded out of the schools.

Need. The need for a skill or for information frequently serves as a catalyst to introduce a new idea, new material, or new activities into the schools. Driver education is an example. Other examples at the elementary level might be typing, safety education, nutrition studies, foreign language in some sections of the country, and perhaps listening, or physical education and recreation. By the same token lack of need has led to the dropping of such studies as gardening, square root, surveying, and certain trade skills.

The Ability of the Learner. Mental capacity must be taken into consideration. No matter how much effort you put into instruction, how good the materials are, and how attractive the surroundings are, the learning is dependent on the ability of the learner to absorb what is being taught. Some striking examples would be teaching a child of three months to talk, a two-year-old to compute mathematical equations, or philosophy to a six-year-old. There is still a limit beyond which one cannot go, in spite of Bruner's (4:33) well-known and oft-quoted statement:

> We begin with the hypothesis that any subject can be taught effectively in some intellectually honest form to any child at any stage of development.

The child with limited experience is not in a position to make comparisons and form judgments. Some abilities are based on native capacity. Some are based on maturity that comes with living and experience. Some are based on varying interests and personality factors. Certainly the learner must possess the capacity and the concern for what is being taught if any degree of success is to be attained.

Content to be Taught. The nature of the subject matter is an influential factor in determining relation of content to curriculum. It influences both whether or not it is to be taught and where it is to be placed

in the scheme of things. Some learnings are more difficult or more complicated than others. There is more need for maturity, experiential background, or instruction to attain some learnings from others. Piaget's
(18:245–246) concept of the development of thinking in children indicates
appropriate ages for certain selected experiences. He identifies these stages
as sensorimotor, preconceptual, intuitive, concrete operations, and formal
operations. Ilg and Ames (15) emphasize the importance of developmental
age in the assessment of readiness. They serve as helpful guides in the
selection of content. Some learnings are built on logical or sequential
organization, with each step based on the one that has gone before. In this
case not only the placement, but also the sequence of curriculum content is
influenced by the nature of the subject matter. New knowledge is constantly
entering various fields. What to teach, and when to include it, as well as
whether or not to incorporate this new knowledge become issues.

BASIS FOR ORGANIZATION

Organized information and related experiences are more useful than
miscellaneous facts and isolated activities. One might have a wide variety
of interesting and stimulating activities without coordinating them into any
meaningful pattern. One might accumulate a vast storehouse of encyclopedic facts without seeing any relationship from one to the other. A
curriculum that drills for skills and feeds for facts may produce learners
who can perform on tests and produce scores. But we must question
whether the learning will function beyond the end of the term. If the goal
is only a high score, the so-called learnings soon may be forgotten. A
curriculum that organizes facts and coordinates learnings to develop
understandings and insights is producing learners who can meet situations,
set goals, make decisions, and become self-propelled.

The basis for organizing the curriculum varies with the goals. The
points of emphasis have varied with time and with perspective. Historically, the curriculum has been influenced by religion, nationalism,
industrialization, culture, and technology. At present, there is a struggle for
curricular influence based on the individual versus the welfare of the social
order. These areas of emphasis lead to the need for orientation in terms of
goals. Which is of more value: knowledge, skills, and attitudes accumulated,
or the processes through which the learner goes in learning how to learn?

Points of Emphasis

Organizing curriculum content for inclusion in outlines, teachers'
manuals, children's textbooks, lesson plans, and stated targets will be
influenced by the emphasis given to instructional goals. Emphases have

been influenced historically and tend to fluctuate with the point of view of curriculum specialists and teachers.

Historical Review   From the time of early discovery and exploration in our country down to the present day we can trace trends which have influenced content. Schools have always reflected the demands of the public. Perhaps it will be permissible to agree with Callahan (5:264) that the schools bow to the demands of society rather than set the pace for a new generation of society. He says:

> America needs to break with its traditional practice, strengthened so much in the age of efficiency, of asking how our schools can be operated most economically and begin asking instead what steps need to be taken to provide an excellent education for our children.

As situations change new demands create new emphases. Following the trends through the years shows a distinct parallel between the history of our country and the points of emphasis in our schools.

Religion was an early dominating factor. The first settlers who founded the colony at Plymouth had stated their objective as freedom of worship. Naturally they wanted to establish schools that would teach their children to read so they could read the Bible and learn to live a good life. The content of the curriculum as well as the nature of educational practices reflected religion, morality, fear of God, punishment for evil doing, and expectation of reward in heaven. Children were taught to accept the dictates of their elders, learn what was presented, obey the rules, and lead a pious life. This religious emphasis dominated the schools of early America for more than a hundred years while the settlers carved for themselves a home in the wilderness.

Nationalism became an influence as the country expanded and the need for unified efforts became evident. Once freedom of worship was established as a national principle, people could concentrate on other issues. As communities grew, a need for some form of self government developed. With expanded relationships between communities came a need for cooperative efforts to achieve the greatest good for all. As relations with other countries, particularly the "mother country," grew, a feeling of independence, self-reliance, and maturity sprang up. Then the citizenry saw a need for banding together for the common good. Thus grew a concern for national interests. People began to see an over-reaching need for leaders who could form governing bodies, engage in foreign relations, and bring unity and order to a growing nation. Then interests turned to government, politics, statesmanship, and also history and geography, as well as the practical studies such as mathematics, surveying, and exploration which went with expansion.

Historical trends place demands upon the schools. When schools respond by expanding and altering the curriculum to meet these new demands, they are recognizing the influence of historical trends.

Industrialization of the country was a natural outgrowth of expansion, increased population, and invention of machines. The mere presence of more people made division of labor a practical reality. Machines reduced the emphasis on hand work and the family unit was no longer an independent entity. Shared skills and divided responsibilities led to mechanization of labor and industrialization of business. No longer did young children learn their life's skills at the side of their parents. It became more profitable for each person to learn a trade, fit into an industrial operation, and specialize in a skill. At once the schools responded by expanding the curriculum to include such technical studies as industrial arts, agriculture, business, and trades. By this time the educated person was the one who was leading a free personal life, participating in self-government through the ballot, and preparing for an occupation which would lead to a productive and useful place in society. On leaving school the student could expect to become established in a business or growing trade and assume a place in the local community.

Culture is often thought of as a leisure time pursuit. When workers secured their place in society with paying occupations, they gained new freedom. With money earned from occupational pursuits, workers were able to purchase necessities and many of the luxuries unknown to their predecessors who had needed to expend all their energies just making enough to live. With the attainment of extra time and money, the citizens of our growing nation took a renewed interest in the humanities, literature, music, art, and personal development. Then they again turned to the schools and said, "We want more than religion, more than patriotism, more than economic efficiency for our children. We want them to lead a better life than we led. We are willing to pay the price. Teach them the finer things of life." As a result of these demands, the schools increased their emphasis on cultural subjects such as literature and the arts. Many citizens in the late nineteenth century found themselves financially able to give their sons an education in European schools and their daughters a cultural background in finishing schools. As a result there was a wide spread growth in secondary education and an extension of European influence in American education. The curriculum of the elementary school reflected these emphases by becoming preparatory for secondary education.

Technology removed much of the drudgery from daily living. Many of the manual skills once thought important began to vanish. No longer was it necessary to do such mundane chores as fashioning shingles by hand, molding candles at home, and even churning butter, weaving cloth, or chopping fuel wood. The curriculum changed to meet new demands.

Even the skills and knowledge once thought essential for the educated person changed. Computation in simple arithmetic as a skill seemed of less importance than it was before the day of the adding machine. With the growth of a well-traveled population, place geography seemed to need less emphasis. Sewing, cooking, and home canning gave way to home economics based on consumer buying and family management. The almost universal use of the typewriter altered the emphasis on penmanship, which was once considered a mark of culture. Radio and television influenced communication from the standpoint of method as well as content. Many of the things which were in the curriculum a generation or two earlier ceased to have value. And new ideas and values are being accepted daily.

Thus we see that history has worn a path which has determined curriculum emphasis through the years. Organization of content and experiences of the learners vary depending on whether the point of emphasis is religion, nationalism, industrialization, culture, or modern technology. What "used to be" will no longer do. What was "good enough for our ancestors" is not good enough for our descendents. This brings us to the point of viewing the curriculum from the present perspective.

Present Perspective. The point of view of the observer determines the perspective on the subject. Some scholars tend to see the individual as a part of the larger social order and personal development in terms of what it contributes to the greatest good for the greatest number. Others tend to see society as the setting in which the individual grows and develops, and the cultivation of a social order that provides for the greatest good for each individual within the total structure. The perspective determines the goals. The goals determine curriculum content and activity.

Social order as a basis for curriculum perspective would lead us to teach universal truths and world concepts. It would tend to teach the learners to view the world as a home for humanity and themselves as contributors to the greater good. Individuals would be seeking to make the world, the environment, the society of which they are a part a better place for themselves, their peers, and posterity. Citizens would be schooled to see the nation as of importance and the state as a part of the total political, economic, and cultural milieu of which they are a part. They would see local concerns as a part of universal goals and themselves as contributors to the ultimate truth and values.

Individual development as a basis for curriculum perspective would lead us to teach discovery of principles and the sacredness of the individual personality. It would teach the learners to view themselves as self-actualizing individuals in a setting designed to support and encourage personal development to the ultimate of one's potential. Attempts to improve the local community would center around providing a richer and fuller life for personal growth and development. Good people make good communities, good states, good nations, and a good world. By emphasizing development of individuals, such a curriculum would hope to plant the seed for a better world in the future. Each generation and each locale would have to arrive at its own definition of what is "good."

Perhaps no curriculum pattern is organized entirely around one or the other of these points of view, but educators must determine what they really believe and what their perspective really is, before they can determine the points of emphasis.

Orientation

All this brings us to the significant question about the targets toward which we are aiming in the development of curriculum for elementary school children. What do we really want? Where are we going? And why? And how? What do we really want the children to be able to do? What do we want them to know? What kinds of persons do we want them to become? And who is influencing these decisions? Is it society at large, professionals outside the school, or professionals on the firing line where things are happening? What is swaying the decisions? Tradition? Need? Abilities of the learners? Demands of content? And how is the curriculum being organized? Will we be more influenced by history or by present day perspective? Will we be guided by the product we are turning out as evidenced through measurable objectives, or by the process through which the learner passes in learning how to learn?

Product Orientation. A curriculum that is completely product oriented puts emphasis on facts and skills measured by uniform standards. Measurement is in terms of performance, correct answers, and established norms. The problem becomes one of determining what facts and what skills are worth learning. Concern is for what level of performance is acceptable and what answers are right. The establishment of standards against which to measure accomplishment is subject to debate, research, opinion, and pressure. Such a curriculum would give little or no attention to the values inherent in human development and how the learners feel about themselves, their society, or the content of their learning. It is doubtful if any curriculum is designed entirely on this premise but there are many curricular practices which strongly reflect this point of view. They can be identified by goals stated in terms of facts to be learned, skills to be mastered, and standards to be attained.

Process Orientation. A curriculum that is completely process oriented puts the emphasis on the activities and the experiences in which the learner engages in dealing with facts and establishing useful skills. It is evaluated in terms of affective principles. Measurement is in terms of personal values and growth. Answers are relative, and standards are flexible. The problem becomes one of determining what experiences and what activities are worth providing. Goals become enjoyment, self-satisfaction, and personal growth. Such a curriculum would give less attention to perfection of skills or mastery of subject matter. It is doubtful if any curriculum is designed entirely on this premise but there are curriculum practices which tend to strongly reflect this point of view. They can be identified by goals stated in terms of personal satisfaction, enjoyment, and self concept.

Perhaps a balance between the two types of orientation might be a reasonable goal. If one learns facts and learns to hate them, then the point has been lost. If one learns a skill but learns to dread the performance, then it ceases to have value. If one learns to love activity but does not become proficient enough in any activity to be successful, then perhaps it has reached the point of activity for activity's sake. If one makes a noble contribution to posterity but leads a miserable life doing so, perhaps altruism has gone too far. If one enjoys life to the utmost, but in doing so gains nothing from life but enjoyment and contributes nothing to the world, then perhaps that person has been merely a parasite for a period of time occupying space which is needed for more constructive purposes.

If, on the other hand, one learns facts because there is use for them and skills because they give satisfaction and value from the performance, the learner is getting both product and process in the curriculum. If one performs some activities with enough proficiency that there is success in the accomplishment, and if one gets personal satisfaction from altruistic acts, then the contributions may be as great as the personal benefits derived.

SUMMARY

A curriculum design that recognizes a balance between product and process involves certain principles. Learning implies learning something. Practicing suggests practicing something. Having experiences necessitates experiencing something. Reading requires reading something. Thinking demands thinking about something. Loving means loving something or someone. Learning does not take place in a vacuum. The product indicates the content of the curriculum. The process indicates the activities in the curriculum. The *target* is to provide each learner with meaningful experiences through which to learn something and activities which will influence the kind of person the growing child is becoming.

Learners should be able to do something, but it is not necessary that they all do the same things. Learners should know something, but it is not necessary that they all know the same things. Learners should become worthwhile persons in their own right, but it is not necessary that they all become miniature images of the same pattern.

Such an approach to curriculum recognizes the innate uniqueness of each individual. It recognizes different targets for different learners. It recognizes personal development within the bounds of social control. It presents the problem, not of determining the goal, but of recognizing different goals for different learners.

Therein lies the problem.

SUGGESTED ACTIVITIES

Select one or more of the following activities for individual or small committee development and report your findings.

1. Make up a list of ten facts which you believe every child should know upon leaving elementary school. Duplicate your list and ask ten people to check the five most important facts.
   Tabulate your responses.
   Summarize and report your findings.
   Do the same for ten skills and ten attitudes.

2. Examine a curriculum guide for a school system and identify the objectives stated. Classify them under the following categories:
   a. Product oriented
   b. Process oriented
   c. Both product and process oriented

3. Review the history of our nation and develop a chart showing the relation between historical and educational events and objectives. The following chart format will help you get organized:

APPROXIMATE DATES	HISTORICAL EVENTS	AIMS OF THE NATION	CURRICULUM OBJECTIVES	CURRICULUM CONTENT
1620–1775	Early settlement	Religious freedom	Ability to read the Bible	Readings Bibles Morals
etc.	etc.	etc.	etc.	etc.

4. Ask ten adults (not school people) what schools have done for them. Try to get positive reactions. Summarize your findings.

5. Consult ten adults (not school people) with the question:
   "What's wrong with our schools?"
   Summarize and report your findings.

6. Debate the issue:
   Resolved: In determining curriculum content the social order should be given preference over the welfare of the individual.
   Affirmative: Emphasis on society
   Negative: Emphasis on the individual

7. Make a list of things you learned in elementary school which have had little value to you and might as well be deleted from the curriculum. Justify your conclusions.

8. Make a list of things you have needed in life and which should have been included in the curriculum but which you did not learn at the time you were in elementary school. Justify your recommendations.

SELECTED READINGS

1. ALPREN, MORTON, "Sources of the Curriculum," in *Educational Leadership*, Vol. 28, No. 3, Dec. 1970, pp. 307–309. Reviews curriculum from 1930 to 1970. Discusses relevance, recent history, current concern for the humanities, and need for balance.

2. Association for Supervision and Curriculum Development, *Perceiving, Behaving, and Becoming: A New Focus for Education*, Yearbook, Washington D. C.: ASCD, 1962. Combs, Arthur W. "A Perceptual View of the Adequate Personality," Chap. 5, pp. 50–64. Rogers, Carl R. "Toward Becoming a Fully Functioning Person," Chap. 3, pp. 21–23.

3. Association for Supervision and Curriculum Development, NEA, *Perspectives on Curriculum Development 1776–1976*. 1976 Yearbook O. L. Davis, Jr. Chairperson and Editor, Washington D. C. 1976. Reviews 200 years of history of curriculum in the schools of America. Highlights outstanding individuals who have contributed to change and progress.

4. BRUNER, JEROME S. *The Process of Education*, New York: Random House, 1960 (A Vintage Book) pp. 97. A summary report of a conference held by 35 scientists, scholars, and educators at Woods Hole on Cape Cod in September 1959 to discuss improvement of education. Emphasizes the importance of structure of learning and the patterns of thinking.

5. CALLAHAN, RAYMOND E. *Education and the Cult of Efficiency*, Chicago: The University of Chicago Press, 1962, pp. 273. (paper) A study of the social forces that have shaped the administration of the public schools during the twentieth century.

6. CLEGG, AMBROSE A. Jr. "The Teacher As Manager of the Curriculum," in *Educational Leadership*, Vol. 30, No. 4, Jan. 1973, pp. 307–309. Sees curriculum as a system and the teacher as the manager. Identifies the role of the teacher as manipulator or designer. Points out the significance of the teacher in implementing a curriculum. Followed by six related articles.

7. COMBS, ARTHUR W. *The Professional Education of Teachers*, Boston: Allyn and Bacon, 1965, pp. 134 (paper). An attempt to take a new look at the need for providing preservice education that will change the perspective of the teachers.

8. DEWEY, JOHN, *Democracy and Education*, New York: Macmillan Co. 1961 (paper). Presents Dewey's philosophy as it relates to present day schools.

9. DOLL, RONALD C. *Curriculum Improvement; Decision-Making and Process*, Boston: Allyn and Bacon, 1970, pp. 440. Discusses bases for curriculum decisions, social forces, and the role of subject matter. Identifies the steps and the process in curriculum development and points out some recent promising strategies.

10. EASH, MAURICE J. "Aberrant Curriculum Designs," in *Educational Forum*, Vol. XXXV, No. 2, Jan. 1971, pp. 197–202. Identifies new forces shaping

curriculum design. Moving from rationalism to existentialism away from subject-centered to emphasis on personal search and relationship with others. Stresses human emotional needs.

11. Elementary English, "Opening Classrooms," in *Elementary English*, Vol. 50, No. 3, March 1973. pp. 351–416. A series of twelve articles focusing on the theme of the *open classroom*.

12. ELKIND, DAVID, "What Does Piaget Say to the Teacher?" in *Today's Education*, Vol. 61, No. 8, Nov. 1972, pp. 47–48. Summarizes three aspects of Piaget's procedures that have implications for teaching. Relates his theories to curriculum.

13. GOODLAD, JOHN I., "The Child and His School in Transition," in *The National Elementary Principal*, Vol. LII, No. 1, Jan. 1973, pp. 28–34. Hypothesizes on the kind of schools we need in the future. Recommends phases, not grade levels, and individual fulfillment rather than conformity to established standards.

14. HYMAN, R. T. (Ed.), *Approaches in Curriculum*, Englewood Cliffs, N.J.: Prentice-Hall, Inc., 1973. A collection of eleven different ways to focus curriculum as written by the various advocates.

15. ILG, FRANCES, and LOUISE B. AMES, *School Readiness*, New York: Harper & Row, 1964. Stresses the importance of readiness and identifies characteristics that indicate readiness for school related tasks.

16. JARVIS, OSCAR T. and MARION J. RICE, *An Introduction to Teaching in the Elementary School*, Dubuque, Iowa: Wm. C. Brown, 1972, pp. 545. Discusses planning and curriculum development. See Chap. 3, "Setting Curriculum Objectives."

17. MUESSIG, RAYMOND H. and JOHN J. COGAN, "To Humanize Schooling," in *Educational Leadership*, Vol. 30, No. 1, Oct. 1972, pp. 34–36. A plea is made for seeing schooling as a human relations experience as opposed to a mechanical impersonal setting in which mastery of facts and skills are stressed.

18. National Society for the Study of Education, *Theories of Learning and Instruction*, Sixty-third Yearbook, Part I, Chicago: University of Chicago Press, 1964. Identifies theories, explains their origins, and points out their applications to teaching goals.

19. NICHOLS, EUGENE D., "Are Behavioral Objectives the Answer?" in *The Arithmetic Teacher*, Vol. XIX, Oct. 1972, pp. 419, 474–476. Makes an eleven-point case against behavioral objectives as a basis for evaluating results in arithmetic.

20. OJEMANN, RALPH H. "Education for Change," in *Educational Forum*, Vol. XXXIV, No. 4, May 1970, pp. 447–456. Identifies types of change to expect. Suggests how to educate for change in the future.

21. PARKER, CECIL and LOUIS J. RUBIN, *Process as Content: Curriculum Design and the Application of Knowledge*, Chicago: Rand McNally, 1966, pp. 66. Settles the controversy over process versus content by suggesting that process *is* content in the curriculum.

22. RAGAN, WILLIAM B., *Modern Elementary Curriculum*, New York: Holt, Rinehart and Winston, 1966, pp. 544. Deals with all the areas of the curriculum plus the problems of classroom organization and control.

23. SHANE, JUNE GRANT, and HAROLD G. SHANE, "Ralph Tyler Discusses Behavioral Objectives," (An Interview) in *Today's Education* Vol. 62, No. 6, Sept–Oct. 1973, pp. 41–46. A question and answer account of an interview between the authors and the educator on the subject of behavioral objectives. Points out the importance of concern with specific behavior and human capabilities.

24. TALMAGE, HARRIET, "The Textbook as Arbiter of Curriculum and Instruction," in *The Elementary School Journal*, Vol. LXXIII, Oct. 1972, pp. 20–25. Raises the question of the dependence of education and curriculum content on the quality of available instructional materials.

25. TANNER, DANIEL and LAUREL N. TANNER, *Curriculum Development: Theory Into Practice*, New York: Macmillan Publishing Co., Inc. 1975. Gives historical background and perspective on curriculum development in America.

26. THORNDIKE, EDWARD L., *Educational Psychology*, New York: Lemcke and Buechner, 1903, Chap. 1. A classic in the field. Some of the principles emphasized more than seventy years ago are still pertinent.

2

GETTING ORGANIZED FOR TEACHING

Gaining Perspective on the Task Ahead

Courtesy, John G. Pitkin

ORGANIZATION

It is the first day of school. The whole year is ahead of you. Do you know what to expect? Have you planned for your goals? Your time? Your materials? Preliminary planning makes for self-assurance.

On what will you base your goals? Books and curriculum outlines? Children and their backgrounds as revealed by records? Activities and experiences? Skills and facts? Or will you think about what you are going to do to help the children develop wholesome personalities and successful lives?

How will you plan your time? What is important? What comes first? How much time will you devote to each activity? How will you plan your daily schedule? Must you account for each minute? How much freedom and flexibility can you permit and still meet your obligations to the school, the curriculum, and the children?

Everything may look neat and orderly as you stand in the doorway surveying the setting. Or perhaps supplies have just been delivered and await your efforts to organize them. Where will you keep materials so they will be available for use as needed? Will you give children access to them? What will you do about materials that must be shared among the children or perhaps with other classes?

Getting organized makes for efficiency.
Do you know how to organize your goals?
Do you know how to organize your time?
Do you know how to organize your materials?

The efficiency expert performs time-motion studies, identifies the minimum of materials and activities needed and the sequence of movements, and then comes up with a formula for accomplishing the greatest amount of production in relation to effort and time expended. In industry that is considered good business. Even though working with human beings in a learning situation cannot be rigidly controlled, there is, nevertheless, a parallel. Teachers who scatter their energies as well as their materials and wait for something to turn up are not making as efficient use of their time as those who have goals, a workable schedule, and the materials at hand. Therefore, we should give some thought to getting ourselves organized for teaching. With more and more demands being made on our time, we need to plan carefully or we may find the day gone with little or nothing to show for it. Let's consider the organization of goals, time, and materials.

ORGANIZING YOUR GOALS

In the preceding chapter we discussed at length the *targets*, or goals, of the elementary curriculum. We identified them as skills, knowledge, and attitudes. We looked at both historical and present-day emphasis in terms of the good of society versus the development of the individual. We viewed the objectives in terms of product and process. We identified the factors influencing the content of the curriculum and concluded that even though influences outside the classroom are evident, the real determiners are the teacher and the pupils working together in the classroom. We concluded that the organization of the curriculum is a decision the teacher makes while working with the pupils. Organization depends on the philosophy the teacher accepts and the objectives to be established.

Goals Based on Curriculum Design

Manning (9:20–28) identifies three basic curriculum designs: subject designs, activity designs, and core designs. Each of these is based on a different set of beliefs and results in a different organization of curriculum content and activities. There may be some overlap from one to the other but basically you, as a teacher, will have to identify yourself with one of them.

Subject Design.   If you see subject matter as the basis for curriculum, you will begin with the textbook. If you organize curriculum in this manner, you will outline the areas to be covered and expect each child to conform. You will see subject matter in terms of segments to be covered which are organized around the disciplines such as history, mathematics, or geography. You will plan logical organization of content and assume the responsibility for presenting it to the children for mastery. Uniform textbooks in the hands of every child will tend to become the chief source of information, and verbal interchange through questions and answers will be the main activity. Results will be measured in terms of skills mastered, information memorized, and marks earned.

Activity Design.   When you see the child as the basis for curriculum design, you will organize curriculum in terms of interests expressed by the children themselves. Not only will children indicate interests which will become the content of the curriculum, but they will participate in planning sequences and activities. You will become guide and leader rather than instigator. You will be alert for expressions of concern by the children and will capitalize on their immediate interests. Your main concern will be the development of the child, and you will see subject matter as the vehicle through which curricular experiences are developed. You will provide the children with many concrete learnings and encourage individual initiative and creativity. There will be many occasions for problem solving and much variety not only in activities but in subject matter. Achievement will be noted not so much in coverage of subject matter and mastery of facts and skills but rather in the child's development.

Core Design.　When you see life's problem as the basis for curriculum design, you will begin with the issues, and the work will be organized around special social situations. Many of the topics covered will involve real-life situations such as how people make a living, how we use transportation to get the things we need, why our country needs to practice conservation, and how people are interdependent in present-day society. Again the activities will involve problem solving and teacher-pupil planning. Real problems will be the controlling element in the organization of curricular experiences. Both subject matter and pupil activity will be in evidence, but the real crux of curricular organization will be the need for solving life-like or even real-life problems.

Before you can organize your thinking in terms of curriculum to be covered, you must decide which of these designs you wish to follow. This will make the difference among whether you list facts to be learned, activities to be scheduled, or problems to be solved. Quite naturally, this organization leads to the next step which is stating the goals in terms of either product or process.

Goals Based on Objectives

In identifying objectives as the basis for organization in Chap. 1, we recognized product orientation and process orientation. We pointed out that either extreme is probably not implemented in most schools and that absolutes are unrealistic. A balance between the two might be a more realistic goal. The problem is how to organize curriculum targets to obtain that balance.

Product Orientation.　Acceptance of the goals and responsibility of education by the learners is shown by accumulating knowledge and mastering skills because they have been found to be useful and interesting. But the children may still be directing their energies toward the product. If this is the case, they see the outcome of learning as better scores on tests and rewards for accomplishments. They count right answers and time performance. They want to know, "What did I get?" To them, education is something that can be quantified and they think in terms of getting it done. If you stress answers and marks and attempt to adhere to standards, you are supporting a product oriented point of view.

Process Orientation.　Pupils who not only learn something but learn how to learn are on the way to self-direction. The ones who also learn to select what is of value are learning how to make judgments. They become self-propelled learners for life. In that case, they ask themselves "Can I do it?" "How can I verify my answer?" "Have I practiced enough to be proficient?" "Do I have enough evidence to support my point?" "Have I covered the topic adequately?" To them, education is something that can be used and they think in terms of continued application. If you stress alternate considerations, evidences of quality, and ability to meet issues and solve problems, you are supporting this point of view. You are helping the children to prepare for learning beyond their school years. They may not know what information and what skills will be needed in twenty years from now, but you can help students prepare to meet new situations independently. When new problems arise, they will be able to identify the information and skills they need and will know how to attain them.

Goodlad (4:1) points out that:

> We cannot predict what society will be like, but only that a dynamic, self-renewing society will require self-renewing individuals.

Frost (2:208) suggests that:

> The current issue about programmed instruction versus teacher instruction relates to the "child centered" versus subject-centered approach.

Furthermore, Frost (2:213) shows the need for a freeing kind of education when he quotes Earl Kelley as saying:

> The person who learns to accept change and looks forward to it has the only security available to humans.

These points of view support the thesis that teaching the child to think, to be a self-propelled learner, and to carry education beyond the classroom and beyond school years is the real goal. What is learned may not be so significant as the fact that the child learns how to learn and to want to learn.

ORGANIZING YOUR TIME

Organizing time calls for a long term view of how the time will be used during the forthcoming semester, school year, or perhaps a period of years. It also calls for a very practical look at the daily schedule in answer to the question, "What shall I do first?" or "What now?" Laying out the format for the daily or weekly schedule is a first priority in organizing time. Never forget that *time* is a commodity, perhaps one of the most important commodities at your disposal in the classroom. Respect it. Plan for it. Use it carefully.

Planning for Long Term Goals

Looking ahead calls for foresight, perspective, and commitment to the future. By identifying targets or goals, you take the first step. When you view the targets in perspective and determine their relative importance, you make choices in terms of curriculum content and practices. By committing yourself to definite goals, you are setting a course which will lead to success. Waiting for something to happen seldom yields worthwhile ends. Deciding which goals are worthwhile and setting about reaching them may be difficult because of the stumbling blocks and detours along the way. But remember—the difference between stumbling blocks and stepping stones is in the use you make of them. Even detours can become challenging innovations if they are not allowed to sway you permanently from the ultimate goal. Therefore, in organizing your time, you need to take three specific steps: (a) establish priorities; (b) determine sequences; and (c) establish time limits. Let's examine them one at a time.

Establishing Priorities. Deciding what is of greatest importance calls for making judgments. Start by writing down some specific objectives. Your list may be long and the items may seem quite miscellaneous. If you are *subject* oriented, you will tend to think in terms of content to be covered and plan for activities which will be appropriate to the desired learnings. Problems will grow out of these lists. Your format may look like the one shown in Fig. 2–1.

If you are oriented to *child development* and plan your curriculum around the interests and activities of the children, your objectives may

CONTENT	ACTIVITIES	PROBLEMS
Science		
Magnetism and electricity	Make a buzzer	What makes electricity work?
Mathematics		
Addition of fractions with unlike denominators	Present Unit II Use drill sheet #9 Give mastery test over fractions	How to reduce fractions to common denominators How to add fractions
Soc. Studies		
Middle Atlantic States	Read pp. 187–216 Make maps of region Assign committees for: products natural resources climate	Location of Middle Atlantic States Identification of products Location of states, capitals, major cities, and land formations
etc.	etc.	etc.

Figure 2-1. *Sample planning chart showing objectives based on content*

look more like the ones illustrated in Fig. 2–2. In this case you tend to think more in terms of the activities you hope the children will experience. You will plan them around a selected topic, probably one already prescribed by the curriculum outline or the textbook. The problems will grow out of the activities.

ACTIVITIES	CONTENT	PROBLEMS

Make a time line
Keep a diary of the
  voyage of Columbus
Dramatize scenes:
  Columbus before the
  Queen of Spain
  Sighting Land
  Talking with the
  American Indians
  Reporting to the Queen
  of Spain
	The voyage of discovery
	  by Columbus in 1492
		In what sequence did the
		  events happen?
		How did the men on the
		  ships feel?
		What prompted Columbus
		  to make the voyage?
		What effect does his voyage
		  have on our life today?
		What if he had turned back?

etc.	etc.	etc.

Figure 2-2.   *Sample planning chart for objectives based on activities*

If you are oriented to a *core curriculum* design and see problems as the approach to organization, your listing of objectives may look more like the ones presented in Figure 2–3. In this case, you start with a problem or a question. It might be a question that has arisen in a class discussion about

PROBLEMS	ACTIVITIES	CONTENT

How do rivers affect
  cities?
	Trace a river system
	Build a table model
	  showing the effects
	  of erosion
	Visit a water
	  purification plant
	Set up a science
	  project on water
	  filtration
	Collect data about use
	  of rivers for:
	  transportation
	  recreation
	  water supply
		Main rivers in U.S.
		  Mississippi
		  Ohio
		  Missouri
		Rivers of the world used
		  for transportation
		Rivers used for city
		  water supply
		Major cities built on
		  banks of rivers

etc.	etc.	etc.

Figure 2-3.   *Sample planning chart for objectives based on problems*

a current or local problem. Perhaps the river bordering the town has been declared polluted, or has flooded the community, or is the subject for a city beautification project. The children might raise the question, "What good are rivers anyway?" "How do they affect cities?" "Why are so many cities built on the banks of rivers?" Using these interests, the teacher guides the children to a study of rivers in general, and in order to solve their problems, the teacher helps them plan related activities. In their research, the children cover considerable content.

After writing down your objectives, whether they are in terms of subject matter, pupil activities, or social problems, you are ready to establish some priorities. You will probably begin with a rather long list. The ideas will be gleaned from local curriculum guides, from teachers' manuals accompanying available text books, and from your own experience and judgment about what is important for these children. Don't let the enormity of the list overwhelm you. Once you have something down on paper, you are ready to organize and select. Begin by putting together those items which seem to be related, for example:

> Put together the time line in social studies and the computation of time by centuries in mathematics.
>
> Relate the discovery of the principle of gravity in science to the period in history when the event took place.
>
> Identify historical events which took place within the same century.
>
> Identify important people who were contemporaries.
>
> While studying the history of the westward movement, read a novel with a pioneer setting or some children's pioneer stories.

Next group together those items which bear a relationship to one another and can be viewed as subtopics under a major heading. For example, the mechanics of punctuation can become a major topic in language while the use of the comma in a series can become a subtopic. The skills related to denominate numbers can be considered a major teaching unit in mathematics. You may think this is too much. If so, back off and look at it in perspective and identify the most important targets. Set some dates. Commit yourself to accomplishing definite ends by a given date. Now you are accepting responsibility for achievement both on your part and on the part of your pupils. You have taken a practical look at some long-term goals and have established some priorities. You are ready for the next step.

Determining Sequences.   After you have listed all the things you hope to do during the year or semester, the next logical step is to determine the sequences. You establish priorities by deciding which things are more important. This means you will list the items in descending order of importance. Some of the sequences may be based on this listing, but others may have to be planned with logical organization of subject matter in mind. For instance, you may see mastery of the fundamental processes of computation with fractions as a major priority, but a survey of your class may reveal some individuals who still have not mastered the fundamental processes with whole numbers. In this case, you may need to readjust your priorities in terms of subject matter. Such priorities are of greater significance in some areas than others. For example, if you are teaching social studies and have a curriculum which prescribes a study of the regions of the United States, there is no good reason why you cannot begin with the local region even if it is Chap. 5 in the text. This will allow you to later study preceding chapters that are about regions farther from where the children live. Establishing priorities and determining sequences need to be done for all the curricular areas for which you are responsible.

Establishing Time Limits.   Once you have listed priorities and established sequences, you are ready to take a look at the calendar and estimate the amount of time needed for each topic or activity. Write down the date by which you expect to complete a given topic or the date on which you hope to be ready to approach a new unit. This will help you in ordering supplies and scheduling such teaching aids as films or recordings. You may not meet all your time limits, but establishing them will help you evaluate along the way. If you get done sooner than you expected, you may find time for some interesting innovations, or you may decide to deal with some of the problems in greater depth. If you find yourself running short of time or extending the unit beyond what you had estimated, you may need to ask such questions as, "Was this unit worth this much of our time? Did I let the children's passing fancy pull us off target and waste time on irrelevancies? What else have we planned that will have to be discarded for lack of time?" These kinds of evaluations are in terms of relative values rather than right or wrong answers. It might even be expedient to discuss the problem with the children. "If we go into that much detail with this project, we will have to eliminate one of the following units. Which one is more important to us?" The children often make surprisingly good judgments in response to such questions. If the decision is to curtail the planned activities, then do so without argument; and if the decision is to continue the activities and omit other units, do so without regrets.

Planning the Schedule

Now that you have thought through your long term goals, established some priorities, and set some time limits, you are ready to answer the question, "What shall I do first?" This means meeting the situation head on and facing your class with a plan of action. In preparation for the very first day with a new group, you may find it helpful to write down the specific things you plan to do, such as:

Take roll and learn names.
Collect lunch money.
Assign books for individual use.
Listen to each child read orally.
Have children write a paragraph about themselves.
Dictate spelling list from Lesson 1.
Collect samples of penmanship for diagnosis.
Discuss room organization with the children.
List plans for "Things we hope to do this year."
List books we will use this year.

In this way, you will be finding out something about the children and their interests and at the same time will be letting them participate in planning for the activities to come.

Eventually you must set up a schedule to follow. Many classrooms must follow a set routine. Bells ring. Buses arrive. Cafeterias maintain time limits. Special teachers come and go. Many of these routines will be decided for you. Your task is to identify these preestablished time limits, survey the remaining time at your disposal, and plan for its use. Some teachers prefer to have a daily schedule with modifications for special occasions. Some prefer a weekly schedule, especially if certain activities are scheduled only on certain days, such as library hour on Tuesday, special music teacher on Monday and Wednesday, or all-school assembly on Friday. Whether you plan by the day or by the week, you still need to determine *what* is going to happen *when* and to identify the events which must appear on your posted schedule.

Deciding on the Activities. You will find it helpful to estimate the amount of time needed for each type of activity and to establish time limits within which you must work. For instance, you may feel the need for a full hour for an art class, but if you don't get started till 2:30 and the bus leaves at 3:00, you will have to quit at the end of a half hour whether the lesson is over or not. Additionally, you may be left cleaning up the mess alone. On the other hand, with proper planning, the children could have the learning experience which goes with getting materials ready, finishing the project, and putting away their own supplies. You may decide to time an activity that calls for bringing things from home first thing on arrival because the children are ready to share their contributions. You may decide that spelling and penmanship can frequently be combined into a single activity and therefore should be scheduled together. You may feel that the sequence in which you meet reading groups should be varied depending on the nature of the day's activities and therefore it might seem advantageous to block a full hour for reading without necessarily designating which group will meet first. All this suggests that you need a flexible schedule or else one with alternates built in.

Allotting Time Segments.   Next you need to determine what is going to happen and when. Some teachers see time broken into segments with fifteen minutes to dictate the spelling list, twenty minutes for each of three reading groups, ten minutes for a break, and thirty minutes for social studies activities, followed by twenty minutes for discussion. This type of schedule keeps everybody, including the children, in a state of nervous tension trying to meet deadlines and justifying violations. Many teachers find a schedule built on larger blocks of time devoted to related activities more comfortable. For example, you might set aside two hours in the morning for language arts activities and try to include in that period all the reading instruction, spelling and penmanship practice, and language activities which result in either oral or written expression. Such flexibility is less frustrating but at the same time less definite. This kind of schedule requires a teacher who is self-disciplined enough to make sure all the work gets done. Also, it allows the children to assume some of the responsibility for deciding when, and within what time block, they will perform certain tasks.

Meeting Obligations.   Program implementation must give consideration to school organization, curricular requirements, and the children to be taught. The school may require instruction in safety to meet a local situation, in nutrition to support the cafeteria program. The curriculum may prescribe that a unit on election procedures precede each state or national election date, or that all children be given instruction in the effects of alcohol, tobacco, or drugs as a part of the health-education program. Your particular children may need extra help in vocabulary development or enriching socializing experiences because of a barren background.

All these factors need to be considered in planning the schedule. Once the long term goals have been identified and the sequences have been established, you are ready to start allotting time segments and fitting the activities into the time slots on the schedule. This calls for a format for laying out the program.

Laying Out the Format

To put your schedule on paper you need a format to follow. There are different forms a class program can take. The ones offered here as samples are only suggestive. You may find some of them helpful. They represent both detailed and flexible schedules and daily and weekly plans, as well as a form for programming activities in an open classroom staffed by a team.

Minute-by-Minute Accounting.   If subject-matter goals must be met, you may find it expedient to account for each ten- or fifteen-minute period thoughout the day. In this case your schedule may look something like the one shown in Fig. 2-4. This schedule establishes rigid time limits and definite sequences. Each day tends to be the same as the one before. One of the advantages is that both children and teacher know what to expect. One of the disadvantages is that interruptions and deviations tend to be upsetting.

DAILY SCHEDULE

Time	Activity
8:30	Arrival, attendance, announcements
9:00	Opening Exercises
9:15	Mathematics
10:00	Reading, Group I
10:20	Reading, Group II
10:40	Reading, Group III
11:00	Spelling
11:20	Language and Writing
11:45	Lunch
1:00	Social Studies
1:40	Science or Health
2:15	Physical Education
2:40	Art or Music
3:30	Dismissal

Figure 2-4. *Sample daily schedule based on subject matter goals and detailed accounting for time periods.*

Larger Blocks of Time.   When related activities are grouped together, you have more freedom in working within a schedule. Then you may find the format suggested in Fig. 2-5 more to your liking. This type of schedule is more descriptive of what is actually happening, while at the same time, allowing for more freedom in adapting to unexpected events, variations to take care of related activities, and deviations to meet special needs.

Weekly Scheduling.   Still another approach is needed when different time allotments are indicated for different days of the week. This kind of schedule is effective when you are working with special teachers who come on designated days and at specified times, or if the school reserves time for all-school activities into which you must fit your schedule. Such a weekly program is illustrated in Fig. 2-6. Some activities are the same every day. Some are planned for one day only, or for alternate days. This program is structured on the assumption that you have been given definite times and days when you may take your class to the gymnasium, times for classes by subject-matter teachers, and definite times for all-school activities to which you must conform. You will need to make frequent deviations from the schedule to meet such requirements as medical inspections when the health clinic visits the school, participation in school pictures, special convocations for holidays, and rehearsals for PTA programs. Additionally, the schedule will be disrupted by holidays which take one day out of the week and leave the total program incomplete. It will be your decision whether to omit the day's schedule, substitute another schedule for it, or try to telescope the time and get all the activities in even though there has been an interruption. Decisions will vary depending on the importance of the work or the convenience of the group.

CLASSROOM SCHEDULE

Time Allotment	Types of Activities
8:30–9:15	Preparation for the day's activities including routine collections, attendance record, etc.
	Opening activity—a song, a story, or a few minutes of music appreciation
	Group discussion of plans for the day
9:15–11:00	Language Arts Block, including:
	group and individual work in reading
	practice in penmanship and spelling
	checking off week's spelling assignment
	oral and/or written language activities as related to current unit of study
11:00–12:00	Unit of Study
	Either Social Studies or Science
	Including Health
	Or some combination of the three areas
12:00–1:00	N O O N
1:00–1:40	Mathematics
1:40–2:20	Art Activities or Music
	Note: These may grow out of the unit of study, becoming an implementation of subject matter, or they may be independent of the unit.
	Activities may be limited to two or three days a week with alternate days devoted to art techniques or art appreciation.
2:20–2:45	Physical Activities
	Note: These will encompass the use of the gymnasium on assigned days. Physical activities may be combined with music through rhythms and dancing.
2:45–3:15	Evaluation and Planning Period
	Indicate accomplishments. Check off tasks completed. List things yet to be done. Discuss plans for future. Individual conferences. Clean-up and put-away.
3:15	Dismissal

Figure 2–5. *Sample classroom schedule based on large blocks of time and interrelation of activities*

WEEKLY SCHEDULE

Time	Monday	Tuesday	Wednesday	Thursday	Friday
8:30	Daily Preliminaries—Routine, attendance, collections, etc.				
9:00	Reading	Reading	Reading	Reading	Library
10:00	Spelling	Writing	Spelling	Writing	Spelling
10:15	Language	Music	Language	Music	Language
10:45	Soc. St.	Science	Soc. St.	Science	Soc. St.
11:45	NOON HOUR				
1:00	Art	P. E.	Art	P. E.	Art
1:25	Art	Health	Art	Health	Art
1:50	Mathematics	Mathematics	Assembly	Mathematics	Mathematics
2:40	Individual Help as Needed, Pupil-teacher Planning				Weekly News
3:30	DISMISSAL				

Figure 2–6. *Sample Schedule based on weekly distribution of time with variation from day to day for alternate activities.*

35

Team Teaching in an Open Classroom.   If your assignment happens to be as a member of a team in an open classroom which accommodates 60–80 pupils, you will be introduced to a still different type of schedule. Figure 2–7 illustrates a format which is used effectively on a large wall bulletin board. The names of the team members and their status roles appear across the top. Time slots and general areas of study are listed down the left-hand side. These slots may be left open to be assigned as the daily or weekly planning is done, or they may be filled in as shown with general assignments that will be altered from day to day. These assignments may be printed on cards that can be moved from one space to another as responsibilities are adjusted. Greater detail can be added by pinning extra notations in each block as current plans materialize. This kind of schedule permits wide flexibility but requires carefully coordinated planning among the team members so that conflicts do not arise and so that each child will be included in the scheduled activities.

Schedules are made to serve as guides. They help you meet obligations imposed by the curriculum as well as obligations to the children. The children's time is important. It must be used to their advantage. A schedule serves as a guide without which your program could become haphazard and fruitless. If you become a slave to it, you may experience frustration and boredom. There is a middle-of-the-road approach that is helpful as well as practical. When you know what you are going to do, you do not experience the frustration of facing a class with uncertainty. When the children know what comes next, they use their time more wisely. Specific time allotments for certain activities insure the activities get done. Open time blocks permit flexibility in varying the sequence to meet the needs. For example, if the planning for the social studies period calls for discussion, it can serve as the oral language lesson, and it can precede rather than follow the history lesson. On the other hand, if the social studies discussion leads to plans for writing summaries, the scheduled language activity can be this written assignment.

Along with scheduled activities comes the need for unstructured or independent time. While you are working with one group or with a committee the rest of the children must be doing something. If you leave them to their own devices without an assignment, or with no guidance in deciding how to use the time, you may find trouble starts. Unstructured time can be planned for if the children have learned to set their own goals and assume responsibility for their own activities. This calls for a planning time with groups as well as with individuals. Children can be taught to keep a library book always at hand, play a game alone or with a partner, move on to an individual assignment without teacher direction, use time for creative activities, or make a list of "things to do in my free time." All

Time	Area	Miss Brown Coordinator	Mr. Andrews Prof. Tr.	Mrs. Payne Prof. Tr.	Miss Banks Tr. Intern	Mrs. Borden Tr. Aide
8:30	Planning	Discussion Leader	Preparation of materials	Preparation of materials	Asst. to Disc. Ld.	Checking attendance
9:00 10:00	Lang. Arts	General Supervision	Reading Gr. 1 and 2 Individual conferences	Reading Gr. 3 and 4 Individual conferences	Spelling dictation Handwriting practice	Checking individual work sheets Record keeping
11:00	Unit Soc. St. or Science	Work with committees and small groups	Science Unit	Soc. St. Unit	Work with committees	Preparation of materials Supervision of clean-up activities
12:00				NOON		
1:00	Mathematics	Presentation of new concepts to groups	Review and reteaching in small groups	Remedial work individual	Drill as needed in small groups	Checking workbooks or drill sheets
2:00	Music or Art Phys. Ed. and Health	Art projects or music	Boys P. E. Health	Girls P. E. Health	Assist with art projects or music	Materials and supplies
3:00	Summary	Group 1	Group 2	Group 3	Group 4	Housekeeping

Figure 2–7. Sample schedule based on open classroom with team teaching and 60–80 pupils.

this requires responsibility and self-reliance as well as planning. Furthermore, unstructured time involves organization of materials and learning centers so the children can find what they need, when they need it. It necessitates that they know the limitations within which they can work without direction. In a room where the children are not permitted to move out of their seats without seeking permission from the teacher, this is not possible. On the other hand, there is likely to be a great waste of time, not to mention confusion resulting in disorder and sometimes even chaos in a room where the children are permitted to wander about aimlessly. There must be organization of materials as well as goals and time.

ORGANIZING YOUR MATERIALS

The old saying, "A place for everything and everything in its place," certainly applies to a classroom. When time is spent hunting materials or supplies, the loss of time is compounded. If you waste ten minutes hunting for something, the waste is multiplied by thirty if there are that many children in the classroom. Ten times thirty comes to 300 minutes which figures out to five hours. If you say, "You may pass the paper, Fred," and there is not enough on the shelf to supply the class, a confusing situation develops which a little foresight could have prevented. Either you have to substitute some other kind of paper not quite appropriate for the task, postpone the activity till a later time, or wait while someone makes a trip to the stock room for more paper. Such a waste of time could easily have been prevented with organization of teaching materials. Then there is the matter of the use of such teaching tools as a globe, for instance. In the midst of the lesson you may hear yourself remark, "That is more easily illustrated with a globe than a flat map." At this point you become aware that there is no globe in the room. The lesson may be weakened by the lack of a globe, or else the children will have to wait while you go for the globe. Either solution reveals a lack of preliminary planning and organization.

Materials to be organized may be classified as those used by each individual or those shared with others. And they may be further broken down into consumables and nonconsumables. Each type presents its own problems in management and classroom organization.

Consumable Materials

Every child needs such materials as paper, workbook, paste, crayons, and pencils. They are consumable items, hence subject to periodic renewal. Waiting for them to run out indicates lack of forethought. Plan to provide more paper before the package is all gone. If you plan ahead, know what supplies will be needed, and check to make sure they are ready, you will find classroom activities move along smoothly and effectively. Pencils can become a major source of irritation. If the children must supply their own pencils, some precaution must be exercised so that in the midst of a working session, Eugene doesn't raise his hand and say, "I ain't got no pencil." Either you must have a supply of spare pencils or the children must be led to plan their own supplies so that they always have more than one pencil available. Other items are subject to similar forethought and planning.

Time spent discussing with the children the importance of having supplies ready, making lists of "things we will need," laying out the equipment and checking it off for the science experiment, and counting to make sure there is enough is time well spent. Many of these responsibilities can be delegated to children. Establish a place for items used daily. Indicate individuals to be held responsible for checking supplies and making sure they are ready. Make sure everybody knows where the paper is kept, where extra pencils may be obtained, where scrap paper is available for creative activities, and where such materials as crayons, paste, scissors, and erasers may be secured as needed without disrupting the class to ask permission.

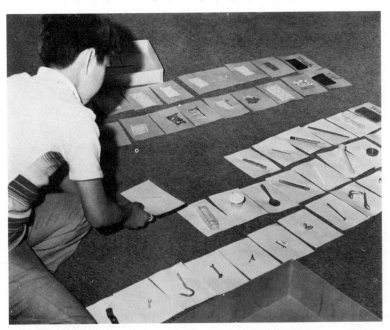

Organizing and classifying are a part of learning that children need to experience. (Courtesy, Skiff School, Phoenix, Arizona)

This kind of pupil-assumed responsibility does not develop suddenly, nor does it come from teacher-imposed rules. It comes after many meaningful discussions with the children about the organization of the materials and the responsibility of each individual for getting work done without infringing upon the rights of others. You don't legislate responsibility; you develop it.

Nonconsumable Materials

Some types of classroom activities require materials in the hands of every child. If the arithmetic or spelling lesson is in a textbook, every child needs a copy, however, they may not all have the same textbook at the same time. Whether textbooks such as readers are kept in the child's desk, or on the shelf in sets when not in use, the child needs to know where they are and when and how to get them if needed. If sets of readers are kept on the shelf when not in use, saying, "Who wants to pass the books?" is not only a waste of time but invites an argument and competition for the privilege. If someone must pass the books, the job should be assigned as a routine task. Perhaps it would be even more expedient if each child were to pick up a copy as the group assembles. Reducing such activity to routine without comment is a great time saver.

The same principle holds true for other nonconsumable materials. Scissors and rulers are not used up. Whether they are kept in individual desks or stored together is a matter of management. Either way may be all right. Much depends on the program and the availability of storage space. Whichever plan is adopted should be used consistently. The children should know where the rulers belong and how to get them, and the plan should be followed consistently. These may seem like trite comments, but more teachers have found themselves engulfed with chaos and what appears to be discipline problems because of lack of organization than because of lack of knowledge of subject matter.

Shared Materials

Some materials and pieces of equipment are not provided on a one-per-pupil basis and must be shared. These items create a different type of problem. There will probably be only one set of encyclopedias of a given kind available. There will probably be only one unabridged dictionary. Globes, wall maps, and charts are usually provided on the basis of one per room. Since not every child will have individual equipment of this kind, a plan must be worked out for expedient use through sharing. If the assignment calls for reference work and all the facts needed are in the same volume of the encyclopedia, then children may be waiting in line to use the same book. A little preplanning could prevent such waste. Either topics should be varied, or time should be scheduled to prevent the conflict. This is better planned *with* the children than dictated *to* them.

Materials shared with other rooms create still different problems. If one projector must serve the entire school, or three or four rooms, then a bit of consideration will relieve conflicts and irritations. There should be a place for the projector. Its extension cord should be a "sacred" attachment. Definite times should be established for its use, or there should be a place to sign up for a requested time so no one will be looking for it and not finding it. If Miss Anderson regularly uses the overhead projector for the art class at ten o'clock, she has every reason to be irritated if she comes with transparencies in hand and finds the projector in use in another room, or finds that someone has appropriated the extension cord for use in the science laboratory. If a sign-up sheet is kept beside the projector and Mr. Adams wants to use it on Tuesday at one o'clock, he can sign his name and indicate the time. Then he has every right to expect to find it in its accustomed place when he comes to get it. If Miss Burdin has used it before noon and has neglected to return it, she might very well expect to find her co-worker a bit irritated. Materials shared with the total school should be subject to a routine that makes them available when needed. Such lack of dependability is what causes some teachers to "give up" and materials to gather dust. Many administrators have experimented with open-stock and self-regulation schedules with considerable success. There is really no need for a clerk to check out books, projectors, or records if teachers will assume the responsibility for indicating when they need these items, for picking them up at the appointed place, and for returning them at the appropriate time. This kind of organization puts the responsibility on the users, and the expediency with which the plan works is as self-disciplining for teachers as it is for children.

SUMMARY

Yes, getting organized for teaching is important. The old saying, "A good beginning is a task half done," certainly applies here. Organizing your goals helps you know where you are going and why. Such organization may be based on subject matter, pupil activities, or social problems. The end result may be product oriented or process oriented. Organizing your time helps you know both the priorities and the sequences. You need to plan for both long term goals and the daily schedule. Daily schedules may be detailed or may provide for large blocks of time with flexibility. Organizing your materials makes sure everything is ready for the learning activities to come. This applies to both consumable and nonconsumable materials, and to items for individual use as well as shared materials.

Now we are ready to take a look at the planning needed for specific lessons within this structure. If the planning is well done, everything will be ready and the lesson should be a success. Let's turn to the structure for the lesson plan in the next chapter.

SUGGESTED ACTIVITIES

Select one or more of the following activities for individual or small group development. Report your results to the class.

1. Collect classroom schedules from five different teachers and compare them from the standpoint of content, sequence, and emphasis.
2. Work out a daily schedule you could use in your own classroom.
3. Visit a classroom and list all the materials you see either in use or available for use.
   Divide them into two groups—consumable and nonconsumable.
   Divide them into two different groups—individual and shared.
4. Take the above lists of materials and organize them by placing them on the following chart:

MATERIALS OF INSTRUCTION

Type	Individual	Shared
Consumable		
Nonconsumable		

5. Design a sign-up sheet to show how you would establish a self-regulating schedule for the use of shared materials kept in the school's stock room.

SELECTED READINGS

1. Association for Supervision and Curriculum Development, NEA, *A Curriculum for Children*, Washington, D. C.: ASCD Elementary Education Advisory Council, Alexander Frazier, Editor, 1969, pp. 138. Describes the setting and the scene in the present day elementary school. Points out the need for some new designs and a new focus for young children. Eight Contributors.
2. FROST, JOE L. and G. THOMAS ROWLAND, *Curricula for the Seventies*. Boston: Houghton Mifflin Company, 1969, pp. 454. Identifies five major curriculum areas and their place in the scheme of elementary education. Discusses background, approaches, methodology, and bases for organization.

3. GOODLAD, JOHN I. "The Child and His School in Transition." in *The National Elementary Principal*, Vol. LII, Jan. 1973, pp. 28–34. Hypothesizes on the kind of schools we need in the future. Recommends phases, not grades, and individual fulfillment rather than conformity to established standards.

4. GOODLAD, JOHN I., *School, Curriculum, and the Individual*, Waltham, Mass: Blaisdell, 1966. Reviews tradition of schools and points out the need and also the difficulty of predicting for the future.

5. JACOBY, SUSAN, "What Makes Sue Nonell's Open Classroom Work?" in *Learning*, Vol. 1, No. 4, Feb. 1973, pp. 58–62. Through interview, description, and full-color illustration, Susan Jacoby, a journalist, seeks to answer the question posed in the title. She emphasizes teacher attitude rather than equipment or money as the key to success.

6. JARVIS, OSCAR T. and MARION J. RICE, *An Introduction to Teaching in the Elementary School*, Dubuque, Iowa: Wm. C. Brown Company Publishers, 1972, pp. 545. See Chap. 19, *Vertical and Horizontal Patterns of Organization*.

7. KELLEY, EARL, *The Significance of Being Unique*, ETC. 1957, pp. 169–184. The title suggests the content.

8. MAGER, ROBERT F., *Developing Attitude Toward Learning*, Palo Alto, California: Fearon, 1968, pp. 104. Seeks to answer such questions as, "Where am I going? How shall I get there? and How will I know I have arrived?"

9. MANNING, DUANE, *Toward a Humanistic Curriculum*, New York: Harper & Row, 1971, pp. 306. Makes a plea for humanism in organizing schools, planning curriculum content, and evaluating results.

10. OLDS, ANITA R., "Making Hard Rooms Soft Rooms," in *Learning*, Vol. 1, No. 1, Nov. 1972, pp. 36–40. Presents the concept of the open classroom through discussion and pictures. Discusses the physical setting and the organization of the learning experiences.

11. PILCHER, PAUL S. "Open Education," in *Educational Leadership*, Vol. 30, No. 2, Nov. 1972, pp. 137–140. Compares the British primary schools with the establishment of the open-school concept in the United States. Identifies the difference in problems and their application.

12. SHAW, JANE S., "Cross-Age Tutoring: How to Make It Work," in *Nation's Schools*, Vol. XCI, Jan. 1973, pp. 43–46. Gives step-by-step suggestions for administrator, teacher, and tutor. Emphasizes careful planning, appropriate matching, and pre-training.

13. SMITH, RICHARD J. and KENNETH L. JENSEN, "Canaries, Sparrows, and Reading Group Placement," in *The Reading Teacher*, Vol. 26, No. 2, Nov. 1972, pp. 166–170. Points out dangers of using standardized tests scores as a basis for grouping, and urges keeping groups more flexible based on teacher judgment and actual accomplishment changes.

3

PLANNING WITH AND FOR THE LEARNERS

Making Sure You Know Where You're Going

Courtesy, Skiff School, Phoenix, Arizona

PLANNING

Have you decided whether you will base your plans on subject matter, children's needs, or problems? If so, you have established a basic philosophy which will influence your relations with your students.

Do you know the difference between a long-term plan, a unit plan, and a daily plan? Do you know what functions each will serve? When you sit down to write a lesson plan, do you know where to begin? Do you know how to organize your thinking and put your ideas on paper? Can you produce a plan that will be helpful, one that is more than a "busy work" exercise for you? Will it be helpful when you face the class? Will it answer such questions as, "What will I do?" "What will I say?"

Do you know the difference between an indirect plan and a direct plan? Each has advantages. Do you know what they are?

Would you like to see some sample lesson plans? Can you produce a plan that will help you think through what you are going to do in the time available? What if you plan more than you can get done? What if you run out of things to do before the bell rings? These are very practical questions which will be answered when you are prepared with a functional plan to meet the occasion.

This chapter is designed to help you with these pertinent problems in teaching.

One teacher said, "I never bother to plan. I don't use plans anyway. I believe in taking advantage of the teachable moment."

Another teacher reacted, "What if nothing teachable occurs? It's easier to change a plan on the spur of the moment than to construct one out of thin air."

Careful planning makes the difference between haphazard teaching and constructive, developmental curricular experiences. If you know how to plan for daily activities, continuous unit experiences, and overall goals, you will accomplish something because you know where you are headed. Such planning calls for answers to two basic questions; namely: On what will you base your plans? and How will you structure your plans?

BASES FOR PLANNING

On what will you base your teaching plans? Should you follow the traditional pattern of organization of subject matter? Should you begin with the children and their needs? Or should plans center around learning activities? The answers to these questions will determine the way you will go about your planning. Each has merit. Perhaps you will use a combination of all three. Perhaps you will emphasize one more than another. Let's examine them one at a time.

Planning Based On Subject Matter

Traditionally, the content to be covered has been the basis for curriculum development. If you see the curriculum in spelling as the list of words in the textbook; the curriculum in arithmetic as addition combinations, carrying, subtraction, fractions, or story problems; the curriculum in reading as the textbook and its accompanying workbook to be covered; then you are basing your plans on subject matter. In this case, the children will be expected to follow the dictates of the subject matter outline. They will be rewarded with praise, marks, and promotions. The entries in your plan book will look something like this:

> Finish the story on page 37.
> Write out the answers to the questions on page 63.
> Give test covering the 100 addition facts.
> Practice writing the spelling words.
> Start the unit on Indians in the social studies book.

This kind of planning may, or may not, meet the needs of individuals. Children will all cover the same territory whether they need it or not. They will all turn in the same assignments for judging. This may result in "covering" the curriculum, but it does not guarantee learning. It only guarantees exposure. This kind of planning is traditional. It is sometimes encouraged because it appears to be organized and objective. But the real curriculum maker here is the writer of the textbook, the manual, or the course outlines. The only part you have in making the curriculum is deciding whether or not to stay on schedule and when to do the assignments. The children are merely the objects receiving the curriculum.

Planning Based on Child Development

If you are a student of child development, you will start by studying the needs of each individual child. Perhaps Susan needs more phonics. Allen needs more self-confidence. Bill needs practice on the multiplication combinations. Fred needs to read more carefully to get the details. Sara needs practice on letter formation. Planning to meet all these needs suggests an individualized approach. But, you say, you have twenty five or thirty individuals and such planning is impractical. Then your first step is to get organized.

Start by listing some of the most obvious needs. Under each item, list the names of children who have similar needs. For example: Drill on multiplication facts—Tom, Sara, Bill, Erma, and John. Now you have a teachable group. Their needs may not be identical but they have enough in common to justify grouping for instructional purposes and thus take care of some individual differences by meeting more than one individual at a time. From this group you have eliminated Betty, Grace, and Carl who seem to be skilled in this area but in need of practice to improve their skills in oral reading. They, along with some others, may form another instructional group.

This kind of planning takes careful study of the children's abilities and needs. It calls for constant reevaluation and frequent regrouping. Children themselves can often decide whether they are in need of certain kinds of help. It means studying materials available and keeping careful records to know when goals have been met. With this approach you are truly the curriculum maker.

Planning Based on Learning Activities

A variety of activities implies listening and participating, observing and doing, practicing and testing, mastering and creating, and remembering and thinking. If you use this approach to planning, you will start with a list of things to do. For example:

> Go on a field trip.
> Practice penmanship.
> Listen to stories on records.
> Sing and play games.
> Read library books.

The balance may come in the school day or over a longer period of time. The important point is that you are aware that children are getting a variety of activities, that each is maintaining a wholesome balance, and developing in keeping with abilities, interests, and level of growth. This kind of planning calls for breadth of ideas and a keen insight into children's abilities. Much of the planning may be done with the children, but even that will need to be preceded by careful planning on your part. Planning with the children may result in a list of:

> Things we need to do today
> Items we have finished
> Things we didn't get done today
> Things we must do tomorrow

This kind of planning is fruitful because the children know where they are going. It puts much of the responsibility for decision making on the learners themselves. They see the job, not as something you have assigned, but as an activity they have identified and accepted. In this kind of planning, the children become partners in keeping records. With this approach, you and the children become jointly responsible for curriculum development.

These three approaches to planning are referred to as *subject-centered*, *child-centered*, and *activity-centered*. The first centers attention on *what* is to be learned. The other two center attention on the children and what they do with what they learn. All three make use of subject matter and materials. The difference is in the approach and the organization. You are now ready to construct a lesson plan.

STRUCTURE FOR PLANNING

Plans don't materialize out of thin air. They must be structured according to some type of organization. If you face your class with a vague idea of what you hope to do, you will find yourself groping for words, hunting for materials, making sudden and sometimes unwise decisions, and changing your mind. Lack of planning and unorganized teaching leads to confusion, lack of accomplishment, and sometimes disinterest and even disciplinary problems. If you know *what* you are going to do and *why* and

Children can help plan for a forthcoming unit by selecting suitable materials to be shared with the rest of the class. (Courtesy, Skiff School, Phoenix, Arizona)

how, you will have everything ready and will be able to move forward with dispatch and confidence. And if the children know what they are going to do and why and how, they too will be able to work efficiently, recognize accomplishments, and assume responsibility for next steps.

Plans that lead to this kind of self-confidence need to be viewed from two perspectives: First, for what period of time should the plans be constructed? Second, what form should they take?

Perspective for Planning

Planning for classroom work can be compared to taking a journey. You need to see the whole trip at a glance. Then you need to know what you will be doing first so you can prepare accordingly. Eventually you must face the issue of taking that first step. For a journey, this involves getting ready, packing, buying the ticket, making the reservations, and perhaps getting immunization shots. This calls for studying the map, anticipating events, and making preliminary decisions. Unless these steps are taken, you may come home from the journey with the feeling that you had been nowhere. Planning for classroom activities demands a long-term view to see the ultimate goal, a closer look to identify the activities related to a particular unit of experience, and eventually a detailed plan for the day which answers the immediate question, "What shall I do now?"

Long Term Plans.   Some plans should be made before you even meet the children. They include:

Looking over the textbooks provided for your new assignment.
Studying the manuals for an overview of their suggestions.
Previewing the curriculum guides provided for the school.
Studying the cumulative records for information about the children you will teach.

After these steps have been taken, you will be ready to make some decisions about plans for *these* children *this* year. Some general plans may be based on subject matter. You may list such topics as:

Social Studies—Three units for the first semester
    Transportation
    Food, shelter, and clothing
    Type regions
Arithmetic
    Review of whole numbers
    Introduction of multiplication and division with two-digit multipliers and divisors
    Introduction to simple fractions
    Work on story problems

Reading
> Review mechanical skills of word recognition
> Complete the textbook
> Plan with the children for an individualized program based on use of library books

Some of your plans may be based on activities. In this case you may make such a list as the following:

> One trip away from school, probably to the railroad station or the airport in connection with the unit on transportation
> A series of library visits to increase interest in independent reading
> An assembly program utilizing language skills to share our completed unit with an audience
> A visiting day for parents of each group
> A once-a-month newsletter to parents

Long term planning is important because it gives direction, provides a visible goal, insures continuity and sequence, and provides a basis for summary and evaluation. But it is not enough. Without more detailed plans you may be led off on tangents that waste time and you may never reach the originally stated goals.

Unit Plans.   Some plans are made for shorter periods of time. A unit plan may be for one day or one or two weeks. With more mature students the unit could extend over many weeks or months, but it would be an unusual situation in which interest would hold attention indefinitely. Planning a unit either for or with the children calls for previewing. Suppose you are going to launch a unit on transportation. Your preliminary planning might include listing of activities such as:

> Reading from references to find needed information
> Writing letters for information
> Writing outlines and summaries
> Discussing facts gleaned from various sources
> Computing mileage, distance and rate
> Learning to spell such words as motorized, amphibian, pilot, conductor and transcontinental
> Collecting pictures from magazines
> Constructing murals or models

Your planning with the children will probably be stated in terms of questions and activities. For example:

> Questions we hope to answer:
> > How do people travel in different parts of the world?
> > How has travel changed over the years?

What kind of travel is most economical?
How would I travel if I were going to India?
How long would it take me to get there?

Ways we can find out:
Read textbooks and encyclopedias.
Collect pictures of kinds of transportation.
Talk with people who work in transportation industries.
Visit the railroad station, the bus station, and the airport.
Take a bus ride, a train ride, or an airplane ride.
Write to companies for information and travel folders.

Things we can do:
Make a mural or a diorama showing different kinds of transportation.
Make a bulletin board for each kind of transportation.
Invite another room to see and hear about our work.

Now you know where you are going. You have an overall view of the unit and its potential. You have included the children in the planning. As you pursue the unit, you should watch for opportunities to check off the items and for other supplementary interests which may occur and seem worth adding to the original plans. But even then, you will have to face the class and ask: What shall I do now? What shall I say? What do I need to work with? Am I ready?

Daily Plans. Eventually the time comes when you must determine what is going to happen *now*. Without plans, you may still be just "going for a ride," instead of getting somewhere. Daily plans take many forms. Consider these possibilities:

A formal and detailed plan handed in to a supervisor

An outline written into the week's plan book

Notes on file cards slipped into the textbook for prompting so you won't omit important elements

Notes to yourself written into the margins of the textbook indicating questions, comments, and activities

Regardless of what form your daily plans take, they must exist if you are going to accomplish anything. Some veteran teachers are so sure of themselves that they think they can "keep their plans in their heads." The risk is that the teacher will repeat what was done yesterday, last week, or even last year. Plans need to be "fresh" daily. You may think something stimulating will come up, but what if it doesn't? You may think you will remember everything, but what if you forget something? Making a list has advantages. It's like shopping list. If you jot items down, you will be sure to remember them, and you won't have to make another trip for something you have forgotten.

It may seem ironic that the longer *good* teachers teach, the more detailed their plans become. When you are a beginner, you may not make detailed plans because you don't know how, you don't realize their importance, or you think you know what you are going to do. After a few experiences with lessons that fail, you will see more and more need for detailed planning. When you know what you are going to do and have everything ready, things move along smoothly.

Form for Planning

Now that you have viewed planning from the long term point of view, from the unit basis, and from the daily needs basis, you are ready to put something on paper. This calls for organizing your thoughts. Your plan must be definite and to the point. Let's first examine some of the weaknesses of typical plans and arrive at some concrete suggestions for implementing planning.

Perhaps two of the primary weaknesses in planning are scheduling either more than you can get done or not enough to "fill the period." Another weakness is indefiniteness. Vague suggestions leave you standing before the class with nothing to say or with the need to repeat because what you said the first time was ineffective. Preliminary planning helps overcome these weaknesses. Perhaps a format or "map" for planning will be helpful. The following suggestions are designed to answer two questions: How shall I organize my lesson plan? and In what form shall I write it?

Organizing the Lesson Plan.   In writing your lesson plan, you must answer three questions, probably in this order:

1. Why am I going to teach this lesson?
2. What subject matter will I cover and what materials will I need?
3. How will I go about it?

The plan itself may take any one of several forms. You may have your own ideas, but it is easier to vary from a prescribed form than to create a totally new one. For this reason, the "map" shown in Fig. 3–1 is presented as a guide. It will help you get started. Study it and the following description to familiarize yourself with the content and purpose for each section.

In Part I of the plan you will be justifying, stating why you are going to teach the lesson. It will have the same type of content whether you are planning for a twenty-minute period, a unit, or a semester's work. You can call this part goals, aims, purposes, objectives, or whatever you will. Some authors differentiate among these terms, but the main point is that in this part you will justify what you are planning to do. This may be stated in terms of what you hope to accomplish or what the children will do. It may be stated as behavioral objectives or instructional goals. You decide, but be consistent. Just make sure you know where you are going before you need to justify your plans to a supervisory official, an inquiring parent, or perhaps even to yourself.

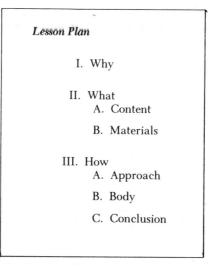

Figure 3-1.　*Format for lesson planning.*

In Part II you are previewing the situation to make sure you know *what* you are going to teach and what materials you will need. It will include an outline of the topics to be covered and a list of the materials needed, including textbooks and references with exact page numbers. And don't forget to include even the minutest detail such as the extra bulb for the projector, the extension cord, the dittoed master sheets, the rulers, or the book markers. Care in this step eliminates embarrassment and confusion resulting from having to hunt for things, apologize for lack of preparation, or chastize the children for having been inattentive while you went for more paper. Having everything ready is what makes a lesson move with dispatch.

In Part III you are thinking about how you will go about accomplishing your objectives, what you will do and say when you actually face the children. You might compare this part of the lesson to the parts of a composition or a sermon. First you must get started. Then you must do something. And eventually you have to stop. This is the traditional introduction, body, and conclusion. But it is not that simple. Lessons often fall flat because you don't actually know how to start or stop. A strong approach and a convincing conclusion strengthen a presentation.

Let's begin with the *approach*. Compare the two sets of approaches in the following parallel columns:

Yesterday we talked about simple machines. What examples did you find in your mother's kitchen?

All right. It is time for spelling now.

We have a new story which is about a boat race. The pictures suggest who won but they don't tell how.

What page are we ready for today?

Who still needs help with the borrowing process?

Did you get all your homework done?

If we are going to write to the mayor, how can we be sure our letter is in good form? What difference does it make?

How many of you found all the answers?

The "starters" on the left suggest problems with satisfactory closures. The approaches include the introduction and the motivation. They begin with something within the background or experience of the children and lead to a reason for pursuing the lesson.

The "starters" on the right imply that the class is going through preestablished routines, covering textbooks, and putting in time.

Be sure you start your lessons with a purpose that is obvious to the children.

Now let's move to the *conclusion*. Compare the two sets of lesson endings in the following parallel columns:

That's a good place to leave our story. You may want to finish it for yourself to find out what happened.

That's all the time we have for today.

If you are sure you understand this new process, you may try the examples on p. 56 by yourself.

All right, you may take up the papers, Fred.

Since it's time for the bus, perhaps you would like to take this home to finish.

Tomorrow we will begin here.

If you have an encyclopedia at home, you may be able to bring in some more information on this.

Put your geography books away and get out your spellers.

The "stoppers" on the left suggest the lesson has been completed or that it has reached a satisfactory place for concluding and that the learners are now ready to proceed on their own. The conclusion may include a summary of points covered, a suggestion for transition to the next day or the next unit, or an assignment for the children to follow up with independent activities or a check on accomplishment.

Be sure you end your lessons by giving the children a feeling of accomplishment.

This still leaves the *body* of the lesson. It will be the longest part of the plan. Knowing exactly what you are going to do calls for making a list. This is an example:

First Step: Look at the map with the children to identify the geographical features of the Mediterranean region. (List them on the chalkboard.)

Second Step: Look at the illustrations in the textbook for tentative answers to questions posed yesterday.

Third Step: Help children preview the sections in the text by identifying the topics indicated in the paragraph headings. List the headings in outline form.

Fourth Step: Help the children transform each heading into a question.

Fifth Step: Then have them read to find answers to questions.

Sixth Step: Discuss with class answers to questions.

Be sure you have the steps in mind. If you find it difficult to remember all of them, provide yourself with some guides.

Writing the Lesson Plan. Eventually you must state your objectives, itemize the content and materials, and indicate your procedures. Objectives or aims may be stated in teacher terms. For instance:

To lead the children to preview the text to get an overview of what is included.

To present information that will lead to discovery and a discussion of cause and effect relationships.

To provide experiences which will help them see the problem of conservation related to local conditions.

These are all things the teacher plans to do. Whether the children accomplish these objectives or not is another matter. On the other hand, objectives can be stated in terms of the pupils and what they will do. For example:

To practice alphabetizing.

To read and outline the material in the dictionary exercises on p. 48 in the workbook.

To find out three things the dictionary tells.

These are all things you plan for the pupils to do. Asserting expectations of accomplishment implies stating the aims as behavioral objectives which are particularly appropriate when accountability is required. Examples are:

Given a list of sentences containing words in a series, the child will be able to insert the commas in the appropriate places with a minimum accuracy of 90 percent.

After reading directions for an experiment, the child will be able to write in sequence the three steps to be taken and will be able to perform the experiment.

When faced with examples, the child will be able to differentiate between facts and inferences.

The important thing in stating the objectives is that you establish a point of view, know why you are going to teach, and are consistent.

Content and materials are identified in the second part of the lesson plan. It is here that you list the topics to be covered and the materials you will be using. Such lists should be concise, easily read, and readily checked off.

Procedures are indicated in the third part of the lesson plan. This is the *how* part where you answer such questions as: What am I going to do? What am I going to say? Talking about something is one thing, but doing it is quite another. Sometimes you meet your downfall because you make vague suggestions such as, "Discuss the picture with the children." Then when you face the class and hold up the picture you may be temporarily in a quandary about just what to say. You may fumble for words and ask such inappropriate questions as:

Do you like this picture?
Look at these children. Did you ever do this?
Isn't this an interesting picture?
What do you see in this picture?

Responses to questions such as these will be either "Yes" or "No" or at best merely agreement. These questions call for little thought and result in very little forward progress.

The difference between poor questions and good questions lies in the depth of thinking and the types of responses they elicit. The examples above are poor because the children are asked simply to agree or disagree, express an unfounded opinion, or identify a one-word response.

Try the following suggested approaches for improvement. Note that these questions call for considered evaluations, reasoning, and problem solving. As you study these questions, think about them in terms of the type of responses the children will make:

Apparently these children have lost something. How do they feel? What makes you think so?

Here we are interpreting the picture. The first question may be answered with one word but it will not be the same word from every member of the class. And the second question certainly calls for some thinking and the use of language to express ideas rather than facts. Here is another approach worth trying:

Johnny is in a predicament in this picture. What would you do about it if you were in his place?

This calls for some thought and a response which goes well beyond "Yes" or "No," a simple nod of the head, or a one word fact that could be supplied after looking at the picture.

If the body of the lesson plan contains such suggestions as, "Study the map with the children," you may again be groping for something to say. Perhaps it would help if you were to write down exactly what you plan to say. Study these examples from the standpoint of expected pupil responses:

Turn to the map of Italy on p. 47.

Using the numbers at the side of the map, determine the latitude of the country.

What does this suggest about the climate?

Using the color key, determine topography of the land.

What does this suggest further about the climate?

From what you know about the climate and topography, what conclusions might you draw about the industries?

Look at the shoreline. What might this suggest about the occupations of the people?

How can we verify our observations?

These questions make sure something happens. The children will end this discussion with a list of facts and some theories about what they will expect to find out. They will see a need for pursuing the content to verify their theories. They will be reading to prove a point or support a conviction. The discussion which follows will be more than a regurgitation of facts to prove they have studied the lesson.

The difference between these two plans is obvious. The one which suggests discussing the map with the children is an *indirect plan.* The one which lists the directions and questions is a *direct plan.*

The indirect or general plan suggests what will be discussed. It is more appropriate for long term and unit planning. (See Sample Plan No. 3 at the end of this chapter.)

The direct plan indicates exactly what will be said and done. Formulating effective teaching questions is very important. Such questions don't come easily. Thinking them through ahead of time with emphasis on anticipated pupil responses makes sure the discussion will yield thinking and learning. In order to know exactly what you are going to say, you will find it advantageous to use the first person in stating the questions and comments and to direct them to the class. The direct plan is more appropriate for daily lessons. (See Sample Plans Nos. 1 and 2 at the end of this chapter.)

If you take an indirect or general approach and write into your plan the direction, "Discuss zoo animals with the children," you may be ready to face the class with an idea but not with an effective plan. If you begin your lesson with a fruitless question such as, "Have you ever been to the zoo?," you are opening the way for a poor or even disastrous response. Some of the children may look blank, shake their heads, or say "No" in unison. That makes no progress toward the goal. Others may shout, "Yeeeeeees," in unison, raising the tempo of the class. You still have made little or no progress. A more aggressive group of children may respond by all talking at once and vying for center stage, thus creating confusion and drawing attention away from the intended goal of identifying animals by directing attention toward popcorn stands and monkey tricks. Another equally fruitless question is, "Do you like to go to the zoo?" The only possible response is "Yes" or "No." If you have decided to teach the lesson in the science book on zoo animals, begin with the assumption that your children know what a zoo is and that at least some of them have been there. Then open the lesson by asking, "What animals do we see at the zoo?" The children can't answer that question with "Yes" or "No," or by submissively agreeing with you. Neither can they stray from the goal by talking about the picnic lunch, the toy train, or the automobile accident they saw on the way. "Our science book tells about zoo animals beginning on p. 43. Turn the pages and look at the pictures. Note the names and see how many of them we have already listed. What others can we add to our list?"

The lesson plan which says, "Discuss zoo animals with the children," is taking an indirect approach. The lesson plan which says, "What animals do you see at the zoo?" is taking a direct approach. The latter implies that the teacher has thought through the goals and the expected pupil responses in order to avoid the pitfalls of ineffective questions and to have ready effective questions which will elicit appropriate responses. Writing down the questions gives you assurance when you face the class. Some teachers use direct plans in the form of questions on file cards or in the margins of the teacher's edition of the text. It is in this *how* part of the lesson plan that you make sure you know exactly what you are going to do and say. It is here that you take the preventive measures which eliminate wasted time and useless detours, and assure yourself of efficient use of time and forward progress toward the stated objectives.

SUMMARY

Lesson plans may be based on subject matter to be covered, needs of the learners, or activities to be developed. The first permits curriculum planning to be done at the "office" level or in the editorial department. The second puts the decisions in the hands of the teacher and is based on what is known about the subject matter and the children. The third takes the children in on the planning and the execution of the plans.

Lesson plans may be structured around long-term goals, units, or daily activities. Each has its place.

Lesson plans need to include the why, the what, and the how. The *why* part seeks to justify what you plan to do. The *what* part make sure you have everything ready before you meet the class. The *how* part of an effective lesson plan provides for introducing the new concept and motivating the children to action. This part of the plan needs to show sequential development through the steps leading to a logical conclusion that has closure. It leaves the class with a feeling of accomplishment and a forward look to next steps. Parts of a lesson plan may be suggestive, general, and indirect, especially in long-term planning. There are distinct advantages in stating directly some parts of the lesson plan such as introductory comments, the specific questions to be asked, and the directions for activities or assignments, that is, stating them in the exact words you will use. This is especially true for daily lesson plans.

Whichever kind of planning you use, you can be assured that you will reap dividends in the form of self-confidence, evidence of results, and cooperation from the learners. The test of the planning is in the teaching. When you plan effectively and teach constructively you are the active agent in curriculum binding.

SAMPLE LESSON PLANS

In order to implement the suggestions in this chapter, it seems appropriate to provide samples for comparison and evaluation. On the following pages you will find three sample lesson plans constructed in accordance with the "map" provided in Fig. 3–1, p. 53. Two of the plans are for one class period each. They are both *direct* plans, stating directly what is to be said and done. The third is a unit plan covering several class periods. It is an *indirect*, or general plan, stating long term goals, organizing materials, and indicating activities.

The first sample, "How to Use Quotation Marks," is designed to show how to teach a specific skill. It is direct and subject-centered. It is appropriate at almost any grade level. Even first graders meet quotation marks in their preprimers. The second sample, "How to Read a Map," is designed to teach the use of the lines of latitude and longitude. It, too, is written as a direct plan but is activity-centered. It is appropriate at the intermediate grade level. While it is a lesson in geography, there are activities which recognize relationships to science, mathematics, and the language arts. The third sample plan, "Rivers," is a unit plan designed to cover several days and to show how to develop a series of related concepts. It is written in a general or indirect format and is problem-centered.

Study the plans, Imagine yourself actually teaching each one. Construct answers to the questions to visualize pupil responses. Evaluate the learning. Read statements and try to visualize what will happen in the classroom. When you have done this, you are ready to try your hand at writing your own lesson plans.

SAMPLE LESSON PLAN NO. 1

A plan for one class period written in direct form and using a subject-centered approach. Suitable for any grade level.

How to Use Quotation Marks

    I. Goals (stated as behavioral objectives)
        A. Given a sample of printed material with direct discourse, the children will be able to identify the direct quotations by finding the quotation marks which set off the exact words of the speaker.
        B. Given the statement including the exact words of a speaker, the children will be able to set off the direct quotation with quotation marks.
        C. Given a sample of their own writing, the children will be able to place quotation marks around direct discourse.

    II. Material to be covered
        A. Subject Matter
            1. Direct discourse
            2. Quotation marks
        B. Materials and equipment needed
            1. Language textbook, p. 121
            2. Reading textbook, p. 36 using direct discourse
            3. Overhead projector and transparencies
            4. Chalkboard and chalk
            5. Pencils and paper for each child

    III. Method
        A. Approach to the lesson
            1. Introduction
                Take a look at these sentences (on transparencies).
                    Dan and Bill went out to ride their pony.
                    The pony balked and Bill said, Help! Help!
                    The pony ran away and Dan said, Stop! Stop!
            2. Motivation
                Who is talking? How can you tell? Most books have a way of showing exactly what someone has said. Comics use the

familiar "balloon" with the line leading to the mouth of the speaker. There is another way. Let's see what it is.

B. Body of the lesson (developing use of quotation marks)
1. First step—Discovery
Examine these illustrations (on transparencies).
Bill said, "Help! Help!"
Dan said, "Stop! Stop!"
Put your hands around the part that tells exactly what Bill said. Notice that you have fenced off his exact words. Notice the marks that appear before and after what he said. These marks fence off, or enclose, his exact words. They are called quotation marks. To quote means to repeat the words of another. That is why they are called quotation marks.

2. Second step—Experimentation
Quotations can come in different parts of a sentence.
Examine these illustrations (on transparencies).
"Bill!" said Dan.
Bill said, "Dan!"
"Look, Dan," said Bill.
"Look," Dan said, "Bill is riding."
In the first sentence who is talking? What did he say? In the second sentence who is talking? What did he say? In the third sentence who is talking? What did he say? In the fourth sentence who is talking? What did he say? Be sure you get it all. Why did it take two pair of quotation marks in the fourth sentence?

C. Conclusion and follow-up
1. Identifying the principle
In a printed story how can you tell exactly what someone is saying? Read the story on p. 36 in the reader and find what each character said. How can you tell who is saying it?

If you are writing a story, how can you tell your readers which one of your characters is talking and exactly what he or she said?

2. Assignment
Find two examples of direct discourse in your reader or in a library book.

Explain the difference in the meanings of these two examples:
Bill said, "Dan, come here."
"Bill," said Dan, "come here."
Write two sentences containing direct discourse.
Place the quotation marks to tell your reader exactly what the speaker said.
Turn to the exercises on p. 121 in your language text and see if you can do them by yourself.

SAMPLE LESSON PLAN NO. 2

A direct plan for one class period appropriate for intermediate grades and using an activities-centered approach.

How to Read a Map

    I. Objectives
        A. To increase skill in map reading through actual practice.
        B. To engage in activities which will aid in map reading through the use of lines of latitude and longitude.

    II. Materials
        A. Maps—The World, Africa
        B. Blackboard, chalk, yardstick
        C. Graph paper and rulers for each pupil

    III. Procedures
        A. Introduction and motivation
            We have been using maps. We have talked about the lines on the maps and how they help us locate places. *I think I can help you see how this works.* (Note: This is the most important point because it implies that the child is doing the learning and it is the teacher who is helping.) Why do we need to locate things? Why is having a method better than just hunting at random?
        B. Development of the concepts
            First step—establishing a point of view
                To locate anything you have to have a place to start. Unless you know where Luis is now, you can't tell him how to go from there to where he wants to go. Similarly, on a map we have to have a starting point. Lay your paper off in squares like this:

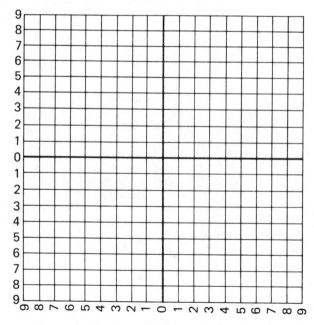

Now draw a heavy line through the center each way at the zero point. Which one is the vertical line? Which one is the horizontal line? If we were going to locate something on that graph where would we begin?

Second step—group practice

Begin in the middle where the two heavy lines cross.
Count to the right four spaces and up two spaces.
Place a dot there. Now begin in the middle again and count to the left five spaces and up four spaces.
Put a dot there. Next begin in the middle, count to the left six spaces and down two spaces. Put a dot there. Now count to the right two spaces and down three spaces. Mark the place.
On a map, right and left and up and down have names indicating directions. What are they? Label them on your graph: North, East, South, and West. Now try these:

Go east two spaces and north four spaces.
Go east three spaces and south six spaces.
Go west four spaces and north four spaces.
Go west four spaces and south five spaces.

Third Step—individual practice

Here is a sheet of graph paper for you. You will also need your pencil and a ruler. Draw a vertical line near the middle. Label it zero. Draw a horizontal line through the middle. Label it zero. This establishes your starting point. Put N at the top, S at the bottom, E at the right, and W at the left. Then locate these places:

E5–N9; E7–N3; E8–N0. Connect them with a line.
W4–N1; W8–S1; E8–N7. Connect them with a line.
Find the point of intersection. (E6–N6)

Fourth step—applying the principle to a map of the world and a map of Africa. (Note: Africa is the only continent from which measurements can be shown from both the equator and the prime meridian in all four directions.)

When you read a map you use the same principle. What are the vertical lines on maps called? What are the horizontal lines called? Where shall we begin? Notice the numbers across the top of the map. Where is the one numbered zero? We call that the prime meridian. It is the point from which all east and west directions are measured. Notice the numbers down the side of the map. Where is the one marked zero? What is another name for it? (equator) Now that you have decided on a starting point where these two lines cross, you are ready to use east and west longitude and north and south latitude to locate any place in the world.

On the map of Africa, find a city 15 degrees north latitude and 17 degrees west longitude. (Dakar) Find a city 18 degrees east and 34 degrees south. (Capetown) Find one 30 degrees north and 32 degrees east. (Cairo)

On a map of the world, find the following and indicate their locations by latitude and longitude:

Manila, P. I.—(15N–120E)
New York City—(40N–75W)
Sydney, Australia—(35S–150E)
Buenos Aires, S. A.—(35S–60W)

C. Conclusion

With this method you can locate any place in the world. It works two ways. If you know where a city is, you can describe it for someone else by telling its latitude and longitude. If you want to find a city and know its latitude and longitude on a map, you can readily locate it. The same applies for other geographical features such as oceans, lakes, mountains, and rivers. This information is important to navigators, pilots, tourists, traveling salespeople, and even armchair travelers enjoying an article in *The National Geographic* magazine.

SAMPLE LESSON PLAN NO. 3

A unit plan covering several days or weeks, written in indirect form, and using a problem-centered approach.

Rivers

I. Justification for Teaching the Unit (Why)
  A. General Objectives
    1. The children will come to appreciate the value of rivers in our system of ecology, and the problems created by people in the misuse of rivers.
    2. The children will be able to identify uses of rivers as sources of power, water, drainage, transportation, recreation, and beauty.
    3. The children will recognize the relationship which exists between a river and its surrounding environment, both natural and man-made.
  B. Specific Objectives
    1. The children will be able to identify the parts of a river as:

       source   distributaries
       channel   mouth
       tributaries   delta
       navigable portion

    2. The children will be able to trace on a map of the world the main rivers on each continent.
    3. The children will be able to locate specifically the following rivers:

       Hudson   Ohio
       Mississippi   Missouri
       Rio Grande   Columbia

    4. For each of the above rivers, the children will be able to:
        Trace from source to mouth.
        Identify major tributaries.
        Locate important cities along the route.
        Discuss the relation of each river to climate, natural resources, and industry.

II. Overview of the Plans for Teaching the Unit (What)
    A. Content to be covered
        1. Why are rivers important?
        2. How are rivers formed?
        3. How do rivers change?
        4. What are some important characteristics of rivers?
        5. How do rivers affect people?
        6. How do people affect rivers?
        7. What rivers in the United States are especially significant in the early settlement and development of our country?
    B. Materials to be used
        1. Globes
        2. Maps—both wall maps and individual desk maps
        3. Transparencies and overhead projector
        4. Sand table
        5. Tape recorder and player
        6. Reference books (list titles and page numbers)
        7. Film, "Rivers" and projector
    C. Activities to be scheduled
        1. Take a trip to a dam to see how water is impounded and power is developed.
        2. Make a sand table model showing a contour map of a river system.
        3. Develop a series of drawings showing how people use rivers for their own good.
        4. Write script to accompany pictures.
        5. Record script on tape.
        6. Plan a program to present pictures and tapes.

III. Sequential Steps in Development of the Unit (How)
    A. Launching the unit (including introduction, motivation, and initial teacher-pupil planning)
        1. Introduce the unit by showing the film, "Rivers."
        2. Let the children discuss the information given in the film and raise questions about problems related to rivers.
        3. Have them add facts they know about rivers.
        4. Lead them to raise questions which will be listed on the chalkboard as a basis for further study.
    B. Step-by-step schedule of activities in pursuit of the unit (Body)
        1. Refer to the questions raised and list sources of information— texts, encyclopedias, maps, local river system, and local settlements related to the river.
        2. Divide the class into committees to assume responsibilities for answering specific questions raised, such as:
            a. How many ways can you find that rivers help people?
            b. How many ways do you know that people use rivers?

      c. What ways have people changed rivers for their own use?

      d. Identify cities located on rivers and find out why they were developed there.

      e. Identify the parts of a river system and make a diagram to demonstrate.

3. Appoint a group of two or three capable children to scan available references and mark sources of helpful information.

4. Allow two or three days for small groups to work.

5. Allow one or two days for committee reports on the above topics.

6. Assign one U.S. river to each of several children, or pairs of children for special report.

7. Work with the rest of the class on local river system:

    source   history

    channel   value to community

8. Plan one or two days for reporting information gathered under items 6 and 7 above.

9. If there is a local dam, artificial lake, or disposal plant, plan a field trip to find out why it was developed and what function it serves in the community.

10. Use language periods for writing scripts and summaries.

C. Culminating activities (Conclusion)

  1. Summarizing content

      a. Have each committee or individual who has done research or made a report illustrate information with drawings, sand-table models, or murals. These can be photographed and made into slides.

      b. Have commentary written to accompany and explain slides.

      c. Have capable readers record summaries on tapes.

  2. Sharing with others

    Invite an audience to see the slides and hear the recordings. This may be used for an all-school assembly program, or the class may invite another room, or parents as an audience.

    In this form the program may be repeated as often as needed.

  3. Checking on learnings

    Give teams a map of a country showing its rivers and some additional information in order to apply what they have learned. The stated problem:

    "If you were planning this country, where would you locate the five major cities? Tell why you choose these particular locations. How would you develop the surrounding areas?"

Estimated Time Schedule for Teaching the Unit:

1. Showing of film	1 day
2. Discussion, listing of facts, raising questions, and identifying sources of information	1 day
3. Planning committee organization and scheduling study sessions	3 days

4.	Reporting of findings	2 days
5.	Planning study of local rivers	1 day
6.	Research and study activities	2 days
7.	Reporting	2 days
8.	Field trip	1 day
9.	Summarizing, photographing, and taping	3 days
10.	Program presentation	1 day
11.	Evaluation	1 day
	Estimated	18 days

Relation to Other Curricular Areas:

Reading—reference and source materials
Language—written—preparing summaries
Language—oral—taping summaries
Spelling—vocabulary as needed
Art—making sketches to illustrate information
Mathematics—distance, volume, cost, and graphs
Music—songs about rivers
Health—sanitation, water supply, sewage disposal
Geography—map reading, locations of rivers
History—Record of settlements, transportation, and explorers
Economics—effect on cost of transportation and cost of products to people

SUGGESTED ACTIVITIES

1. Find at least two sample lesson plans in curriculum reference books and compare them with the samples given in this chapter as to content, format, and organization.
2. Consult two or three in-service teachers who are willing to share with you their lesson plans and compare them for content and format.
3. Select a subject matter area at a given grade level. Consult a textbook (or books), the accompanying teachers' manual, and the curriculum outline:
   a. List the topics you will cover during the year.
   b. List the materials you will use.
   c. List the activities you will carry out.
4. Select one unit within the subject matter outlined above. This may be a topic that will cover a week or two.
   a. List the related subtopics.
   b. List the needed materials for this one unit.
   c. List the specific activities for this unit.
   d. Estimate the time needed to complete the unit.
5. Select one part of the unit–a lesson you plan to cover in one class period in from 30 to 60 minutes.
   a. Write a lesson plan including only those learnings and those activities which you can cover in one period.
   b. Make your plan specific and direct.

6. Condense this lesson plan into notes you can place on 3 × 5 file cards to have in your hands for ready reference while teaching.

7. If possible, arrange to teach the unit or at least one lesson of it to a group of children in an actual classroom. Note: This may be done in cooperation with a local school, or during your student teaching.

SELECTED READINGS

1. BAIRD, HUGH W., Dwayne Belt, Lyal Holder, and Clark Webb, *A Behavioral Approach to Teaching*, Dubuque, Iowa: Wm. C. Brown, 1972, p. 252. A spiral bound 8 ½ by 11 book. Discusses planning, objectives, assessment, sequencing, questioning, and concept teaching.

2. BURNS, RICHARD W., *New Approaches to Behavioral Objectives*, Dubuque, Iowa: Wm. C. Brown, 1972, p. 118. Uses programmed instruction form with self-testing to differentiate between goals and objectives, terminal and instructional objectives, overt and covert behaviors, and open and closed objectives. Explains how to evaluate and use objectives in teaching. Chapter tests with answer keys.

3. DAWE, ROBERT, "You May Not Agree, but Plan Books Are A Waste of Time," in *Today's Education*, Vol. 60, No. 6, Sept. 1971, p. 49. Arguments for and against plan books. Invitation to send in reactions.

4. GAGNE, ROBERT M., "Behavioral Objectives? Yes!" in *Educational Leadership*, Vol. 29, No. 5, Feb. 1972, pp. 394–96. Identifies behavioral objectives and justifies them.

5. GODBOLD, JOHN VANCE, "Oral Questioning Practices of Teachers in Social Studies Classes," in *Educational Leadership*. Vol. 28, No. 1, Oct. 1970, pp. 61–67. Divides questions into categories. Identifies most commonly used types.

6. JOYCE, BRUCE, and MARTHA WEIL, *Models of Teaching*, Englewood Cliffs, N.J.: Prentice-Hall, 1972. This book is written for the classroom teacher. It offers practical suggestions and describes models of effective teaching.

7. KNELLER, GEORGE F., "Behavioral Objectives? No!" in *Educational Leadership*, Vol. 29, No. 5, Feb. 1972, pp. 397–400. Analyzes behavioral objectives. Speculates about their uses and dangers. Presents the case against them.

8. MAGER, ROBERT F., *Preparing Instructional Objectives*, Palo Alto, California: Fearon, 1962, p. 61. Paperback book showing exactly how to prepare objectives for classroom teaching. Provides self-test at the end.

9. MANNELLO, GEORGE, "Resource Unit Versus Instructional System," in *Educational Forum*, Vol. XXXV, No. 1, Nov. 1970, pp. 65–70. Points out the attractions of "package" programs. Identifies the professional teacher as one who is involved in the curriculum with the children. Recommends retaining the resource unit as a base but freeing teachers to organize on their own.

10. NICHOLS, EUGENE D., "Are Behavioral Objectives the Answer?" in *The Arithmetic Teacher*, Vol. XIX, Oct. 1972, pp. 419, and 474–76. Makes an eleven-point case against behavioral objectives as a basis for evaluating results in arithmetic.

11. POPHAM, W. JAMES, and EVA L. BAKER, *Establishing Instructional Goals*, Englewood Cliffs, N.J.: Prentice-Hall, 1970. Tells how to select appropriate objectives and establish performance standards. Programmed learning. Mastery tests. Answer sheets.

12. POPHAM, W. JAMES, and EVA L. BAKER, *Planning Instructional Sequence*, Englewood Cliffs, N.J.: Prentice-Hall, 1970, p. 138. Tells how to provide appropriate practice and provide the learner with knowledge of results. Shows how to analyze learner behaviors and to evaluate results. Programmed lessons. Mastery tests. Answer sheets.

13. SHANE, JUNE GRANT, and HAROLD G. SHANE, "Ralph Tyler Discusses Behavioral Objectives," (An Interview) in *Today's Education*, Vol. 62, No. 6, Sept.-Oct. 1973, pp. 41–46. A question and answer account of an interview between the authors and the educator on the subject of behavioral objectives. Points out the importance of concern with specific behavior and human capabilities.

14. STEWIG, JOHN WARREN, "Instructional Strategies," in *Elementary English*, Vol. 50, No. 4, April 1973, pp. 647–50. Focuses on questioning techniques as a means of teaching. Analyzes types of questions and structure of pupil responses.

15. WENDEL, ROBERT, "Inquiry Teaching: Dispelling the Myths," in *The Clearing House*. Vol. XLVIII, Sept. 1973, pp. 24–28. Distinguishes between totally unstructured, student-centered teaching and cooperative teacher-pupil planning as a means of learning. Identifies the teacher's role not as one of explaining content but rather as one of guiding learning.

4

MANAGING THE CLASSROOM

Getting It All Done and Keeping Everything Properly Managed

Courtesy, Skiff School, Phoenix, Arizona

CLASSROOM MANAGEMENT

You're the general manager. You have a roomful of children. You may have the same ones all day or a different group each period. When the bell rings and the door closes, you are in charge. Do you know how to manage the situation in order to get all the work done and keep everything under control? Sometimes this is more difficult than mastering the subject matter or planning the lessons.

Here come the children! You must accept all who come and create a place for each one regardless of the situation and the individual's age and achievement level. Will you try to put together children with like abilities or work with heterogeneous groups? And after the term has ended, how will you handle plans for progress to the next level or the next year?

Will the classroom be self-contained or departmentalized? Will you be alone or a member of a team? Will you have any nonprofessional help? Will you teach the class as a total group or subdivide it? And if you establish teaching groups, on what basis will you make the divisions? How will you meet the needs of individuals who do not seem to fit?

Once you are organized, can you keep things going? Why do the children behave as they do and what can you do about it? Will you meet behavior problems negatively or positively? Will you correct them or try to prevent them?

All this must be considered before the actual teaching can take place. Are you ready? Can you do it? This chapter is designed to help you visualize the problems, anticipate the situations, and be prepared to meet whatever comes.

The dictionary defines the word "teach" in two ways. The first definition is "to impart knowledge." The second is "to cause one to learn." It is the second of these definitions with which we are dealing in this chapter. Knowledge is essential to the teacher, but no matter how much knowledge you possess, it will do no good unless the pupil learns. Your expounding on the subject matter may or may not result in learning. Your major task is "to cause the children to learn." This implies managing the classroom in such a way that learning happens. This depends on the skill with which you and your administrators set up a situation in which learning can take place. It involves such problems as grade-level assignments, grouping, promotion, organization, pupil behavior, routine, and discipline. Unless these problems are met and solved before actual instruction begins, attempts to cause the children to learn may meet with frustration. When they are met satisfactorily and a learning environment has been created, the daily schedule should work and the lesson plans should yield results.

The principal is responsible for the management of the total school. This is an administrative job. The teacher is the key person responsible for the management of the classroom. That is an instructional job. Both are important. But let us never forget that the only reason for the existence of the administrative organization is to make the instructional program work. We shall begin then with a look at the administrative problem of the organization of pupil personnel.

HOW TO CLASSIFY AND GROUP THE PUPILS

By the time the children come into the classroom on the first day of school, much preliminary planning has already gone into preregistration, both at the end of the previous year and in the before-school period in late summer. Even so, no one is ever quite sure exactly how many children there will be once school starts, where each one should go, and what arrangements will have to be made to receive them. There are two steps involved in organizing pupil personnel. The first one has to do with building organization. This is the responsibility of the chief administrator who may or may not consult with teachers in making room assignments. The second step has to do with room organization. This is the point at which you, the teacher, assume control. Whether you are new in the profession, new in this particular set-up, or a veteran with previous experiences on which to build, you still have certain responsibilities for fitting into the total program. Since the whole school exists for the benefit of the pupils, a suitable place must be found for each one.

Accepting the Children Who Come

The child who is made to feel wanted and accepted has crossed the first bridge toward learning. The public school is in no position to accept or reject children on the basis of abilities, ethnic origins, social status, personal preferences, or any other factors differentiating one child from another. If the child falls within the age limits covered by the school program, belongs in the district or has been legally assigned to the school, and has potential for benefiting from public school education, then that child has a right to be there and it is the responsibility of the school not only to accept but to create a place for each one.

Once the children are there, they have to be sorted out. Each one must be given a station to provide a feeling of belongingness. Each child has the right to feel that this is "my school," "my room," "my desk," and "my teacher." They all need to feel that they belong and that there is a place for them. There are many different ways of sorting children and placing them in a setting where teaching and learning can take place. But children don't stay put. Time passes, children grow, lessons are learned, and the situation changes. Therefore, the next step in organization involves watching the growth process and moving the children along according to some kind of plan.

Let's examine what kinds of plans are made to meet the problems of building organization.

Creating a Place for Each Child.   The first contact the children will have with the school is usually in the general office where they and perhaps their parents form a first impression. A harrassed principal or overworked clerk may leave them with the feeling that they represent one more burden too great to bear. On the other hand, if the school personnel provide a cordial welcome and show genuine interest in obtaining necessary information to be recorded on enrollment forms, they may provide the children and parents with a sense of security. Guiding the children to the right room where they meet the right teacher may create a warm feeling. The room assignment may depend on total enrollment, policy for organization, and the philosophy of the instructional program. Even then there may be need to make adjustments for children who reveal family problems, illnesses, or unexpected spurts of progress. Many different plans have been tried, altered, abandoned, and sometimes reinstated over the years. All of them are merely devices for putting children into groups conducive to teaching and learning.

One-room schools were originally developed in sparsely settled communities, such as those which existed in pioneer days, and still exist in some of the more remote regions. *Graded schools* began to make their appearance in the middle of the nineteenth century. These were based on a plan instituted by Horrace Mann in the Quincey School in Boston in 1848. *Primary* and *intermediate schools* were designed to lessen the rigidity of the graded structure and to permit a child to move along for a period of two or three years before a decision was faced as to the ability to work at the next level. *The junior high school* was originally designed as an attempt to bridge the gap between the elementary school and the high school. This plan tended to introduce the formal organization of the high school sooner and so *the middle school* was an attempt to correct this problem. *The nongraded school* represented still another innovation. It has appeared in the literature regularly but exists less often in actual practice. This was intended to remove the lock-step system of assignments, standards, and promotions and to permit the child to move at a pace commensurate with ability and to grow in a continuous pattern. It eliminated failure because children moved on only when a sequence of tasks had been completed.

Regardless of which of the above patterns of organization exists, with the possible exception of the one room school, there is still the problem of sorting the pupils into teachable groups and moving them along to the next level at stated intervals. These two problems involve classification and promotion.

Sorting Them Out. In addition to chronological age and grade classification, many other administrative factors need to be considered. If there are only twenty-five or thirty eight-year-olds in the community, the problem of placement in classrooms is relatively easy because a natural grouping of the children exists. The third-grade teacher and the eight-year-old children will become a teaching-learning group in the classroom. When more children at a given age or grade level appear and more teachers are assigned to the same level, then the problem of which children will be assigned to each room or teacher becomes an issue. This plan is usually referred to as *horizontal organization*. The question is how shall the children be divided within the grade level. Many ways have been tried. Each one solves some problems but in doing so creates other problems.

Homogeneous grouping is a plan which places together individuals who are similar according to some one criterion such as age, mental ability, or scores on standardized tests. In attaining homogeneity in one area, one automatically creates differences in other areas. For instance, if the criterion is mental ability, differences such as in age, sex, ethnic background, social status, interest, physical size, and perhaps many other factors will exist within the group. The plan has both advantages and disadvantages as set forth in Fig. 4–1.

Homogeneous Grouping

ADVANTAGES	DISADVANTAGES
Reduces preparation of subject matter for the teacher.	Leads to false assumption that same learnings will do for all.
Provides "fair" competition for the learner.	Reduces challenges for fast worker because this child can equal or exceed goals of the group.
Develops unity and cohesion within the group.	Eliminates extra challenge for slow worker because this child never sees a higher level of performance.
Unifies goals in terms of subject matter.	
Places major emphasis on group attainment and conformity.	Reduces emphasis on development of the individual.
Makes for economy of time and funds in management and buying of materials of instruction.	Leads to waste of time and material when used with individuals for whom the program is inappropriate.
Makes objective testing and record keeping systematic and uniform.	Expects the child to fit predetermined pattern and meet preestablished goals.
Provides for comparison of groups based on standards and common goals.	Invites comparison based on standards outside the child and the stage of development.

Figure 4–1.   *Advantages and disadvantages of homogeneous grouping*

Heterogeneous grouping is a plan which attempts to place together individuals who represent differences. This kind of organization is not a laissez faire approach. In order to achieve true heterogeneity some planning must be done to make sure the group actually contains representatives of different types—both sexes, different races, old and young, upper and lower social status, bright and dull, and high and low achievement. The plan has both advantages and disadvantages as set forth in Fig. 4-2.

Random grouping occurs when the administrator merely lets the children go to the rooms they wish, or merely fills one room before starting to enroll in another. Some schools claim to have heterogeneity in their grouping because they have not sorted children according to any particular characteristics. In actuality they have failed to achieve true heterogeneity because they have not given careful consideration to making each group representative of the various types of children in the total school population. Children allowed to enroll in rooms at random tend to develop some elements of homogeneity through choice of teachers, maintenance of friendship groups, and a show of timidity in asserting themselves. This approach is truly a laissez faire attitude of noninterference. It is an avoidance of responsibility.

Multiage or cross-level grouping has some similarities with the traditional one-room school. Comparison with family life, the popularity of

Heterogeneous Grouping

ADVANTAGES	DISADVANTAGES
Encourages the teacher to see each child as an individual within the total group.	Increases and differentiates preparation on the part of the teacher.
Provides challenges for all, even the most capable.	May lead to "unfair" competition if slower learner is expected to keep up with peers.
Gives slower learner a higher goal and an opportunity to learn from others who may make a contribution to the child's meager background.	May divide rather than unify the group.
	Makes for variety, duplicity, and sometimes waste in buying of materials and supplies.
Puts emphasis on individual rather than total group.	Makes objective testing, measurement in terms of standards, and evaluation in terms of attainments difficult.
Encourages use of both time and materials in terms of needs.	
Encourages planning in terms of individual learning needs.	Demands a teacher who is oriented to a child-development approach instead of a standards approach.
Invites evaluation in terms of growth rather than competition and comparison.	Demands an open mind toward children on the part of the administrators.
Eliminates need for excessive emphasis on grades and awards.	Is often misunderstood by parents and laypeople who believe in standards, honor rolls, and awards.
Puts emphasis on growth and learning.	Ignores individual differences in some areas.
Allows children to proceed at their own pace.	

Figure 4-2. *Advantages and disadvantages of heterogeneous grouping*

the British Primary School, and disillusionment with rigid grouping plans have caused many educators as well as parents to look to the past and see some of the advantages of such a plan. This changed perspective has led to thinking of children as belonging to a peer group not strictly limited to those within a few months or a single year of their own age level. In a family situation, children associate with others both older and younger than themselves. Working out such a multiage grouping plan for a classroom takes some thoughtful planning. Figure 4–3 shows how some individuals might fit into the situation and how a total building organization might work out. Figure 4–4 shows the flow through one room over a four-year span. Study the examples of Freddie and Alan in this figure to see how their positions in the total group change from year to year. Freddie

AGE LEVELS	TEACHER ASSIGNMENTS		
	Miss Black	*Mrs. Horn*	*Miss West*
6 year-olds	Alice	★★★★★★★★★★★★★★★★	★★★★★★★★★★★★★★★★
	★★★★★★★★★★★★★★★★	★★★★★★★★★★★★★★★★	★★★★★★★★★★★★★★★★
	★★★★★★★★★★★★★★★★	★★★★★★★★★★★★★★★★	★★★★★★★★★★★★★★★★
	★★★★★★★★★★★★★★★★	★★★★★★★★★★★★★★★★	★★★★★★★★★★★★★★★★
	★★★★★★★★★★★★★★★	Pauline	★★★★★★★★★★★★★★★★
	★★★★★★★★★★★★★★★★	★★★★★★★★★★★★★★★★	★★★★★★★★★★★★★★★★
	★★★★★★★★★★★★★★★★	★★★★★★★★★★★★★★★★	★★★★★★★★★★★★★★★★
	★★★★★★★★★★★★★★★★	★★★★★★★★★★★★★★★★	★★★★★★★★★★★★★★★★
	★★★★★★★★★★★★★★★★	★★★★★★★★★★★★★★★★	★★★★★★★★★★★★★★★★
	★★★★★★★★★★★★★★★★	★★★★★★★★★★★★★★★	Betty
7 year-olds	★★★★★★★★★★★★★★★★	★★★★★★★★★★★★★★★	Thelma
	★★★★★★★★★★★★★★★★	★★★★★★★★★★★★★★★★	★★★★★★★★★★★★★★★★
	★★★★★★★★★★★★★★★★	★★★★★★★★★★★★★★★★	★★★★★★★★★★★★★★★★
	★★★★★★★★★★★★★★★★	★★★★★★★★★★★★★★★★	★★★★★★★★★★★★★★★★
	★★★★★★★★★★★★★★★	Anne	★★★★★★★★★★★★★★★★
	★★★★★★★★★★★★★★★★	★★★★★★★★★★★★★★★★	★★★★★★★★★★★★★★★★
	★★★★★★★★★★★★★★★★	★★★★★★★★★★★★★★★★	★★★★★★★★★★★★★★★★
	★★★★★★★★★★★★★★★★	★★★★★★★★★★★★★★★★	★★★★★★★★★★★★★★★★
	Martha	★★★★★★★★★★★★★★★	★★★★★★★★★★★★★★★★
8 year-olds	Barbara	★★★★★★★★★★★★★★★★	★★★★★★★★★★★★★★★★
	★★★★★★★★★★★★★★★★	★★★★★★★★★★★★★★★★	★★★★★★★★★★★★★★★★
	★★★★★★★★★★★★★★★★	★★★★★★★★★★★★★★★★	★★★★★★★★★★★★★★★★
	★★★★★★★★★★★★★★★★	★★★★★★★★★★★★★★★★	★★★★★★★★★★★★★★★★
	★★★★★★★★★★★★★★★	Cathy	★★★★★★★★★★★★★★★★
	★★★★★★★★★★★★★★★★	★★★★★★★★★★★★★★★★	★★★★★★★★★★★★★★★★
	★★★★★★★★★★★★★★★★	★★★★★★★★★★★★★★★★	★★★★★★★★★★★★★★★★
	★★★★★★★★★★★★★★★★	★★★★★★★★★★★★★★★★	★★★★★★★★★★★★★★★★
	★★★★★★★★★★★★★★★★	★★★★★★★★★★★★★★★	Helen

Figure 4–3. *Organization based on a multiage grouping plan.*

started school young and immature. He spent four years in the same room without ever experiencing the uprooting from a total group because turnover was gradual from year to year. Alan started school older and more mature than Freddie and spent only two years in the room without missing anything because he could work with other groups in the room. He scarcely knew when or how he made the adjustment to a different group.

As the various plans for grouping children have been tried, it has become evident that each one has both advantages and disadvantages. A long-term perspective, however, soon revealed that as one problem was solved another was created. No plan has been found that has all the advantages and none of the disadvantages.

AGE LEVELS	MISS SAMPSON'S ROOM			
	1st year	*2nd year*	*3rd year*	*4th year*
6 year-olds	Freddie ★★★★★★★★★★ ★★★★★★★★★★ ★★★★★★★★★★ ★★★★★★★★★★ ★★★★★★★★★★ ★★★★★★★★★★ Alan	★★★★★★★★★ ★★★★★★★★ ★★★★★★★★★★ ★★★★★★★★★★ ★★★★★★★★★★ ★★★★★★★★★★ ★★★★★★★★★★ ★★★★★★★★★★	★★★★★★★★★ ★★★★★★★★★★ ★★★★★★★★★★ ★★★★★★★★★★ ★★★★★★★★★★ ★★★★★★★★★★ ★★★★★★★★★★ ★★★★★★★★★★	★★★★★★★★★ ★★★★★★★★★★ ★★★★★★★★ ★★★★★★★★★★ ★★★★★★★★★★ ★★★★★★★★★★ ★★★★★★★★★★ ★★★★★★★★★★
7 year-olds	★★★★★★★★★★ ★★★★★★★★★★ ★★★★★★★★★★ ★★★★★★★★★★ ★★★★★★★★★★ ★★★★★★★★★★ ★★★★★★★★★★ ★★★★★★★★★★	Freddie ★★★★★★★★★★ ★★★★★★★★★★ ★★★★★★★★★★ ★★★★★★★★★★ ★★★★★★★★★★ ★★★★★★★★★★ Alan	★★★★★★★★★ ★★★★★★★★★★ ★★★★★★★★★ ★★★★★★★★★★ ★★★★★★★★★★ ★★★★★★★★★★ ★★★★★★★★★ ★★★★★★★★★	★★★★★★★★★★ ★★★★★★★★★★ ★★★★★★★★★★ ★★★★★★★★★★ ★★★★★★★★★★ ★★★★★★★★★★ ★★★★★★★★★★ ★★★★★★★★★★
8 year-olds	★★★★★★★★★ ★★★★★★★★★★ ★★★★★★★★★★ ★★★★★★★★★★ ★★★★★★★★★★ ★★★★★★★★★★ ★★★★★★★★★★ ★★★★★★★★★★	★★★★★★★★★ ★★★★★★★★★ ★★★★★★★★★★ ★★★★★★★★★★ ★★★★★★★★★★ ★★★★★★★★★★ ★★★★★★★★★★ ★★★★★★★★★★	Freddie ★★★★★★★★★★ ★★★★★★★★★★ ★★★★★★★★★★ ★★★★★★★★★★ ★★★★★★★★★★ ★★★★★★★★★★ ★★★★★★★★★★	★★★★★★★★★ ★★★★★★★★★★ ★★★★★★★★★★ ★★★★★★★★★★ ★★★★★★★★★★ ★★★★★★★★★★ ★★★★★★★★★★ ★★.★★★★★★★★
9 year-olds	★★★★★★★★★ ★★★★★★★★★★	★★★★★★★★★ ★★★★★★★★★★	★★★★★★★★★ ★★★★★★★★★★	Freddie ★★★★★★★★★★

Figure 4-4. *Year by year turn-over of pupil personnel in a classroom organized on a multiage plan*

Moving Them Along.   Under our present school calendars we have a "first day of school" in the fall and a "last day of school" in the spring. It has become customary to move children along from one level to another. Thus, the end of the year calls for decisions. This process of moving children along from one level to the next is known as *vertical organization*. It involves the whole area of pupil *classification* and *promotion*. It is set up on the assumption that the prescribed curriculum has been covered and that each child did do it or didn't do it and therefore either *passed* or *failed*. What we know about growth patterns of children is convincing enough to countermand this plan. Unfortunately, tradition has kept us in the "rut" of the graded program and the pass-fail syndrome. A review of admission plans, promotion practices, and individual progress will show the problem in a new light.

Admission plans in most school systems are regulated by the calendar. In order to expedite the admission policy, the administration sets a "cut off" date on or before which a child must be a given age in order to enter school. In most cases, this date is different from the compulsory age for school attendance. In any case, it is arbitrary and results in a full year's difference, lacking one day, between the oldest and the youngest child in the entering group. Add to that the possibility of variation in maturity and intelligence and there is an even wider span of ability levels. Some schools have attempted to provide flexibility in the admission policy on the basis of maturity, test results, or available space, but too often this has resulted in succumbing to parental pressure rather than in an adjustment for the benefit of the child. (See Figure 4–3.)

Promotion practices determine the manner in which children are moved along after they are in the school. Some believe children who cannot keep up should be "failed" or "retained." Such a plan results in retentions, overageness, and failure. Others believe that nothing is gained by having children repeat a grade level and that they are actually harmed by being labeled a "failure." The question is should the school adjust to the child's needs or ask that the child's growth pattern adjust to the school's requirements.

Individual progress calls for planning both content and activities to keep pace with the growth pattern of the child. This means that there will be many different levels of work in a given classroom and that an individual child may be working at one level in one area and at a different level in another area. This makes possible a program of *continuous growth* where the child is no longer expected to cover a prescribed body of content in a given period of time to be completed by the end of the year. Such a plan, however, does change the system of uniform admissions and promotion policies. (See Figure 4–4.)

Flexible admissions policies would change the concept of both horizontal and vertical organization. When a school system recognizes the principles of individual differences, it cannot justify an admission policy based on chronological age with a fixed date. It cannot support a promotion policy determined by subject matter covered in a given period of time. Jones (17:195–202) describes a plan for continuous admissions and compares it with the traditional system, pointing out the problems encountered and the advantages gained by both. McLain (20:472–75) describes an all-year plan which operates schools the year around with no beginning and no ending. He advocates that children enter school whenever they are ready and move along at their own individual rates. With these plans sometimes children will work alone and sometimes in small groups based on needs, interests, and abilities.

Organizing Children Within the Classroom

A teacher, plus a number of children, plus four walls do not necessarily make a good teaching-learning situation. The patterns of curriculum organization identified in Chap. 3 will be evident in the way the room is organized and the instructional program is carried out.

Deciding Who Will Teach What to Whom. Historically we have moved from one pattern to another in an attempt to find the "best" way. Each time an innovation is launched, there are those who hope they have found "the answer." Unfortunately, each alteration in the plan of organization solves some problems and creates some new ones.

The self-contained classroom is one in which the entire curriculum is contained in a single setting. In such a setting the teacher has a continuing relationship with the children over an extended period of time. Knowing the children and their families gives insight difficult to attain in a situation subject to constant change.

Departmentalization was introduced as content became more complex on the premise that better learning experiences might result if each teacher taught a specialty. The strongest argument for this plan was in the area of special subjects. Another strong argument was in the economy of materials and their multiple use by different groups. This plan meant that either children or teachers had to move from station to station. One of the apparent weaknesses of it was that the targets became subject-matter centered and all the children tended to be exposed to the same content at the same time.

Team-teaching, differentiated staffing, dual progress, and *block programs* have been introduced to help the teacher know the children better and still work in a given curriculum area. Team teaching has been differentiated from departmentalization in that in one case, two or more teachers are planning and working together to combine their talents whereas, in the other case, the responsibilities are divided in order to strengthen subject matter. Carrying out such a program demands that each member of the team be aware of the total program. Giving different types of assignments to different staff members and moving children in "blocks" provides continuity for both teachers and children. This makes it possible for learners to progress at different rates in different areas.

Aides and paraprofessionals may be volunteer, paid, or part of a special project, sometimes federally funded. Care must be exercised in the use of such help in order that it benefit the child. A helper assigned to "hear a child read" may be accomplishing little except removing an objectionable child from the group and listening to and recording the child's mistakes. Such assistance in the classroom is not intended to make things easier for you, but it should be a means whereby you can render more professional services to more children because someone else is taking care of such routine duties as counting lunch money, preparing supplies, or copying information on record forms while you engage in "teaching," which is what you were trained to do.

Facing the Class.   This is the point at which you actually begin teaching. There they are! What will you do? How should you manage the group? Should you try to talk to all of them at once? Where should you be stationed in the room? If you talk to an individual or a small group what will the rest be doing? If you decide to break the children up into subgroups within the room for instructional purposes, on what basis should the grouping be done? If you work with individuals each on his or her own level, how will you be able to keep it all straight? How much time can you spend with each child? And what happens to the unit plans and the daily schedule?

Total group instruction is practical at times. Singing a song calls for unison work since part of the group can't very well work independently while singing is going on in the room. The same may be true of listening to a story, planning room activities, watching a film, or listening to announcements. However, if you do all the teaching in this manner, you are subscribing to the book-centered curriculum on the assumption that, "This is what I teach and if the children can't keep up they should not be here." There are, however, some areas of the curriculum where there can be a common thread of interest without everyone necessarily doing the same things at the same level. This could be true in a content area such as social studies. We will discuss this later and in more detail in the chapter on social studies.

Subgroups within the classroom seem advantageous in some areas of the curriculum. Identifying the group with which to work and deciding what to do with them is not as difficult as helping the others to become self-propelled and independent while you are occupied with another group. The question of how the groups will be organized is a major one in classroom management. A rigid grouping plan that puts Betty in a slow group or a fast group and leaves her there in all the curricular areas for the entire year fails to recognize differences within the child and variations in growth patterns in some areas as time progresses. A flexible plan of grouping is more in keeping with the nature of the children. There are times when ability grouping may be advantageous. At other times common needs will determine the people in the group. And when the need has been met, the group will dissolve. If a group shares an interest in horse stories, science experimentation, play acting, or a topic like nutrition, then interest groupings may cross ability levels. Groups may be large or small. Sometimes paired learning will be effective with two children working together. Sometimes the members of the pair may be of equal ability and at other times of contrasting abilities.

Individualized instruction has gained momentum since the advent of programmed materials and technology. Perhaps "individualized learning" would be a more appropriate designation for what actually takes place. You are responsible for a number of children. Each one has unique abilities, interests, and needs. Your job is to set up conditions which will enable the child to proceed independently. You can provide the materials, the know-how, and the stimulus, but you cannot do the learning. That, the individual must do. When you are able to see yourself as the creator of the learning situation rather than the dispenser of knowledge, you will truly be able to individualize the curriculum for the children. This is true whether they constitute a homogeneous group or a heterogeneous group, whether the program is set in a self-contained classroom or in a departmentalized or team-teaching situation.

HOW TO KEEP A CLASSROOM RUNNING SMOOTHLY

Keeping the machinery well oiled is partly a management problem and partly an instructional problem. In order to meet and solve it successfully, you must be aware of patterns of pupil conduct. Techniques for influencing behavior and establishing routine help create an effective climate for learning. You must be aware of types of problems that may arise, and you must have workable ideas about how to handle them. You will find it advantageous to anticipate problems and create a learning environment that is preventive rather than corrective. This involves motivation, personal relationships, and emphasis on a positive approach to learning. Let us take a look at typical patterns of pupil behavior before we attempt to suggest ways of influencing behavior.

Why Children Behave as They Do

"What makes him act that way?" is a pertinent question. If you view children as people before you see them as pupils, you may be more likely to establish a positive relationship with them than if you think of them as receptors for the subject matter which you plan to dispense. The second attitude suggests the acceptance of content as the curriculum target. Seeing them as people implies that the curriculum targets are centered around pupil activities or problems. This necessitates an analysis of the nature of the children and their personal relations with others, both peers and adults.

What Children Are Like.   The work of Gesell in the clinic with Ames and Ilg (4, 5, 6) has resulted in the publication of extensive studies based on developmental patterns. These studies give a detailed analysis of physical development and corresponding behavior patterns that can be expected of children at given stages. They are built on the theory that certain stages of development are inextricably related to chronological age and are a matter of maturation. This implies a wait-and-see attitude and encourages the school to take a passive position on growth and development. Nevertheless, it is advantageous to study observable behavior patterns in order to determine "what is" before you attempt to plan teaching strategies in terms of "what might be."

The nature of the child is important information. Young children tend to be active. They are curious about their environment. They are self-centered. They are person oriented. They are constantly growing and changing, both physically and mentally. Unless they have learned fear and passivity from their environment, they are trusting and open to new experiences. The task of education is to recognize the tendency toward activity and to nurture and cultivate natural curiosity. This means relating curriculum targets to the children's world, helping them relate to their associates, and providing for their ever-changing physical and intellectual needs. It means accepting children as individuals and leading them to new experiences and new acquaintances without violating their trust in the world and in people. Keeping the learners alert and receptive is the key to increasing knowledge and understanding.

Young children depend on their senses to learn about the environment. They need to see, to touch, to hear, to taste, to smell. They need to repeat these experiences until the learning becomes a part of their being. Only after they have felt many things which are smooth or rough, cold or hot, soft or hard, can they generalize about the concepts. Only after they have reached the generalizations, can they deal with the ideas as abstractions. Curricular experiences that recognize this need for sensory contact in the formation of understandings will deal with the concrete in the learning situation. Only when deep understandings have been established can they be dealt with in the abstract. Moving curricular experiences from the concrete to the abstract before understandings are developed leads to verbalism, regurgitation of facts, rote performance of skills, and answer-seeking behaviors.

Personal relations are influential in the child's life. No two children have exactly the same relations with others. Each child relates to a family, comprised of siblings, parents, and relatives, and to neighbors, as well as to peers. Many of these relationships are well established before the child comes to school. An only child relates to other children differently than a child from a family of two or more children. Even two children in the same family do not have the same environment. The older one does not know what it means to have an older brother or sister, and the youngest child in the family cannot know what it is like to have a younger sibling who looks up to or depends on him or her. The child who comes to school meets an entirely new situation. The adults in this new setting do not focus on personal activities. Such a child becomes a member of a group and frequently sees the teacher as a parent substitute but without the accustomed individual attention a parent usually gives. Peers are not so much playmates and coworkers as rivals for the attention of the significant adult in the new setting.

What to Expect.   These new perspectives on the environment may cause the child to become aggressive and competitive or sometimes to feel defeated and become withdrawn and passive. In fact, the same child may react in one way in some situations and just the opposite in others. This is why Billy sometimes refuses to talk and sometimes tries to talk louder than the others. This is why Gary sometimes stands back and waits to be told what to do, while at other times rushes pell-mell into the situation trying to be first. This is why Patty sometimes hesitates and acts afraid, or else grabs for more than her share. If you are a sensitive teacher, you will be aware of these evidences and recognize them as expressions of trust, fear, jealousy, insecurity, and so on and will adjust your reactions to the advantage of the child. If you help the child establish cooperative relationships with peers and mutually trusting relationships with adults, you will be helping build an environment in which learning, growth, and development can be unfolded. If you understand what children are like, you will have a good idea of what kinds of behavior patterns to expect. This all helps you make decisions and plan strategies centered around the problems of classroom management.

How to Influence Child Behavior

Let us begin by defining teaching as setting up conditions for learning. This means creating an environment that will be conducive to the kinds of activities resulting in changed behavior. The child needs to learn to perform new tasks, assimilate and recall new knowledge, understand new concepts, respond in more mature ways to others, and accept more and more responsibility. Many classroom problems identified by the novice as disciplinary are actually matters of routine and management. Many of the attitudes are actually matters of motivation and manifestations of self perception. As a teacher, you have two major problems; first, handling the problems which arise; and second, creating a situation which anticipates and prevents problems.

Meeting and Solving Problems.   A negative approach to discipline and the control of pupil behavior waits for problems to arise. A cartoonist depicted the old school with a bundle of switches above the map case, a dunce cap and stool in the corner, and the teacher with a sour look and pointed finger as a reflection of autocratic discipline. In such a classroom the teacher ruled by "divine right," and the children were expected to obey because "teacher knows best" or "does not allow." Rules were adult imposed. Punishment was the consequence of infringement. Any forth-coming rewards were more in the nature of bribes than achievements. Such an approach to classroom control develops fear and inhibitions. It leads to submission to authority and anticipation of release from restrictions. The child learns to "be good" either because of fear of the consequences or because of coveted rewards. This teaches dependence on authority for standards of conduct. Such a child grows up to be an adult who respects the law because of fear of the consequences, rather than because of regulations viewed as standards that are for the greatest good for the greatest number in a complex society. Such an adult sees work as a device for attaining rewards rather than as a means of contributing to the good of humanity, and views conforming behavior as a restriction on personal "rights," rather than as an adjustment to society which makes it possible for us to live together in peace and harmony.

Preventing Problems.   A positive approach to classroom control means creating a climate in which children move and work with purposes related to tasks. It means self-control motivated by the desire to grow and improve. It means planning in which pupils have a part so that they know what they are going to do and why. It means evaluation in which pupils assume responsibility not only for judging the quality of work but also for deciding next steps in the on-going process. It means teachers who lead and

Pupils often assume responsibility for routine chores in the classroom. This utilizes their abilities and frees the teacher to teach. (Courtesy, Lowell School, Mesa, Arizona)

suggest rather than dictate and direct. It means teachers who help children learn rather than teachers who assign tasks and check up on the students to see if the tasks were done.

In order that you may have a more realistic appraisal of the difference between a negative and a positive approach to the problem of influencing pupil behavior patterns, consider the following contrasts in approaches to classroom management:

> Do you say, "I want everybody to do p. 37," or "How many of the exercises on p. 37 can you do before noon?"
>
> Do you say, "I won't accept papers without margins," or "Remember, you'll need a margin for space to punch the holes for your notebook."?
>
> Do you say, "If you don't finish you'll have to stay after school," or "If you don't have time to finish, perhaps I can find time to help you after school."?
>
> Do you post a sign saying, "Talking prohibited in the library," or "Remember. Others are studying. Talking disturbs them."?
>
> Do you say, "Do you want to hear a story?" or "Here is a story that illustrates that point. Let's listen to find out what it has to say."?

It is easy to identify the approaches based on a negative point of view and to recognize them when they are transformed into positive approaches. One encourages submission and sometimes resistance. The other invites cooperation and responsibility.

SUMMARY

Managing the situation so learning can take place involves classifying and grouping pupils and then working with them in the classroom. Classifying and grouping pupils must be done first at the building level and later at the classroom level.

The school must accept the children who come, create a place for each one, sort them horizontally, and move them along vertically. All kinds of plans have been tried for sorting children ranging from the one-room school in the small community to the highly structured graded school in the city. Grouping has been tried to achieve homogeneity or heterogeneity, and sometimes random grouping has been permitted to develop in the name of avoidance of interference. Admissions have been based on age, size, ability, space, and personal preference. No one plan has been found that solves all the problems, but forward-looking educators have been giving consideration to flexible admission policies and continuous-growth programs that take into consideration not the demands of the curriculum, but rather the development of the child.

Classroom organization is a teacher problem. Whether you are solely responsible for a group of children or are sharing the responsibility with others through plans involving departmentalization, team teaching, and use of paraprofessionals, you must still face a class and decide how you will manage the situation. You may work with a large group, a small group, or one child. Even then you will still need to be aware of what the other children are doing.

When you understand children and why they act as they do, you will be able to meet them with confidence. Your influence on their behavior may be either negative or positive, depending on whether you meet and solve problems or anticipate and prevent them. Effective classroom management helps prevent discipline problems and is a route to success in teaching.

SUGGESTED ACTIVITIES

Work individually, in pairs, or in a small team to explore one or more of the following attitudinal studies.

1. Consult five different teachers with these two questions:
   a. Do you prefer homogeneous or heterogeneous grouping?
   b. Why?
   Summarize the responses and report your conclusions to the class.

Try to classify the above responses under these two headings:
   a. Child-centered curriculum targets.
   b. Subject-matter centered curriculum targets.

2. Consult five different school administrators with these same two questions and analyze your findings in the same way.
   Compare these with the responses from the teachers.

3. Consult five different adults (not teachers) with these same two questions and analyze the findings.
   Compare these with the responses from teachers and administrators.

4. Interview at least five teachers with the question:
   Which do you prefer: a self-contained classroom, departmentalization, or team teaching? Why?
   Summarize the responses in table form under the headings:
   a. Advantages
   b. Disadvantages

5. Ask this same question of five school administrators and summarize their responses in a similar manner.

6. Ask this same question of five adults (not teachers) and summarize their responses in the same manner.

7. Compare the points of view of teachers, administrators, and laypeople on the preferences for the self-contained classroom, departmentalization, and team teaching.
   What conclusions can you draw?

SELECTED READINGS

1. BRAUN, CARL, "Johnny Reads the Cues: Teacher Expectation," in *The Reading Teacher*, Vol. 26, No. 7, April 1973, pp. 704–12. The teacher gives out cues as to her expectation of levels of achievement. Johnny reads the cues and performs accordingly. Negative self-image is highly resistant to change.

2. BUSH, ROBERT N., "Can We Develop Curriculum-Proof Teachers?" in *Educational Forum*, Vol. XXXIII, No. 4, May 1969, pp. 417–25. Discusses scheduling, computer use, pupil and teacher behaviors and evaluation. Identifies power as the emerging new word in education.

3. ERB, JANE, "Use of Paraprofessionals," in *Educational Leadership*, Vol. 29, No. 4, Jan. 1972, pp. 323–26. Points out duties and rewards. Describes how to develop the program and orient the participants.

4. GESELL, ARNOLD, and FRANCES L. ILG, *Child Development*, New York: Harper and Row, 1949. Describes child development in the early years.

5. GESELL, ARNOLD, and FRANCES L. ILG, *Child from Five to Ten*, New York: Harper and Row, 1945. Describes child development in five-year period.

6. GESELL, ARNOLD et al., *The First Five Years of Life*, Harper & Row, 1940. Describes child development before age five.

7. GINOT, HAIM, "I Am Angry! I Am Appalled! I Am Furious," in *Today's Education*, Vol. 61, No. 8, Nov. 1972, pp. 23–24. Tells how to handle discipline cases without emotionalism.

8. HARING, NORRIS G. and E. LAKIN PHILLIPS, *Analysis and Modification of Classroom Behavior*, Englewood Cliffs, N.J.: Prentice-Hall, 1972, pp. 224. Presents techniques for analyzing behavior and makes recommendations for modification in the classroom. Case studies.

9. HARRIS, MARY M., "Learning by Tutoring Others," in *Today's Education*, Vol. 60, No. 2, Feb. 1971, pp. 48-49. An account of sixth graders who benefited from their reading sessions with their younger tutees in Brookline, Mass.

10. HARRISON, ALTON, Jr., and ELDON G. SCRIVEN, "Individualized Instruction—A Word of Caution," in *Kappa Delta Pi Record*, Vol. 8, No. 4, Apr. 1972, pp. 105-6. Compares current emphasis on individualized instruction to some of the basic principles of progressive education of the 1930's. Differentiates between the philosophies of individualism and socialism.

11. HOLLAWAY, OTTO, "Problem Centered Team Teaching: Viewpoint," in *Educational Leadership*, Vol. 28, No. 3, Dec. 1970, pp. 311-13. Identifies characteristics of team teaching at the elementary and the secondary level.

12. HOWARD, ALVIN W., "Discipline is Caring," in *Today's Education*, Vol. 61, No. 3, Mar. 1972, pp. 52-54. Sets up fourteen helpful guidelines to keep minor problems from becoming major ones.

13. HOWES, VIRGIL M., *Informal Teaching in the Open Classroom*, New York: Macmillan, 1974, p. 220 (paper). Explains theory and offers concrete examples through description, photography, sample forms, and check lists.

14. JARVIS, OSCAR T. and MARION J. RICE, *An Introduction to Teaching in the Elementary School*, Dubuque, Iowa: Wm. C. Brown, 1972, p. 545. Chapter 21 discusses classroom management and teaching.

15. JETER, JAN, "Teacher Expectancies and Teacher Classroom Behavior," in *Educational Leadership*, Vol. 30, No. 7, April 1973, pp. 677-81. Review of research related to topic. Bases conclusions on the assumption that pupils' performance is influenced by what the teacher expects of them.

16. JOHNSON, GLENN R. and ARTHUR J. LEWIS, "How Individualized Is the Non-graded School?" in *Educational Leadership*, Vol. 29, No. 2, Nov. 1971, pp. 139-41. Replacing grade levels with some other designation does not guarantee individualized instruction. Identifies the role of the teacher as helping individuals learn.

17. JONES, DAISY M., "A Feasible Plan for Continuous Admission," in *Education*, Vol. 89, No. 3, March 1969, pp. 195-202. A description of a proposed plan for admitting children to school throughout the year. Chart compares proposed plan with traditional plan.

18. JONES, DAISY MARVEL, *Teaching Children to Read*, New York: Harper & Row, 1971, p. 423. A practical approach to reading written from the standpoint of the classroom teacher.

19. MADSEN, CHARLES H. Jr. and CLIFFORD K. MADSEN, *Teaching, Discipline, Behavioral Principles Toward a Positive Approach*, Boston: Allyn and Bacon, 1970, p. 139. Why and what of discipline. Problems and how to meet them. Behavior modification. Positive approaches.

20. MCLAIN, JOHN, "Developing Flexible All-Year Schools," in *Educational Leadership*, Vol. 28, No. 5, Feb. 1971, pp. 472-75. All year plan for entering and leaving school. Operate on a continuous basis.

21. MEASEL, WES and GLEN FINCHER, "Team Teaching in Canton's Model School," in *Educational Leadership*, Vol. 29, No. 6, Mar. 1972, pp. 520–22. Describes the experimental program under ESEA, Title III.

22. PRATT, TERESSA MARJORIE, "A Positive Approach to Disruptive Behavior," in *Today's Education*, Vol. 62, No. 1, Jan. 1973, pp. 18–19. Describes an eight-week experimental program with ten intermediate-grade boys who had a history of disruptive behavior in the classroom.

23. RESNIK, HENRY S., "The Open Classroom," in *Today's Education*, Vol. 60, No. 9, pp. 16–17 and 60–61. Dec. 1971. Identifies the room and its philosophy. Answers questions and compares with the self-contained classroom concept.

24. ROBBINS, GLAYDON, D., "New Preparation for Teachers," in *Educational Forum*, Vol. XXXVI, No. 1, Nov. 1971, pp. 99–102. Lists as newcomers: individualization, nongradedness, flexibility, continuous progress, team teaching, differentiated staffing, and use of media and technology.

25. ROGERS, VINCENT R., "Open Schools on the British Model," in *Educational Leadership*, Vol. 29, No. 5, Feb. 1972, pp. 401–404. Diary account of a visit to Britain. Gives reasons for change.

26. ROTH, THEODORE C., "Expanding the Concept of Individualized Education," in *Educational Forum*, Vol. XXXVI, No. 1, Nov. 1971, pp. 61–66. Discusses grouping, class size, one track curriculum, basal reading programs, intra-class groupings, rate of progress. Recommends a look at variable content.

27. SKINNER, B. F., "On Punishment and Permissiveness," in *Today's Education*, Vol. 61, No. 3, Mar. 1972, pp. 53–54. From his controversial book, "Beyond Freedom and Dignity," Alfred A. Knopf, 1971.

28. STAPLES, I. EZRA, "The 'Open Space' Plan in Education," in *Educational Leadership*, Vol. 28, No. 5, Feb. 1971, pp. 458–63. Open space in action. Plan in Great Britain, the United States, and other areas.

29. SWIFT, DAVID W., "Changing Patterns of Pupil Control," in *Educational Forum*, Vol. XXXVI, No. 2, Jan. 1972, pp. 199–208. Discusses discipline. Summarizes the history of disciplinary methods in older traditional schools and the reasons for changes in modern schools. Identifies four major changes and three causes for change.

30. TAYLOR, ALBERT J., "Those Magnificent Men and Their Teaching Machines," in *Educational Forum*, Vol. XXXVI, No. 2, Jan. 1972, pp. 239–46. Criticizes teaching machines and programmed learning as based on predetermined "right" answers and as conducive to memory rather than thinking.

31. WILES, HILDA L., "A Multi-Age Team Teaching Program," in *Educational Leadership*, Vol. 29, No. 4, Jan. 1972, pp. 305–308. Describes a pilot program in the P. K. Yonge Laboratory School, University of Florida.

32. YAMAMOTO, KAORU, "Better Guidance for the Individual," in *Educational Leadership*, Vol. 29, No. 4, Jan. 1972, pp. 319–22. Discusses current approaches to school guidance.

5

ACCOMPLISHING GOALS THROUGH WORKING WITH OTHERS

*How to Relate to Children,
Parents, and the Staff*

Courtesy, Skiff School, Phoenix, Arizona

PERSONAL RELATIONS

Many good teachers have failed, not because they didn't know the subject matter, and not because they didn't know how to teach, but because they couldn't get along with the people with whom they were working. If you become "a thorn in the side" of the school staff, you will eliminate yourself no matter how right or how capable you are.

Do you know how to establish yourself with the public? Are you aware of the many kinds of children with whom you may work? Do you know different approaches for different children?

Do you dread meeting the parents? Has it ever occurred to you that they may dread meeting you? Do you know how to approach them to "build bridges" of good feeling? Do you know what to say to win them over instead of antagonizing them?

And the public—that means the laypeople who may be the school's severest critics: What will you say to them? Will you wait or take the initiative? How will you answer their questions?

The most important people of all are probably your coworkers. What is the role of the administrator? What is your responsibility to her or him? Who else works with the same children? Is theirs a separate responsibility or a shared one? Whose move is it? Do you know how to work with the nurse, the librarian, the special teachers, the teacher across the hall, the secretary, and the custodian?

Have you identified your role in the total organization? Remember you are not on a solo flight. You are a member of a working team. What are you doing to make teamwork work?

Aubrey Haan (12:293) says that, "What the teacher *is* educates children." He further states:

> The basic structure of motivation for young children lies in their identification with adults around them. Children absorb the characteristics of the teacher throughout the time they are in the classroom. His attitudes, his anxieties, his seeming omnipotence are all taken in by children. Many of the things children learn from the teacher are not consciously learned.

If we accept this philosophy, it means we must examine ourselves as teachers, our relationships with others, and our relationships with the children. We must determine to what degree what we are is basic to curriculum targets in the classroom.

HOW TO ESTABLISH YOURSELF WITH THE PUPILS

Shumsky (24:247, 255, 281) differentiates between the repetitive teacher and the creative teacher when he says:

> . . . the most important factor in determining whether the elementary school teacher will move forward toward creative teaching or seek the security of the repetitive mode of behavior is his relations with the children.

> . . . the child senses whether the teacher believes that it pays to try, or whether it is useless. If the teacher feels the child cannot do it, why should the latter try?

> . . . It is difficult to achieve when the "significant person" does not believe that one is capable of achieving. It is difficult both for the child and his teacher.

This point of view suggests that the first and most important step in working with the children is to establish rapport. Since each child is unique, this becomes a person-to-person relationship. This means recognizing differences so that curriculum targets can be set in terms of reality.

Establishing Rapport

Children come to school with some preconceived notions of what a teacher is. They get their ideas from previous experiences and from comments made by parents and other children. Combs (2:70–71) clarifies this perspective by saying:

> . . . perceptions are within the individual and will not be brought out unless the climate outside is safe for them. . . . They come out only when the perceiver feels that he wants them to be presented, and he will not bring them out in the classroom or anywhere else if there is danger that they will be attacked or ridiculed.

Furthermore, Combs (5:9) defines the effective teacher as:

> . . . a unique human being who has learned to use himself effectively and efficiently to carry out his own and society's purposes in the education of others.

If we accept this definition of a teacher and teaching, we must create a climate for learning before we can hope to pursue curriculum targets based on subject matter to be learned, skills to be acquired, or activities to be carried out.

Person-to-Person Relationships.   You need to establish yourself with each child to win cooperation. When you are able to make friends with them as individuals, you have won their confidence. Then they will be receptive to you and to what you have to teach. Establishing this kind of relationship calls for maturity and dignity. If you offer support, if you know when to release the "apron strings," the children will have the courage to move out on their own. Hicks (14:306) calls these the "ground rules" for establishing and maintaining classroom climate. He cautions against such informalities as use of nicknames, careless posture, and aimless roaming. He warns of the dangers inherent in the use of sarcasm, scolding, criticism, arguing, and verbal discipline. This means that you must be poised and purposeful and take a positive approach toward pupil conduct and learning behavior.

Classroom Atmosphere.   An atmosphere is something you can feel or sense. It is not definable in terms of objects, degrees, or decibels. Ragan (20:196–97) identifies classroom climates as reflections of the weather. He uses the terms *cold* or *chilly*, *stormy*, *foggy*, and *warm*. In some rooms the children find the atmosphere unreceptive and forbidding. In some they find it violent and dangerous. In some they are so uncertain about what to expect that they are in a *fog*. And in some they find a breath of *sunshine* inviting them to explore and learn.

Atmosphere is partly influenced by physical facilities. Try to picture yourself in a classroom. The size and shape may make a difference. Furniture arrangement suggests an atmosphere. Consider the settings created by the arrangements illustrated in the accompanying diagrams.

Figure 5–1 shows a classroom that is teacher oriented. The children **are all facing the teacher. They see only backs of heads of their classmates.** The implication is that all communication is between teacher and pupil. This is a testing and reciting atmosphere. The furniture will probably remain in these neat rows indefinitely. It might as well be screwed to the floor.

Figure 5–2 shows a classroom where the children are able to look one another in the eye. They are encouraged to communicate with each other. The implication is that they will be sharing information and exchanging ideas rather than repeating facts gleaned from teacher-imposed assignments.

Figure 5–3 shows groups of children involved in self-imposed tasks. They may be constructing a model, collecting data for a chart, enjoying a good story, or working in pairs to practice needed skills. The implication is that learnings are purposeful and that the children know what they are doing and why. The teacher is a very important resource for learning but not a dictator.

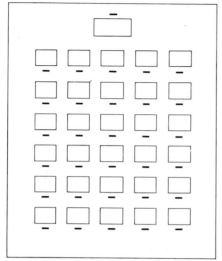

Figure 5-1. *A formal classroom. Teacher centered.*

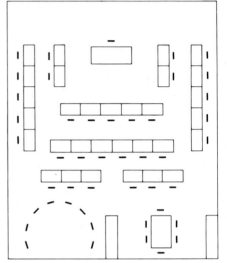

Figure 5-2. *An informal classroom. Pupil centered.*

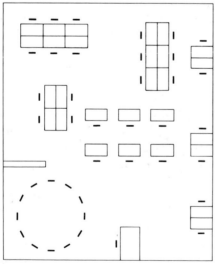

Figure 5-3. *An informal classroom oriented to group work.*

Figures 5–4 and 5–5 represent openness. The room does not even need the conventional four walls and square corners. In these two drawings, the classroom is conceived of as an area where learning can take place. Movable walls and openings without doors make the space adjustable. Carpeting and sound proofing create quiet areas conducive to conversation without confusion. The implication is that learning is influenced by freedom to move, access to nearby library facilities, use of the teacher as a

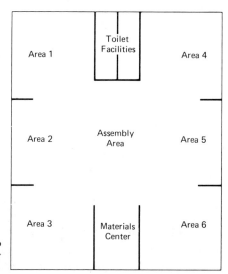

Figure 5-4. An open-area classroom to accommodate a large group and as many as six teachers plus aides.

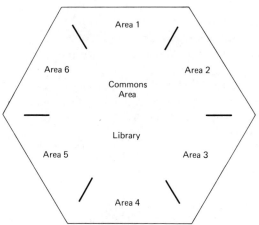

Figure 5-5. Open-area classrooms for large groups and several teachers and aides. Notice the irregular form.

guide and resource, and verbal interchange between groups or individuals. Isolation is no longer practiced. This kind of atmosphere can become confusing unless both teachers and pupils accept responsibility for their own curriculum targets. Openness is determined by freedom from feelings of inadequacy and the attitude of confidence in coworkers. It depends on mutual trust and cooperation between teachers and pupils as well as among teachers.

Recognizing Individual Differences

Schools exist because children need to learn. If it weren't for this fact, we could eliminate all the rest of the accouterments, the trappings that make up the school. This includes not only the buildings, furniture, books, and physical facilities, but also the teachers, administrators, and special-service personnel. This being the case it behooves us to look at the children who need educating.

When you face a classroom you will see all kinds of children—the handicapped and the gifted, the privileged and the disadvantaged. There are no such things as "average" students or "normal" children. These terms refer to hypothetical children who form a composite representing the different qualities that exist in varying combinations in many individuals. Some children seem to have so many things interfering with their educational potential that meeting and solving their problems is a necessary step even before curriculum targets can be set. Others seem to have so much going for them that accomplishment seems a foregone conclusion when they appear in the classroom eager and ready to learn.

The Educationally Handicapped.   Each child must be received and helped with problems so that an opportunity to succeed is possible. And success does not mean "keeping up." It means learning and growing in accordance with personal needs and abilities.

Retarded children are slow in academic development. This may be caused by some kind of physical or mental deficiency interfering with normal development.

Slow learners may or may not be retarded. Such children may be just moving at a more leisurely pace and may reach maturity at a later period. Alpren (1:422-424) lists the characteristics of slow learners. They may have one of or any combination of the following:

1. He has difficulty with symbols and abstract concepts.
2. He has poor auditory and visual discrimination.
3. He has difficulty anticipating outcomes, understanding consequences, forming associations, making generalizations, and setting long range goals.

4. He is weak in storing information and remembering facts.
5. He is less likely to be motivated.
6. He has a low frustration tolerance and short attention span.
7. He is frequently aggressive and hostile.
8. He is demanding of time and attention.
9. He often does not try or gives up.

Emotionally disturbed children may be unable to concentrate on school learnings because there are so many uncertainties in life that they have learned to see themselves as unable and unfit. Such children may be withdrawn and hard to reach, or aggressive and disturbing to others in the classroom.

Physically disabled children may have some kind of bodily limitation that prevents their taking part in normal activities. Disabling conditions could include blindness, deafness, paralysis, or a crippling condition affecting locomotion or muscular coordination. Meeting such problems might be a matter of adjusting to the limitations rather than trying to eliminate the difficulties. Recognizing which conditions can be corrected and which must be accepted may be basic to their mental health. Learning to live with their limitations may be the necessary solution.

Culturally different children have received increased attention during the current decade. This change is caused by a social philosophy based on a belief that the way to a better society is through eliminating interferences to learning and through building a better self concept which will enable the disadvantaged to become upwardly mobile in society.

Linguistically different children may or may not be at a disadvantage. There is a tendency to attribute the term bilingual to any child who does not speak English as a first language. This is not necessarily the case. Multilingual children may speak another language adequately but find themselves at a disadvantage in a school setting where all communication is in English. The linguistically disadvantaged child may speak only English and that so inadequately that communication channels are limited. Such a child is linguistically different and disadvantaged. A truly bilingual child communicates adequately in more than one language. This child is gifted.

The Educationally Advantaged.   Children classified as advantaged may or may not present problems in the classroom. If you receive such children with a warm welcome, recognize their superior abilities, and present them with challenges, you will be meeting their needs. If their exceptional abilities are curbed by adherence to a rigid subject-matter centered curriculum, the advantaged pupils may learn to waste time, get by, and lose that high potential.

Talented children possess special abilities in artistic areas such as music or art. Some have unusual grace and physical beauty. Some seem to have wholesome personalities and to have been fortunate in their environment. In spite of their talents they may be deficient in certain basic skills and sometimes they develop superiority concepts that create personality conflicts.

Intellectually gifted children are different from those with special talents. Whether intellectual capacity is a matter of heredity or environment is not the issue. Some children seem to be more capable than others. Intellectually gifted children are alert and attentive. They have inquiring and receptive minds. They rank high on measures of intelligence. Academic achievement seems to come easily. They need to be stimulated and challenged. They are the ones who possess the capacity for making contributions to the progress of civilization. You must see these educationally advantaged children as individuals and as challenges to your ability to bring out the best they have to offer. Alpren (1:397) identifies the characteristics of the gifted as:

1. Curiosity
2. Good school achievement
3. Enjoyment of reading
4. Impatience with routine and drill work
5. Concentration power
6. Effective expression of ideas
7. Critical thought and suggestions for improvement of ideas and activities
8. Desire for the challenge of dealing with difficult problems
9. Ability to form concepts
10. Creative imagination
11. Critical thinking
12. Ability to memorize and retain information

Once you have established yourself with your pupils, you must build bridges between their backgrounds and the school environment. Children bring to school all their past experiences. They live in homes in a community. They may have had many experiences in the local setting including trips to the store, visits to the zoo, Saturday afternoons at the movies, rides on buses or airplanes, and contacts with relatives, neighbors, and friends. You and the school represent one more step in the establishment of their place in the total society. When you recognize that, you are fitting the targets of the curriculum into the life patterns of the children. You are their link with the school world and they are your link with the public with whom you also must communicate.

HOW TO COMMUNICATE WITH THE PUBLIC

You can't spend all your professional time inside the classroom. The school walls should not insulate you from the public. Parents and other community members are out there. You must work with them. Knowing what they expect and how to approach them will help you get the job done.

Parents

All children have parents or guardians. Some children may come from broken homes or one-parent homes, but it is a most unusual situation in which a child does not have at least one or more adults with whom to relate before coming to school. Parents or guardians are a part of the team. They can be partners or rivals. Much of the role they assume is determined by the initiative taken by the school. Some parents may be highly educated, socially affluent, and financially influential. Thus, they see the school and school personnel in a subservient role. Other parents may feel inferior or inadequate in the presence of professional educators. It is your responsibility to take the initiative in establishing desirable relationships. A positive approach to this responsibility is to view the parents first as partners and then as resources in the educational program.

Parents as Partners.   In a good educational program, the talents and efforts of both teachers and parents are combined for the benefit of the children. Parents need to know what is going on in school. Parents can be the "sounding board" so essential to the young learners who need someone to listen to their problems, achievements, and learning experiences. This does not mean someone to find fault with what they are doing, but someone to lend an appreciative ear to their efforts at **self-evaluation**. If parents will but listen, the children will decide for themselves whether progress is being made or not. Parents are often a source of information as well as inspiration for children. A truly concerned parent can come to school to see what the child is doing there, listen to practice in reading or spelling, stand by while homework is being done, make sure there is a time and a place for necessary study, and support and encourage the child and the school.

This positive approach does much for the child's attitude toward learning. Communicating with the parent who is serving in the role of partner depends on the insight and the tact of the teacher and/or the administrator.

We should not say, "You'll have to help Bob," but rather, "This is what he is doing. How can you help?"

Avoid implying that the kind of help offered at home is wrong. Instead, suggest that, "If you would like to come to school to see how we are doing it, you might be able to continue the same procedures at home."

Refrain from waiting until something is wrong before contacting the home. Instead, watch for opportunities to report little successes by calling on the telephone to say, "I thought you would like to know how much we appreciated the pictures Billy's brother brought home from the islands."

Keep the channels of communication open. Strive for at least as many positive comments as negative ones. Perhaps they will crowd out the need for negative comments entirely.

Parents as Resources.   Parents can be a constructive resource in the pursuit of educational targets. If you are a wise teacher, you will find out who the parents are, what they do, what experiences they have had, and what facilities they have which could enrich the school program. If Jim's father is a police officer, invite him to share with the children the nature of his work and its importance to them. If Ann's mother sings or plays an instrument, she just might be the accompanist you are looking for to help with the upcoming program. If Patrick has lived in a foreign country with his parents, invite them to school to enrich the children's backgrounds. If Paul's father is a cartoonist, ask him to help the children with some of their drawings. If Edith's father or mother happens to be in the legislature, capitalize on the direct contact to learn more about how our country is governed. If Thelma's mother is an expert seamstress, perhaps she would be willing to help with the costumes for the program. One teacher made a special effort to find out as much as possible about the contributions the parents might make and catalogued the information on file cards for future reference. The findings were shared with the rest of the faculty and the idea grew into an all-school project which became a continuing file of community resources. Parents do not usually criticize adversely what they are a part of or are making a personal commitment to.

Community

There are others in the school community who are equally concerned about the school program and curriculum content. They are the tax payers who support the schools. They represent not only the local businesses and industries but also the social and service groups working for a better community.

Business and Industry.   Business and industrial groups who employ the products of the schools are concerned about the standards of performance. They want students to achieve a high standard of computation and communication skills and are vocal in their demands and their criticisms. Soliciting their help might be the route, not only to better education, but to a more positive approach to their criticisms. They might appear in the schools, or the pupils might have a look at what goes on in the business world.

Social and Service Groups. In most communities special organizations exist for altruistic purposes. They contribute to the school program and draw on the school for support of their special programs and projects. They can help by their work, their interest, and their good will. Bringing them into the program is good business. When the school takes the initiative, it is preventing the skepticism that comes from the uninformed and the negative reactions that come from the doubters. Hicks (14:366) points out that different members of the community see the products of the school differently:

> *Economists* view youth as the richest of natural resources.
> *Business men* see them as potential customers, employees, and even competitors.
> *Militarists* see them as defenders of the nation.
> *Politicians* know that they are the electorate of the future and that they are already influential lobbyists with the present electorate.
> *Scholars* want to hang all the knowledge accumulated in the past upon them so as to motivate them to climb to new levels of understanding.
> *Democrats* stake all on their ability to preserve and extend the democratic ideal.

HOW TO GET ALONG WITH THE REST OF THE STAFF

Consider all the people it takes to make a school for even a few hundred children function adequately. Somebody has to select and employ the teachers. Somebody has to coordinate the efforts of the group. Somebody has to have an overall view of the curriculum. Somebody, or a number of somebodies, must meet the special needs of the children. Teachers who work at parallel assignments must live and work in the same general environment. Many of the duties in and about the school do not necessarily involve teaching, but they must be done in order that the teaching and learning can take place. Unless the work of all these people is synchronized, there can be much waste of time and effort. When you are in the classroom, you need to see yourself in relation to all these other members of the organization. Sometimes you play a leadership role and sometimes a supporting role. Always your concern is for the best possible curricular program for the children.

Professional Staff

The professional staff may be designated as administrators, other professional workers, and fellow teachers. Each has a unique role to play in making the curriculum work for children.

Administrators. An administrator is one who iş designated to manage the affairs of the group. This includes the responsibility for seeing that the organization functions smoothly. It requires an overall view of the workings of the organization. It need not necessarily be viewed as a superior position. In actuality, it may be a position subservient to the real work of the school, that is, teaching the children. If the administrator's assignment includes a less confining schedule, it may be because of proven ability to assume responsibility. If remuneration is greater it may be because the leader has assumed more responsibility and is giving more time to the job.

The superintendent is the titular head of most school systems. Such a role is one of leadership and management. Most likely, this is the person you will contact first when you are employed. One of the jobs of the superintendent is to select staff members who can carry out the work of the school. A good superintendent makes wise selections and then permits staff members to assume the responsibility for their own acts.

The principal is usually in charge of a school which is a localized part of the larger oganization. The person filling this role has the duties of coordinating the efforts of all the personnel working in the community served by the school. Responsibilities cover administration and supervision of both certified and noncertified staff. They cover physical facilities as well as curriculum. This is a management job. It is closer to the work of the individual teacher and the children in the classroom than is that of the superintendent. Ideally, the principal has had enough classroom experience to be familiar with the work of the teachers and the needs of the children.

Supervisors, consultants, directors and/or *coordinators* are employed in many school systems. Titles vary in an attempt to describe their roles more accurately. Whatever they are called, they are service personnel. Their chief function is to facilitate your work as a teacher with the children. They may be curriculum specialists in subject-matter areas such as music, art, or physical education. They may be generalists with an overview of the total curriculum. Their services may be available on schedule or on call. Their function is to provide you with help in materials, know-how, and evaluation. They are chiefly interested in improving the instructional program for the children. Theirs is not an evaluative function in terms of teaching effectiveness but rather a constructive role in terms of learning effectiveness. It is to your advantage to take the initiative in seeking such services. You can ask them for information, solicit counsel on planned programs, and invite participation in curriculum activities. You can also volunteer your services in on-going district-wide programs.

Other Professional Workers. There are a number of professionally educated workers serving the school in roles not limited to the classroom. They, too, have unique positions in serving the children. They should not be viewed as superior or inferior in professional status. Their work supplements and augments the work of the classroom teacher.

The school nurse is concerned about the health needs of the children. Services are available for emergencies. You need to know how and when to secure help in order to render direct service to the children. In addition to emergency service, the nurse helps with inspection, health surveys, and preventive techniques. The nurse's major function is to encourage good health habits and to teach the children how to keep well.

The speech and hearing therapist is concerned with very special problems of individual children who have hearing defects, loss of hearing, or speech problems which interfere with effective communication. These problems may be either physical or functional. The therapist identifies the problems, renders therapeutic aid where possible, and refers problem cases to medical technicians when necessary. As the classroom teacher, you may be the first to see that a child has need for a therapist. It is your responsibility to refer to the specialist those children who can benefit by such services.

Psychologists and counselors are also on the staff in many schools. They deal with problem cases. They may not be aware that problems exist unless someone refers cases to them. If you are an observant teacher, you will detect problems and see that children receive the help they need. Such referrals should be followed up for action.

Other special personnel may be serving the needs of corrective teaching in such areas as reading or arithmetic, or they may be providing enriching experiences in such areas as music, art, drama, dance, creative expression, physical education, and so on. Again it is your function to be aware of these services and to secure them for the children who need them or who can benefit from them. If you take the initiative, more benefits will result for the individual child than if you wait for the services to come to you.

Fellow Teachers. Most schools have a number of teachers who fill parallel positions. They fit into the horizontal organization of the school by assuming the responsibility for the instructional program of one of the groups at a given time. They fit into the vertical organization of the school by working with one of the groups during an interval of time, usually a year or more, as they move through the school from the time of entrance to graduation.

Horizontal relationships involve getting along with coworkers. This means sharing time, facilities, materials, and sometimes responsibilities. If you use the duplicator and leave it with ink running out of it for the next user to clean up, you are inviting conflict. If you leave children unsupervised while you visit in the hall, you may cause a disruption in the work of others and create antagonisms. On the other hand, if you see a need for an orderly school and meet the situations which present themselves, you are acting in a helpful and mature manner. It makes no difference whose fault it is or whose responsibility it is, if the job needs doing, the mature teacher will act. Winning the respect and good will of fellow teachers may go as far toward insuring success as planning a decorative classroom which wins public plaudits.

Vertical relationships involve building bridges which make for smooth crossings. Find out what the teacher last year did with the children. Listen to this teacher's evaluation and advice. The evaluation may give you insight. You may, or may not, use the advice, but it won't hurt to listen. And don't argue. Share with the next teacher what you have found out about the children. Provide a record of materials used and content covered. Be free with your counsel but not insistent. Above all, do not be disturbed if your advice is not taken.

Team relationships exist whether there is a formal planned team teaching program in progress or not. The teacher whose children achieve high scores on the tests, but who creates conflicts among fellow teachers is a liability. Many a principal has kept a teacher on the staff even though the records are sometimes late or inaccurate, or the classroom is less effective than might be wished, because that staff member is a peacemaker and a supporter who welds together the faculty when the "chips are down."

Non-certified Workers

There was a day when the teacher taught in the one-room school, kept all the records, swept and dusted the room, built the fires, carried in the wood, helped the children after school, and even "boarded around" in the community, thus adding homework to the regular duties. In our complex society, that picture has been altered. Special help is provided in most of these areas.

Clerical Help.   Most modern schools have clerks or secretaries to type stencils, fill out attendance forms, obtain factual data from new enrollees, run the duplicator, answer the telephone, keep a record of supplies on hand, make out purchase orders, stamp books, and a thousand and one other chores which are time consuming. These persons are invaluable assets to the school. Sometimes such persons are the first contact with the school made by a new pupil, a parent, a salesperson, or even an applicant for a professional position. They are important. They should be treated in such a manner that they are able to maintain this role and to create a positive image for the school. You must recognize them.

Custodial Help.   Custodial help in today's schools has freed the time of the teacher for teaching duties. Custodians are not servants. Theirs is an important part in the functioning of the school. They are not to be ordered around, but are to be welcomed as team members with specific services to render. When you see them as coworkers with different roles to perform and solicit their help and cooperation, you will get beneficial results. They deserve consideration. You and your children can assume responsibility for putting things in their proper places, cleaning up your own litter, and using the school facilities with care. You can express a word of appreciation for favors and help. You will then feel free to request help when needed to expedite the instructional program. Custodians are pleased to be asked to lend a hand as long as they are recognized as a part of the total team and their other duties are not so burdensome that there is no time or opportunity to be helpful. Sometimes such a remark as, "We put everything away and cleaned up the room as best as we could so you would have time to help us with the model we are building," is just the right word to make such a team member feel pride in work and support for the kinds of learning activities going on in the school. Never forget that they, too, are a part of the total community and have their influence on the public relations of the school.

Paraprofessionals.   Aides have become useful in our schools. The prefix, "para" means "alongside." Aides who work alongside teachers are called paraprofessionals. Perhaps one of the better services they render is in public relations. The parent or aide who sees what is going on in the classroom gains a new respect for the work of the teacher. And people are less likely to be critical of something they have a part in. In whatever capacity they serve, paraprofessionals are there because they are interested in providing a better educational experience for the children. It is your responsibility to help them assume their roles and to see that their services result in better learning opportunities. Some of them may organize a team and give vision or hearing checks on a routine basis for the records. Some may check papers or workbooks. Some may catalog books and supplies. Some may listen while children practice reading at an independent level. Some may type or run the duplicator. Some may help with buttons, zippers, or overshoes. Whatever their assignments, they should always be recognized as supporting aides who free you to teach. They are not there to relieve you so you will have less to do, but to provide you with more time to engage in the professional role of teaching for which you are educated.

SUMMARY

In this fifth chapter we have gained some perspectives on your job as a teacher. You are a member of a team. The teaching-learning team consists of pupils, parents, and other workers, both professional and non-certified. Pulling together helps make it possible for everyone to hit the targets.

You need to recognize children as individuals—the retarded child, the slow learner, the emotionally disturbed, the physically disabled, the culturally and linguistically different, as well as the talented and the intellectually gifted. Even the talented and the gifted can create problems if their needs are not met. Remember, the children all have parents or other significant adults in their lives and come from a community which has certain expectations regarding outcomes for the schools. Parents and other community members can be a resource for hidden curriculum and can help with special services.

No longer is a teacher isolated in a rural one-room school as in the early days in our country. Today's teachers are members of a professional staff including administrators, nonteaching professionals, fellow teachers, and noncertified workers. Each makes a contribution. The successful teacher understands all these relationships, respects the contributions of others, and finds a way to make a contribution to the learning of the children. Getting along with others may be as important as knowing the subject matter and preparing the lessons.

SUGGESTED ACTIVITIES

Select one or more of the following activities for individual or small-group development and report your findings to the class.

1. If you teach for forty years and then retire; and if you have thirty children in your room each year, how many lives will you influence during your teaching career?

   Add to that children moving in and out of the class to make a total of more than thirty per year and refigure the number you influence.

Change the problem to a team-teaching or departmentalized organization where you contact more different children each year and estimate the numbers again. How many lives are you likely to influence during your teaching career?

2. If you teach beginners, they will be five or six years old.

   If you teach till you are sixty five, what will be the date of your retirement? Probably you will then be teaching children who will be born forty years from now.

   If they live to become adults, and voters, and business people, and teachers, what will be the span of their influence? Approximately to what date would their influence extend?

   Write a letter as of that future date describing some of the changes that will have taken place in the interval. Let your imagination run rampant here.

3. Role play one or more of the following situations in two episodes each, one with a negative approach and an unhappy consequence, and the other with a positive approach and a more satisfactory culmination:
   a. A disciplinary encounter with a child
   b. A conference with a parent
   c. A faculty meeting
   d. Or think up your own situation

4. Identify a child who is educationally handicapped and work up a case study describing the problems and recommending appropriate measures for his or her learning.

5. Identify a child who is educationally advantaged and work up a case study describing his or her personality and the setting in which this child lives. Make recommendations for meeting the child's educational needs and challenging abilities.

SELECTED READINGS

1. ALPREN, MORTON, *The Subject Curriculum*, Columbus, Ohio: Charles E. Merrill, 1967, Chap. 15 and 16. Describes curriculum for the gifted and for the slow learners.

2. Association for Supervision and Curriculum Development, Yearbook, *Perceiving Behaving Becoming: A New Focus for Education*, Washington: D.C.: ASCD, 1962. In Chap. 5 Arthur W. Combs describes "A Perceptual View of the Adequate Personality," and in Chap. 3 Carl R. Rogers discusses the steps in moving "Toward Becoming a Fully Functioning Person."

3. BLOOM, JOHN H., "The Potential of Teacher Aides in Instruction," in *The Education Forum*, Vol. XXXVII, Jan. 1973, pp. 195–99. Recommends expansion of the role of teacher aide to improve learning opportunities for the pupil.

4. COLEMAN, ALWIN B., "The Disadvantaged Child Who Is Successful in School," in *The Educational Forum*, Vol. XXXIV, No. 1, Nov. 1969, pp. 95–97. Identifies behavior patterns in disadvantaged children who are successful in spite of their disadvantages.

5. COMBS, ARTHUR W., *The Professional Education of Teachers*, Boston: Allyn and Bacon, 1965. Describes effective teaching characteristics and types of training that invite them.

6. CRISCUOLO, NICHOLAS P., "PR and the Reading Program," in *The Reading Teacher*, Vol. 26, No. 8, May 1973, pp. 817–19. Public criticisms are usually caused by misinformation or lack of information. Instead of becoming defensive, educators should assume the initiative in keeping parents informed.

7. EASH, MAURICE J., "Aberrant Curriculum Designs," in *Educational Forum*, Vol. XXXV, No. 2, Jan. 1971, pp. 197–202. Identifies new forces shaping curriculum design, away from subject-centered to emphasis on personal search and relationships with others. Stresses emotional needs.

8. *Educational Leadership*, Vol. 29, No. 8, May 1972. Theme articles on "Community Involvement in Curriculum."

    ALEXANDER, WILLIAM M., "Community Involvement in Curriculum," (An Editorial) pp. 655–57.

    FANTINI, MARIO D., "Community Participation: Many Faces Many Directions," pp. 674–80.

    HAMILTON, NORMAN K., "The Decision-Making Structure of a School System," pp. 668–71.

    HASKINS, KENNETH W., "Implications: New Conceptions of Relevancy," pp. 687–89.

    JACKSON, SHIRLEY A., "The Curriculum Council: New Hope, New Promise," pp. 690–91, 93–94.

    McCOY, RHODY A., "Ingredients of Leadership," pp. 672–73.

    WILCOX, PRESTON, "Changing Conceptions of Community," pp. 681–86.

9. ERB, JANE, "Use of Paraprofessionals," in *Educational Leadership*, Vol. 29, No. 4, Jan. 1972, pp. 323–26. Points out duties and rewards. Describes how to develop the program and orient the participants.

10. GEORGIADY, NICHOLAS P. and LOUIS G. ROMANO, "Ulcerville, U.S.A.—Viewpoint," in *Educational Leadership*, Vol. 29, No. 3, Dec. 1971, pp. 269–72. Stepped up kindergarten program. Good grades at any cost. Pressures in high school. A winning team or else. The social whirl. Cheating. Importance of the individual.

11. GOOD, THOMAS L. and JERE E. BROPHY, "The Self-Fulfilling Prophecy," in *Today's Education*, Vol. 60, No. 4, April, 1971, pp. 52–53. Pygmalion in the classroom, findings, teacher behavior, low expectations, desirable attitudes, and expectations.

12. HAAN, AUBREY, *Elementary School Curriculum: Theory and Research*, Boston: Allyn and Bacon, 1961. Chapter 12 discusses teacher personality and its effects on curriculum.

13. HENRIKSON, HAROLD A., "Role of Teacher Attitude in Educating the Disadvantaged Child," in *Educational Leadership*, Vol. 28, No. 4, Jan. 1971, pp. 425–29. Identifies the influence of self-fulfilling prophecy.

14. HICKS, WM. VERNON, *et al.*, *The New Elementary Curriculum*, New York: Van Reinhold Nostrand and Company, 1970. Chapter 10 is on classroom management and pupil behavior.

15. KOWITZ, GERALD T., "Trends in Elementary School Counseling," in *Educational Forum*, Vol. XXXIV, No. 1, Nov. 1969, pp. 87–93. Identifies four distinct movements in counseling. Predicts trends for the future.·

16. KRAVETZ, NATHAN, "The Creative Child in the Un-Creative School," in *Educational Forum*, Vol. XXXIV, No. 2, Jan. 1970, pp. 219–22. Identifies creative children and their problems. Suggests what you as a teacher can do to help them.

17. MANNING, DUANE, *Toward a Humanistic Curriculum*, New York: Harper & Row, 1971. Identifies the teacher as the humanizing agent in the classroom.

18. MOUNTAIN, LEE HARRISON, "Telling Parents About Transformational Grammar," in *Elementary English*, Vol. XLIX, No. 5, May 1972, pp. 684–87. Compares transformational grammar to assembling a basic wardrobe and puts it in language the parents can understand.

19. O'BRIEN, CARMEN A., *Teaching the Language-Different Child to Read*, Columbus, Ohio: Charles E. Merrill, 1973, p. 168 (paper). Identifies the linguistic problems that emerge because of differences in speech sounds, the cultural problems that exist because of differences in background, and the reading problems that develop because of unfamiliarity with both the language and the concepts.

20. RAGAN, WILLIAM B., and CELIA BURNS STENDLER, *Modern Elementary Curriculum*, New York: Holt, Rinehart and Winston, 1971. Chapter 7 discusses organizing the class for living and learning.

21. RESNIK, HENRY S., "The Open Classroom," in *Today's Education*, Vol. 60, No. 9, pp. 16–17. Identifies the room and its philosophy. Answers questions and compares with the self-contained classroom concept.

22. ROGERS, VINCENT R., "Open Schools on the British Model," in *Educational Leadership*, Vol. 29, No. 5, Feb. 1972, pp. 401–404. Diary account of a visit to Britain. Reasons for change.

23. ROSENBERG, MAX, "Community Relations—Approaches Educators Use," in *Clearing House,* Vol. XLVIII, Sept. 1973, pp. 50–53. Suggests that "our" attitude helps to establish relations with the community. It is our school, our community, and our children. Educators and citizens must work together for better schools.

24. SHUMSKY, ABRAHAM, *Creative Teaching in the Elementary School*, New York: Appleton-Century-Crofts, 1965. Chapter 10 discusses relations with children.

25. STAPLES, I. EZRA, "the 'Open Space' Plan in Education," in *Educational Leadership*, Vol. 28, No. 5, Feb. 1971, pp. 458–63. Describes the open space concept in education.

26. TAYLOR, CHARLOTTE P., "The Expectations of Pygmalion's Creators," in *Educational Leadership*, Vol. 28, No. 2, Nov. 1970, pp. 161–64. Questions control of the experiment and the validity of the data.

27. Today's Education, "A Life-Time Life-Space Perspective," A Special Feature on Home-School Cooperation, in *Today's Education*, Vol. 62, No. 2, Feb. 1973, pp. 28–40. A series of six articles dealing with the central theme. Parental assistance, home starts, child progress, parental interest, and teen-age parents.

28. TODD, CHARLES C. Jr., "Should Reading Be Taught at Home?" in *The Reading Teacher*, Vol. 26, No. 8, May 1973, pp. 814–16. Early reading experience is an individual experience and it occurs whether the school wills it or not, and attitudes formed before school entrance are significant in success in formal reading instruction in school.

part two

Putting Curriculum Into Practice Through Selection of Content in the Subject Matter Areas

AN INTRODUCTION

The terms skill, knowledge, and attitude are often attributed to the various subjects in the traditional curriculum. These terms are not mutually exclusive. No subject is strictly a skill subject, a content subject, or an affective subject. There are elements of all in each.

Learning how to do something involves mastering a skill. A person may learn how to spell, how to calculate, how to type, how to read, how to write, how to sing, how to play a piano, how to drive a car, how to diagram a sentence, how to punctuate, and how to do many other useful or challenging things in life. But one doesn't learn how to history, how to geography, or how to literature. Skills are observable and most of them can be measured objectively. One can measure how far an athlete jumps, count how many words the typist types per minute, weigh the amount of cotton produced, count the number of words spelled accurately, judge the quality of penmanship against an established standard, and so on. These are performance skills. The value of the skills is another matter.

Accumulating knowledge is cognitive learning. One may memorize rules and correct form, facts about art, information about literature, background data about history, and a storehouse of vocabulary words, but

this type of learning does not necessarily imply application or even understanding. Factual learnings are measurable. One can count the correct
answers marked on an objective test, itemize the facts reproduced accurately, and indicate the amount of information stored for recall. Whether
or not the content is worth learning is also another matter. Selection of
content to be learned is a matter of opinion, and decisions vary with
objectives expressed by the evaluator.

Developing attitudes toward learnings is developing insights and
understandings which influence affective behavior and learning. One may
learn to want to spell correctly and to care whether or not spelling
conforms to accepted standards. One may learn to want to write legibly
and to feel a deep concern for the reader who may struggle with the written
message. One may learn to care about ability to speak correctly and to
communicate with ease and effectiveness. One may learn to appreciate
good literature, art, music, and other forms of human expression. One may
develop a desire for a strong body, an appreciation for good health, respect
for honesty and fair play, and an enjoyment of living. These learnings are
less objective, but very real nonetheless. They may be of lifelong benefit,
but they are more difficult to pin down and measure. What is beneficial to
one may not necessarily be beneficial to another.

Skills may deteriorate through lack of use. Knowledge may be altered
through new discoveries. But attitudinal learnings are continuous. The goal
of the school curriculum should be to make the individual a lifetime learner
and a self-propelled student. True, pupils must learn something, but
whether the emphasis is placed on the measurable product and the process,
or on the effect of the learning on the students will influence the perspective
on the curriculum.

It is the purpose of Part Two to explore the content of the curriculum
in the elementary school from the standpoint of what is worth teaching and
what experiences are worth providing in order to implement the program.
Separate chapters are devoted to mastering the art of communication,
understanding the social studies, relating to the sciences, understanding
and using quantitative relationships, and appreciating the arts and the
humanities. Each is explored in turn from the standpoint of skills to be
mastered, knowledge to be gleaned, and attitudes to be developed. In other
words: to do, to know, and to be. Each chapter seeks to do two things: (1)
identify the areas of the curriculum that can be categorized under that
discipline; and (2) identify the objectives in terms of the three original
premises—namely; doing, knowing, and being.

The five chapters in Part Two have the same basic organization, but
not necessarily the same treatment. Each chapter has three major divisions:
(1) an analysis of the nature of the subject matter; (2) a justification for
teaching it at the elementary level; and (3) concrete suggestions about how
to organize the teaching-learning situations to achieve the stated objectives.

In the second section of each chapter, you will find a chart organizing the content of the discipline. In the third section of each chapter you will find another chart identifying the objectives of the discipline under skills, knowledge, and attitudes.

Treatment varies with the nature of the discipline. The chapter on communication emphasizes language as a medium of exchange of ideas. The chapter on social studies concentrates on group processes as they relate to the individual. The chapter on science looks at the environment and how it affects life. The chapter on mathematics stresses both concepts and skills as practical aspects of quantitative relationships. The chapter on the humanities views the cultural background and helps the reader develop an appreciation for the arts.

Throughout Part Two there is a repeated emphasis on pupil activity, questioning techniques, lesson sequences, discovery learning, inductive thinking, and classroom organization for effective teaching and learning. The child is led to learn not only from experiences but from thinking about those experiences.

6

HELPING CHILDREN MASTER THE ART OF COMMUNICATION

Developing Facility in Using Language to Listen, Talk, Read, and Write

Courtesy, Arizona State University Photo Services

USING LANGUAGE
TO LISTEN, TALK, READ, AND WRITE

Try getting along without language for awhile. Even one day or one hour should convince you of the need for and importance of language. Have the children list all the ways they use language. The length of their list should be amazing.

Do you know how you learned your language? Do you know what you can do to help the children expand their language? Do you know what skills the child needs to use language effectively? What is the difference between hearing and listening? between talking and communicating? between reading mechanically and comprehending? between writing mechanically and expressing ideas? Which are major objectives and which are supporting goals for language development? How are they related?

What information do you have about language? How much of it can you, or should you, pass along to your pupils? What activities should you plan to provide learning? Do you know when language is functional and when it is creative? What is the difference?

What is you own attitude toward language? Can you convince children that they need language? Can you create an interest in language as a skill? as content? Can you help children establish their own goals in the use of their language? That is what curriculum building requires.

Skills, knowledge, and attitudes are all important. They are interrelated. The purpose of this chapter is to point out these facets of the curriculum, show their interrelationships, and help you identify your part in curriculum development through the language arts.

Language is one important element that raises people from the realm of lower animals to the highly structured and civilized society of human beings. The origins of written language can be traced back as far as the beginning of recorded history. There is no way of tracing the origins of spoken language. Schools are one of society's organizations for passing on the heritage of preceding generations. Language is the chief medium for such communication. Thus the teaching of language is probably the most significant responsibility of the curriculum. It is our purpose here to survey the skills to be developed, the knowledge to be presented, and the attitudes to be encouraged.

LANGUAGE AND THE SOCIAL STRUCTURE

Since language is a part of our social structure, we need to know what it is, how it is acquired, and what forms are available and useful in using it to communicate.

Language As Communication

Language is communication and it might include gestures, facial expression, and even grunts or sighs. Some would include music, pictures, numbers, and signs. Here we are chiefly concerned with the language of words. Language is oral and the written symbol is merely an abstract device to preserve and record the spoken word. Language is orderly and has structure and pattern. It is learned and transmitted from one generation to another. Each language is meaningful only within the culture to which it applies.

How Language is Acquired

Spoken language is acquired through association. Infants experiment with sounds and learn to associate certain sounds with specific meanings. They experiment with their vocal organs and gain reinforcement when they make accepted sounds and associations. They acquire language gradually through hearing, experimenting, and imitating. What language each child acquires and the quality of language are determined by the environment.

Forms of Communication Through Language

Direct communication through language calls for person-to-person contact. This implies speaking and listening. The advent of the telephone, the radio, and television has made direct communication possible over great distances. This makes the human voice even more potent as a means of carrying messages. The importance of accurate speech and clear enunciation has increased and attentive listening has become more essential.

Indirect communication depends on the printed or recorded word to relay the message. Both sender and receiver must have command of a set of skills for expressing and interpreting messages. This implies reading and writing. Printed materials provide a means of indirect communication circumventing the person-to-person contact. Indirect communication places greater demands on both the writer and the reader. Sometimes the writer does not even know who may read the message. Therefore, the writer must exercise great care in putting information, ideas, and opinions into print and the reader should exercise equally great care in interpreting or quoting the words of another. Recorded materials bear many of the same characteristics as printed materials. The sender may be addressing an unknown audience and the message may be dependent on the interpretation of the listener. The close proximity of direct communication has thus been sacrificed for broader coverage.

Language and the Cultural Background

Language is a determiner of culture. A specific language is neither good nor bad, right nor wrong. Since the purpose of language is to communicate, the first and most important question is, "Did it communicate? And how effectively?" It is just possible that the slang of the teen-ager communicates to the peer group more effectively than the language of the classroom. The same might be said for local dialect. It is quite appropriate for an individual to have more than one language, more than one dialect, and even more than one set of standards. People who know which form of communication to use in each setting are more effective than those who adhere to only one form for all occasions and are unable to adapt to their audiences.

LANGUAGE AND THE LEARNER

Language is a two-way street. The learner must be seen as both a receiver and a sender of language. This calls for mastery of both the oral and the written form of language in order to effectively use this important tool of communication.

Figure 6–1 illustrates language as communication. Intake involves listening and reading. The user is the receiver of the message. Outgo involves speaking and writing. The user is the sender of the message. Listening and speaking are primary or direct communication. Reading and writing are secondary or indirect communication.

The Learner as a Receiver of Language

From their earliest contacts with other human beings, young children learn to listen to sounds and to interpret them into meanings. They add to this skill of interpreting meaning upon initiation into the world of the written word, when they learn to read as one more means of finding out what the messages are as communicated through language.

Listening. Listeners are receiving language to learn about people and things. They are learning to attach definite forms to specific ideas. Perhaps the sense of hearing rivals the senses of sight, touch, taste, and smell as a source of information. But listening involves more than hearing. Not only must listeners have good auditory reception but also good auditory perception. It is this latter which enables them to sort out the many sounds and attach meanings to them. They learn to interpret sounds such as the opening of a door, the ringing of a bell, the clatter of dishes, and the running of water as related to such experiences as the approach of another person, the call of the telephone, the preparation of a meal, or the advent of the daily bath.

Language as Communication

	INTAKE	OUTGO
Primary or Direct	**Listening** *Auditory Skills* Reception—hearing Perception—listening *Perception Skills* Information patterns words—vocabulary Ideas--comprehension Meaning patterns Sentences Word order Syntax	**Speaking** *Vocal Skills* Vocalization Articulation Enunciation Intonation Pitch—volume Stress—emphasis Juncture—pauses Usage Syntax Grammar Sentence patterns *Knowledge* Words—vocabulary Ideas—comprehension
Secondary or Indirect	**Reading** *Mechanics* Alphabetic principle Decoding—phonics Linguistic structure of words of sentences of syntax of grammar Rules *Meanings* Words—vocabulary concrete abstract Sentences—structure phrases word order sentence patterns syntax grammar Ideas—comprehension single words words in context	**Writing** *Mechanics* Penmanship Letter forms Movement Spelling—encoding Linguistic structure words—vocabulary word patterns—rules Capitalization Punctuation Usage Syntax Grammar *Meanings* Functional writing Record keeping Narration Creative writing Prose Poetry

Figure 6-1. *Interrelationships of the four phases of language*

In addition to these sounds they learn the meaning of the human voice. They can readily distinguish between danger and security, admonition and praise, rejection and acceptance. These understandings often come more through the tone of the voice than through the actual words spoken. As they progress in knowledge of language, they learn to associate spoken words first with concrete objects, and finally with ideas. These come through commands, explanations, and conversations. Fortunate indeed are those children who live with adults who take the time and effort to talk with them. As they expand their environment to include the neighborhood, the school, and eventually society in general, they are constantly expanding the use of listening as receivers of language. The school plays a major role in the development of such language facility. Listening is not automatic. It is a learned skill. There is much you can do to help children improve in this area.

Reading. As children become aware that oral speech can be recorded through printing, they approach readiness for learning to read. For some children this comes quite early as they watch their parents record information, make shopping lists, write letters to friends, and read the daily paper. When children enjoy a good story with a parent or other significant

Selecting a book for independent reading is the ultimate goal of reading instruction. Having a wide choice and a place to read makes it doubly enjoyable. (Courtesy, Lowell School, Mesa, Arizona)

adult, they are developing not only a concept of what reading is but also a desire to read by themselves. Whether reading begins at home or at school, whether it is a formal presentation for rote learning or an emerging experience from which one derives understandings, it is still a process of using language as a source of information and enjoyment. When children are functioning as readers, they are using language as receivers. The school has long considered the teaching of this complex skill as an important part of the curriculum for the young child.

The Learner as a Sender of Language

Language production develops simultaneously with listening skills. Listening represents the intake and speaking the outgo. When people speak they are using language in oral form. When they write they are using language in written form. Both have as their major goals communication with others. Communication can be person-to-person or indirect.

Speaking. Did it ever occur to you that most animals have all the organs of articulation yet they do not speak, at least not in an intelligible language which human beings can interpret? Of course, devoted owners are convinced they can tell the difference between a frightened whimper and a joyful bark coming from their pet dogs, but the dog's language never develops beyond that point. Young children may also produce these same sounds, but additionally as they mature they are able to imitate the language they hear and translate ideas into abstractions which we call words. Anyone who has ever had the privilege of observing a young child develop meaningful vocabulary and build a language has truly seen a miracle happen.

Children learn to speak by observing, listening, imitating, and experimenting. Most of them would probably speak adequately for the social setting if they never attended a school. The responsibility of the school through the curriculum is that of refining and extending the language in order that communication skills through oral speech may be more effective.

Writing. Writing is produced to be read. It is another facet of the communication process. The child who learns to write is using the skill to record information for future use or to transmit information to others. Labeling possessions, making lists of things to bring to school, and identifying objects in the environment all are techniques for recording information. Writing a note, an announcement, a story, a poem are all techniques for communicating thoughts to others.

The content of the written message is the important element. Unless the child has something to say there is no point to writing. The phase of writing that concerns contents comes under the heading of composition. It may be the telling of an incident, the description of an object, directions for doing something, or presentation of a point of view. What the writer has to say is important.

The form in which the written message is presented is also important, but it is secondary to the content. It is only when the message is to be read by another that penmanship, spelling, usage, and punctuation become significant. The mechanics are more a courtesy to the reader than a concern for the writer. Whenever children feel that what they have to write is worthy of the effort on the part of another to read it, they are truly communicating. When they care enough for the ease and the convenience of the receiver of the message to want to make it readable, they have not only created their own motive for the mastery of the mechanics but have also become social beings concerned about others.

LANGUAGE AND THE TEACHING-LEARNING PROCESS

It is your responsibility as a teacher to bring together the children and the language. In so doing you will help them acquire skills and the information that will make them effective in all their communication efforts. You need first of all to be an accomplished user of the language yourself. Then you need to know what to teach the pupils at their present level of development. When you teach them to be independent users of language and to have pride in their verbal ability, and when you teach them to enjoy the role of receiver and to care about the role of sender, you have freed them to soar on their own.

Developing Language Facility

A preview of the relationships shown in Fig. 6–2 will provide perspective on the place of language in the elementary curriculum. It shows the various facets of language and differentiates among the things one does, the things one knows, and the way one feels about language.

Developing Skills.   Listening, speaking, reading, and writing are the well-known and often-quoted foursome encompassing the language skills. Reading also can be subdivided into mechanics and comprehension. This division is based on two assumptions (1) mastering the mechanical skills does not necessarily guarantee understanding, and (2) understanding, which is the ultimate goal of reading, is dependent on the mastery of the skills. Writing can also be broken down into mechanics and expression. Mechanics include penmanship, spelling, punctuation, and capitalization. Expression of ideas includes both functional communication and creativity. The balanced curriculum considers all these factors in planning a program that will result in understanding of grammatical structure and effective use of language not only in school but throughout life.

Listening is a means of personal development, a source of information and ideas, a social and a cultural accomplishment, a learned skill, and an art. In spite of all the advancements made by civilization through the use of the written word, listening still remains the primary source of information. The child listens at home, at school, on the street, in public, and in private. Knowing what to listen for, how to discriminate among the sounds one hears, and how to listen effectively are learned achievements which the school can cultivate.

There's more than one way to enjoy a story. Looking at the pictures and listening to the story teller is evidently fun! (Courtesy, Lowell School, Mesa, Arizona)

Tidyman (46:81) identifies seven different kinds of listening, namely:

1. Simple listening
2. Discriminative listening
3. Listening for relaxation
4. Listening for information
5. Listening to organize ideas
6. Critical listening
7. Creative listening

Strickland's list (45:131) of types of listening includes eight levels progressing from the less mature to the more mature as follows:

1. Little conscious listening
2. Half listening
3. Listening passively
4. Off again—on again listening
5. Listening and responding
6. Listening with some reac⁻ ⸱ ᵢs
7. Listening with some part⸱⁓ ᵃtion
8. Listening—meeting of min ᵢ⸳

Other authorities give similar lists of types of listening—some more detailed and lengthy and some shorter and simpler. The point is that listening is not a simple one-formula skill but a complex set of skills used in different ways at different times for different purposes. The user of language needs to know the differences and how to apply them. These skills can be learned and therefore can be taught. Thus they become a part of the curriculum. The skills, knowledge, and attitudes essential to effective listening are itemized in the first row of Fig. 6–2.

Speaking is a learned skill. If society attempted to delay beginning speech until there was evidence of readiness and to control the acquisition of speech through an orderly sequence of carefully graded skills, there might be more speech problems than there are now. The young in any culture seem to "pick up" speech from others. Both the quality and the quantity of speech are influenced by what the child hears. That is not to say that we should practice a "hands off" policy and wait for speech to develop on its own. There is much that can be done both at home and at school to improve the effectiveness of speech. Setting a desirable pattern, encouraging attentive listening, providing for adequate practice, and helping with constructive evaluation are all techniques for growth and improvement. They should be a part of the curriculum.

Using a child-size podium to read to an audience gives the young reader security and ease of performance. (Courtesy, Lowell School, Mesa, Arizona)

Speaking is essential for the development of other communication skills. Better speakers are more likely to become effective listeners. The child who likes and uses language adequately both in listening and speaking is better able to master the reading skills, and speaking bears a positive relationship to written language. Donoghue (8:211) says:

> The child must communicate orally before he can express himself in written form. Speaking and listening habits have a profound influence upon the pupil's ability to write. If he is not taught to think and express himself precisely through oral means, he will never attain the thorough comprehension of the richness and variety of the English language which is the source of writing skill.

The skills, knowledge, and attitudes for effective speaking are identified in the second row of Fig. 6–2.

The mechanics of reading involve the how-to-do-it part. If learners learn only the mechanics and do not use the skill to find out what the writer has to say, they have missed the whole purpose of learning to read. Row three of Fig. 6–2 indicates what mechanics the learner should master in order to do, to know, and to be an effective performer in both silent and oral reading.

Comprehension is the ultimate goal of reading. Without it the rest of the reading skills are of little value. And unless the reader reads both in school and after the school years, the effort that has gone into learning how to read has been wasted. Stauffer (44:199) expresses it well when he asks:

> What does it avail a pupil if he learns to say words and parrot texts, if in the process he loses his ability to read and think creatively and critically, if he loses all desire to apply what he has learned, and above all, if he loses a love for reading?

125

Mastering the Art of Communication

AREA	TO DO	TO KNOW	TO BE
Listening	The learner will be able to hear accurately discriminate accutely attend purposefully	The learner will know wide vocabulary meaningful ideas other languages as needed	The learner will develop varied interests receptive attitude interpretive ability evaluative criteria
Speaking	The learner will be able to articulate clearly enunciate accurately pronounce correctly express ideas effectively	The learner will know useful vocabulary sentence patterns syntax linguistic structure correct usage other languages	The learner will develop concern for others in receiving oral language feeling of responsibility in speaking
Reading—Mechanics	The learner will be able to recognize words use phonic skills decode sound-symbol patterns in words	The learner will know the alphabet sound-symbol relations phonics generalizations syntax sentence patterns	The learner will develop a desire to read pleasure in achievement appreciation of orderly structure of patterns in our language
Reading—Comprehension	The learner will be able to set purposes for reading recognize meaning-bearing patterns in words, phrases, and sentences interpret evaluate react apply to new situations	The learner will know language structure related to meaning vocabulary phrasing	The learner will develop enjoyment in reading appreciation of content respect for reading as a skill

Writing—Mechanics	In *penmanship* the learner will master such basic skills as accuracy speed alinement legibility In *spelling* the learner will be able to associate symbol with matching sound encode sounds into both letters and words The learner will be able to use *capital letters* and *punctuation marks* to clarify meanings	In *penmanship* he will know correct letter formation correct writing position effective habits In *spelling* he will know correct spelling for basic words word structure basic rules and their application He will know correct forms and uses for *capital letters* and for marks of *punctuation* in writing.	In *penmanship* the learner will develop pride in good form desire for quality In *spelling* the learner will concern for correctness courtesy toward reader desire to achieve pride in work In use of *capitalization* and *punctuation* the learner will develop concern for clarity desire for accuracy
Writing—Expression of Ideas	The learner will be able to use writing as a functional tool through clarity of expression accuracy of facts fluency of ideas He will be able to use writing as an outlet for creativity and language as a tool for recording ideas in written form.	The learner will know such forms as announcements record keeping reporting advertising He will develop awareness of content knowledge of effective forms of expression knowledge of what content is worthy of expression	The learner will develop respect for accuracy concern for influence of propaganda respect for opinions The learner will develop enjoyment in the act of creativity itself satisfaction in sharing with others
Grammar and Usage	The learner will acquire skill in the use of correct forms habits of usage appropriate to the time, the place, and the audience	The learner will have knowledge of grammatical structure of language in keeping with his level. rules governing such structure and usage	The learner will develop appreciation for the orderly structure of language as a tool of communication desire for correct use of standard English

Figure 6-2. *Essential learnings in communication through the use of language*

The skills, knowledge, and attitudes needed for successful comprehension in reading are pointed out in the fourth row of Fig. 6–2.

There are two opposing points of view on the approaches to beginning reading. Some would have the learner master the mechanics as rote learning and then attempt to use the skills to find out what the writing says. Others would begin with the ideas and seek to show the learner the patterns used in recording the ideas in print, and would let the skills emerge through purposeful and continued usage. The dichotomy between these two points of view is illustrated in Fig. 6–3. The two ladders thus presented differentiate between a prestructured program and an emerging program. The ladder on the left suggests a prestructured program. It implies that the child must first learn the letters and their sounds and then put them together to form phonograms and words *before* expecting to read for meaning. This is a mechanical approach. It builds on the structure of the discipline and depends on rote learning, drill, deductive thinking, and synthesis. The ladder on the right suggests an emerging program. It implies that the child can begin with ideas and see them expressed in sentences and phrases made up of words *before* analyzing them to discover that they are represented by symbols that fit together in an orderly pattern. This is a meaning approach. It builds on the learning pattern of the child and depends on insight, understanding, inductive thinking, and analysis. Both programs teach exactly the same elements. The difference is in the sequence and the method rather than in the content. The problem in each case is in the follow-through to completion of the program.

Children who approach reading as a mechanical process may become the ones who pronounce the words correctly but miss the meaning. If they see reading only as a mechanical skill and are allowed to stop when they have mastered the techniques of word recognition, they will be handicapped when it comes to comprehension, phrasing, expressive oral reading, interpretation, inference, and application. Children who approach reading as a thought-getting process may turn out to be capable of getting the general idea but may lack independence in mechanics. If they are allowed to stop when they become facile at word recognition in context, they may never master the tools which will give them insight into the structure of the language and consequently independence in reading. The secret to the success with either approach is in following the program through to the end. Don't let them stop half way up the ladder!

Those who advocate the prestructured, mechanical approach point out early achievement as indicated by measurable scores. Those who oppose this approach claim that it will ultimately result in slow, laborious reading habits which are hard to break and which will interfere with effective comprehension. Those who advocate the emerging-meaning approach recognize that it may not produce measurable scores as early in the learning-to-read process, but claim that it will ultimately result in efficient reading habits which are conducive to comprehension and intimate communication with the author. Followed through to the end, it gives the child both meaning and structure. It is this dichotomy which is the basis for much of the current controversy over reading materials and the methods used to teach. It is not the purpose of this chapter to settle this argument, but rather to point out that some of the same learnings are essential with either approach.

It is doubtful if many teachers or published programs pursue either sequence completely and exclusively, because meaning goes with words and the two develop simultaneously. However, the philosophy and the sequence are evident in the emphasis. A program that puts heavy initial emphasis on mastery of mechanics and rote memory may intersperse meanings along the way, but the children are learning that reading is a mechanical word-recognition process in which they translate symbols into sounds. A program that puts initial emphasis on meanings through language experience or story content may intersperse some mechanics along the way, but the children are gathering the idea that reading is finding out what the print tells. The sequence may be one of presenting skills which are used to get meanings, alternating the two, or it may be one of presenting meanings and examining the forms in which they are expressed to find out how they function, again alternating the learnings. In either case the children who become adept at word recognition without either getting meaning or finding out how the system works are left without

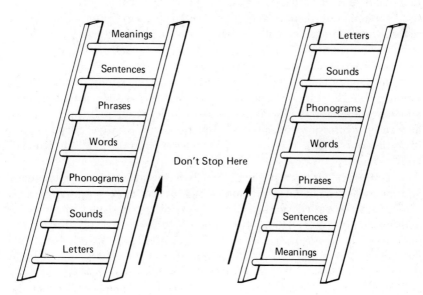

Figure 6-3. *Climbing the ladder to success in learning to read. Two opposing points of view regarding sequences*

purpose or without independence. Learning to read must go beyond word recognition. It must include both mechanical skills and comprehension.

The mechanics of writing, like reading, may be interpreted as a how-to-do-it process. And like reading, if one learns only the mechanics and does not use the skills to express ideas, the whole purpose for learning to write has been missed. The mechanics of writing include *penmanship* and *spelling* plus the amenities of *capitalization* and *punctuation.* At one time fancy penmanship was considered a mark of culture, and much time was devoted to rhythmical practice to perfect form. Currently simplicity of style, ease of performance, and legibility are considered more desirable curricular targets. At one time the ability to spell long lists of unusual words was considered a mark of knowledge. A more practical point of view is currently recognized as an objective in spelling. Both penmanship and spelling are tools of communication that are useful only when one attempts to put thoughts into writing. The use of clear, legible penmanship and the ability to apply accepted spelling patterns are matters of respect and consideration for the reader. Capitalization and punctuation are merely tools for conveying to the reader the designations of important points or the pauses, stops, and inflections of the voice which are lost when oral speech is recorded in print. For a listing of skills, knowledge, and attitudes related to the mechanics of penmanship, spelling, capitalization, and punctuation refer to row five in Fig. 6–2.

Written expression of ideas serves two basic purposes. One is *functional* and the other is *creative.* When the writer sends a message, writes an announcement, makes a list, records facts for future reference, or reports on findings, writing is being used in a practical sense. Ideas recorded or shared through original prose, or occasionally poetry, are creative. An idea need not necessarily be new in order for it to be creative or original. It may be new to the writer or it may be expressed in a new or unique way. The important point is that the writer wishes to express ideas and views language as a medium through which to express them. Learnings in written expression, whether for functional or creative purposes, are identified in Fig. 6–2, row six as things for the pupil "to Do," "to Know," and "to Be."

Grammar implies a systematic study of the structure of the language and the arrangements of words into sentences that convey meanings. This arrangement is called syntax. Grammar is often construed to mean, in addition to syntax, the study of morphology (the study of word patterns), phonology (pronunciation of words), and semantics (study of word meanings). There have been numerous studies about the relationship between the understanding of grammatical structure of language and the ability of the user to conform to basic accepted principles. Whether the knowledge of the structure of language results from formal study and analysis or from application of principles which are observed in listening and reading, there are still certain grammatical principles that do affect meanings. For example, the tense of a verb indicates when an event happened, thus:

> The boys walk to school.
> The boys walked to school.

The word order in the sentence, particularly in the English sentence, makes a difference in the subject or agent doing the acting and the object or recipient of the action, thus:

> The boy burned the match.
> The match burned the boy.

Usage refers to the form of expression commonly applied to both speech and writing. Good usage means adherence to socially acceptable forms applied in communication. What is good in one situation might not necessarily be good in another. Perhaps appropriate usage might be a more descriptive term in referring to acceptable patterns of expression. See the last row in Fig. 6–2 for a detailed list of skills, knowledge, and attitudes to be established through a study of grammar and usage.

Building a Background of Information. Learning is a result of awareness of experience. Learning results in changed behavior. When these concepts are applied to language skills, they indicate that the learner must first be aware of the nature of language and then must have experience in the use of the tool. Given these concepts, behavior in the use of language should be changed to conform to accepted practices and effective usage. In order to help the child grow in the use of language as a tool of communication, you need to select thoughtfully the content to be taught and plan carefully the activities to be provided.

Selecting the content to be taught is more than a mere listing of skills, knowledge, and attitudes. Content must be associated with recognized targets and carefully planned activities. Covering the items listed does not constitute teaching. Real teaching has taken place only when the learner has assimilated the information, mastered the skills, and assumed the desirable attitudes specified in the goals. Deciding what the learner should know is one of your responsibilities. In language some learnings are rather specific. The ones listed below are customarily considered practical and useful at the elementary level.

Vocabulary adequate to understand the spoken word and to express ideas orally enhances communication. The same vocabulary becomes the foundation for reading and expressing ideas in writing. Some vocabulary is acquired incidentally and informally. Carefully planned teaching can do much to increase vocabulary both in quantity and in quality.

Sentence pattern and *syntax* are basic elements in the use of language. Most children master much of the structure of language long before entering school. They are aware of and use subjects and verb forms. They follow the rules of word order and subordination. They know and use modifiers. They can express tense, number, and degree. Sometimes they err when they follow systematic patterns applied to irregular English forms, but this proves their knowledge of the structure of the language. For example, when Fred says, "I runned all the way home," he is applying the principle of forming the past tense of the verb by adding the "ed" to the verb. Language can be greatly expanded and enriched through constructive help in the understanding and use of sentence patterns.

Linguistic structure of language adds much insight into meaning-bearing patterns. Sometimes a word's meaning is changed through the addition of a prefix or a suffix. Sometimes a phrase or a sentence is changed through the arrangement of words into thought units. The child who learns the principles is not dependent on memory for details and specifics. Lefevre (25:343) emphasizes the importance of structure of language when he says:

> Reading comprehension can be greatly improved with increased emphasis upon the sentence as the basic meaning-bearing unit instead of the word; such an emphasis should be one strand of reading instruction from the very beginning.

Alphabetical principles of language provide a basis for many generalizations about word structure, pronunciation, and meaning. The learner who establishes such a base early in the learning experience is building a foundation for independence in both reading and writing. This foundation involves both encoding through spelling and decoding through reading. When pupils realize the multiplicity of words and ideas that can be expressed with only twenty-six symbols they develop a keen respect for the alphabet.

Capitalization and *punctuation* are tools that enable writers to tell prospective readers more accurately what they want to say. Capitalization points out what is important in the way of comparison and change of thought. Punctuation shows the readers where they would pause in articulation. It indicates when to stop with one thought and start a new one. It tells whether the sentence is inquiring instead of telling and whether it is to be expressed with strong emotion. Punctuation also shows when the words of another are being quoted. The writer who knows how to use these tools can express ideas more accurately and the reader who understands them can read with greater comprehension. The school curriculum assumes the responsibility for acquainting children with these devices to enhance their abilities in communication.

Usage implies the manner in which the communicator uses language to convey ideas. One point of view sees the grammarian as the dictator of correct usage. Another sees the grammarian as the recorder of accepted usage. According to the latter point of view, usage changes with time. As forms become more commonly accepted among users of the language, they enter the dictionaries and the language textbooks as a part of the description of the language. Usage might be considered acceptable if it communicates effectively in the situation; an interpretation that allows acceptable usage to vary from one situation to another. It is the responsibility of the school curriculum to acquaint children with the standards of usage that are generally acceptable and that are the measure by which they will be judged in the world of work, the world of society, and the world beyond the confines of the immediate home or neighborhood.

Rules are of consequence only when they help the learner make more efficient use of knowledge. Rules memorized verbatim and regurgitated on command without understanding are of little value. Only when children understand the situation from which the rules have been derived and have helped in the formulation of the statement through discovering the basic principles for themselves have they learned generalizations that will be helpful to them in meeting new or unfamiliar situations. In discussing the importance of redundancy in learning of language principles Frank Smith (40:228) says:

> The child has to learn how the rules of syntax are related to the written aspects of language, together with the relation of visual configurations and semantic interpretations. All this can come about only if the child is given examples, if he is shown what is the same and what is different. He has to be given the raw material so that he can develop the rules for himself. He can only look for the 'regularities' that are the basis for all cognitive activity if he is exposed to a large enough sample of 'evidence.'

Forms of written expression are varied. Children who learn to adapt listening and reading to various forms as the occasion demands will be more effective than those who follow one set pattern. Sometimes they listen for details such as how to play a game. Sometimes they listen for general impressions in a story. Sometimes they listen for sequence of events or relevancy of points as in an essay or a sermon. Sometimes they listen for beauty in the expression itself. These same principles apply to reading. The most important concept in describing facility in either listening or reading is *adaptability*. Children who learn to adapt to various forms for various purposes as receivers of language are better equipped to use language as a medium of expression through either oral speech or written communication.

A *second language* and its use is dependent on the situation and the individual. Sometimes more than two languages may be needed. There was a time when children could expect to grow up and live out their entire lives in the small community where they heard only one language. For them a second language had no functional use. If they learned it in school, it was textbook-oriented study and served no purpose beyond school. This is not so common in today's society. Many children travel while growing up or move to places where they have a real need for understanding and speaking another language. Many live in border localities where different cultures and different languages are intermingled. Whether or not a second language should be a part of the elementary-school curriculum is controversial. If a second language is taught, we still need to answer such questions as what language should this be? When should the teaching begin? By whom? And how? A language appropriate to the Southwest where Spanish is commonly spoken might not be appropriate for a locality bordering a Canadian province with many French speaking citizens. Timing the teaching of the language involves finding the right time in the child's life as well as the right time in the school day. Then there is the problem of the teacher. Should we have bilingual teachers or should a specialist be brought in on a regular schedule? And should the language be taught with an oral-aural approach or with a structured grammatical approach? These are definite curricular problems any elementary school must face when it considers the addition of a second language to its curriculum. The answers will vary with the situation.

Selecting the activities to be provided includes both curriculum content and experiences. Since language experiences constitute such a major portion of the school day and are basic to most other learnings, certainly language activities are one of your concerns in curriculum planning. They include both the informal experiences as well as the direct instruction in planned practice sessions, and they cannot stop short of the independent application of language skills practiced by the pupil.

Informal experiences in *communication* begin the moment children enter the school. They answer questions about their names, their homes, their ages, and their needs. These experiences include the spontaneous communication which takes place the first thing in the morning when the children come bursting in with something to tell. They are clearly evident during "sharing time" when the child has something to share with the group. They continue on the playground and in the corridor whenever the child has a need to communicate with you, with peers, or with other school personnel such as the principal, the caretaker, the nurse, or the librarian. Children spend most of their time communicating. Perhaps more of it is spent in listening than in any other form of communication. Today's schools are also seeing a greater need for providing experiences in oral communication than in the past when schools put the prize on sitting still and being quiet. Reading follows listening as a means of communicating and that need gradually increases over the years. Writing is a much used mode of communication throughout school and life.

Direct instruction in the communication arts is a traditional part of the elementary curriculum. Practically every classroom at the beginning levels considers the teaching of reading, writing, spelling, and language as a major responsibility. Such instruction may be provided on an individual basis or in groups. Sometimes it is in the form of mass instruction to the total group, but regardless of the form it is still very much a part of the planned program. Instruction in these language arts areas may be based on textbooks or workbooks, or it may be an emerging experience based on the activities of the children, but it is still evident in the plans. You must feel a definite responsibility for indicating correct forms, needed skills, and definite learnings in this area. You must teach skills, knowledge, and attitudes.

Planned practice is also a part of the program because the children learn when they perform. Sometimes the planned practice is informal and elicits oral responses on the basis of interests. Sometimes the practice is in the form of written assignments and routine work. These may be dictated, placed on the chalkboard, or provided as duplicated or printed material. Many of the exercises may consist of blanks to fill in or questions to answer. Their value may be debated but the plan for practice exists nevertheless.

Independent *application* and *self-evaluation* may be a part of the curriculum plan and of the teacher's goals, or they may be self-initiated by the learner. Regardless of the method, such activities do occur in the classroom and therefore are a part of the curriculum. You may provide an author's corner which invites children to come and create. You may provide materials to which they may help themselves if they have an idea to express. You may encourage free writing as a spare-time activity. You may discuss with each child informally written or oral expression and offer help in deciding what has been accomplished and what needs to be done to improve the work. Each child may be encouraged to keep a library book at hand for spare-time reading. There may be an interesting reading table that beckons the young reader. All these are indications that communication through oral and written expression is very much a part of the planned activities throughout the school day in every classroom.

Encouraging and Maintaining Lifelong Habits and Attitudes. The ultimate goal in learning the communication arts in the elementary school is to be able to communicate effectively with others not only in the classroom but in all situations. This includes communication with peers, family members, school personnel, business associates, social acquaintances, and even politicians and foreign diplomats. Being able to share information, ideas, and ideals with others on a meaningful basis is the key to world understanding. Those who have learned such skills have taken the first step. The use of language is the single most important means of such communication. Therefore, the school that is providing functioning curriculum in this area helps the child to see the needs, to create an interest, to develop concerns, and to establish independence.

Establishing needs for communication is part of curriculum planning. Children are aware of the need for communication long before they enter school. Up to that time they have already used language to communicate with family members, playmates, and others. They have used language to express wants, find out about the environment, satisfy curiosity, and share feelings. The school must cultivate the need which already exists. A school setting that puts the premium on "being still" discourages rather than extends that need. Children need many opportunities to talk with the teacher, with each other, and even to themselves. They gain this experience through telling about their experiences, role playing in imitation of adult activities, reliving the experiences of literary characters in dramatization, asking questions, and exchanging ideas with classmates and teachers.

Creating interests depends on attitudes of curiosity, fascination, or absorption. Interest cannot be delivered on demand. It comes from within. The best you can do is make learning attractive and hope to win the interest

Children who lose themselves in the identity of a story character become totally engrossed in what they are saying and not in what the audience thinks about it. (Courtesy, Lowell School, Mesa, Arizona)

of the learner. Only the child can decide what curricular experiences will be accepted. When you are skillful at arousing and holding the attention of the pupils, you have taken the first step. Unless the pupils get some kind of pleasure, satisfaction, or gratification from the learning act, they will accept passively and turn away when the influence of the school has been removed. Their reactions may be negative or positive. If they are negative, the child may seem to cooperate not because of interest in the activity but because of concern about the consequences which might be punishment or withdrawal of rewards. When reprimands or low marks are used as motivation, the attention of the child is lost as soon as the influence of the school is removed. Even a seemingly positive motive may be negative in its effect. The promise of praise or reward as a reason for learning only causes the child to work for the reward not the learning.

Developing attitudes means leading children to be concerned about accomplishments. They need to be led to see themselves as persons who can and therefore who do. They need to be concerned not with winning or being the best but with achieving. When children are led to see language as a personally useful tool, when they have the desire to master it for their own use, and when they have developed pride in accomplishment, then they are ready to pursue the learning for personal use rather than for the reward. When children appreciate language for its intrinsic worth, they no longer need an external reward for their efforts. As you develop these attitudes you are placing the learner in the "driver's seat" and are offering your support in the enterprise of self-education. Such attitudes do not come on command and do not develop instantly. It takes time to change or develop attitudes. It takes persistence and repeated efforts. Evidences of such attitudes are noted when a child volunteers information, listens because of a desire to know, asks for reading matter to satisfy curiosity, and creates in writing without having an assignment with a deadline.

Establishing self-direction means attaining independence in the use of language. When Ann can work without a teacher to tell her what to do or to pass judgment on her work, she is independent. This is a very mature response in the use of language. Perhaps not everybody reaches it to the point of complete independence but all do reach it to some extent.

Organizing the Curriculum

Language is not a "subject" taught between 10:30 and 11:15 daily. You cannot outline language skills in your curriculum notebook, plan daily lessons to accomplish the goals, and check them off when they are done. Language is something that functions all day every day. That is true in the classroom. It continues to be true as long as a person lives in contact with others.

Relating Language to the Rest of the Curriculum.   Children do not "turn off" language when the period is over and they put away the language text. They use language all day in social studies, science, arithmetic, spelling, physical education, writing, art, music, in fact, in everything they do. Language is a two-way street. They travel the street in both directions.

Finding out what one needs to know is a basic use for language. Children listen and read for information and entertainment, to find out the assignment, what information classmates can contribute to the topic under discussion, and what others think about ideas. They read to find out about the past, about plans for the future, and about what others have thought. They read to gather information basic to the pursuit of daily assignments in all other school subjects.

Communicating information and ideas means traveling the street in the other direction. Pupils share with others what they have found out, what they know, and what they think. This is just as important as finding out in the first place. When they ask questions about the assignment, plan with classmates for the making of a mural or the building of a model, relate to the rest what they found out from an interview with the school nurse or from reading in the encyclopedia, they are using language to communicate. When they give directions for a game, explain the meaning of a production in art, pronounce the spelling list to a partner, verbalize the solution to a mathematics problem, or participate in a dramatization, they are using language.

Language is a finding-out process and a communicating process. Whether children spend all of the school day with one teacher or move from one teacher to another, the carry-over is still needed. It is your responsibility to see that language skills continue to function in all areas of the curriculum.

Relating Language to Life.   Children no more "turn off" language when they leave the classroom than when they reach the end of the language class period. They carry language with them to the playground and to the home. They use language all summer. They continue to use language after they graduate. If you help them lay a firm foundation of language skills, knowledge, and attitudes, they will continue to grow in language power as long as they live.

A *source of information* that makes one independent is one of the most valuable uses of language. When children learn to see reading and listening as sources of information rather than as school related skills to be tested, they are moving into independence. This is the reverse of drilling on skills in anticipation of future needs. Only when they enjoy the reading act for its own sake and the story for its content will they be acquiring lasting habits and attitudes. If they read library books only for the "certificate of merit" or for credit, they will cease to read when school is out. If they read because they enjoy the story, the reward will no longer be necessary. If they continue to see need for reading outside the classroom, they will read newspapers, current periodicals, directions that go with purchases, editorials, advertisements, announcements, and communiques received. They will continue to be informed persons.

Personal and social contacts are enhanced through the use of language. The mature person sees writing not as a skill in producing perfect penmanship and spelling, but as a means of recording and sharing ideas. The adult who writes a letter and exercises enough care to make it readable is showing that kind of independence. Even the person who assumes such adult responsibilities as taking the minutes for a club meeting, reporting the actions of a civic committee, or dictating a business letter to a secretary has come to view language as a useful and valuable tool. A pleasant "good morning," a cultivated telephone manner, a polite conversational pattern, a well modulated voice, all these are a part of the use of language which makes a person an accepted member of a social group.

SUMMARY

Language is a part of our social structure. It is a means of communication and is acquired from the environment. Communication through language may be direct through person-to-person use of oral language, or it may be indirect through the use of mass media. What language one acquires and the quality of that language are products of the cultural background.

The user of any language serves alternately in the role of a receiver or a sender. The receiver of language is a listener or a reader. The sender of language is a speaker or a writer. It takes both to complete the cycle and make language truly a communication agent.

The teaching of language is a curricular responsibility in the elementary school. You are in a position to help the child develop needed skills, knowledge, and attitudes leading to ability to listen effectively, speak meaningfully, read with comprehension and understanding, and write correctly the ideas and information needed to record or communicate. This implies building adequate vocabulary, establishing effective patterns of speech, understanding principles of alphabetization, punctuation, capitalization, and syntax, and improving ability to use language, or languages, to communicate.

These learnings in the classroom come from informal experiences, direct instruction, planned practice, and eventually independent self-evaluation. Not until the learners recognize the needs, acquire personal interests, and develop concerns for learning have they really established their own targets in language.

SUGGESTED ACTIVITIES

Select one or more of the following suggested activities as a basis for expanding your personal understanding of how language is developed in children. Share your findings with the rest of the class.

1. Observe a young child learning to talk. Over a period of three or four weeks keep a daily record of:
   new words added to the vocabulary
   first evidences of sentence structure
   indications of insight into the structure of the language
   growth over a period of time

2. Monitor a television or radio program over a period of a week or two. Collect evidences of language used for different purposes:
   to impart information
   to influence thinking
   to entertain

3. Examine the daily newspaper and sort the content into:
   factual information versus opinion
   statements of fact versus propaganda
   information versus entertainment

4. Select ten popular magazines from the newsstand. Try to identify each in terms of:
   their intended audience
   their purposes
   their types of content
   their style of writing

5. Take a pupil's textbook in some subject other than language arts. Read carefully and make a collection of words that bear special meanings in this setting. For example:
   rabbits *multiply* rapidly—*multiply* six times seven
   draw a picture—*draw* your money from the bank

6. From the same source identify sayings or figures of speech that are basic to the understanding of the content and that may need explaining to the child. For example:
   as cool as a cucumber
   laughed till his sides split
   left in the dark
   traffic flowed

7. Select a portion of a story in which there is conversation recorded. Copy the selection omitting all the punctuation marks. Present it to a classmate for reading and interpretation. Notice the difference in meaning or the confusions caused by lack of punctuation.

8. Write reviews for ten children's books and try to "sell" them to a group of children.

9. Prepare a set of suggestions you could use with a parent group to help them help their children in language.

SELECTED READINGS

1. AGEE, HUGH, "Zonking in the Classroom (or, Language Lessons from the Market Place)" in *Elementary English*, Vol. XLIX, No. 5, May 1972, pp. 780–82. Plays on linguistic structure of language to help children discover how new words are created, how language grows, and how meanings are derived.

2. ANDERSON, PAUL S., *Language Skills in Elementary Education* (2nd edition), New York: Macmillan, 1972, p. 517. Treats the whole area of language including speech and listening, children's literature, handwriting, reading, composition, spelling, and grammar.

3. BLOCK, J. R., "ita and Other Alphabets," in *Elementary English*, Vol. 50, No. 1, Jan. 1973, pp. 49–59. Describes Traditional Orthography, Initial Teaching Alphabet, Unifon, Diacritical Marking System, Words in Color, and World English Spelling. Quotes research evaluating results. Concludes teachers are a major variable.

4. CALLAWAY, BRYON, et. al, "Five Methods of Teaching Language Arts: A Comparison," in *Elementary English*, Vol. 49, No. 8, Dec. 1972, pp. 1240–45. Research report on specific methods.

5. COSTANZO, FRANCES S., "Language of the Six-Year-Old Child," in *Elementary English*, Vol. XLIX, No. 3, March 1972, pp. 382–86. Traces growth from 2–8. Differentiates between types of children.

6. CROSBY, ROBERT M., "Reading: The Dyslexic Child," in *Today's Education*, Vol. 60, No. 7, Oct. 1971, pp. 46–48. Outlines causes and symptoms. Suggests steps for remediation.

7. DALLMANN, MARTHA, et. al., *The Teaching of Reading* (4th edition), New York: Holt, Rinehart and Winston, 1974. Follows same pattern as earlier editions. Reflects current trends in skills and free reading. Gives emphasis to comprehension.

8. DONOGHUE, MILDRED R., *The Child and the English Language Arts*, Dubuque, Iowa: Wm. C. Brown Co., 1971. Outlines needs and specific techniques. Many classroom examples.

9. DUFFY, GERALD G. and GEORGE B. SHERMAN, *Systematic Reading Instruction*, New York: Harper & Row, 1972, p. 311 (paper). Presents the skills, identifies objectives, provides examples and tests.

10. FICHTENAU, ROBERT L., "Teaching Rhetorical Concepts," in *Elementary English*, Vol. XLIX, No. 3, March 1972, pp. 376–381. Differentiates between writing as transcription and as composition.

11. FISHBEIN, JUSTIN, and ROBERT EMANS, *A Question of Competence, Language, Intelligence, and Learning to Read*, Chicago: Science Research Associates, 1972, p. 231 (paper). Puts emphasis on the child rather than the method.

12. FUNK, HAL D. and DEWAYNE TRIPLETT, *Language Arts in the Elementary School: Readings*, New York: J. B. Lippincott, 1972, p. 500 (paper). Comprehensive collection of about 70 articles by recognized authorities.

13. GOODMAN, KENNETH S., "Orthography in a Theory of Reading Instruction," in *Elementary English*, Vol. 49, No. 8, Dec. 1972, pp. 1254–61. Suggests excessive concern for phonics induces reading for sounds or words and evades reading for meaning. This endangers comprehension. Sees meaning as basic to the reading process.

14. GUNDERSON, DORIS V., "New Developments in the Teaching of Reading," in *Elementary English*, Vol. 50, No. 1, Jan. 1973, pp. 17–21. Television, individualized learning, open classroom, programmed materials, etc. Concludes teacher is important factor.

15. HEILMAN, ARTHUR W., *Principles and Practices of Teaching Reading* (3rd edition), Columbus, Ohio: Charles E. Merrill, 1972. Emphasizes language process and teaching both meaning and mechanics concommitantly, not in sequence.

16. HEILMAN, ARTHUR W., and ELIZABETH ANN HOLMES, *Smuggling Language into the Teaching of Reading*, Columbus, Ohio: Charles E. Merrill, 1972, p. 109 (paper). Emphasizes intonation, word meanings, word structure, context clues, inferences, sentence patterns, etc. as a part of the comprehension process. Exercises, games, puzzles.

17. JACKSON, MARY, "Let's Make Foreign Language Study More Relevant," in *Today's Education*, Vol. 60, No. 3, pp. 18–20, March 1971. Discusses teacher, methods, and curriculum.

18. JARVIS, OSCAR T. and MARION J. RICE, *An Introduction to Teaching in the Elementary School*, Dubuque, Iowa: Wm. C. Brown, 1972. Chap. 6. Communication Arts, Chap. 10. Reading, Chaps. 11, Language and Communication.

19. JONES, DAISY M., "All Children Have Language Problems—Which Ones Are Special?" in *Elementary English*, Vol. 49, No. 6, Oct. 1972, pp. 836–41. Identifies problems and tells what to do about them. Identifies communication as the basic purpose of language.

20. JONES, DAISY MARVEL, *Teaching Children to Read*, New York: Harper & Row, Publishers, 1971. A practical approach to reading, written from the viewpoint of the classroom teacher. Chap. 5. Word Patterns.

21. KENNEDY, EDDIE C., *Classroom Approaches to Remedial Reading*, Itasca, Ill.: F. E. Peacock, 1971. Emphasizes remedial reading. Suggestions for classroom rather than clinical use.

22. KENNEDY, EDDIE C., *Methods in Teaching Developmental Reading*, Itasca, Ill.: F. E. Peacock, 1974. Evaluates both basal and nonbasal programs. Analyzes both skills and comprehension. Shows application in other curriculum areas.

23. KUNKLE, JOHN F., "Now that FLES Is Dead, What Next?" in *Educational Leadership*, Vol. 29, No. 5, Feb. 1972, pp. 417–19. Points out lacks in foreign language teaching in elementary schools. Gives Canadian model as an alternative.

24. LEFCOURT, ANN, "Spelling and the Dictionary," in *Elementary English*, Vol. 49, No. 8, Dec. 1972, pp. 1228–32. Suggests relationship between sounds heard and symbols seen and, though not always consistent, they are a clue to spelling.

25. LEFEVRE, CARL A., *Linguistics, English, and the Language Arts*, Boston: Allyn and Bacon, 1970. Shows how meaning bearing patterns are basic to effective speaking, listening, reading, and writing. Stresses ideas rather than mechanics.

26. LUND, ARLINE, "Reading: Teaching Migrant Children," in *Today's Education*, Vol. 60, No. 7, Oct. 1971, pp. 49–51. First grade teacher identifies special problem and what she has done about it.

27. MILLER, WILMA H., *Elementary Reading Today: (Selected Articles)*, New York: Holt, Rinehart and Winston, 1972, p. 331 (paper). Forty-five articles on reading process, readiness, approaches, individual differences, and remediation.

28. MILLER, WILMA H., *The First R, Elementary Reading Today.* New York: Holt, Rinehart and Winston, 1972, p. 276 (paper). Written for preservice teachers. Describes process, approaches, mechanics, and comprehension. Emphasizes prevention rather than remediation.

29. NELSON, THEODORE F., "We're Failing to Teach Effective Talking," in *Today's Education*, Vol. 60, No. 7, Oct. 1971, pp. 43–45. Stresses need for communication courses in elementary schools.

30. O'BRIEN, CARMEN A., *Teaching the Language-Different Child to Read*, Columbus, Ohio: Charles E. Merrill, 1973, p. 168 (paper). Identifies problems caused by differences in speech sounds and reading problems that develop because of unfamiliarity with both language and concepts.

31. OTTO, WAYNE, *et. al.*, *Focused Reading Instruction*, Menlo Park, Cal.: Addison-Wesley, 1974. Stresses individualization and accountability. Focuses on specific problems and provides examples of what to do to remedy the situation.

32. RICKETTS, MARY E., "Reading: Remedial Reading via TV," in *Today's Education*, Vol. 60, No. 7, Oct. 1971, pp. 51–52. Discusses impact of Sesame Street and The Electric Company.

33. ROWELL, C. GLENNON, "A Prototype for an Individualized Spelling Program," in *Elementary English*, Vol. XLIX, No. 3, Mar. 1972, pp. 335–40. Techniques and strategies for individualization.

34. RUDDELL, ROBERT, *Reading-Language Instruction: Innovative Practices*, Englewood Cliffs, N.J.: Prentice-Hall, 1973. Combines language and reading. Presents practical activities based on research.

35. SCHNEIDER, MARY, "Black Dialect: The Basis for an Approach to Reading Instruction," in *Educational Leadership*, Vol. 28, No. 5, Feb. 1971, pp. 543–49. Different, not deficient.

36. SEBESTA, SAM LEATON, and CARL J. WALLEN, *The First R, Readings on Teaching Reading*, Chicago: Science Research Associates, 1972, p. 490 (paper). Forty contributions in eight sections with statement of objectives, rationale, and study questions.

37. SHELDON, WILLIAM D. *et al.*, "A Summary of Research Studies Relating to Language Arts in Elementary Education," in *Elementary English*, Vol. 50, No. 5, May 1973, pp. 791–839. Summarizes 179 studies.

38. SMITH, DORA V., "Trends in Elementary School Language Arts Today," in *Elementary English*, Vol. XLIX, No. 3, Mar. 1972, pp. 326–34. Recent trends with examples. Comparison with British schools.

39. SMITH, FRANK, "Phonology and Orthography: Reading and Writing," in *Elementary English*, Vol. 49, No. 7, Nov. 1972, pp. 1075–88. Emphasizes alphabetic principle in reading and writing. Emphasizes meaning and points out that decoding is only for oral reading.

40. SMITH, FRANK, *Understanding Reading, A Psycholinguistic Analysis of Reading and Learning to Read*, New York: Holt, Rinehart and Winston, 1971. A description of language and the process of learning to read.

41. SMITH, LEWIS, *et. al.*, "Communication Skills through Self-Recording," in *Today's Education*, Vol. 60, No. 1, Jan. 1971, pp. 18–20. An account of a project with second graders making recordings.

42. SPACHE, EVELYN B., *Reading Activities for Child Involvement*, Boston: Allyn and Bacon, 1972. A collection of activities for classroom use.

43. SPACHE, GEORGE D. and EVELYN B. SPACHE, *Reading in the Elementary School* (3rd edition), Boston: Allyn and Bacon, 1972. Practical helps to understanding and teaching reading.

44. STAUFFER, RUSSELL G., *Teaching Reading as a Thinking Process*, New York: Harper & Row, 1969. Emphasizes comprehension. Sees mechanics as an outgrowth rather than a preparation for reading.

45. STRICKLAND, RUTH G., *The Language Arts in the Elementary School* (3rd edition), Lexington, Mass.: D. C. Heath, 1969. Explores acquisition and use of language in all areas of the curriculum.

46. TIDYMAN, WILLARD F. *et. al.*, *Teaching the Language Arts* (3rd edition), New York: McGraw-Hill, 1969. Outlines phases of the language arts program. Part 4 describes steps in planning a language-arts curriculum.

47. WALCUTT, CHARLES C. *et. al.*, *Teaching Reading, A Phonic-Linguistic Approach to Developmental Reading*, New York: Macmillan, 1974. The title is descriptive of the theory and the recommended approach to the teaching of reading.

48. WALLEN, CARL J., *Competency in Teaching Reading*, Chicago: Science Research Associates, 1972, p. 513 (paper). Identifies purposes. Sets up problem situations. Gives examples. Provides self-tests. Covers both skills and comprehension.

49. WOODFIN, MARY JO, "Whatever Happened to Reading?" in *Educational Leadership*, Vol. 30, No. 7, April 1973, pp. 619–22. New programs, methods, materials, processes, approaches, and accountability. Sees quality as related to instruction.

50. ZIEGENFUSS, W. BEATRICE, "Special Feature on Reading: Recipe for Reading," in *Today's Education*, Vol. 60, No. 7, Oct. 1971, pp. 44–45. A third grade teacher tells how she does it.

HELPING CHILDREN UNDERSTAND THE SOCIAL STUDIES

How Human Beings Behave and Why

Courtesy, Lowell School, Mesa, Arizona

UNDERSTANDING SOCIAL STUDIES

Take a look at the past to see what it can teach you and what you can help the children learn from it. That is history. Knowing the facts is not enough. Where did they happen and how have they been affected by weather and climate, and by the presence of human life. That is geography. Should these two areas be explored separately or together? You may have one unified text, two separate texts, or a collection of references. What will you do with them?

Knowing what and how is not enough. You also need to know why people behave as they do. Children need to delve into the minds of people, the trends in society, and the influences of government, business, and the world of work. Will you begin at the local level and expand or take an overall view as a basis for understanding the here and the now? Social studies are influenced by such disciplines as psychology, sociology, political science, civics and government, economics, business, and even the trades and professions. Can you help the children make the connections?

How can you help children satisfy their needs for human relations, make a living, being protected, and participating in government? What information will they need? What skills will they use? What decisions will be facing them? The decisions they make will determine the kinds of people they become.

The social studies provide the content. Mastering skills and memorizing information may help them pass the tests, but the real measure is in how they perform when they meet the real situation. Knowing the "right" answer is not good enough. You need to create a social setting in which attitudes function. Do you know how?

> History is the story of great events in the lives of men. If you would understand the story of the past, study about the great men who lived in each age and find out what they did. Some great men have been explorers. Others have been rulers, inventors, scholars, missionaries, merchants, teachers, and so on. Time and place are important in social studies. Events are important. Most important of all are the people you read about and the lasting effect their work has had on the world.

This is the advice offered by Jones (17:92) to intermediate grade children in the introduction to a social studies unit. Hicks (12:124) suggests that the purpose of the social studies curriculum is "the induction of young people into our society." Haan (11:238) reiterates this same point of view when he says:

Broadly the purpose of the social studies is that of socialization of children so they can live in and shape a society of free men. . . . The creative job of the curriculum maker is the building and finding of experiences appropriate to children which will allow for growth in the children's ability to cope with the social situations in which they live.

And Piercey (24:81) brings the topic right up to date when she tells how to use the newspaper as "A Daily Text for Thinking" saying:

How man behaved yesterday is told on the pages of history. How he behaves today is written across the pages of the daily newspaper.

Just as today becomes yesterday, current events become the chronicle of the human race. The newspaper keeps a written, running account of man's debits and credits, often interpreting both, but leaving for history the final settlement of the account.

History, geography, economics, government are immobilized in textbooks. Set apart is a course called current world affairs, or current events. Its official textbook is the daily newspaper along with the other communications media. Current events, however, can no more be separated from the other courses than the motion can be separated from man in repose. By means of the newspaper, parallels, examples, comparisons, contrasts,—all current, all today—can be made with history—the yesterday which once was today.

Students can exercise their reasoning powers by second-guessing historians with inquiries involving the newspaper.

The content of the social studies curriculum revolves around the questions of how humanity has arrived at its present state and why people behave as they do. In order to justify the teaching of this discipline at the elementary school level, we need to know what society expects, what the individual needs, and what the curriculum is trying to do. This leads us to question how to teach and how to organize for teaching. Some things the children will be able to do; some things they will know; and some things will affect the kinds of persons they become. Exploring these ideas will give us perspective on what we can do to help children understand the basic concepts in social studies.

SOCIAL STUDIES CONTENT

When we study about people and how they have arrived at the present state in civilization, we need to take a look at the past and the setting in which events have occurred. This embodies the area of history, including anthropological concepts, and geography, which is a description of the earth's features and ecology in the environment. These concepts may be studied separately or may be fused into a unified course to help the child become aware of and appreciative of humanity's accomplishments.

How Humanity Has Arrived at its Present State

A backward look helps us to recognize origins. A historical look helps orient us in terms of time sequences. A geographical look provides perspective in terms of space and distance. A composite known as *the social studies* enables us to see humanity as it has been, as a factor in present day life, and as a potential influence on the future.

History.   Frost (8:366) defines history as a "narrative account of the past." This can be explained to children by playing with the word history. Help them to see it as Man, His Story. The events can be told in sequence. The pupil can watch them unfold and can study them to observe cause and effect, interpret actions, and predict the future. It has been said aptly that the person who knows history need not repeat the mistakes of the past. That is one of the marks of civilization—we can benefit by transmitting the culture and progressing without having to recapitulate the entire history of civilization.

Geography.   On the other hand, a description of the setting in which achievements take place involves a study of geography and an understanding of ecology. Place geography merely gives loci to events. Geographical features influence human's actions through their adapting to or changing of the lay of the land, the courses of the rivers, and the actions of weather and climate. Ecology looks at the effect people have on the environment and, in turn, its effect on the future. When pupils study geography, they seek answers to such questions as, How has the environment affected crops, industries, movement of people and materials, and of food, shelter, and clothing? Another question answered by the study of geography is, What can we do about it? People have not only adapted to existing conditions but actually have changed the conditions through irrigation of the land, building of dams, construction of highways, leveling of the earth, and even by heating and air conditioning buildings. Cities have grown up where natural settings exist, but settings have also been created that are amenable to the development of planned communities, for example Brazilia and Canberra.

Human beings live in a physical setting. They continue to add to and recreate the setting for their own advantage. The story of civilization is an account of the changes which have come about because of people's use of or contribution to the environment. The study of social studies should be more than a study of historical facts and geographical information. It must be extended to include the other disciplines which have to do with people's relations to each other in the world today.

Why People Behave as They Do

In order to understand why people behave as they do, we need to delve into more sophisticated fields once considered too advanced for the young child. Today's curriculum recognizes the contributions to the thinking of children which can be made by the disciplines of psychology and sociology, political science and government, economics and business, and the trades and professions. The hypothesis that we can teach any subject to any child at any time in an intellectually honest form comes from the report of the 1959 Woods Hole Conference. Bruner (4:33) says:

> It is a bold hypothesis and an essential one in thinking about the nature of curriculum. No evidence exists to contradict it; considerable evidence is being amassed to support it.

Then let us examine what these more sophisticated disciplines have to offer the elementary school pupil and how they can be applied in the social studies curriculum.

Psychology and Sociology.   A study of the mental processes of human beings and their social behavior includes principles of psychology and sociology. Even quite young children can discuss what they think about things, how they happened to remember a story, how they feel about their playmates, toys, and family, and what they are planning to do tomorrow. They think; and they can talk about what they think. Children of all ages live and work and play with other human beings. What they do, and say, and think are all influenced by other people with whom they come in contact. Out of respect for others one learns to say, "Thank you," to walk behind a visitor, and to obey the police officer. One learns to see the family as a part of a community and to look forward to some day establishing a family of one's own. These are some of the "intellectually honest" forms of these topics which can be taught to children at an early age. Children can learn how to get other people to agree with a point of view, how to influence the class in a group project, how to win a school election, and how to improve the quality of living in the local community. When children join a club, take part in a class election, or campaign for better meals in the cafeteria, they are practicing principles of sociology. When they see themselves interacting with others in these situations, they begin to analyze how they feel and why they think as they do, and how they can influence thinking of others. This is an application of the principles of psychology at an early level and again in an "intellectually honest" form.

Government, Politics, and Civics. Human beings have long attempted to control their own actions while living in groups. The methods used in managing the affairs of government are based on political relationships, while a study of government deals with the manner in which organized society attempts to govern itself. Even the kindergartener is engaging in self-governing practices when he helps decide that since there are only four easels in the room, the students will have to take turns using them. Primary children who decide to appoint a committee to set up rules for the use of the new playground equipment are practicing politics in that they are willing to accept the decisions of a representative group in managing their affairs. Robert, who serves as a representative for his room in the Junior Red Cross or the School Council, is getting his first taste of representative government. These experiences prepare him for an in-depth study of local, state, and national governing bodies and how they work. From these experiences and his study of civics, he learns about control and the rights and responsibilities of a citizen.

Economics and Business. Living and working in the world sets up conditions that cause people to want things. Money buys things. Work earns money. Work must produce either goods or services other people want. Anne, who learns to make a contribution to society through her own efforts, is engaging in business enterprises that provide her either with the things she wants or the where-with-all to buy what she wants. In primitive communities people supplied most of their own wants—food, clothing, shelter—and since they seldom traveled far from their place of birth, they were self-sufficient. But as society became more complex, individuals were able to supply fewer of their own needs and become more dependent on the work of others. This interdependence leads to the division of labor and the management of financial affairs based on economic principles. The work of Lawrence Senish (27) in the schools of Elkhart, Indiana demonstrates quite clearly the ability of young children to understand these basic principles. He refers to the principle as the conflict between limited resources and unlimited wants. The elementary school child who helps with a cupcake sale to raise money for a trip to the zoo, participates in a school banking project, serves as a treasurer for a club, or acts as manager for the team is learning and applying the principles of business and economics. Such a child is beginning to assume a place in the world of work by laying a foundation of meaningful experiences on which to base a more formal study of a more mature discipline in later years. This child is adding to the understanding of why people behave as they do.

Professions, Trades, and Employment. Living in society makes people interdependent. Young children can talk about the kinds of work they observe among adults, explain what their parents do, and discuss what they want to be when they grow up. They soon learn to identify with an adult who serves as an ideal. They recognize that the community needs people such as teachers, lawyers, doctors, dentists, nurses, and librarians to meet its special needs. They learn to recognize the services contributed by the grocer, postal clerk, patrol officer, sales person, and legislator as contributions to their personal welfare and convenience. These understandings begin at an early age. They are a part of social studies experiences throughout the school years. They develop in a spiral that extends knowledge and expands understanding. As pupils become selective in making a place for themselves in the world of work and at the same time earning a living, an appreciation for the work of others develops.

Figure 7-1 identifies the social studies as a problem-centered discipline and suggests that all the related disciplines are called into use in the attempt to think through a problem and decide on a course of action.

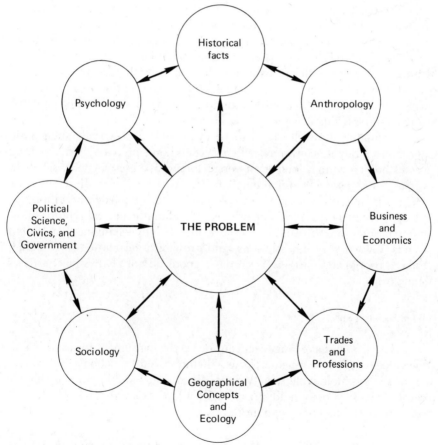

Figure 7-1. *The contributions of the various related disciplines to the solutions of social problems*

Content of the social studies is implied through listing of disciplines. Problem approach is suggested through the interrelatedness of the disciplines.

WHY WE TEACH THE SOCIAL STUDIES

A study of the social sciences should help the child develop a value system. It is through understanding the kind of world in which we are living that children will be able to arrive at decisions about how to meet present problems and those in the future. We are living in a period of great change and the pupil who knows how to adjust to change and deal with new situations will be the one most capable of coping with life. Since we cannot know what the future will bring, it is impossible to teach today's children what they will need to know to meet tomorrow's problems. The best we can hope to do is to teach them how to adjust to change and to make decisions. Learnings in the social studies are not so specific as addition combinations or correct spellings, and many of the questions have **multiple answers with no assurance that one is right and the others are** wrong. For this reason we need to look at the targets in this area in terms of what society expects, what the individual needs or wants, and what the curriculum is trying to do.

Changing life styles need to be evaluated in answering such basic questions as buying convenience items versus home prepared items, renting versus home owning, long term versus temporary use of goods, self help versus hired services, and immediate versus delayed gratifications. The same principle of changing concepts applies to knowledge pertaining to science, architectural styles, health needs, and mathematical relationships. Even moral and spiritual values are affected by changing population trends, revised personal relations, and growing interrelationships among today's people and nations. Yesterday's goods do not always meet today's standards.

What Society Expects

The schools have long been considered the instrument for carrying on the values of society. Whether society dictates what the schools shall teach, or the schools mold what society shall become is debatable. But one thing is certain. Society does hold great expectations from the schools that it supports both financially and morally.

Civic Responsibility. One of the expectations of society for its citizens is they assume responsibility for a better community. If children are to grow up to be constructive members of the community and the nation, they must do more than occupy space. They must be informed about government and must participate in it at least as voters. They must understand the regulations imposed by authority, and must not only obey them but help others to do likewise. They must develop respect for authority and concern for the welfare of others. They must see the future of the community and the country as personal responsibilities. Perhaps they need to follow the advice of President Kennedy in his inaugural address:

> Ask not what your country can do for you but what you can do for your country.

In order to assume such a civic responsibility, pupils in the elementary school need more than information. They need experience in democratic living and an attitude that will cause them to think and to act.

Moral Character. A logical outgrowth of civic responsibility is the development of a set of high ideals resulting in good morals. The citizen cannot work for a better society without first being a better person. While "right" and "wrong" are relative, individuals cannot decide for themselves which is which without knowing the standards on which they are based. Children who meekly follow the dictates of others, be they parents, teachers, or law-enforcement officers, are giving little thought to becoming morally responsible persons whose actions are based on values which they support. Only when they have had experiences and have explored ideas can they make decisions for themselves. Social studies provides an opportunity to analyze the behaviors of human beings, both past and present, as a basis for deciding what is best for the individual as well as for society, and therefore what is the "right" thing for each one.

What the Individual Needs or Wants

Children come to school to learn. Because they live in a nation that requires that all children attend school, some of them actually come as a matter of course and do not necessarily have real purposes or definite ideas about why they come. But most of them really do want certain things whether or not their desires are expressed verbally. And most of them have certain basic needs that the school can fulfill. Some of these needs and wants are best provided for in the area of the curriculum known as the social studies.

Self Realization. Who am I? And why am I here? What does life have to offer me? These are unasked but very real questions. Every individual needs self-realization and self-fulfillment. All children need to see themselves as worthy persons respected for what they are. They all need to feel that they have a place in the scheme of things. The social studies give them an opportunity to explore the nature of people, what they are, how they came to be, what they are like, and what they may become. This includes not only a look at one's self as a person, but as a member of a family, a member of a community, a worker in a worthwhile occupation, and a contributing member of society.

Satisfying Human Relationships.   Who are my parents? My friends? My acquaintances? My fellow citizens? What can they do for me? What can I do for them? These questions need to be answered by each individual. Developing satisfying human relationships is a basic part of becoming a social being. Human beings tend to be gregarious. Children want to be where significant adults are. They want someone to play with. They want to "belong." They want to do what others are doing. They want recognition from their elders and from their peers. These are the things that make them feel competent and accepted. These learnings do not come out of a book. They cannot be "given" to the pupil by a teacher. They are developed through living with people. The teacher can plan curriculum experiences in social studies that will permit the child to develop satisfying human relationships.

Economic Competence.   What young child has not said, "That's mine."? Possession gives a feeling of importance and power. Economic competence is a desirable goal. The person who is dependent on others for possessions lacks the feeling of independence that comes with maturity. Young children put their money in the piggy-bank or in a savings account. They soon learn to respect the intrinsic reward in the form of pay for effort expended. They like to feel that what they do is of worth to others and that they are earning their right to ownership. The adolescent eagerly looks foward to earning enough money to buy a first car. The young person who wants a summer job may be more interested in the economic independence the job will bring than in the mowing of the neighbor's lawn. Social studies provides the opportunity for the young child to learn how others have attained such competence and independence. It provides ideals and patterns to direct planning toward a similar competence. The curricular experiences you provide help children experiment with and develop skills which make them citizens who meet these requirements.

Protection.   Young children are trusting. Infants have no fear when strong adults toss them about. They will take an adult's hand and go wherever this person leads. They are unafraid until they meet an unfortunate experience that teaches them distrust. Then they look for protection from that which threatens their security. They need protection from the danger of fire, weather, traffic, cruelty, or mistreatment. When they venture forth into the community outside the home, they need more protection than the family can give. They soon learn to depend on other adults—the teacher, the police officer, the doctor, the nurse, the fire fighter—to offer protection. They learn through the social studies where to turn for such protection and to respect the society which provides it.

What the Curriculum is Trying to Do

The school attempts to meet the demands made on it. Curriculum planners are constantly reaching out to offer the help needed. In the social studies, there is need for skills, information, and attitudes. These can all be supplied through the experiences you provide in the classroom.

Developing Needed Skills.   Skills in gathering information will be useful beyond the school years. Skills in organizing and interpreting facts as a basis for making decisions will be used throughout life. Skills in group processes and discussions are essential for living in the world with others. All these skills are developed through the social studies experiences. Only as children have the opportunity to recognize these skills and practice them, will they become skillful in the use of them. These skills call for reading from various sources, making lists pointing out cause and effect relationships, working on committees, discussing issues, and making decisions.

Providing Useful Information.   Information is valuable only when it serves a purpose for living. Being able to name the states and their capitals may have little or no immediate value beyond passing the test, but the child who travels with parents, mails a letter to a relative in another state, or reads a story with a setting in a distant land is finding use for the information gleaned in the study of place geography. Being able to name the dates and the generals in a series of battles may have little or no value in itself, but the pupil who follows the thread of action through a series of events that bring supremacy to the leaders in a cause is building up a storehouse of information to help decide why one was more successful than the other. The sequence of events, the time line that puts happenings in perspective, the character traits of the leaders, the significance of the outcomes all serve as a basis for evaluating the historical events. Such evaluation helps build a foundation of skills and facts on which to base decisions and plan acts for the future.

Creating Attitudes.   Positive attitudes toward society and toward the future provide the building blocks on which advancement is made. Pupils who learn to respect home, family, community, and government will be the ones who will support these social institutions and lend a hand to improve them for the next generation. Children who learn to face the new and the unexpected with confidence will be the ones who will meet problems, do something about them, and progress. The area of social studies perhaps makes its greatest contribution not in the skills it develops and the knowledge it imparts, but in the attitudes it develops for future citizens. If that is the target of the curriculum, then teaching must be directed toward that goal. That is your task and your responsibility. You, as teacher, can point out these changing needs by calling attention to new discoveries and inventions, by commenting, "That's a new way, let's try it," and by being willing to explore alternate approaches yourself.

HOW TO TEACH THE SOCIAL STUDIES

An examination of the relationships illustrated in Fig. 7–2 will give perspective on the place of the various facets of the social studies, and will differentiate among the things children will learn how to do, the information they will accumulate, and the attitudes they will develop. Each of these areas is explored in terms of how humanity arrived at its present state through the influence of history and geography, and why people behave as they do through a study of related disciplines emphasizing psychology, sociology, political science, civics and government, economics and business, and the trades and professions. When you understand these relationships yourself, you will be in a better position to decide what to teach and how to organize for teaching.

What and How to Teach

Deciding what to teach is a curriculum question. It includes not only the subject matter to be covered but also the experiences to be provided. The content is inherent in the curriculum targets. They include skills, knowledge, and attitudes indicated in Fig. 7–2 as things the child will do, know, and be.

The Skills.   One might ask, "Does the pupil practice the skills so they can be used, or are the skills a by-product of repeated usage?" Either point of view results in skills. Overton (1:105–106), writing about "A New Look at Progressive Education" in the 1972 Yearbook of the Association for Supervision and Curriculum Development, interprets Piaget's theory of intellectual development as related to progressive education to mean that:

> . . . the business of educators in arranging experiences is not the rote **training of connections between particular responses and specific stimuli, nor** is it merely the providing of an "enriched" environment.

Hines (1:140–141) in the same yearbook describes progressivism in practice by saying:

Learning took place when the pupil's ways of behaving changed along desirable lines rather than when he was able to give parrot-like responses to teachers' questions. . . . Learning was much more than memorizing; it was incorporating experience into behavior.

These two points of view imply that the skills result from experiences and exploration of knowledge rather than prepare for such learnings. With either approach, however, pupils who are effective in the study of content material in such a field as social studies must have at their command some basic skills for study and research. These are listed in the "To Do" column in Fig. 7–2. All these skills are essential to life in a world where the individual is a member of a social group. They are learned through the pursuit of the social studies in the classroom as well as in life outside the school.

Knowledge. Much information is gleaned throughout the social studies. Many of the facts learned have limited values unless they are related to daily living. These are listed in the "To Know" column of Fig. 7–2. Knowing about all these things may, or may not, contribute to the type of citizen the child becomes. Reading the text, collecting the facts, repeating the information in the recitation period or on the examination may not necessarily make a difference in how one uses information as a citizen. One must take the next step, which is acting in accordance with the attitudes developed.

The library is an appropriate place to find out what you want to know. Writing it down is important when you want to share it with others. (Courtesy, Skiff School, Phoenix, Arizona)

Assimilating Social Relationships

AREA	TO DO	TO KNOW	TO BE
History *A study of the past including Anthropology*	The child will be able to: read factual information locate needed facts record information listen observe discuss generalize organize summarize	The child will know about: dates, names, places, and events origins and development of mankind archeology, religion, languages, linguistics, and ecology sequences of events causes and effects cultural relations influence of historical events on people	The child will become: a concerned citizen a useful and constructive member of society The child will develop attitudes of: tolerance for others respect for differences among peoples and among cultures
Geography *A study of the setting in which history takes place*	The child will be able to: locate places on a map interpret map symbols key latitude and longitude color codes scale direction read symbolic forms diagrams charts time lines graphs tables	The child will master facts concerning: place geography regional geography such as oceans, continents, countries, states, and cities physical features such as rivers, mountains, bays, capes, straights, plains, deserts, peninsulas, and islands The child will understand: relation of climate to business and industry relation of topography to lives of people relation of geographic features to culture importance of conservation of natural resources	The child will become: respectful of natural phenomena concerned about the ecology reverent about the creation of the universe willing to cooperate with nature

	The child will be able to:	The child will know about:	The child will become:
Psychology and Sociology *A study of the person's mental processes and social behavior*	remember information think through problems behave in acceptable ways share materials take turns help others	family life religions of the world welfare of others minority groups social systems delinquency and correction crime and prevention	mentally healthy socially acceptable confident in own ability tolerant of differences other people other cultures
Political Science *Civics and Government*	listen to facts and opinions serve as a representative of the group vote on actions and problems participate in group processes	public services public utilities community resources personal rights and responsibilities of citizens justice interdependence town, city, state, nation	a responsible citizen a contributing member of the group and of society a participant in plans and actions respectful of majority respectful of rights of others
Business and Economics	read factual information keep a budget compute essential accounts keep records of costs compose a simple business letter	the value of money the costs of services the costs of commodities credit and investment insurance wages and salaries buying and selling profit and loss	economically competent sensitive to propaganda aware of advertising vocationally skilled personally responsible trustworthy
Trades and Professions *Education Home Economy Law Engineering Agriculture etc.*	follow directions learn and teach cook and sew manage a home plant and reap interpret laws drive a car obey traffic signs	public health communicable diseases cure and prevention public projects contracts and obligations food and nutrition transportation consumer needs jobs and work	a healthy person a responsible member of a family and of a community a contributing member of the world of work a respector of all kinds of work

Figure 7–2. *Concepts related to the social studies.*

Attitudes and Understandings.   The real target of the social studies is the development of social beings. Society expects children to become adults who realize their own potential in human relations and who exercise self-sufficiency in the social and economic world. Mastering skills and accumulating information does not necessarily guarantee this goal. It is only when pupils become different kinds of persons that they have really attained the goal. This calls for more than drill and recitation. It calls for doing. The activities in which children engage in pursuit of these studies will lead toward becoming. These attitudes are listed in the "To Be" column in Fig. 7–2.

The skills the children master and the knowledge they accumulate are only the means to the end. Out of all this the children acquire tolerance for others, respect for differences in cultures, understandings of sequence, cause and effect, and influence of historical happenings and geographical

Art, Social Studies, Reading, and Language are blended in the study of a unit on Transportation. (Courtesy, Skiff School, Phoenix, Arizona)

features on events and people. They learn to understand the relation of climate and topography to human life. They come to respect natural resources and to recognize their responsibility for conservation and ecology. As a result of these responsible reactions, they become mentally healthy persons, socially acceptable citizens, and individuals who are confident in their own abilities; in other words, they become responsible and contributing members of society. As contributors they not only participate in group action, but respect the contributions, the rights, and the responsibilities of others. As economically competent people, they will be aware of the influences of advertising and propaganda, and will be able to make wise decisions that will lead to vocational competence, making their chosen occupations more than a means of earning a living. Work will become a contribution to society. They will see work as something they can do, want to do, and will do as a part of the ongoing improvement of society, and they will be paid for their efforts. Thus the "pay check" becomes the byproduct, not the target of life's work.

Finally they will grow up to become persons with healthy minds in healthy bodies capable of assuming responsible positions as members of a family, a community, and a nation. This is the goal of the social studies program. It is what society expects. It is what the individual wants and needs. And it is the target of the curriculum. In order to move in this direction in curriculum planning, you must move beyond skills to be mastered, facts to be memorized, and pages to be covered. You must think in terms of experiences to be engaged in, attitudes to be developed, and understandings to be attained. Wilson (31:176–179) criticizes much of the traditional curriculum in the social studies when he says:

> In all the schools' experiences with problem-centered curricula, efforts have tended to stop somewhat short of the target of decision making. . . . Most of the topics have still retained an informational emphasis rather than an invitation to decision making.

He recommends a break with the tradition of chronology and issues an invitation to comparison, contrast, and debate. This is what he calls an open access curriculum.

How to Organize for Teaching

In order to meet these objectives of the social studies, you need far more than a time schedule and a textbook. You need to move forward into a curricular plan based on a problem-centered approach. You need to see subject matter not as a goal but as a means to a much broader target. The real target is based on understandings that will affect behavior. This approach calls for experiences that will cause the learners to analyze events, note cause and effect, and discover relationships for themselves. Through inductive reasoning a study of climate, topography, and natural resources in a variety of types of regions will lead to the conclusion that these factors influence how people live and in turn how they are adapted or altered by the people who live there. A study of great leaders, political events, and social settings will lead to discovery of the interrelationships of one to the other and a determination to contribute to society through participation in local, state, national, and world events. A study of the many kinds of work to be done will lead to a comparison of personal capabilities with the needs for goods and services, and will help the children assess their own potential and discover their particular niche through career education. Most of the significant outcomes of the social studies are discoveries the children make about themselves in relation to others.

Accomplishing these goals involves two problems, namely, the organization of the teaching act and the organization of the content to be taught.

Unit Plan Versus Textbook Approach. A unit plan as opposed to a textbook approach implies a problem-centered curriculum as differentiated from a subject-centered curriculum. This takes the emphasis off the content to be covered and places it on the process in which the learner engages. It changes the target from information accumulated to understandings developed as a result of experience. For example, as a representation of life in a hot, dry land one group might study about the Sahara Desert and another group might study life as it is lived in the American Southwest or the desert regions of Central Australia. One group might study life in the African jungles along the Congo River and another life along the Amazon River in South America. One group might study the life of the Laplanders and another that of the Eskimos. One group might study life in the mountainous regions of Switzerland and another life in the Himalayan highlands. As a result of their various studies, each may learn some place geography, some physical geography, and perhaps some facts about the history of the peoples who inhabit these regions. But these facts will all lead to the concept that people adapt their ways of life to the geography of the land in which they live. The studies also should produce a profound respect for the ability of human beings to adapt to, or make adaptations in, the environment in seeking a livelihood.

In order to use the unit approach effectively, first you need to see social studies in terms of problems rather than facts and skills. Then you need resource materials from which to collect information and activities on which to build the experiences. Jarolimek (14:1967) refers to these as resource units and teaching units. Shumsky (29:186) defines the unit as:

> . . . an attempt to organize learning experiences around a social problem and draw on subject matter from any area which contributes to a better understanding of the topic.

Crosby (5:260–262) makes this same point when she says:

> Common learnings can never be common content. Common learnings must always be expressed in terms of common concepts. . . . In no area of the curriculum is there greater potential for the school to fulfill its commitment to children and to society than through the utilization of the social studies.

Dunfee and Sagl (7:Preface) advocate a problem solving approach as a challenge to elementary-school children and teachers. They say:

> Teaching social studies through problem solving is not a new approach to learning in this area of the curriculum. . . . The teaching of social studies through problem solving is a marked departure from traditional teaching in this area of the curriculum. To implement it requires change in the perspective with which goals are conceived as well as in the means for achieving them. . . . The trend in social studies instruction is clearly in the direction of more emphasis on learning how to learn—on the process of learning by inquiry, problem solving, and discovery.

The lesson plans at the end of Chap. 3 on "Map Reading" and "Rivers" illustrate the problems approach and the unit organization.

Separate Subjects Versus Fusion. Fusion of subject matter seems best to meet the needs of the above stated targets. If the center of the curriculum target is to be the problem as suggested in Fig. 7–1, then no one separate discipline can solve the problem. History may tell the story of what happened. Geography may describe the places or the conditions under which things happen. Psychology may help interpret the thinking of people as they deal with events. Sociology may help in understanding how people work together for a common solution to mutual problems. Political science and civics may help picture the pattern of government with the accompanying rights and responsibilities of its citizens. Economics and business may lead to an understanding of monetary system, the principles of buying and selling, profit and loss, and investment and income. A study of labor, trades, and professions may help pupils see their places in the work-a-day world where they will make a living. But it takes all of these blended into a whole or fused into one topic to solve the problems presented by such questions as: "If I moved to Boston, what would I do to make a living? Where would I live? What would it cost? What would I need?"

In discussing the differences of opinion concerning whether the social sciences should be combined in the curriculum or taught as separate disciplines, Neagley says: (22:296–297)

> The argument. . . is likely to continue into the 1980s. Strong pleas will be made for the addition of areas receiving little emphasis at present. The structural approach will become less important and there will be a gradual swing back to a search for common elements. This will require that scholars and teachers representing the different social sciences work together in the development of the curriculum.
>
> Another important task which must be assumed by the social sciences is assisting pupils to prepare for the cultural shock resulting from tremendous changes that are constantly taking place around them.
>
> The schools in the 1980s must prepare students for this cultural shock. Opportunities must be provided for pupils to discuss these changes and their implications. In addition they must be encouraged to look into the future to anticipate changes that are almost a certainty. Finally, they should be stimulated to do some dreaming on their own.

SUMMARY

Social studies is the study of human beings in the environment and their relations to others with whom they come into contact. The content of the social studies at the elementary level includes the story of the past in its geographical and ecological setting. It presents the problems of people as affected by such disciplines as psychology, anthropology, sociology, political science, civics, economics, and the professions. Society expects us to develop responsible citizens with good moral standards. Individuals expect us to help them realize their own highest potential both as persons and as members of their social group. This calls for economic competence, self-realization, and adequate protection.

In doing these things for society and for the individual, the targets of the curriculum are to develop needed skills and to provide a background of useful knowledge as a basis for creating positive attitudes and understandings which lead to becoming a competent person. In doing this the schools seek to develop skills in the use of informational media, knowledge about the world, and attitudes and understandings which will lead the individual to make decisions and act responsibly in society. Curriculum makers tend to see the problem approach based on a unit plan as more directly related to the ultimate goal, and fusion of content rather than separate subjects as the means to problem solutions.

SUGGESTED ACTIVITIES

Plan to carry out one or more of the following activities, working individually or in teams, and bring to the class the findings and conclusions you reach about the contributions a study of the social studies can make to child development.

1. Make a list of twenty-five historical facts you think are important for children to know at the end of their elementary-school years.

   Submit your list to your classmates and ask them to check the ten they consider to be the most important.

   Tabulate the results and report your findings to the class.
2. Do the same for twenty-five geographical facts.
3. Select a college text book in one of the following disciplines:

Psychology	Government
Sociology	Civics
Economics	Political Science
Business Arithmetic	Real Estate
Taxation	Labor and Management
Trade Unions	Any Profession

   Go through the text and select ten basic principles you believe you can teach to an elementary school child in "some intellectually honest form."

   Write a lesson plan to show how you would go about it.
4. Debate the following:

   Resolved: The citizen's first responsibility is to the social order.

   Affirmative: Individual responsibility to the state.

   Negative: Individual rights to state protection.
5. Observe a child in a classroom, in the home, or on a playground with other children and collect specific instances which give evidence of the child's concept of self. Categorize your examples as negative self-concepts and positive self-concepts.

   Identify ways you might improve this self-concept through the social-studies curriculum in the classroom.
6. Point out specific ways in which a child can attain economic competence. Discuss the following issues:

Allowances	Competition
Family responsibility	Cooperation
Pay for chores	Privileges

   How will these decisions affect your social-studies curriculum content and activities in the classroom?
7. Discuss the issue of fused versus separate subject courses in history and geography at the intermediate grade level.

   In two parallel columns prepare a summary contrasting the advantages of each. Keep all your points in the positive vein. Thus:

History and Geography
Separate Subjects Versus Fusion

ADVANTAGES OF SEPARATE SUBJECTS	ADVANTAGES OF FUSION COURSES

8. Find out what the practice is in a selected school system by examining their curriculum outlines, their basic adopted texts, and their supplementary and library materials.

9. Secure the opinions of selected children on one or more of the following topics:

Allowances	Pay for home chores
Employment of minors	Compulsory school attendance
Family councils	Parental authority

SELECTED READINGS

1. Association for Supervision and Curriculum Development, NEA, *A New Look at Progressive Education*, Washington, D.C.: ASCD Yearbook Committee, 1972. p. 400. Reviews purposes of progressive education in early part of this century. Identifies goals of "learning how to learn" as recurring today. Points out progressive pattern in curriculum as environment for learning.

2. BEYER, BARRY K., *Inquiry in the Social Studies Classroom: A Strategy for Teaching*, Columbus, Ohio: Charles E. Merrill, 1971, p. 192 (paper). Applies inquiry teaching to the content of the social studies curriculum. Develops actual lesson plans and units.

3. BRUNER, JEROME S., *Man: A Course of Study*, Cambridge, Mass.: Social Studies Curriculum Program, Educational Services, 1965. A philosophical model posed to answer the question: What is human about human beings? Man is unique in his adaptation to his environment and in contrast to the existence of other forms of life.

4. BRUNER, JEROME S., *The Process of Education*, New York: Random House, 1960, p. 33. A report of a conference held at Woods Hole on Cape Cod in September 1959. Emphasizes the importance of structure in learning and the patterns of thinking.

5. CROSBY, MURIEL, *Curriculum Development for Elementary Schools in a Changing Society*, Boston: D. C. Heath, 1964. Emphasizes human relations. Gives real experiences of boys and girls. Stresses importance of curricula with value for children.

6. DOUGLAS, MALCOLM P., *Social Studies: From Theory to Practice in Elementary Education*, Philadelphia: Lippincott, 1967. Moves into practical application of recommended theories.

7. DUNFEE, MAXINE and HELEN SAGL, *Social Studies Through Problem Solving: A Challenge to Elementary School Teachers*, New York: Holt, Rinehart & Winston, 1966. Each chapter begins with a dialogue presentation illustrating the problem. Helps with cooperative planning, use of experiences, activities, creativity, culmination, and evaluation.

8. FROST, JOE L. and G. THOMAS ROWLAND, *Curricula for the Seventies*, Boston: Houghton Mifflin, 1969. Chapter 11 on "Developing Literacy in the Social Sciences" identifies recent developments, points up objectives, and helps with planning and teaching through integration.

9. GILLESPIE, MARGARET C. and A. GRAY THOMPSON, *Social Studies for Living in a Multi Ethnic Society: A Unit Approach*, Columbus, Ohio: Charles E. Merrill, 1972. Helps with unit building. Gives framework for planning. Identifies multiethnic society and demonstrates approach to teaching.

10. GODBOLD, JOHN VANCE, "Oral Questioning Practices of Teachers in Social Studies Classes," *Educational Leadership*, Vol. 28, No. 1, Oct. 1970, pp. 61–67. Identifies most commonly used types of questions.

11. HAAN, AUBREY, *Elementary School Curriculum: Theory and Research*, Boston: Allyn and Bacon, 1961. Chapter 9 discusses frontiers in curriculum development in the social studies. Identifies changes, problems, and evaluation techniques. See Chart, p. 239.

12. HICKS, WM. VERNON, *et. al.*, *The New Elementary School Curriculum*, New York: Van Nostrand Reinhold, 1970. Chapter 5 defines social studies, indicates origin, and points out place in the curriculum. Justifies unit teaching and outlines content and activities by grades.

13. JAROLIMEK, JOHN, "In Pursuit of the Elusive New Social Studies," in *Educational Leadership*, Vol. 30, No. 7, April 1973. pp. 596–99. Sees funding agencies and materials producers as decision makers.

14. JAROLIMEK, JOHN, *Social Studies in Elementary Education*, New York: Macmillan, 1967. Concrete helps in unit teaching.

15. JARVIS, OSCAR T. and MARION J. RICE, *An Introduction to Teaching in the Elementary School*, Dubuque, Iowa: Wm. C. Brown, 1972. Chapter 7 is on social studies. See also Chap. 14 on "Democracy and Citizenship."

16. JOHNSON, ROGER E. and EILEEN B. VARDIAN, "Reading, Readability and Social Studies," in *Reading Teacher*, Vol. 26, No. 5, Feb. 1973, pp. 483–86. Gives readability levels of popular social studies texts. Emphasizes teacher responsibility for building conceptual backgrounds, vocabulary, and materials.

17. JONES, DAISY M. and J. LOUIS COOPER, *From Coins to Kings*, Evanston, Ill.: Harper & Row, 1964. A sixth-grade reading text in the subject matter areas.

18. MEHLINGER, HOWARD D., "Social Studies—Yesterday, Today, and Tomorrow," in *Today's Education*, Vol. 63, No. 2, Mar.–Apr. 1974, pp. 66–70. Takes a look at the teaching of the social studies, where it has come from, where it is now, and where it is going. Takes an optimistic view.

19. MICHAELIS, JOHN W., *Social Studies for Children in a Democracy* (4th edition), Englewood Cliffs, N.J.: Prentice-Hall, 1968. Inquiry and conceptual approaches to social studies instruction. Objectives, organization, techniques, media, and evaluation.

20. MICHAELIS, JOHN W. and EVERETT T. KEACH, JR. (Editors), *Teaching Strategies for Elementary School Social Studies*, Itasca, Ill.: F. E. Peacock Publishers, 1972. An anthology. Methods, principles, guidelines, editorial comments.

21. MILLS, PATRICIA, "A Philosophical Base for Curriculum Decisions," in *Educational Leadership*, Vol. 29, No. 7, Apr. 1972, pp. 631–37. Presents five dimensions for curriculum decisions: abstraction, subjectification, survival, integration, choice. It is the ability to make choices that makes humans unique.

22. NEAGLEY, ROSS L. and N. DEAN EVANS, *Handbook for Effective Curriculum Development*, Englewood Cliffs, N.J.: Prentice-Hall, 1967. Puts curriculum decisions into everyday practice. The practical approach is pertinent to the social studies.

23. NICOLL, G. DOUGLAS, "Why Study History?" in *Educational Forum*, Vol. XXXIII, No. 2, Jan. 1969. pp. 193–99. Justifies the teaching of history through analysis of data, critical attitude, and insight into contemporary social structures.

24. PIERCEY, DOROTHY, *A Daily Text for Thinking*, Phoenix, Ariz.: The Arizona Republic and Gazette, 1970. Based on the use of the newspaper in the classroom for the teaching of reading and thinking skills.

25. ROGERS, VINCENT R. and THOMAS P. WEINLAND (Editors), *Teaching Social Studies in the Urban Classroom*, Reading, Mass.: Addison-Wesley, 1972. Account of actual teaching of teachers working in inner-city. Case studies, practical helps, different solutions. Theories with applications.

26. ROOZE, GENE E. and LEONA M. FOERSTER, *Teaching Elementary Social Studies: A New Perspective*, Columbus, Ohio: Charles E. Merrill, 1972. Identifies roles of teacher, student, and material. Provides a model and sample lesson units. Treats skills, content, and values.

27. SENESH, LAWRENCE, *Elkhart Indiana Experiment in Economic Education*, Lafayette, Ind.: Department of Economics, Purdue University. Materials for teachers available from Science Research Associates, Chicago, Ill.

28. SHAFTEL, FANNIE R. and GEORGE SHAFTEL, *Role-Playing for Social Values: Decision-Making in the Social Studies*, Englewood Cliffs, N.J.: Prentice-Hall, 1967. Explains how to use role playing in teaching children to meet situations and make decisions.

29. SHUMSKY, ABRAHAM, *Creative Teaching in the Elementary School*, New York: Appleton-Century-Crofts, 1965. Chapter 8 shows how social studies can be a repetitive or a creative learning experience. Emphasizes concept formation and productive thinking.

30. SMITH, JAMES A., *Creative Teaching in the Social Studies in the Elementary School*, Boston: Allyn and Bacon, 1967. One of the books in a series emphasizing creativity in teaching in the various areas of the curriculum.

31. WILSON, L. CRAIG, *The Open Access Curriculum*, Boston: Allyn and Bacon, 1971. Chapter 10 identifies the disciplines included in the social sciences and indicates projects and learnings suitable for each grade level.

8

TEACHING THE RELATIONSHIP OF SCIENCE TO LIFE

Helping Children Find Out How Science Affects Them Daily

Courtesy, Arizona State University Photo Service

SCIENCE EVERY DAY

How are you affected by science in your daily life? How are children affected? Do they recognize scientific principles in their personal contacts? How can you help them?

Plants are more than flowers or food. Animals are more than pets or beasts of burden. How do they fit into the plan of the universe? What responsibility do children have for ecology? How can they help with conservation? What needs to be conserved? Why? And how can it be done?

Knowledge of the physical sciences and the universe has expanded rapidly in this century. What are the implications for the lives of children? For the future? What is your responsibility for orienting children to these facts? There are far more facts than anyone can hope to assimilate. How can you deal with the problem?

Do you see science as a product or a process? What is the difference? How does a scientist think? Can you think like a scientist? Can you help children do so? Do you know sequences that lead to scientific problem solving? How can you help the children draw conclusions and become independent learners?

Will you need a textbook or a generous supply of references? Do you know how to use them? What equipment will be available? What is the function of experimentation? Of demonstration? How and when will you use each?

Do you know what to do if you don't know the answer?

The place of science in the elementary curriculum has become well established within the past two decades. Home economics and agriculture were introduced at the upper grade levels before the beginning of the present century. These gave only token attention to scientific principles. Up through the first quarter of the present century science took the form of occasional lessons in nature study. According to Frost (9:307) the first series of science textbooks for children were published in 1932. Pioneers in the field of teaching science to young children, such as Gerald S. Craig and Glen O. Blough, led the way in producing textbooks for children and professional books for teachers. Schools began to take notice of the trend and in the late 1940's and early 1950's local curriculum committees were working on content outlines and suggested activities. Many of these were indicated as general science, drew from the various areas of science, and were often allocated to the upper elementary grades.

The National Defense Education Act (NDEA), signed by President Eisenhower in 1958, gave added impetus to the teaching of science in the elementary schools through the provision of federal funds for programs and materials. Immediately leaders moved into action. Summer workshops were organized. Key projects were launched. Local programs were put into operation. Science specialists took new interest in the possibilities for teaching the discipline to young children. Elementary teachers became involved in the area of science, often with considerable apprehension and sometimes with outright resistance. Publishers were quick to realize the sales potentials and began producing textbook materials for children. Science supply houses began making up laboratory kits and catalog listings of experimental equipment and apparatus. Key projects were launched in various places and their curriculum guides were made available for use by others.

The introduction of science into the elementary curriculum not only presented new content from such disciplines as chemistry, physics, astronomy, geology, meteorology, biology, and zoology, but also led the way to new approaches in teaching. Alpren (1:179–180) reviews the history of the science curriculum in the elementary school. The use of observation and experimentation as sources of information to supplement textbook reading changed the role of the teacher from that of lesson-assigner and information-giver to that of organizer of learning experiences and leader in activities. Memorization of facts became less important and development of scientific thinking became more important. Inductive reasoning based on accumulated evidence and discovery learning replaced question-and-answer textbook approach. Attention was drawn away from accumulation of facts and directed toward interrelationships in nature. This new emphasis caused curriculum makers to ask not only what we should be teaching to young children about science but why. They showed concern for attitudes to be developed as well as skills and facts to be mastered. Recognizing the sequences in learning, the complexities of concepts, and the rapid increase in science information caused them to question the organization of the content as well as the learning experiences. A broad perspective is needed in order to meet the problems and provide for the needs of the children.

WHAT CHILDREN LEARN IN SCIENCE

The attempt to provide you with a complete outline of the content of science would be impractical from the standpoint of space and ill-advised from the standpoint of information. New knowledge is being discovered daily in the scientific world. Some of the facts that were taught yesterday are no longer true. Your job in teaching science is not to become a source of information but a leader in the search for information. Your pupils will find their information in the textbooks, current periodicals, the mass media over the air waves, and often from their own observation and experimentation. What you need to know in order to help your pupils become students of science is how the information is organized, where the sources of information are, and how to use teaching time in leading the children to become thinkers and doers as they discover truths for themselves. Let's begin with a look at the organization of the science content. It falls into four general categories—life sciences, physical sciences, earth sciences, and personal science. These are schematically represented in Fig. 8–1.

The Life Sciences

The study of living things makes up much of the content of science for younger children. A study of *plant life* (botany) and *animal life* (zoology) will give young children a deeper appreciation and understanding of nature and its place in the order of things. One of the earliest concepts to be recognized is that all living things can be divided into these two major classifications. From observing, experimenting, reading, and listening, children will learn this concept and will come to understand that many human needs are supplied by the use of the environment. This will lead to the concept of orderliness in the environment and the need for *conservation* (ecology) of the natural resources to maintain, perpetuate, and improve life in harmony with nature.

The Physical Sciences

The physical environment in which we live is an orderly system controlled by the elements. When children learn what these elements are and how they are organized, they are developing not only a respect for principles of science but basic information that will enable them to adapt to or make use of these principles in daily living. All around us we find *air*, *water*, and *land*. Learning about these elements constitutes a study of *matter*. That they exist is a statement of fact. Knowing the extent to which they exist and the properties they possess adds insight to information. Information about their relationships to each other and to life can be discovered through observation and experimentation.

Some of the properties the elements possess such as *heat*, *light*, and *sound* make up another area of physical science known as *energy*.

When they are affected by these properties, they are put into motion, that is, matter is affected by energy and we get *forces* which move *simple machines*. This constitutes that phase of physical science called *mechanics*. Children do not need to be shown how simple machines work. They can observe them for themselves as they climb a stair, sharpen a pencil, lift a weight, or propel a bicycle. Another force which nature provides to aid in the use of energy and matter is found in *magnetism*, which has led to the use

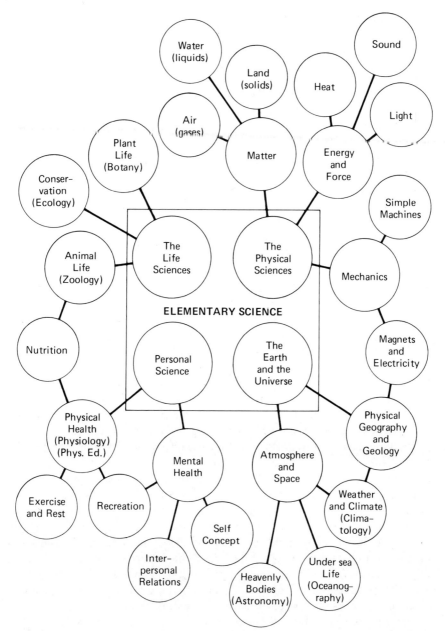

Figure 8-1. *Interrelationships of the content fields in the areas of Elementary Science*

of *electricity.* Young scientists who can assimilate all these factors and turn their uses to their own purposes have become more than mere receptacles for information. They have become self-propelled learners, discoverers, and perhaps innovators. These experiences provide the sources of future scientists and future scientific discoveries.

The Earth and the Universe

Ancient people were curious about their environment. They spent time studying the immediate vicinity but their concern did not stop there. People have always wondered about what they could observe as they gazed into the night sky. They have often worshipped what appeared to be the life-giving properties of the ball of fire as it produced both heat and light for their comfort and convenience. The heavenly bodies (astronomy) have long fascinated scholars. Because of this interest, they have been led to make observations, record findings, and invent new and better ways of satisfying curiosity. Out of this has come the invention of such instruments as the telescope, the microscope, and the camera, and the development of such devices as the calendar and the clock.

As people looked at that part of the environment closer at hand, they became concerned about *the earth* and its composition. *Physical geography* provides a description of the features of the earth and the orderly arrangement of the elements. *Geology* is a scientific study of the origin and history of the physical environment. Together, the two sciences answer questions about what the earth is like and how it came to be. The search goes on and on through explorations into space and to the bottom of the sea. The astronaut and the aquanaut continue to add to our knowledge of the heavens and the depths of the ocean through *astronomy* and *oceanography*.

But the elements do not remain constant. Their changes are affected by movement of air and variations in temperature. Observing these changes has led scholars to study the *weather* conditions that exist at any particular place at any given time and the effect they have on plant and animal life. Recording these observations has helped scientists arrive at some generalizations about the conditions prevailing over a given region during an extended period of time. This is known as *climate* and its study is called *climatology*. These kinds of scientific observations have enabled observers to predict weather and anticipate climate changes. This knowledge has aided in planting crops and developing industries. There is an old saying that everybody talks about the weather but nobody does anything about it. That may no longer be true. People with knowledge of scientific principles are beginning to do something about the weather and climate. Today's young scientist in the elementary classroom might well be tomorrow's pioneer who will make the discoveries and invent the methods that will provide progress on this front. And you may be the teacher who inspires that action.

Personal Science

The physical body is very personal. Only you can own it or do anything about it. Knowledge is not enough. Unless you use what you know to alter or adapt to a way of life, the body can be destroyed. The study of *physical health* is probably the most important single learning not only in the field of science but in the entire elementary curriculum. *Physiology* gives the pupil the knowledge of the human body and how it works. A study of *nutrition* helps with understanding of essential elements in maintaining the body. The field of *physical education* helps the individual understand and use the principles of *exercise, rest,* and *recreation* in maintaining a sound and healthy body. Knowing about them is not enough. Regular and daily practice of these principles is what the school physical-education program is designed to do.

Increasingly, the field of health is coming to recognize the importance of *mental health* as well as physical health. The mind influences the body. It determines the attitudes and practices that lead to a positive or negative *self concept*. These concepts of self influence *interpersonal relationships*. These in turn contribute to both physical and mental health. Children who learn how both the body and the mind work are learning to be masters rather than servants of their own being.

Sources of information are readily available in curriculum outlines planned by experts and in textbooks written by authorities in the various fields. Alpren (1:187–189) outlines scope and sequence for elementary science and Beauchamp (2:154–161) identifies basic areas and major concepts. No doubt you will teach in a situation where there is leadership in curriculum planning and where books and other source materials are provided. These are not designed to tell you what to do but to provide you with source material helpful in the organization of the experiences of the children. It is still your responsibility to set the curriculum targets for your children in the field of science. Lead them to observe the science all around them. Help them to organize, record, and use their discoveries. Encourage them to raise questions and explore new frontiers. If they learn to repeat facts, they will be merely storehouses of information, but if they learn to use facts, they will become innovators and doers. When they answer the questions they are passive, but when they raise the questions they become active scientists. They may explore new frontiers comparable to those pursued by pioneers in the fields of disease control, prevention of disease, exploration of space, and many other remarkable feats.

WHY WE TEACH SCIENCE IN SCHOOL

Science is all about us. It is a way of life. It is life. Teaching science in school is merely an acknowledgment that it affects our daily lives and we cannot live without it. The introduction of science as a study in the elementary curriculum presented a whole new approach to teaching and learning. Carin (7:18) says:

> Science education should emphasize the development of scientific principles and methodology instead of the memorization of facts. Teachers should employ the experimental or discovery approach to science with emphasis upon inductive learning, problem solving, and critical thinking.

Before you can transmit this point of view to your pupils, you must recognize the many uses of science in daily life. Then you, too, must learn to think like a scientist through discovery learning. That makes you a learner along with the children. You will no longer be saying:

> "This is the way it is." or
> "Look it up in the text."

but rather,

> "Let's work it out together."
> "What information do we already have?"
> "What else do we need to know?"
> "What did you observe?"
> "What do you think might be the cause?"
> "Let's try out those ideas and see which ones work."

Your first step in setting curriculum targets in science then, will be to recognize its value.

Recognizing the Uses of Science in Daily Life

Recognition is only the first step. It must be followed by application. Recognition without application is merely verbal learning. Attempts at application without recognition result in aimless action and fruitless effort.

Evidences of Science All About Us.   Before you can teach children to be observant, you must be observant yourself. Learn to take note of evidences of science all about you. Call attention to them. Lead the children to make similar observations and report their findings to the group. Watch a plant grow. Take care of a pet. Experiment with soil and water to find out how it contributes to plant growth. Experiment with foods to see how they affect animal growth. Analyze the content of air or water and find out how it relates to life. Keep a record of temperature fluctuations. Learn to measure light amplification. Experiment with the sound of a bell or a stringed instrument to find out what causes pitch and volume. Collect examples of simple household tools that represent the principles of mechanics. Experiment with forces to see what causes them and how they can be controlled. Try different arrangements of magnets to find out what happens. Wire an electric bell. Record observations about the time of sunrise and sunset over a period of time. Go out at night and have a look at

Watching living creatures in action makes science learning real and enables children to identify the animal life discussed in the text books. (Courtesy, Lowell School, Mesa, Arizona)

the stars. Keep a record of the phases of the moon. Dig in the earth for fossils. Trace a stream from its source to its mouth. Count the surfaces on solid figures. Climb a mountain—or at least a hill. Dig in the sand. Watch the ocean waves ebb and flow. Compare crops with temperatures, rainfall, and lengths of growing seasons. Keep a weekly record of your own weight fluctuations. Keep a record of growth in height from year to year. Keep a daily record of health habits. Learn a routine that results in physical fitness.

As you are doing these things to note the evidences of science all about you, you are setting the example for the children. You will be doing things with them, not for them. You will be leading them in a way of life that recognizes the principles of science and how they influence our own lives.

Uses of Scientific Principles.   Before you can teach children to use scientific principles in their daily lives you will have to be able to do it yourself. Help them figure out how to make a garden more productive. Work with animals at the zoo to improve their living conditions. Find out how to use the principles of air pressure with a siphon to move water from one fish tank to another. Experiment with fertilizers to find out what effect they have on plants. Heat milk to preserve it. Figure out how to use an inclined plane or a set of pulleys to lift a weight. Wire a buzzer board for drill in arithmetic. Melt some snow or ice for water supply. Build an earthen dam to prevent erosion on the playground. Create your own instruments for a toy band. Do something about the weather. Do something about your own body to make it more healthful. Put on a campaign for community health through sanitation and immunization programs. These are all applications of principles of science. Children who learn to use them when they are young will grow up to be citizens who not only recognize them and cooperate with community projects, but who take the initiative in launching programs for a better world through the use of science principles.

Learning to Think Like a Scientist

Before you can teach children to think like a scientist, you must learn to think that way yourself. This may be practiced in your own teaching techniques as well as in your approach to subject matter in science. Frost (9:315–323) says:

> Stressing scientific activity rather than subject-matter content helps the child to learn information-seeking strategies. (p. 315)
>
> Rather than teaching fragmentary, isolated lessons, the content is to help children to operate very much as the scientist operates when attacking a problem. (p. 323)

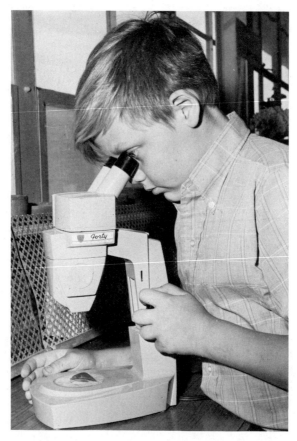

A closer look is sometimes needed to understand what a leaf is like. This student will now read the science text with more insight and understanding. (Courtesy, Lowell School, Mesa, Arizona)

The scientist works in a laboratory which may be anything from the sand pile in the back yard, the kitchen sink, the photography dark-room in the basement, the miniature set purchased at the local hobby shop, the classroom laboratory set up with a minimum of simple equipment, the formal laboratory of the high school or college science department, the experimental laboratory in industry, or even the space program facilities with extensive outlays. In order to find answers to self-imposed questions, the scientist follows a definite sequence in thinking. Learning what that sequence is and practicing it in inquiry will lead children to follow inductive procedures in thinking and to discovery of truths.

Using Laboratory Techniques. An approach to learning that is especially adaptable to science is one based on experimentation. A laboratory is a place to work. Note the root word "labor" in the word laboratory.

Finding out how things work is one of the tasks of the scientist. Carl starts with a question. He may have a "hunch." He is trying to find out. The facts he discovers may be new to the field as in the case of the discovery of bacteria, radium, vaccine, or a new planet, or they may be new only to him. In either case he is learning to think like a scientist.

Proving a point or verifying a fact may lead to further experimentation. Only by repeating experiments over and over again can one prove that an original hunch is true.

Using Scientific Sequences in Thinking. The scientist soon learns not to accept a statement just because "That's what the teacher said," or "It's in the book." Pupils must find out for themselves. They must use discovery techniques to produce evidence applicable to learning beyond the classroom. The steps through which a scientist goes in thinking through a problem and arriving at a conclusion are evidence of scientific thinking. This approach to subject matter is based on natural curiosity, an inquiring mind, challenging problems, and a willingness to seek answers rather than to accept authoritative statements. Often the scientist works at random, first experimenting and then drawing tentative conclusions. Sometimes the scientist has a conviction before all the evidence is in. Sometimes the evidence is a basis for a conclusion and sometimes a support for a conviction. While the sequence may vary, the basic steps remain the same.

Sensing a problem or question is usually the first step. And the question is not necessarily raised by the book or the teacher. It may be raised by the child who comes to school asking why spiders have eight legs while ants have only six. It might be initiated by a child's curiosity to learn why the door bell chimes instead of buzzing. Whatever the question or problem, the pupil wants to find out.

Making a guess or forming a hypothesis comes next. If you ask Ann what makes it rain, she may say, "God makes it rain," or "The water is heavy and it falls." Whatever her explanation she starts with a hunch or a belief. If she bases her hunches on shallow evidence or superstitions and shows no curiosity, she is missing much of the thought process of the scientist. But when curiosity leads her to question hunches, she is ready for the next step.

Gathering evidence is the next step in scientific thinking. Techniques include observing, listening, reading, experimenting, and recording which call for gathering information and lead to a conclusion that can be proved.

Drawing the conclusion comes next. No longer will expressions of beliefs or superstitions suffice. Evidence must be produced to support conclusions. No longer does the child say, "I think . . ." but now can say with certainty, "I know because I have proved it."

Verifying the conclusion is a very necessary final step. The true scientist is not satisfied until there is proof. This means trying again and again. If one gets the same results repeatedly, there is basis for saying with confidence, "I know this is the way it is because every time I do it, this is the way it comes out."

In emphasizing this approach to learning in science, Shuster (20:300) says:

> The public elementary school science program then is not for developing specialists, but for building understandings, skills, and appreciations in the future scientists and others from all walks of life who will work and study together.

HOW TO TEACH SCIENCE TO CHILDREN

You may know some of the facts of science and why we teach science in the elementary school. You may be able to follow scientific principles in your own life and teach children to think like a scientist. But there is so much to know and do that your task as a curriculum worker is selecting what to teach and deciding how to get organized.

What to Teach

Each science experience in the classroom has a threefold purpose. To say that a specific science lesson is for the purpose of developing skills, accumulating knowledge, or creating attitudes is to fail to see the total perspective. Nearly every lesson, every experience, every experiment will include all three areas. Even so, it may help you to orient yourself in terms of the objectives if you view each of the goals separately. Figure 8–2 identifies the three types of learnings for each area.

Mastering the Skills.   Skills in science are somewhat different from those in other areas. Language or mathematical skills will be useful in developing science skills. Skills in the use of laboratory equipment and thinking like a scientist have to do with how one performs. As a result of using discovery techniques, the pupil will learn to be careful and accurate, specific and logical. These skills relate directly to science activities and are itemized in the "To Do" column of Fig. 8–2.

Accumulating the Information.   Scientific facts are interesting and useful. They function when they are used to solve problems, improve living conditions, and make advancements toward insight into the nature of the universe. Ragan (18:377) suggests that:

> The facts of science are important, but they are tools used in problem solving rather than ends in themselves.

Listing facts to be gleaned from a study of science is endless. All children need not learn the same facts. The important point is that they discover the generalizations resulting from an organization of factual information, summarized in the "To Know" column of Fig. 8–2.

A study of life sciences may include such specific information as that insects have six legs, oak trees produce acorns, bears hibernate, birds migrate, butterflies come out of cocoons, ducks can swim, turtles may live as long as 150 years, snails carry their houses on their backs, ladybugs are helpful, orchids are parasites, and some trees are deciduous. These are specific and isolated facts, which are only the bases for forming generalizations. What pupils should get from such study is a statement of principles which the facts will lead them to discover through inductive reasoning. Examples are: All living things are either plants or animals. All living things grow and reproduce their own kind. Plants are fixed in position. Plants reproduce through seeds or spores. Animals are free to move about. Some animals are mammals and produce their young alive. Others produce eggs from which the young are hatched. Both plants and animals adapt to their environment. Hibernation and migration are forms of adaptation. All life follows a cycle from conception, to birth, growth, maturity, reproduction, decline, and death.

These are only representative statements of general principles. A complete list would be repetitive and exhaustive. Curriculum guides and science texts will aid you in the selection of content. These are offered only

AREA	TO DO	TO KNOW	TO BE
Life Sciences Plant Life Animal life Conservation	The child will be able to: observe accurately recognize details measure precisely compute accurately experiment reliably manipulate skillfully control carefully define accurately classify exactly infer logically hypothesize reliably predict responsibly speak precisely communicate effectively	The child will know about: organization of living things into: animal life plant life reproduction fundamental processes life cycle birth growth death structural forms human needs human use of environment human adaptation to the environment	The child will develop: willingness to accept life cycles in self as well as in nature respect for ability to adapt to environment concern for adapting the environment to personal uses reverence for life-giving properties respect for accuracy
Physical Sciences Matter Energy Mechanics Magnetism and Electricity	The child will be able to: observe accurately recognize details measure precisely compute accurately experiment reliably manipulate skillfully control carefully define accurately classify exactly infer logically hypothesize reliably predict responsibly speak precisely communicate effectively	The child will know about: matter air—gas water—liquid land—solid energy and force heat light sound mechanics forces simple machines magnetism and electricity	The child will develop: respect for natural resources logical thinking about sequences and scientific relationships acceptance of need for adaptation to natural forces willingness to accept natural phenomena careful attitudes desire for specificity

The Earth and the Universe
Astronomy
Oceanography
Geology
Geography
Weather
Climate

The child will be able to:
observe accurately
recognize details
measure precisely
compute accurately
experiment reliably
manipulate skillfully
control carefully
define accurately
classify exactly
infer logically
hypothesize reliably
predict responsibly
speak precisely
communicate effectively

The child will know about:
the heavenly bodies
    stars
    sun as source of heat,
        light, and energy
    moon
    planets
    galaxies
the earth
    rocks and soil
    atmosphere
    weather and climate
    natural resources
    seasons
    day and night
    fossils and glaciers
    earthquakes and tides
    currents

The child will become:
aware
curious
respectful
reverent

Personal Health
Physical Education
Mental Health
Physiology
Nutrition
Recreation

The child will be able to:
control own body and its
    functions
establish a suitable routine
observe rest periods
regulate eating habits
follow health routines
    affecting sensory organs
    such as teeth, eyes,
    ears, skin
exercise sensibly
control mental attitudes
maintain positive outlook
relate to others
live within own capabilities
use talents effectively

The child will know about:
the body and its parts
body functions
senses
diseases and their cure or
    prevention
immunizations
public health
sanitation
sex and reproduction
exercise and rest
food and nutrition
effect of mental attitude
    on general health

The child will develop:
desire for a healthy body
attitude of willingness to
    cooperate in the interest
    of public welfare in
    matters of:
        sanitation
        disease control
respect for human life and
    reproduction
concern for safety
responsibility for self

Figure 8-2. *Concepts related to the teaching of science.*

to illustrate the difference between a fact and a principle. After children have studied numerous plants and have identified their parts, they will begin to draw generalizations about their likenesses. After they have seen seeds produce young plants, they will begin to generalize on the principle of seed bearing as a reproductive process. Then they are ready to follow the thinking of a scientist by concluding that if one plants a seed, a new plant will grow. They will be able to predict that planting an apple seed will produce an apple tree which will produce more apples, and planting a peach seed will produce a peach tree which will produce more peaches. Children need not all study the same kinds of plants to arrive at the generalization that each form of life tends to reproduce its own kind. Similarly other principles of science can lead to discovery of generalizations and predictions of outcomes. The child who has lived on a farm and has seen kittens, puppies, calves, colts, or lambs born has no unsatisfied curiosity about human birth and reproduction.

A study of the *physical sciences* may include such specific bits of information as air has weight, water expands when it freezes, water vapor is lighter than air and therefore floats, rocks are heavy, heat comes from the sun, sound pitch may be high, an egg beater is a simple machine, an inclined plane makes lifting a weight easier, magnets attract, electricity may be dangerous, and wind blows. These are facts. As information, they may be interesting. When pupils have experienced enough examples of one concept from which to generalize, they are ready to apply inductive thinking and reach a conclusion. Jane has a pile of rocks which she tests one at a time and finds that they all sink when she puts them in water. She is ready to generalize that in proportion to their volume, rocks are heavier than water. She is now ready for the term "density," which describes the phenomena just discovered. Similarly, Dan may discover that a pulley enables him to lift a heavy weight with less effort than direct lifting and that increasing the number of pulleys decreases the required force. These are generalizations. Other examples are: All matter is *liquid, solid,* or *gas.* All energy comes from the sun. Energy is expressed in the form of *heat, light,* or *sound.* Forces employ energy through mechanics to do work. *Magnetism* and *electricity* are natural forces. The list is endless.

Again a complete list of the principles of physical science will need to come from the curriculum guides or textbooks. You need to be aware of the differences between isolated facts and general principles. Remember that the basic principles can be derived from a variety of facts. There are numerous experiments that demonstrate the fact that air has weight. Some children may crush a can with air, some may pop an egg into a milk bottle, some may siphon water from one can to another, some may hear liquid gurgle as it comes out of the neck of a jug, and some may sail paper airplanes. They are all working with the principle of air pressure. They all reach the same conclusions, that is, that air has weight and air occupies space. These conclusions permit them to generalize and to predict.

A study of *the universe* may include such bits and pieces of information as names of specific stars, identification of constellations, names of kinds of rocks, and descriptions of natural phenomena. These are all facts. They lead to such generalizations as: The earth turns on its axis. As it turns it alternately faces toward and away from the sun. This causes day and night. The earth revolves around the sun in an orbit, maintaining a steady slant controlled by the polar star. The inclination of the earth on its axis causes the sun's rays to strike the surface of the earth at different angles causing the changing seasons. The sun is the source of *heat, light,* and *energy.* Rocks are classified as igneous, metamorphic, and conglomerate depending on their origin. Fossils tell the geological history of the earth. Weather is a present local condition. Climate is a summation of weather conditions in a given region over a period of time. Weather and climate affect crops. Natural resources come from the land and the sea.

Again these sample generalizations are offered to help you determine the difference between factual information and principles. One group might study the climate of the desert and another the climate of fertile plains. Both groups reach the conclusion that climate, including rainfall, temperature, and length of the growing season, determines what crops can be grown. In a given class different groups can study the climate of different regions, and pool their findings through class reporting and discussion. Each group contributes to the collection of data and in turn learns from the data collected by others. The class discussion involves both the sharing of information and the stating of generalizations based on the facts collected. This is scientific thinking and discovery learning.

Through a study of *the physical body* pupils may learn such facts as the number of bones in the body, the four basic food groups, the names of the five senses, and the kinds of blood vessels in the human body. They may learn the rules of health such as brushing teeth, chewing food thoroughly, washing hands before eating, sleeping so many hours each night, and exercising regularly, but unless they associate these rules with good health and practice them, they have missed the point. Being able to pass a paper-and-pencil test on parts of the body, body functions, rules for good health, principles of fair play, and the nature of disease and germs does not constitute a health program. Health is something you do and something you develop, not something you know. This applies to both physical health and mental health, and to regulations about public health, sanitation, and immunization, and facts about sex and reproduction. The child who learns these generalizations is applying the principles. All learners do not have to traverse the same route or collect identical information to arrive at the desired goals.

Developing Attitudes and Understandings.   A person who looks at the world from a scientific point of view sees it differently from the one who is superstitious, uninformed, and prejudiced. Blough (3:17) sees scientifically-minded people as those who are open minded—willing to face evidence, and change their minds. He sees them as deliberate—those who do not jump to conclusions but make many observations. He sees them as challenging facts—as making sure the evidence is reliable. He sees them as those who are not superstitious but look for causes. And furthermore, he sees them as those who are curious, careful, and accurate in all their work. These characteristics can be applied to the young child who is still a pupil, to the mature scholar engaged in research, to you as a teacher, and to the adult living in today's world. Haan reiterates this same point of view when he says (10:215):

> Science helps the child see the order, rhythm, and inevitability of change.

The really significant contributions the study of science can make to human beings are the changes it makes in the kinds of persons the students are becoming. The skills mastered and the information stored are only the vehicles that develop attitudes and understandings that change responses to the environment and to oneself. These are listed in the "To Be" column of Fig. 8–2.

As a result of perusal of facts about plant and animal life and experiences with real live objects, children will develop certain attitudes and understandings that will alter their relationships with nature. As a result of their studies they will develop:

> an understanding of the interdependence of various forms of life and a recognition that life and death are an essential part of the overall plan not only for others but also for themselves.
>
> an insight into the life cycle of all living things that will give an appreciation of human birth, growth, and death.
>
> an understanding of the ability of both plant and animal life to adapt to the environment and from this understanding learn to see the ways of people in various regions of the world not as "queer" and different, but as practical adaptations to existing conditions.
>
> an insight into the ability of human beings to make adaptations in the environment through such acts as building dams, heating and air-conditioning buildings, and irrigating the soil, and will learn to accept these changes as a part of the on-going plan of civilized people and perhaps make constructive contributions themselves.
>
> an understanding of the orderliness and balance in nature which causes all living things to set up protective barriers for themselves while at the same time preying on other living things for their own benefit. From this insight they should gain a new perspective on the acts of human beings in controlling nature through the use of pesticides, the dispersion of plants, the killing of animal life for food, and the interference with balance in nature.
>
> a respect for the life cycle and a reverence for life giving properties.

As a result of a study of matter, energy, and mechanics in the physical world, children will develop insights and understandings which will influence adaptation to and use of natural resources. They will learn:

> to see air, land, and water as commodities to be used with respect and consideration, and therefore as endowments to be preserved. This will lead to an understanding of the need for conservation.
>
> to see systematic and logical organization in the world.
>
> to see the properties of magnetism and electricity as predictable reactions to force and therefore will be able to use them with care and at the same time to their own advantage.
>
> to recognize the forces that have been adapted through the use of simple machines as contributing to their own well being and therefore will gain a respect for such inventions as the wheel, pulley, lever, and more complex forms.
>
> to accept certain natural phenomena.

As a result of the study of the earth and the universe, children will gain insight and understanding which will affect their attitudes toward both the immediate and far reaching studies of the human race. They will develop:

> an awareness of the need for conserving natural resources in order to perpetuate life.
>
> a respect for the explorations of scientists beyond the immediate environment in order to understand humanity's place in the scheme of things.
>
> an understanding of the movements of the earth causing seasons, day and night, tides, weather, and climate, and the ability to adapt or adjust to these phenomena.
>
> an understanding of such apparently natural phenomena as earthquakes, glaciers, floods, storms, and disasters.

What is more intimate and personal than the ability to understand oneself? When one learns to understand the physical body and how it functions and the mind and how it responds, then this person will become an individual as well as a member of society. These understandings influence how people use their bodies and their own unique personalities for the rest of their lives. Unless pupils learn to see themselves in relation to the environment, they have missed the point. Unless they learn to feel responsibility for contributing to life, they have failed to use knowledge of science to extend personal development. They should:

> develop a desire for a strong physical body.
>
> assume increasing responsibility for personal hygiene.
>
> develop concern for preserving a clean environment and willingness to cooperate in public health and disease prevention.
>
> assume responsibility for their own acts and for dissemination of information that will deter others from harmful use of the body.

In addition to the above specific attitudes and understandings related to separate areas, children will also develop some general insights applicable to all areas, such as:

a renewed respect for accuracy
an appreciation for the orderliness of science
a respect for careful research through reading and observation
a desire for specificity
an appreciation for the contributions of scientists
reverence for the overall plan of the universe
wholesome curiosity about the environment
willingness to cooperate with the laws of nature
a feeling of responsibility for their personal place in the scheme of life

How to Organize for Teaching

Being organized for teaching puts you in control of the learning environment. You will determine whether to take a problems approach or a textbook approach. You will determine whether topics will be repeated in greater depth from time to time or treated exhaustively when initially presented. Hicks (11:109) says:

> . . . you, not the prescribed curriculum, will make the difference between a good and a poor science program in your classroom.

Textbook Versus Problems Approach.   No doubt you will be teaching in a situation where there is a curriculum guide to help you in planning the science experiences for your children. Perhaps you will have a basic text adopted by the school system. Copies of such text may be supplied in quantities sufficient for each child to have one, or there may be a limited number of texts and a supply of other source material. The other material may be textbooks in sets of from five to ten copies, or encyclopedic or pamphlet type material, one copy for the entire group. Whatever the type of source material, it is your responsibility to decide: (1) Will I have every child read the same material and answer the same questions? or (2) Will I introduce a topic or a question and encourage each child to read within personal capabilities and contribute in the discussion which takes place in the class period? This is the difference between a textbook approach and a problems approach. Support for the problems approach is expressed by such authorities as Shuster (20), Alpren (1), Neagley (16), and Wilson (24). Shuster (20:303–330) says:

Science should no longer be thought of as an organized body of knowledge from which children are expected to memorize certain principles or a set number of generalizations relating to each experiment. Modern science teaching is problem-centered. Through a study of science, children come to a better understanding of themselves and their environment, and this cannot be accomplished through memorizing a series of what was formerly termed 'universal laws.' *A curriculum design for science education must concern itself with the world in which the child finds himself. That is, the child must learn skills, appreciations, understandings, and attitudes which will help him to understand the changing, dynamic nature of his social and physical environment.* (p. 303) (Italics in original).

To achieve these objectives children must participate—science learnings require activity. (p. 305).

When children have had a variety of concrete experiences, reading takes on new meanings. (p. 307).

Science facts, for example, are important, but these facts are only useful to the learners to the extent that they are related to broader understandings which will lead to some modification in the learner's behavior. (p. 329).

Therefore, the emerging design for elementary school science must provide first-hand experiences for all children in rediscovering basic science principles which are already known. (p. 330).

Alpren (1:205–206) concludes his discussion of the significance of science in the elementary curriculum by pointing out that:

1. Science is for all students.
2. Science should be laboratory-centered.
3. There should be more emphasis on individual thinking and acting.
4. The only worthwhile science is that which will continue beyond the confines of the classroom.
5. Science is a continuum.
6. Science sources should not be stereotyped.

In pointing out the place of textbooks in a problem-centered approach to the teaching of science, Hicks (11:109–111) says:

The adoption of a particular textbook series is still the most prevalent manner of determining a school science program. Chances are, the textbooks that you find in your classroom will be a real asset to you if you use them properly.

Textbooks are not, nor are they intended to be, a total science program. The main benefits of elementary school science derive from active participation of children with objects, events, and ideas. Reading about these things is no substitute for involvement with them.

Neagley (16:295–296) makes a prediction about the use of textbooks in science when he says:

Because they are out of date so quickly, science texts will be replaced by loose leaf manuals or annual supplements will be issued in the same manner in which encyclopedias are kept current today. By the end of the 1980's schools will be linked to large computer centers. With the flick of a switch a student sitting in a soundproof carrel in the school library will be able to view on a small screen the latest developments in any aspect of science, or even to receive a photocopy of a digest of this material.

And finally, Wilson (24:203) points out the effect of packaged programs and cautions against over-dependence on published materials when he says:

With large corporations entering education, there are many programs now on the market and more being produced. All seem to have one thing in common—they are all packages. . . . This seems to stem from an effort to make the curriculum as teacher-proof as possible.

Spiral Versus Ladder Organization.   Organization of science content involves the question of in-depth pursuit of a topic versus expanding repetitions at spaced intervals. The latter provides for the child's ever broadening perception of the environment and deepening understandings. This point of view is supported by such authorities as Haan (10), Carin (7), Beauchamp (2), and Alpren (1). Haan (10:220) in discussing the place of science in the schedule says:

Depending upon the kind of topic or unit being learned, science should occur in the schedule in such a position that at times it may be taught in connection with the social studies and at other times in connection with mathematics. There should also be times when the science unit is pursued without integration with other subject areas. The special opportunities for teaching science, such as show-and-tell periods, health and safety programs, and free periods, can all be utilized if an over-all flexible plan for science exists. Certainly there are times when science should be brought into music, art, and crafts.

Alpren (1:187–189) gives a scope and sequence chart for primary and intermediate grades that exemplifies the expanding spiral organization of subject matter. Beauchamp (2:154–161) also gives a scope and sequence chart prescribing content at each grade level under five basic headings repeated grade by grade and in spiral development to extend the learnings as the child progresses through school. This will vary from text to text and with the authority. The best way is for you to use a text as a guide, expand upon it by using other texts and references, and plan around the experiences of the children. Carin (7) provides a book on the teaching of science which sets up a framework, gives step-by-step activities for organizing and planning, offers enrichment activities, and provides lesson plans with teaching suggestions, experiments, demonstrations, and pictorial riddles for science learning through discovery.

All these quotes support the theory that a spiral organization of subject matter is preferable. Hicks (11:109–110) says in pointing out the importance of the teacher that:

> . . . . elementary school pupils, even the very youngest, are quick to detect uneasiness, insecurity, or bluffing on the part of a teacher in any subject. (p. 109)
>
> Successful teaching of any subject requires an enthusiasm and a commitment to the task that is discernible to the children. (p. 109)
>
> Knowledge is well suited to the giving of answers, but a sincere desire to obtain knowledge makes of the teacher a learner among learners. (p. 110)

SUMMARY

Yes, science teaching is here to stay. Its place in the elementary school curriculum has been well established. In science children learn about life, the physical universe, life beyond our planet, and about themselves. They learn to recognize the many uses of science in daily life and to use the discovery method in learning to think like a scientist. In order to teach science effectively in the classroom, the teacher needs to know what to teach and how to organize for teaching. Knowing what to teach includes the mastery of skills, the accumulation of information, and the development of attitudes affecting behavior beyond the classroom. Organizing for teaching includes a proper respect for sources of information including the textbook, recognition of problems as an approach to science, and an understanding of the spiral organization of subject matter to meet the needs of the child's unfolding perspective on the environment.

Crosby (8:307) describes the contribution of science to the curriculum when she says:

> In a world in which science has so often become a football of competition, with supremacy of one people over another or annihilation as an end goal, it is obligatory that teachers help children learn early in life that science's greatest advancements have come through cooperation. This is one of the great social contributions which science has made to modern life.

SUGGESTED ACTIVITIES

Select from the following ideas at least one to develop as a research project. Work independently, with a partner, or with a committee. Report your findings to the rest of the class.

1. Select a college textbook, a high school textbook, and an elementary school science textbook and study the treatment of a topic at each level. Identify

concepts common to all of them. Look for evidences of spiral unfoldment of an idea from one level to the next. Select from one or more of the following curriculum areas:

Astronomy	Ecology
Biology	Genetics
Botany	Geology
Chemistry	Physics

2. Differentiate between political geography and physical geography. Illustrate with examples from science texts at different levels.

3. Watch a newspaper daily for a week or more and clip news stories with science content that could be used in an elementary classroom. Classify them as to content. Arrange a bulletin board to demonstrate the point or share with the rest of the class.

4. Plan to demonstrate a science experiment for the class. List objectives, materials, steps, and outcomes.

5. Write a lesson plan for a science learning using the inquiry and discovery approach. (Note: Refer to the chapter on planning for format.)

6. Compile a list of equipment and supplies useful in the teaching of science in the elementary classroom. Divide the items into three categories:
   a. Those which can be secured about the ordinary home from the kitchen, the bathroom, or the workshop.
   b. Those which can be purchased for a nominal sum at local stores.
   c. Those which may need to be provided by a science supply house.

Justify the inclusion of each item, especially the more expensive ones.

SELECTED READINGS

1. ALPREN, MORTON, *The Subject Curriculum*, Columbus, Ohio: Charles E. Merrill, 1967. Chapter 8 is devoted to science. It points out newer programs and outlines scope and sequence of topics.

2. BEAUCHAMP, GEORGE A., *The Curriculum of the Elementary School*, Boston: Allyn and Bacon, 1964. Chapter 7 is on science. It outlines sequence of topics by grades.

3. BLOUGH, GLEN O. and JULIUS SCHWARTZ, *Elementary School Science and How to Teach it*, New York: Holt, Rinehart and Winston, 1964. A methods book devoted to the teaching of science.

4. BOYER, JOHN L, M.D., "We Need a New Emphasis in Physical Education," in *Today's Education*, Vol. 61, No. 8, Nov. 1972. pp. 44–45. Points out the need for physical education to meet current needs as differentiated from athletics for competition.

5. BRONARS, JOANNE REYNOLDS, "Tampering with Nature in Elementary School Science," in *Educational Forum*, Vol. XXXIII, No. 1, Nov. 1968, pp. 71–75. Criticizes experimentation with living things in the elementary school. Recommends sharpening powers of observation.

6. BRUNER, JEROME S., *Toward a Theory of Instruction*, New York: W. W. Norton, 1966. A series of eight essays. Describes patterns of growth and the relation of education to society. Patterns applicable to science. Chap. 4—"Man: A Course of Study."

7. CARIN, ARTHUR and ROBERT B. SUND, *Teaching Science Through Discovery*, Columbus, Ohio: Charles E. Merrill, 1964. Emphasizes discovery learning in science. Gives classroom examples. Utilizes problem solving techniques and inquiry. Experiments. Demonstrations.

8. CROSBY, MURIEL, *Curriculum Development for Elementary Schools in a Changing Society*, Boston: D.C. Heath, 1964. Emphasizes human relations with examples of real experiences of boys and girls living in present-day society. Stresses the importance of curricula that have value for children.

9. FROST, JOE L. and G. THOMAS ROWLAND, *Curricula for the Seventies*, Boston: Houghton Mifflin, 1969. Chapter 9 is devoted to science. Emphasizes a process approach. Lists national elementary science curriculum projects.

10. HAAN, AUBREY, *Elementary School Curriculum; Theory and Research*, Boston: Allyn and Bacon, 1961. Chapter 8 on science and mathematics emphasizes science as thinking. Stresses importance of accuracy, value of science, and importance of organization.

11. HICKS, WM. VERNON, *et. al.*, *The New Elementary School Curriculum*, New York: Van Nostrand Reinhold, 1970. Chapter 4 describes current curriculum projects. Emphasizes importance of the teacher, materials, and content.

12. HONE, ELIZABETH B., *et. al.*, *A Sourcebook for Elementary Science* (2nd edition), New York: Harcourt, Brace, Jovanovich, 1971. Practical suggestions in elementary science. Good coverage on space travel.

13. JARVIS, OSCAR T. and MARION J. RICE, *An Introduction to Teaching in the Elementary School*, Dubuque, Iowa: Wm. C. Brown, 1972. Chapters 8 and 13 deal with science and teaching of science.

14. LANSDOWN, BRENDA, and PAUL E. BLACKWOOD, *Teaching Elementary Science: Through Investigation and Colloquium*, New York: Harcourt, Brace, Jovanovich, 1971. Suggestions for activities. Emphasis on conceptual approach.

15. LEE, CHESTER M. "Learning from the Moon," in *Today's Education*, Vol. 60, No. 1, Jan. 1971, pp. 50–52. Science, age dating, solar wind, lunar materials.

16. NEAGLEY, ROSS L. and N. DEAN EVANS, *Handbook for Effective Curriculum Development*, Englewood Cliffs, N.J.: Prentice-Hall, 1967. Puts curriculum decisions into everyday practice. The practical approach is pertinent to the area of science.

17. PORTER, LORENA R., "The Movement Movement," in *Today's Education*, Vol. 61, No. 5, May 1972, pp. 42–44. A study of the aims of physical education. Suggests content and program.

18. RAGAN, WILLIAM B., *Modern Elementary Curriculum*, New York: Holt, Rinehart and Winston, 1966. Chapter 12 outlines objectives and main features of a science program for elementary grades. Treats the problem of gifted children in science.

19. RUTLEDGE, JAMES A., "What Has Happened to the 'New' Science Curricula?" in *Educational Leadership*, Vol. 30, No. 7, April 1973. pp. 600–603. Identifies what's "new" in science and the extent to which the new has been accepted in the school curriculum. Sees action as improvement.

20. SHUSTER, ALBERT H. and MILTON E. PLOGHOFT, *The Emerging Elementary Curriculum*, Columbus, Ohio: Charles E. Merrill, 1963. Chapter 10 shows how to guide children in science experiences. Gives scope and sequence chart. Discusses use of materials. Lists basic minimums.

21. SUND, ROBERT B., WILL W. TILLERY, and LESLIE W. TROBRIDGE, *Elementary Science Discovery Lessons*, Boston: Allyn and Bacon, 1970. Three paperback books subtitled: *The Physical Sciences, The Earth Sciences*, and *The Biological Sciences*. Lists materials, teacher questions, and student activities.

22. VICTOR, EDWARD, *Science for the Elementary School* (2nd edition), New York: Macmillan, 1970. Covers content, methods, and activities.

23. WAGAR, J. ALAN, "Special Feature on What Schools Can Do About Pollution— What Elementary Schools Are Doing," in *Today's Education*, Vol. 59, No. 9, Dec. 1970, pp. 25–27. Diary accounts of experiences in four schools with comments and tips for ecology-conscious consumers.

24. WILSON, L. CRAIG, *The Open Access Curriculum*, Boston: Allyn and Bacon, 1971. Chapter 11 discusses opening the access to science. Lists national elementary science curriculum projects.

9

TEACHING THE USE OF MATHEMATICAL CONCEPTS

Helping Children Learn To Use Numbers in Daily Living

Courtesy, Skiff School, Phoenix, Arizona

MATHEMATICS

When you plan your daily schedule, what time of day will you set aside for mathematics? Why? How much time will you devote to it? Will you use a textbook or depend on incidental learnings? How will you justify your decisions? What about a workbook? Does it have value? If so, what? And when and how will you check it? What use will you make of concrete materials? What will you need? Do you know how to set up a learning center for mathematics so the children can discover number relationships for themselves? What are the advantages of such procedures over abstract drill?

What about drill? Will you use it? If so, when and how? And for what purpose? How can you be sure the children have mastered the skills? What skills are worth mastering? Will you encourage them to use tables and adding machines, or is that considered to be cheating?

Is mathematics a skill or a content subject? Which is more important? And what about modern math? Is it the answer to the teaching of arithmetic, or is it just a current fad? What will you tell the parents about it? Should mathematics be taught by an "expert" in a departmentalized situation, or can you handle it for your own pupils? How can you be sure performance is based on understanding rather than on rote learning?

These are curriculum questions you will have to answer for yourself. Let's explore some of the angles.

Are you confused about whether mathematics is a skill subject or a content subject? It is both. Are you concerned about whether to call it numbers, arithmetic, or mathematics? Take your choice. We are all talking about the same things. Does some of the terminology in the so-called modern math leave you with the feeling that you are out of date? Don't let it. Many mathematicians as well as educators are beginning to believe that much of the change in the field of mathematics is more a matter of vocabulary and methodology than of content. However, Hicks (17:53) says that:

> During the past few years, vast changes have occurred in the content and teaching methodology of elementary school mathematics.

There are changes taking place and you should be aware of what they are and how they will affect your teaching. The purpose of this chapter is to help you get an overview of what to teach, why it is important, and how to go about it. We will develop the concept that number is a language used to communicate ideas about sequences and amounts, justify the need for skills in numeration and computation, emphasize the value of understanding how numbers work, and analyze learnings in terms of skills, knowledge, and attitudes. We will take a look at organization for teaching by noting the relation of mathematics to the rest of the curriculum, compare traditional patterns with recent trends, and conclude with a plea for inductive reasoning, concrete experiences, and discovery learning.

WHAT CHILDREN NEED TO LEARN IN MATHEMATICS

The mathematics program is based partly on tradition, partly on utility, partly on current research, and perhaps partly on the opinions of teachers. Children need to see numbers as a language used to express quantitative relationships, to recognize the use of numbers as a means of expressing amounts and sequences, to compute accurately and quickly, and to understand and appreciate the many uses they have for number in their daily lives. These learnings build up in a pyramid based on an understanding of numbers as a language of quantity and culminating in skills and knowledge leading to application and appreciation. They are diagrammed in Fig. 9–1.

The Language of Numbers

Just as young children learn a language of words, they learn a language of numbers. They are using number concepts when they ask when, where, how long, and how far. They are recognizing number relationships when they say bigger, higher, older, more than, and as much as. Through the use of comparisons they are learning the relationships of size, amount, position, and time. These are all number concepts related to measurement, quantity, and position leading to a vocabulary that is mathematical; for example: equal, diagonal, perpendicular, horizontal, congruent. They recognize quantitative relationships when they reach for the largest piece of candy, the coin of greater value, the longest ribbon, or the tallest glass of milk.

Eventually they add such precise terms as addition, subtraction, multiplication, and division, and their counterparts addend, sum, total, minuend, subtrahend, difference, remainder, multiplicand, multiplier, product, dividend, divisor, and quotient. They learn names for mathematical forms such as triangle, plane, square, pentagon; for time measurements such as day, hour, week, year, century; for number concepts such as

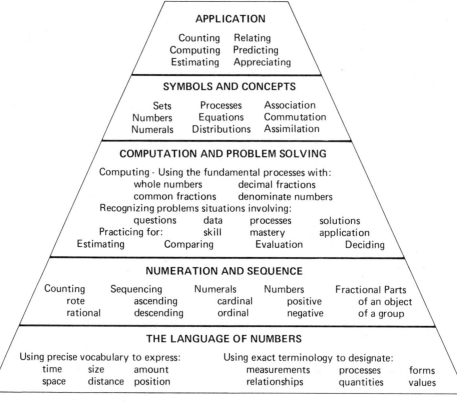

Figure 9-1. *Building a pyramid of mathematical skills and concepts.*

fraction, numerator, denominator, decimal, percent; for forms such as angles, obtuse, acute; for operations such as bisect, intersect, divide; and for relationships such as sets, distributive, associative, and commutative. They learn about positive and negative numbers by playing "Old Maid" and going "in the hole." They even learn to use such terms as algebra, geometry, and computer.

All this is a basic foundation for communicating in the language of numbers. It comes through association with others as well as through direct teaching. Some of it has changed as curriculum targets have been redirected in the elementary school. Parker (23:34–35) points out that:

> In its deeper sense, mathematics is a means of communication with a language of its own. A mathematical sequence is essentially a statement concerning numbers. . . . One of the more important objectives of the reform in mathematics teaching, now making its way into the elementary and secondary schools, has to do with providing students with a mathematical vocabulary.

Numeration and Sequence

The language of number becomes more precise when it is used to designate definite amounts and specific sequences. Rote and rational counting make use of cardinal numbers. Serial sequencing makes use of ordinal numbers.

Rote and Rational Counting. Children may learn to say numbers in rotation long before they are aware of the concept of how many. The child who counts one, two, three in a sing-song manner without relation to real objects is merely counting by *rote*. That kind of counting has little real value beyond an awareness of number and sequence. Children are learning to do *rational counting* when they begin to make a one-to-one association between number and object by pointing to the first book saying, "One," to the second book saying, "two," and so on, and when they are able to end the number naming with an awareness of how many books. This is using *cardinal numbers* to tell how many. This is a much higher level of response than mere rote counting. It recognizes number names as a language expressing quantity.

Serial Sequencing. The child who becomes aware that the one in front is first, the one that follows is second, then comes third, fourth, and fifth in that order is recognizing *sequence* and is using *ordinal numbers*. This gives the concept of sequence in daily life. Sunday comes before Monday. Tuesday follows Monday. Yesterday, today, and tomorrow follow in order. The days of the week and the months of the year follow one another in a fixed pattern. It must be one o'clock before it can be two o'clock. You must be six years old before you can be seven years old. The scores in a game begin at the beginning and build up one at a time. The miles on the odometer accumulate in ascending order, and a count-down at the race or in the space center comes in descending order. These are all learnings which come from the environment. Calling attention to them will give the child an insight into the number system and how it works. Hicks (17:54) points out that:

> The traditional emphasis on computational skills and drill for mastery of facts is being replaced by a search for number patterns and an emphasis on structure of the discipline itself. The mathematics classroom is being transformed into a laboratory where pupils explore for themselves.

Problem Solving

Problem solving calls for more than counting. One must first identify the problem and then arrive at a solution. This calls for manipulation of quantities to arrive at an answer. Sometimes this demands precise computation. Sometimes an estimate is more practical.

Computing.   When children want to know:

How many will I need?
How many will it take?
What will be left?
How much is there?

they are seeing number as a means of finding out, and computation as a process using numbers to answer questions. They compute amounts, distances, sizes, and time. The questions determine the processes. The child who comes to recognize the fundamental processes as devices for answering questions rather than as mental puzzles to be solved in a subject called mathematics is establishing a basis in number knowledge.

Estimating.   Actually in real life situations one has as many, or more uses for estimating as for computing. If one has a dollar and wants to buy two items costing 69¢ and 29¢ respectively the question is, "Will my dollar bill be enough to pay for them?" The one who can estimate by saying "Not quite 70¢ and not quite 30¢ would be not quite a dollar. Yes, I will have enough," is using both understanding of number and estimating skills. Both computing and estimating are necessary. One is a check against the other. They help answer such questions as, what answer can I expect? and does my computation yield a reasonable answer?

Numbers and How they Work

Numbers are symbols used to represent quantities. In mathematics the student learns to use these symbols to communicate and to interpret the environment. Simple integers are used to express quantities in whole numbers such as 1, 2, and 3. Modern mathematics terminology makes a point of differentiating between a number and a numeral. It states that the number is the quantity itself and the numeral is the symbol representing the quantity.

Number relationships are orderly and systematic. Once pupils understand the system, they not only can compute but also predict. It is essential that the beginner in the study of mathematics understand these relationships before attempting to manipulate the symbols for purposes of computation. Such insight and understanding leads to inductive thinking and discovery learning. Bruner (5:72) puts it this way:

We teach a subject not to produce little living libraries on that subject, but rather to get a student to think mathematically for himself, to consider matters as an historian does, to take part in the process of knowledge-getting. Knowing is a process, not a product.

If children learn the language of number by acquiring the appropriate vocabulary and meanings attached thereto; if they learn to use numbers to count and determine sequence; if they attain understanding basic to skill in computing and estimating; and if they understand how numbers work; then they are ready to think like a mathematician. Such an approach to the subject will result in an appreciation of the orderliness of the system and the dependability of the discipline. Such a respect for number relationships will make of mathematics targets a positive goal. Knowledge will be perceived as useful and skill will be viewed as essential. These are the elements that make study and drill purposeful and motivation self imposed by the student.

WHY WE NEED TO TEACH MATHEMATICS

You must be convinced that mathematics is of value and that the teaching of mathematics is a valuable use for classroom time. If children study mathematics only because it is required, because the books have been purchased, or because the teacher says they must, they may see it only as a school related chore and their objective may be merely passing the course, getting an A, or pleasing the teacher. But if they are led to see mathematics as a useful skill with information they can apply daily, they will have more effective motives for reading, counting, computing, and understanding numbers.

To Read Number Language

To be able to read the language of numbers intelligently is a worthy curriculum target. One uses numbers in reading the quantities in a recipe, a formula in science, a clock, maps, graphs, diagrams, tables, figures, page numbers, chapter headings, and index references in a book, and in locating information in the library. One needs a knowledge of numbers to read a bus or plane schedule, a time schedule for a program, the speedometer or odometer on a car, road signs, directions for assembling a do-it-yourself project, and countless other daily activities. One needs a knowledge of numbers to pay bills, collect a salary, keep a bank account, compute income tax, give to charitable organizations, get to work on time, locate favorite television programs, and even to go to bed and get up on a schedule that makes a daily routine fit into the demands of society:

As a teaching-learning strategy, one teacher and the pupils decided to abolish numbers for one day. They eliminated clocks and calendars. They omitted page numbers in the texts. They could not use the telephone or eat in the cafeteria. Finding their classrooms and their homes became more laborious. In fact, before the day ended they simply could not function without numbers. Try it. It's convincing.

To Count and Measure

Tangible things exist in some amount. We can count the number of oranges in a bag, the number of pencils in a box, the number of blocks to school, the number of pupils in the room, the number of minutes we have for a given task, the number of chairs needed for the audience, the number of pages to read, and the number of books on the shelf. Measuring is a counting device to determine how many inches of ribbon, how many quarts of milk, how many pounds of potatoes, how many acres in a field, how many miles per hour, how many minutes till noon, how many hours of sleep, how many days till Christmas, and how many years in school. Ned counts and measures when he tells how old he is, how tall he is, how much he weighs, and how much he has grown in the past year. Peggy compares when she measures her height or weight and compares it with that of a friend to determine who is taller or heavier.

When considering counting and measurement in today's schools, we must not omit the impact of the metric system. The United States is one of the few major nations that does not use that system for measuring. Most of the measurements in the scientific world adhere to the metric system. International trade, medicine, engineering, and manufacturing use metrics. There are many who contend the system is already in our business and industrial world and that it must be introduced into our schools. Bright (4:16–19) says children should be taught to think metric. Hallerberg (16:247–255) insists that it is a program whose time has come. And Jones (18:21–27) insists schools will be teaching it and you'll be living it very very soon.

In order to prove the usefulness of number have the children keep a record for one day of all the things they have counted or measured. Then have them indicate the measuring devices they used and the scales they applied. They will make lists such as rulers, yard sticks, tape measures, meter sticks, measuring cups, pint and quart measures, scales, clocks, calendars, odometers, speedometers, thermometers, and barometers. They will discover such relationships as inches in a foot, feet in a yard, cups in a pint, pints in a quart, quarts in a gallon, minutes in an hour, hours in a day, days in a week, weeks in a month, months in a year, ounces in a pound, pounds in a ton, and on and on. These discoveries will be the organized information they will use in further problem solving.

To Compute

We add to find out how many people in a number of groups when we know the number in each group, how much money it will take to purchase two or more items, how many cards in two or more boxes, and the score in a game. We subtract to find out how much money we have left, how many more people we have room for, and how much more we need. We multiply when we want to double a recipe, find out how much we earn in a week if we earn the same each day, how many pieces of paper we need for five children if each one gets four pieces, and how much money we will make on admissions to the program. We divide when we have twelve dollars and want to know how many dollars each boy will get, or to how many boys we can give three dollars each. We use all these processes with whole numbers, fractions, and decimal fractions as well as with denominate numbers. We call this computation. It means we are using numbers to help us calculate amounts. This is a very practical use for numbers and one which the pupil needs to learn to appreciate and use.

One of the major targets of the elementary curriculum in mathematics is to give children first understanding and appreciation, then the know-how which enables them to do it, followed by purposeful practice to make them skillful enough to serve personal needs. How much knowledge they need will eventually depend on their roles in the adult world, but practically everybody needs the simple skills of computing for daily living and estimating for practical purposes. Beyond that, the use of a computer or the charts of square roots, tax schedules, interest rates, and house payments may take the place of the more complicated forms of calculation. Even so, understanding the basic principles and practicing enough to gain insight into what the computer is doing or the table is telling will make the language of number serviceable.

To Understand Numbers

Which comes first, understanding or process? That is like asking how one learns to ski, or drive a car, or type. William might study the instruction guide to techniques of skiing until he could explain all the positions and movements, but he still would not be able to perform until he puts on the skis and moves. Fred might memorize the typing manual or the driver's manual, but that would be no assurance that he could either operate the typewriter or the car. To say that understanding precedes practice or that practice precedes understanding is to miss the real point of how learning takes place. Both process and understanding must be learned simultaneously. Real understanding emerges as the learner meets the situation, tries out the alternatives to see what happens, discovers what works, and figures out how. From these experiences children gain insight into the system. This in turn helps them make generalizations they can apply to further learning and practice.

Applying this concept to the learning of mathematics, let us see how Cathy arrives at an understanding of the principle of multiplication. She does not memorize a definition or manipulate figures according to a rule. Instead, she meets a situation where she has three pencils in one box, three in another box, and three in another box, and discovers she can find out how many there are altogether in several different ways. One way would be to count the pencils one by one. Another way would be to add three and three and three. From this last experience she discovers that she has three threes, or three pencils three times, and that's what multiplication really is. Experience leads to understanding. Understanding makes experience meaningful. Repeated experiences lead to skill. This principle works for the understanding of all the processes even through higher mathematics. One of the major targets in teaching mathematics in the elementary school is achieving understanding and insight into how the number system works and an appreciation for its pattern. To get skill without understanding is to reduce mathematics to rote performance. To get understanding without skill is to become aware of a process one cannot use. It takes both. They must be developed simultaneously.

HOW TO TEACH MATHEMATICS IN THE ELEMENTARY SCHOOL

Now that you have considered what to teach and why, you are ready to turn your attention to two relevant problems: (1) How to teach skills, facts, and attitudes; and (2) How to get organized for teaching.

How to Teach

There are some things children will need to learn how to do. These are called skills. There is some knowledge they will find useful in the study of mathematics. This refers to content. There are certain basic understandings they need to help them appreciate the discipline. And mathematics does have orderliness, rhythm, pattern, and form. It possesses beauty if one but knows how to find it. These are some of the things we will try to justify as curriculum targets and to demonstrate on a how-to basis in the following pages. They are summarized in Fig. 9–2.

The Skills. The reasons for teaching the skills and the means of perfecting them have varied from time to time. Hicks (17:55–62) identifies three basic theories: (1) the drill theory; (2) the social needs theory; (3) the meaning theory. He defines the drill theory as an approach that assumes that knowing how to do it is the major objective. In this approach little or no attention is given to meaning or interest, and drill precedes understanding. The social needs theory is based on the assumption that the facts and skills are best learned when a situation arises to cause the child to use the skill in a real life situation. Here practice may be haphazard or incidental. The meaning theory is based on the assumption that as the children learn the structure of mathematics, they will discover the broad relationships and basic principles. In this case new ideas are studied for meaning and understanding before practice takes place.

The fundamental processes in arithmetic are commonly known as addition, subtraction, multiplication, and division. Young children can be led to discover that *addition* is putting things together. They need experiences in manipulating objects in groups, in moving the groups about to form new combinations, and in the *commutative* principle that reveals that 5 plus 3 and 3 plus 5 results in the same total. They need to experiment with number relationships and discover that *subtraction* answers three basic questions. Namely:

1.   How many are left? If I have 5 and give away 2, how many are left? This is called the *subtractive* concept.

2.   How many more are needed? Five children are coming to the party. I have only four chairs. How many more chairs do I need? This is known as the *additive* concept.

3.   What is the difference? Mary weighs 87 pounds. Alice weighs 82 pounds. How much more does Mary weigh than Alice? This is the *comparative* concept.

They need experiences in arranging things in groups so they can discover the principle that *multiplication* is a short method of adding and works only when the addends are alike. If Tom wants to know the total of the addends 4, 8, 7, and 5, he must add. but if he needs to know the total of 6, 6, 6, and 6, he can discover that there are four 6's or the quantity 6 is repeated four times.

They need experience in sorting objects into groups so that they can discover that the process of *division* answers two basic questions. Namely:

1.   How many in each group? I have 18 sheets of paper. I am going to give them to six boys. How many sheets will each boy get? Here he deals them out like dealing the cards for a game. One for Tom, one for Harry, one for Fred, one for Alan, one for Billy, and one for Robert. He goes around once. He goes around again. He goes around again. When he uses all the sheets, he counts the ones in each group or each of the parts. How many does Tom have? Three. Billy? Three. The answer three which tells how many in each part is known as the *partition* concept of division.

2.   How many groups? He can answer another question by means of division. This time he has eighteen sheets of paper. But the question is, "To how many

Mathematics Concepts

AREA	TO DO	TO KNOW	TO BE
The Language of Number	The child will be able to: use number names recognize number symbols read numbers use number terms such as: addend minuend multiplier dividend numerator denominator apply number knowledge to the reading of graphs, tables, maps, charts, and schedules	The child will know: the meanings of mathematical terms such as: perpendicular rectangular horizontal parallel diagonal the units of measure the terms of comparison and contrast the nature of the number system and how it works the uses for numbers in other curriculum areas	The child will become: precise in the use of number language appreciative of the value of mathematics as a discipline concerned about accuracy in own work with number relationships
Numeration and Sequence	The child will be able to: count by rote count objects rationally recognize numbers and associate quantities with numerals use both positive and negative numbers in a sequence recognize fractional parts part of an object part of a group associate number names with numerals	The child will know: number sequence the difference between cardinal and ordinal numbers the tables of weights and measures rules governing number sequences the uses for counting the relative sizes of numbers the principle of tens base of our number system	The child will develop: an enjoyment in the manipulation of number sequences a respect for the development of measuring devices based on quantitative relationships a desire for skill in keeping with his own personal abilities and current needs

	The child will be able to:	The child will know:	The child will develop:
Computation and Problem Solving	add, subtract, multiply, and divide using: whole numbers, common fractions, decimal fractions, denominate numbers; recognize problem situations and interpret them for purposes of computation; recognize more than one way to solve a problem; estimate number relationships and quantities	how to compute; which processes to use; how and when to estimate; how to use tables and computers; the three concepts of subtraction: additive, subtractive, comparative; the two concepts of division: partition, measurement; the relationships between the processes	a respect for accuracy; a desire for skill; an appreciation of the contributions of the computer
Symbols, Concepts, Application	use symbols to express relationships for plus, minus, times, divide, equals, greater than, less than, etc.; arrange objects in order according to size, time sequence, etc.; discover number relationships through manipulation of objects	the principle of the fundamental processes; the relation of whole numbers to fractional parts; the relation of common fractions to decimal fractions; the difference between positive and negative numbers; the difference between cardinal and ordinal numbers	a respect for mathematics as an exact science; an appreciation for the orderliness of the number system; a recognition of the many uses for number in daily living

Figure 9–2. *Concepts related to the teaching of elementary mathematics.*

boys can I give three sheets each?" Now he begins by giving three to Tom, three to Bill, and so on until the paper is all gone. In order to answer the question, he must count the boys, or the number of groups. The three was the unit of measurement and the answer is six. This is known as the *measurement* concept of division.

Once these processes are understood in the manipulation of whole numbers, they can be applied to common fractions, decimal fractions, percentages, denominate numbers, and to both positive and negative numbers. Fractions can be presented as parts of wholes or as parts of a group. When Margaret gave her brother half of her candy bar she was dealing with fractions long before she met them in a mathematics textbook. Half of an object or half of a group of objects represents two different concepts. This kind of experimenting will reveal the term *denominator* as denoting or naming the size of the parts. Then the child is ready for the concept of more than one of the parts. If paper is divided into six equal parts, one of the parts is one-sixth of a whole. If Billy takes two of the parts, he has two of the sixths or two-sixths of the paper. The two tells how many. It counts or numerates. Therefore it is called the *numerator*.

Decimal fractions can be presented as another kind of fraction, only this time the denominator is always ten or a power of ten. This fact makes it possible to omit the denominator and use the decimal point to indicate what the denominator is. To develop this concept, it is essential that the word "decimal" be used as an adjective rather than as a noun. The term "decimal fractions" is a more accurate expression than merely the term "decimal" by itself. Such care in the use of terminology is related to understandings and discovery as opposed to deductive learning of rules and rote drill.

Problem solving is the real reason for learning arithmetic. Life is composed of daily incidents which pose problems that are quantitative relationships and the language of number needed to express them is the basis for teaching mathematics. Ragan (24:346) says:

> A mathematics curriculum consisting of sound and meaningful mathematical concepts is not sufficient; pupils must learn to use these concepts in problem solving situations.

Barney (2:57) points out the relation between reading and problem solving. He suggests that the skills needed in this process are both word perception and comprehension, and that the pupil will use these skills to structure, rearrange, edit, sort, and relate concepts in order to translate information into computation processes. He suggests to the teacher helpful steps in rewriting and interpreting problem situations which will lead the child to:

1. Read the problem quickly for an overview.
2. Reread to determine data given.
3. Determine the problem to be solved.
4. Review the facts and select appropriate data and process.

One might well add to this:

1. Estimate probable or reasonable answer.
2. Compute for an exact answer.
3. Compare derived answer with estimate.
4. Answer original question or problem to be solved.

Numbers are more than problems to be solved and exercises for practice. It sometimes helps to see number relationships and relate them to daily experience. (Courtesy, Lowell School, Mesa, Arizona)

Estimating of answers as a part of computation with the fundamental processes and as a part of problem solving is a useful skill. Sometimes it is more practical to estimate than to calculate precisely. In order to become skillful in the use of numbers for estimating, however, the child must first learn to read the language, count and numerate, compute with accuracy and speed, and recognize and use the symbols. Children estimate when they use such expressions as: "Could Washington and Lincoln have talked to each other? Will the room be large enough to seat the entire student body? Is Tom taller or shorter than I am? About how long will it be until lunch time? Do I have enough money to buy both the ball glove and the ball?" This is a practical skill. It is used daily. It must follow understanding of number relationships and some skill in numeration and calculation.

Games are fun, but they also concentrate attention on numbers. (Courtesy, Skiff School, Phoenix, Arizona)

Using the computer has relieved us of much of the time consuming labor required to calculate amounts, but the computer cannot do the thinking. The one who uses the computer still has to know what the question is and what information to feed into the machine in order to get answers to questions. We still must know what to tell the computer to do to find out what we want to know. Computers are a relatively recent invention, and they have made it possible to assemble much more information in a given time than would otherwise be possible. Children can be introduced to simple tables and adding machines which will give "the answers," but they must also understand what it is they are asking the machines to do. Botts (21:455–456) writing for the *69th Yearbook of the National Society for the Study of Education* suggests that:

> The computer's profound effects on the capabilities of our technological era are already everywhere in evidence, and the potentialities of even present-day computers have only begun to be exploited.

Deciding how to teach skills in computation, problem solving, and estimating leads to the question of the use of time and materials. Even though you put meaning first and depend on understanding as an approach, there are still certain learnings that must be reduced to automatic response if they are to be useful. No doubt you will teach where a basic text in mathematics is available. You may have workbooks or multiple copies of drill sheets to place in the hands of the children. If these are used as assignments and are "graded" in order to arive at a mark or evaluation, they may become drudgery. If they are used to provide extra practice for which the child feels a need, they can become a self-imposed challenge. Practice material must be checked, otherwise the child becomes more and more skillful in repeatedly making the same mistakes. That is not the same as their being graded. Gary needs to know how well he did and how much he has improved, but most of all he needs to know what questions or examples he missed and why. Only then can he improve his performance. Workbooks are not tests. They are not "busy work." They are practice material designed to improve needed skills. A complete skills program begins with insight, recognizes application, and provides practice as needed.

Knowledge.   Mathematics as a discipline has a definite content of its own. There is considerable backlog of information that is basic to understanding and appreciating the relationship of numbers to daily living. The targets of the mathematics curriculum should go far beyond writing numerals, practicing on computational skills, learning rules, and getting answers to be checked as right or wrong.

Number as content is a basic principle of modern math. The curriculum includes basic vocabulary to communicate number relations. Understanding relations based on size, quantity, sequence, comparison, and prediction gives content to the discipline.

Background information adds meaning and appreciation to the use of number. Children are challenged by a look at primitive people and how they used numbers. A study of such primitive devices as ropes with knots, water clocks, tally marks, and digits proves interesting. Relating the "tenness" of our number system to the fact that we have ten digits on our appendages, and showing how early people used this as a basis for developing a number system, adds to the content of the discipline. A look at ancient civilizations where people studied the heavenly bodies and developed quite sophisticated calendars and time keeping devices relates number to history. A study of the number system with a base of 2 will help the learner understand the principle of a simple computer. Such knowledge may not necessarily make the pupil more skillful in manipulation of numbers, but it will make the whole discipline more meaningful and as a consequence serve as motivation for learning.

One of the most important values of the computer is its predictive possibilities. When home buyers compute interests or costs and compare them with anticipated income, they are able to predict ability to assume responsibilities and meet obligations. The computer has made it possible to predict movements of the heavenly bodies and land human beings on the moon.

Some information about the number system can be taught directly. Much of it is assimilated through experience. A number table in a classroom provides a learning center where children can handle objects, experiment with shapes and quantities, read signs, and study relationships as they manipulate materials. This type of setting invites children to ask why and what. It encourages their curiosity and helps them learn on their own. It takes the teaching of mathematics out of the category of a once-a-day textbook lesson followed by a workbook exercise, and puts it into a practical setting with application to daily activities. It adds knowledge to skill and makes the discipline product as well as process.

Attitudes and Understandings.   There is beauty in mathematics. One who learns to recognize it, appreciate it, and respect it has arrived at true understanding.

Recognition of the place of numbers comes first. Numerical relationships control the rhythm of music, the repetition of line and form in art, the movement of dance, and the pattern of poetry. Shumsky (27:146) says:

> The real goal for the learner is to "think" arithmetic and not merely to "do" arithmetic!

By that he means the learner should develop an understanding of how numbers work, how they influence life's patterns, and how they can be used to make life more fruitful.

Appreciation leads to application. The musician repeats a time sequence. The artist repeats a color pattern. The athlete times performance and synchronizes skills. The writer plans sequences and repetitions for emphasis and effect. The speaker uses pitch, pauses, and rate to create an effect or convey a message. All these are related to the discipline of mathematics.

Respect for the power of numbers leads the youngster to streamline the boat model, the costume designer to use line to create an illusion of height or width, and the cook to alter a recipe. All these are examples of making mathematics serve a purpose based on attitudes toward life. Developing a profound respect for how number knowledge can influence our lives and how we can use it for our own aims is a vital target for the teaching of mathematics in the elementary school.

How to Organize for Effective Teaching and Learning

Mathematics learnings are directly related to the rest of the curriculum. The daily plans should be made accordingly. This also involves pointing out the applications in the other areas of the curriculum. While mathematics is a sequential discipline, some of the learnings can be used as the problems arise. This calls for effective use of a planned program plus incidental application in real situations. Since the content of the mathematics curriculum has tended to change over the current two decades, a different approach from the one we used a few years ago or from the way we were taught when we were in school is required.

Relation to Other Areas of the Curriculum. We have already given numerous examples of the uses we have for mathematics in our daily lives. Sometimes the problems in the mathematics textbook lack relevancy either because the situations presented are not within the experiences of the children, or because the book is outdated and the situations, the prices, and the facts are no longer true to life. In such cases you either may adjust the content or justify it to the pupils for the purpose of practice. Advertisements from the daily paper are one way of updating the facts. This makes mathematics real and puts it within the experience of the pupil. The same use can be made of mail-order catalogs. By using such sources, the pupils can be led to apply the principles presented in the textbook to make up their own problems.

Mathematics is related to other subjects in the curriculum. Mathematics principles are used all day long whether the time schedule says "mathematics" for that particular period or not. In geography the children may compare sizes of countries or cities from the tables given in the appendix, compute distances using the scale of miles accompanying the map, figure latitude and longitude as a means of locating places, or compare annual rainfall or mean average temperatures as a means of drawing conclusions and predicting conditions. In history they may compare dates to determine which leaders were contemporaries, construct a time line to show sequences of events, or compute time to find out how long a given period lasted, how much time elapsed between one event and another, or how much overlap there was between relevant events. This calls for using the fundamental processes to answer real questions.

In science they will need numbers to use formulae, perform experiments, compare, keep records, and draw conclusions. In music they will learn the time value of notes, rhythm patterns, and tempo. In art they will use geometric principles including parallels, perpendiculars, horizontals, plane surfaces, and perspective to show distance, size, or volume as well as third dimension. Also, they will use fractional concepts in balancing color schemes and points of emphasis in a composition. Even numbering the pages of a theme is a mathematical concept, and making a table of contents or an index carries the application one step farther. In physical education they will march to a rhythmic beat, count off for games, keep score, time performances, and measure growth. Even penmanship has an element of mathematics in it. Writing two spaces tall, one space tall, or estimating the middle for half space letters all are activities involving mathematical concepts. Spelling papers need to be numbered. Errors need to be counted. Percentages of accuracy can be figured. Quantitative thinking enters into practically everything the children do in every subject all day long. Pollak (21:325), writing in the *69th NSSE Yearbook*, offers one caution about such applications when he says:

> The major point which we have learned about applications of mathematics is that applications are about real things and must be connected honestly to the real world.

Mathematics has its place in the schedule. In Chap. 2 we discussed the daily schedule. Should mathematics be pinpointed for a specific time daily? When should it be scheduled? Morning? Afternoon? Before the other content areas? The choice is yours. Two exceptions are if you are working in a school situation where special teachers come and go and you have to plan your schedule around theirs or if you are working in a cooperative situation where some reorganization is done along subject-matter lines and it is necessary for a group of teachers to plan for mathematics to come at the same period daily. The important point is that mathematics gets done. If interest is high and the will to learn is present, the work can be done at any time of day. Mathematics, however, is a sequential subject and needs to be pursued daily. One might pursue a special interest in literature with concentrated attention for a week or so and accomplish something, but that is not true in mathematics. And the part of mathematics that calls for practice is served better by a program that calls for frequent spaced drill periods rather than long concentrated periods. For these reasons you will have mathematics included in your daily schedule for an allotted amount of time and at a regular time each day.

Whether you adhere rigidly to the schedule or keep it flexible enough to capitalize on the uses in daily life and in other areas of the curriculum partly depends on you and how well you can discipline yourself to keep records and make sure the curriculum targets are met. Most teachers find it advantageous in a sequential subject like mathematics to follow a basic text for content and a set time for the daily work allowing for deviations to meet the varying needs of individuals. Some will not be ready for the level of work assigned and some will find it insufficient to challenge their abilities or to fill their time. Even with a textbook and a schedule you will still need to plan carefully for individual differences in ability, level, and rate of work. A block of time reserved on the schedule should suffice. What goes into that block of time is the problem you must solve in terms of the needs and abilities of the pupils. Some may pursue individual programs. Some may participate in group practices. Some presentations may be made to a small group. It will be an unusual class in which you find it expedient to present a new topic, such as division of fractions, to the whole room at once.

In discussing the function of the textbook or of a detailed course of study, Willoughby (21:279) in the *69th NSSE Yearbook* points out that in a sequential subject like mathematics it is well to have some overall plan. He suggests that in a large school where several teachers are involved at a given level, it is advantageous to have some uniformity. This does not restrict you to a day-by-day lesson plan prescribed by a textbook or a supervisor. He suggests that the classroom teacher should be given as much freedom as possible in determining activities for the pupils and that sometimes more than one textbook might be used, or occasionally no textbook. He concludes, however, that:

> The teacher should have some overall, community-wide plan in mind as he guides individual children through their study of mathematics, and he should report to the next teacher any major deviations from such a plan.

Mathematics is a sequential discipline which calls for a predetermined order of some topics. Wilson (32:211–212) recognizes the sequential development of the program in mathematics when he points out that:

> Mathematics is more dependent than many fields on published materials; consequently, the curriculum director's options are directly related to what the commercial press makes available for adoption or adaptation. (p. 211)

He then identifies a number of commercial options available and suggests that the commercial competition may be both beneficial and restrictive. He recognizes the need for sequences prescribed by the nature of the subject matter and suggests the organization of curriculum targets around the sequential nature of the discipline itself rather than around the developmental pattern or experiential background of the learners.

To what degree one approach can supercede the other is a matter for consideration, but it must be recognized that in mathematics more than in some other areas, learnings are built one on another and demand an element of sequence. It would be a waste of time to attempt to teach the process of long division to children who had not yet mastered the concept of subtraction because they will be using the process in their calculations. Similarly, teaching them the fundamental processes in the use of decimal fractions would be frustrating if they could not handle these same processes with whole numbers. While automatic mastery of the basic combinations in addition, subtraction, multiplication, and division may be seen in a different light when taught by the discovery method and the skill may come about through repeated use rather than in anticipation of use, still children who have to count on their fingers or look on a table for the product of 6 and 7 will be greatly hampered in the attempt to multiply a number like 468 by 75. When mastery of one step is achieved, the learners are ready to move on to the next. In using the previously learned skill, they may further improve mastery. Beauchamp (3:70) suggests that "grade placement assignment of topics is but a means of distributing the package." But in that same connection, Ragan (24:349) points out that:

> Experimental programs dealing with elementary school mathematics have caused a revision of notions about the inherent difficulty of topics and subjects.

Traditional Versus Modern Math.   During the current two decades, much of the revision that has entered the curriculum at the elementary level in the area of mathematics has centered around what has come to be known as "modern math." The pressures for change have come from scholars in the discipline rather than from the educators in the classroom. Much of it has grown out of concern for standards in subject matter. It has been influenced somewhat by the work of such scholars as Bruner studying the process of education and Piaget studying the thinking of children. Many parents and laypeople are confused about the terminology. Many traditional teachers are concerned about their need for updating their own learnings. Many children are confused by the change of program in their sequence of learning. Publishers have put considerable effort into providing suitable material for this new emphasis in mathematics. A look at the chart in Fig. 9–3 will help to make some comparisons of modern math with traditional programs in arithmetic. The success of the program depends largely on the ability of the teacher to use the materials and the concepts in a meaningful way with the children. If the new terms in modern math are reduced to verbalisms that the children can "mouth" in a rote fashion, little of value has been accomplished. It is an interesting observation that "good" teachers traversing the road of modern math with children for the first time are probably doing their best work because they are "discovering" the principles with the children. On the next round, the teachers already have made the discoveries and since they already know, there is the danger that they will merely tell instead of leading the pupils to make the discoveries for themselves.

AREA	TRADITIONAL MATH	MODERN MATH
Aims	Skill in computation Mastery of facts Knowledge of subject matter Mental discipline	Insight into the structure of the discipline Precise terminology for naming the concepts Reasoning
Content	Number names Number sequence Computation Notation and numeration Fundamental processes	Vocabulary and sets Theory and logic Principles of association, distribution, and commuta tion Generalizations
Approaches	Present the facts Memorize the processes Drill for perfection and skill Use processes to solve problems	Meet the situation Experiment with possibilities Discover the patterns and the principles Practice for needed skills
Procedures	Explain the processes Provide repetitive drill Test and reteach Memorize rules and formulae Use deductive reasoning Move from definition to theorem	Set the stage Lead the children to experiment Question for insight and understanding Help them draw conclusions Encourage more than one way Use inductive reasoning Move from theorem to definition
Outcomes	Mastery of skills Rote learning Routine application	Insight into the structure of the discipline Appreciation for the orderliness of number relations Independence in approaching new concepts
Advantages	Quick Accurate Easily tested for mastery Objective measurement Parents think they understand it	Leads to: permanent learnings interest for the learner challenge for the teacher independence for future learnings appreciation for the disci- pline of mathematics
Limitations	Learner becomes dependent on rules and rote Subject becomes dull and boring to creative child Pupil lacks insight which leads to independence Provides drill on computation better done by tables or the computer	Takes longer to arrive at mastery of the process Permits trial and error and inaccuracies while insights are being established Real objectives are not easily measured by objective tests Less emphasis on computation Parents do not understand

Figure 9-3. *Traditional versus modern math: comparison and contrast.*

Opinions differ on the significance of the introduction of so-called modern math into the elementary curriculum. Doll (12:121) predicts as follows:

> In the elementary schools, attention to the "new Mathematics" is continuing. Some efforts are being made to achieve a balance between the newer and the more traditional arithmetics. The search for a truly spiral curriculum in mathematics is continuing. In many classrooms where teachers understand the 'whys' of mathematics, the reasons underlying the principles, and practices are being taught along with ways of working. In-service education of teachers in mathematics continues its upswing.

Neagley (22:295) says:

> The new mathematics will continue in popularity during the next two decades. Children in the elementary school will learn to appreciate the meaning of the language of mathematics, but there will be a growing re-emphasis on its utilitarian values.

Wilson (32:210) says:

> The evolution from traditional to modern (the new math) has reached a point of no return. Yet, many educators are convinced that much of the "new math" is not really new. . . . The variations are in technique—not the discipline.

Manning (20:220) expresses considerable skepticism about the value of the "new math" in the elementary school curriculum. He says:

> A substantial portion of the revolution in elementary mathematics has now occurred, leaving some happy, some gasping, some alienated, and some merely bewildered. Was this radical curriculum change wise and well conceived, or did it take a wrong and unfortunate turn? In general the movement seems to be regarded as acceptable, and it amuses one to wonder whether the widespread acceptance is based upon solid convictions that the changes were in fact good, or whether the situation reflects instead a general condition of confusion, apathy, and mass capitulation.

Manning also brands as "nonsense" the use of symbols (20:223), the introduction of formal logic into elementary school mathematics (20:224), the teaching of place system of numeration in bases other than 10, the computational algorithms in these other bases (20:224), educating elementary children as though all these learnings applied to all of them (20:224), and the stress on the distinction between number and numeral (20:224). He suggests that some of the mathematicians who started "this nonsense" are now recanting. (20:225). He concludes that (20:224 and 236):

The emphasis should be upon understanding, use, and skill, not on abstract patterns (p. 224).

Whatever form mathematics takes in the elementary school in the years to come, problem solving will still be of major importance (p. 236).

Relation of Math to Learning. When you face your children in a classroom, you will be setting curriculum targets for them. Whether you ask them to learn facts by rote or to develop insight into the concepts will be determined by what you really believe about how mathematics is learned and what the goals are.

Rote learning must be reexamined. It assumes that skills are essential, that responses must be automatic, and that mastery of the facts must precede their use in problem-solving situations. Rote learning may yield immediate results on test scores, but one needs to press beyond immediate results to find out how these learnings are applied and how lasting they are. Beauchamp says: (3:61)

> There is always the danger when dealing with the fundamental processes that the pupil will learn to utilize the skills in only a rote and meaningless manner. For this reason, curriculum planners and classroom teachers must do everything in their power to insure that the meanings of the concepts involved are taught prior to the use of drill processes.

And Haan (15:203) pushes the matter of rote learning versus meaningful learning beyond that point into creativity when he says:

> Few of us have any notion what it is to be creative in the field of mathematics. Partly because of this we have tended to emphasize rote learning and deductive kinds of teaching in mathematics.

Discovery learning is recommended. If Bob has twelve blocks, pencils, apples, or any other concrete object he is ready to make discoveries about the number 12. If he arranges them in a long row and counts them, he is learning sequence and rational counting. If he arranges them in groups, thus:

11 and 1, 10 and 2, 9 and 3, 8 and 4, 7 and 5, 6 and 6,
1 and 11, 2 and 10, 3 and 9, 4 and 8, 5 and 7,

he is discovering the various combinations that make 12 and also the commutative principle. If he arranges them in the groups showing multiples thus:

2 groups of 6 each	3 groups of 4 each
6 groups of 2 each	4 groups of 3 each

he is discovering the multiplication concept. Or he can reverse this process and discover the principles of division. He can carry the division process further and discover both the partition concept and the measurement concept by dividing the twelve pencils among six boys and counting the number each boy receives, or by giving two pencils to each of the boys and counting how many boys received pencils. He can move one step farther by using thirteen pencils and discovering that when he divides by 2, 3, 4, or 6 he has one left over or remaining. Through such multiplication of concrete objects, he adds meaning. Through discovery he gains insight into principles which he can apply to new situations. Through repetition of the processes he gains practice resulting in skill. All mathematics learnings can be presented through the discovery approach by means of inductive reasoning. The values come in the understanding.

Ragan (24:327, 347), in speaking of discovery learning, emphasizes thinking and points out the role of the teacher as follows:

> Emphasis on the discovery approach shifted the interest in teaching mathematics as a way of doing something toward teaching mathematics as a way of thinking (p. 327).
> Since it is not possible for pupils to acquire all the information available in the field of mathematics, the role of the teacher has become increasingly one of helping pupils develop the skills, understandings, and concepts that will enable them to become increasingly self-propelling during a lifetime of learning (p. 347).

In advocating discovery learning as a creative type of teaching, Shumsky (27:143, 148) says:

> Too often, teachers undermine the process of discovery through manipulation by calling for articulation of rules before the learner is ready to structure them (p. 143).
> When movement toward the ultimate formula is rushed, the end result tends to be a mechanistic adherence to a rule with no insight into the structure (p. 148).

Smith (28:179) also links creativity with discovery learning in mathematics when he says:

> In learning mathematics the elementary school child no longer is asked to remember long lists of facts and rules. He is, instead, placed in the most creative of situations. He goes through stages of manipulating and exploring materials. He gains insight into concepts and algorithms. He learns through discovery.

Present day elementary programs recognize a philosophy based on meaning, discovery, and insight. Wilson (32:213) lists titles of currently published programs to demonstrate this point thus:

Modern Arithmetic Through Discovery—Silver Burdett
Seeing Through Arithmetic—Scott Foresman
New Mathematics—Ginn and Co.
Discovering Mathematics—Merrill
Modern School Mathematics, Structure and Use—Houghton Mifflin

One example of discovery learning is illustrated in Fig. 9–4. This table should be built up with the children one row at a time so that they discover one new principle before they are exposed to the next. From the table the children can organize what they have discovered about the multiplication facts. This will help them see order in the system. It will also serve as a motivating device because they can see the task becoming progressively easier as they go along. This will also help them to reiterate the commutative principle as illustrated in 4 × 8 and 8 × 4. This same principle can be applied to the organization of the addition and subtraction facts, fractional relationships, percentages, and decimal fractions.

	0	1	2	3	4	5	6	7	8	9	Sub-totals	Cumulative Totals
0	0	0	0	0	0	0	0	0	0	0	19 facts, all new all answers 0	19
1	0	1	2	3	4	5	6	7	8	9	19 facts, 17 new 9 new answers	36
2	0	2	4	6	8	10	12	14	16	18	19 facts, 15 new 8 new answers	51
3	0	3	6	9	12	15	18	21	24	27	19 facts, 13 new 7 new answers	64
4	0	4	8	12	16	20	24	28	32	36	19 facts, 11 new 6 new answers	75
5	0	5	10	15	20	25	30	35	40	45	19 facts, 9 new 5 new answers	84
6	0	6	12	18	24	30	36	42	48	54	19 facts, 7 new 4 new answers	91
7	0	7	14	21	28	35	42	49	56	63	19 facts, 5 new 3 new answers	96
8	0	8	16	24	32	40	48	56	64	72	19 facts, 3 new 2 new answers	99
9	0	9	18	27	36	45	54	63	72	81	19 facts, 1 new 1 new answer	100

Total number of combinations 100
Zero times any number = zero 19
1 times any number = the number itself | 19
Any number times 1 = the number itself |
Number of different answers 46
Number of commutative pairs 36
Number of doubles 10

Figure 9–4. *Table of products of one-digit numerals.*

SUMMARY

The objective of the elementary-school mathematics program is to teach children to think quantitatively. In order to do this, children need to learn the language of number, counting and sequencing, computing and estimating, and understanding of the principles. As they do this, they will be able to read number language intelligently, compute accurately and quickly, and understand how the system works. This calls for the teaching of skills, that is, how to do it; the knowledge, that is, the facts; and the understandings and attitudes which determine what kinds of thinkers they will be.

In the past the mathematics program put the emphasis on facts and skills. The trend toward modern math has been in full swing for almost two decades and the emphasis is on precise vocabulary, insight into the system and how it works, and appreciation of the discipline. Both traditional and modern math have their merits and their limitations. The success of either approach is dependent on your understanding and your skill as a teacher. If you relate the work to life both in and out of the classroom, devote adequate time to the subject, and adjust the content to the needs and abilities of the pupils, the learnings will be assured. If you see the advantages of discovery learning over rote learning, you will provide the pupils with objects for manipulation and concrete experiences for understanding. You will lead them through inductive thinking to discover the principles for themselves. Through repeated use the skills will emerge.

SUGGESTED ACTIVITIES

Select one or more items from the following list of suggestions to follow through as an application of mathematical concepts.

1. Make a list of all the uses you find for numbers in your activities for one full day.
2. Make a collection of words which have meanings in their mathematical settings different from their meanings when used in other situations. For example:
   left hand—how many *left*
   peck on the window—a *peck* of grain
   less able—three *less* than
3. Prepare a report on time keeping devices throughout history; for instance, kinds of clocks or kinds of calendars.
4. Prepare a report on the history of money as a medium of exchange.
5. Make a collection of monetary units used throughout the world today. Prepare a table of their relative values.

6. Select some examples of two-step and three-step problems from an elementary-school textbook in arithmetic.

   For each example illustrate more than one way to arrive at a solution.

7. Consult five teachers for their opinions on modern math. Summarize your findings and share with the class.

8. Consult five parents for their opinions of modern math. Summarize your findings and share with the class.

9. Select one subject area in the elementary curriculum and identify as many uses for number as you can find in its study. For example:

geography	music	physical education
history	art	science

10. Write two lesson plans showing how you would develop a specific skill such as adding unlike fractions, carrying from one's place to ten's place in addition, or dividing when there is a remainder.

    Develop the first lesson plan as an inductive discovery learning process.

    Develop a second lesson plan as a deductive rote learning process.

    Explain the difference.

SELECTED READINGS

1. ARMSTRONG, JAMES W., *Mathematics for Elementary School Teachers*, New York: Harper & Row, 1968. The theory of arithmetic from the point of view of the elementary teacher. Takes up mathematics topics one by one and shows how to develop them. Emphasizes importance of subject-matter scholars and professional educators in teacher preparation.

2. BARNEY, LEROY, "The First and Third R's," in *Today's Education*, Vol. 62, No. 3, Mar. 1973. pp. 57–58. Presents the importance of reading in arithmetic, concept load, vocabulary, interpretation, and application to arithmetic skills.

3. BEAUCHAMP, GEORGE A., *The Curriculum of the Elementary School*, Boston: Allyn and Bacon, 1964. Chapter 4 outlines the mathematics program and suggests grade placement of topics.

4. BRIGHT, GEORGE W., and CAROL ANN JONES, "Teaching Children to Think Metric," in *Today's Education*, Vol. 62, No. 4, Apr. 1973, pp. 16–19. Describes procedures used with a fourth grade class to clarify concepts in the use of the metric system.

5. BRUNER, JEROME S., *Toward a Theory of Instruction*, New York: W. W. Norton & Co., 1966. Chapter 6 on theory of instruction gives examples from the discipline of mathematics.

6. COLLIER, CALHOUN C. and HAROLD H. LERCH, *Teaching Mathematics in the Modern Elementary School*, London: Collier-Macmillan, Ltd. 1969. A conservative book based on fundamental processes. Stresses structure. Points out the way in which today's mathematics is going. Surveys current texts.

7. CONKLIN, KENNETH R., "Why Prefer the New Math?" in *Educational Forum*, Vol. XXV, No. 4, May 1971, pp. 439–46. Reviews the trends during the past decade. Compares and contrasts traditional math and new math. Gives reasons for its success.

8. COPELAND, RICHARD W., *How Children Learn Mathematics: Teaching Implications of Piaget's Research*, New York: Macmillan, 1970. As the title suggests, an attempt to show how Piaget's theories apply to the learning of mathematics.

9. D'AUGUSTINE, CHARLES H., *Multiple Methods of Teaching Mathematics in the Elementary School*, New York: Harper & Row, 1968. Points out different ways of teaching same content.

10. DEANS, EDWINA, "The Laboratory Approach to Elementary Mathematics," in *Today's Education*, Vol. 60, No. 2, Feb. 1971, pp. 20–22. Setting up the laboratory, enrichment materials, horizontal and vertical organization, enjoyment in collecting materials, limited funds, listening centers, special rooms, and evaluation.

11. DELON, FLOYD G., "A Field Test of Computer-Assisted Instruction in First Grade Mathematics," in *Educational Leadership*, Vol. 28, No. 3, Nov. 1970, pp. 170–80. Research report. Results: Measurable benefits in the form of increased achievements by disadvantaged first grade pupils resulting from the use of computer-assisted instruction in mathematics.

12. DOLL, RONALD C., *Curriculum Improvement, Decision Making and Process*, Boston: Allyn and Bacon, 1970. Part Two discusses the process in curriculum improvement and the roles of the various people including the classroom teacher.

13. DUMAS, ENOCH, *Math Activities for Child Involvement*, Boston: Allyn and Bacon, 1971. Practical classroom activities, construction projects, games, puzzles, riddles, tricks, verses, and music for K-6.

14. GLENNON, VINCENT J., "Current Status of the New Math," in *Educational Leadership*, Vol. 30, No. 7, Apr. 1973, pp. 604–08. Reviews history of the "new" approach to math. Sees it as aimed at the above average student. Evaluates results up to now and makes predictions for the future.

15. HAAN, AUBREY, *Elementary School Curriculum: Theory and Research*, Boston: Allyn and Bacon, 1961. Chapter 8 emphasizes thinking as a mathematical process. Points out importance of accuracy.

16. HALLERBERG, "The Metric System; Past, Present—Future?" in *The Arithmetic Teacher*, Vol. XX, Apr. 1973, pp. 247–255. Describes origin and development of the metric system and concludes that it is a program whose time has come in the schools of the U.S.

17. HICKS, WM. VERNON, *et. al.*, *The New Elementary School Curriculum*, New York: Van Nostrand Reinhold, 1970. Chapter 3 identifies theories of math instructions and gives concrete examples.

18. JONES, PHILIP G., "Metrics: Schools Will be Teaching it and You'll be Living it—Very, Very Soon," in *The American School Board Journal*, Vol. XLX, July 1973, pp. 21–27. Predicts early transition, estimates costs, and points out advantages.

19. KRAMER, KLAAS, *Problems in the Teaching of Elementary School Mathematics*, Boston: Allyn and Bacon, 1970. Anthology of materials from authorities in the field. Problems, background, issues.

20. MANNING, DUANE, *Toward a Humanistic Curriculum*, New York: Harper & Row, 1971. Chapter 12 is entitled "Making Mathematics Sensible," and is just that. Emphasizes meaning and discovery learning. Indicates mathematics should be both functional and fun.

21. National Society for the Study of Education, *Mathematics Education*, Sixty-Ninth Yearbook, Part I, Chicago: University of Chicago Press, 1970. Series of papers by authorities in the field. Reviews historical background, identifies curriculum content, and predicts the future.

22. NEAGLEY, ROSS L. and N. DEAN EVANS, *Handbook for Effective Curriculum Development*, Englewood Cliffs, N.J.: Prentice-Hall, 1967. Puts curriculum decisions into everyday practice. The practical approach is pertinent to the area of mathematics.

23. PARKER, CECIL, and LOUIS J. RUBIN, *Process as Content: Curriculum Design and the Application of Knowledge*, Chicago: Rand McNally, 1966. Sees the process of learning as content for learning. Gives illustrations from the discipline of mathematics.

24. RAGAN, WILLIAM B. and CELIA BURNS STENDLER, *Modern Elementary Curriculum*, New York: Holt, Rinehart and Winston, 1966. Chapter 11 is on quantitative relationships. Describes projects in operation.

25. REISMAN, FREDRICK K., *A Guide to the Diagnostic Teaching of Arithmetic*, Columbus, Ohio: Charles E. Merrill, 1972. Sample lesson plans, diagnostic inventory, teaching techniques, analysis of common errors.

26. SCHULT, VERYL and JAMES D. GATES, "Mathematical Education: Yesterday and Today," in *Today's Education*, Vol. 59, No. 9, Dec. 1970, pp. 50–51. Questions and answers about new programs, materials, textbooks, and changes.

27. SHUMSKY, ABRAHAM, *Creative Teaching in the Elementary School*, New York: Appleton-Century-Crofts, 1965. Chapter 6 on arithmetic contrasts repetitive and creative teaching.

28. SMITH, JAMES A., *Setting Conditions for Creative Teaching in the Elementary School*, Boston: Allyn and Bacon, 1966. Identifies creativity and suggests ways to nurture it.

29. SUID, MURRAY, "Starting Points: Classroom Ideas with Teaching Posters," *Learning Magazine*, Vol. 1, No. 4, Feb. 1973, pp. 31–42. Presents ideas for teaching about size, measuring and the coming of the metric revolution. Gives a brief history of the metric system, explains metric conversions, and raises the question of what we are going to do about it in our country, and in our schools.

30. TROUTMAN, ANDRIA PRICE, "Strategies for Teaching Elementary School Mathematics," in *The Arithmetic Teacher*, Vol. XX, Oct. 1973, pp. 425–36. Outlines six specific strategies for the improvement of the teaching of mathematics.

31. UNDERHILL, ROBERT G., *Teaching Elementary School Mathematics*, Columbus, Ohio: Charles E. Merrill, 1972. Programmed chapters, behavioral objectives, self tests, methodology.

32. WILSON, L. CRAIG, *The Open Access Curriculum*, Boston: Allyn and Bacon, 1971. Chapter 12 describes elementary programs and the implications of mathematics for an open curriculum.

10

PRESENTING THE ARTS AND HUMANITIES

Developing an Appreciation of Our Cultural Background

Courtesy, Lowell School, Mesa, Arizona

THE HUMANITIES

What does it mean to be human? Why is there increased emphasis on humanism in the curriculum? How do human beings differ from other forms of animal life? What is the responsibility of the school in cultivating humanism?

Will you teach art in your own classroom? Or will it be taught by a specialist? How about music? Drama? Dance? And other forms of expressive arts? If you must teach it yourself, will you have a curriculum guide? Will you have a special place on the program for it? Will there be a textbook? How will you decide what to teach? And when? And how?

What about your own philosophy of education? Have you established one yet? Do you really know what values you hold? How can you help the children establish their own values about good and bad, right and wrong, relevancy, and worthiness? Will you have a time for it, or will it emerge as a part of the total curriculum? How can you be sure it gets done?

How many of the children will eventually become performers in the arts? Is appreciation of the arts enough? How can you provide for both? And how will you work with creative children? Are they necessarily different? How do they fit into the routine you have established?

Are you accountable? Must humanism be measured? If so, how? If not, how can you justify it? Yes, people are human. Skills and facts are not enough. Consider the humanities a part of the total curriculum.

If you believe that each child is a human being, an individual entitled to his or her place in the world, then you will be willing to assume some responsibility for helping each one recognize that place, develop a positive self image, and establish a position in relation to fellow human beings. That is the concern in the teaching of the humanities. Each individual is a part of an on-going stream of human heritage, including culture, and each person has an investment in the future. In order to live life at its fullest, one needs to know something of the background of human development, to be able to participate in the richness of life, and to see a vision of a better life ahead for posterity. When people learn to live beyond self interests and try to make the world a better place for their having been here for a period of time, then they are truly humanistic in their relations with others. The trend toward humanizing the curriculum has given new impetus to cultural pursuits. It is affecting what is being taught and what is happening in the elementary classrooms today. This chapter is planned to give you perspective on these trends and to show you how you can plan your children's experiences toward that end.

WHAT ARE THE HUMANITIES?

The humanities include those branches of knowledge concerned with people and their cultures, such as philosophy, literature, and the fine arts. They are distinguished from the sciences in that they deal with the ethical and the aesthetic rather than with the scientific and the practical. Wilson (27:224) identifies them as "expressions of man's creative nature." They include a study of how human beings have expressed themselves through the ages and how they use these modes of expression in their daily lives.

How People Have Expressed Themselves Through the Ages

From earliest time human beings have shown evidence of the need to express observations and ideas. They have used various forms of expression, many of which have come down through the ages as a record of the development of civilization. Some of these forms can be experienced through the senses. Some can only be imagined. Historical remains have been preserved and restored. Museums have been established. Records have been kept. Societies have been formed for the perpetuation of those ideas people have valued. Learning about them in the elementary classroom helps children gain perspective and appreciate their heritage. Sometimes it even stimulates them to contribute to the preservation of what is, or the creation of what might be. There are many media for expression.

Art and Architecture.   Art has long been established as a part of human heritage. People use drawing, design, ceramics, crafts, painting, figure drawing, sculpture, water color, and some art history. They delve into ancient architecture, study line, shape, color, and texture, and go to see museum collections. Values are expressed through landscaping, construction materials, and form. Mitchel, writing in the *Sixty-fourth Yearbook of the National Society for the Study of Education* (13:225), suggests that children should learn *about* art as well as *through* art if it is to have permanent value in their education.

Drama and Dance.   From ancient times human beings have used their bodies to interpret ideas and beliefs. For instance, many rituals performed through the dance represent various cultural beliefs; e. g. the rain dance, the dance of the harvest, the interpretations of the seasons, and so on. Before the time of the written word re-creations of significant events through impersonation and dramatization were used to relay the happenings and traditions of the people. These have been a part of human experiences through informal dramatization, play acting, role playing, and pantomime. Different cultures engage in folk dancing, modern dance, creative dance, creative dramatics, designing, stage setting, and play writing. They study the history of dance and drama. All these activities help students gain appreciation of the heritage of the past, understanding of attempts to communicate, and expansion of potential for personal development.

Language and Literature.   Language has been recognized as the most important single contribution to the development of civilization. Through language people have been able to communicate experiences, ideas, and hopes for the future. The advent of written language made it possible to preserve thoughts for future generations and to communicate with others in distant places. Wherever people have produced a civilization, a language has developed. There are many languages throughout the world. The mother tongue is the one the child finds in the environment while growing up. Acquiring more than one language is a learning process dependent on a bilingual environment or direct instruction. Language has been used not only to communicate with others but to preserve records. It is the means by which we communicate and preserve both information and ideas. One of our most significant contributions through language has been in the field of literature. Story telling has taken the form of both prose and poetry. Folk tales passed down through the ages have been collected and preserved as a literary heritage. Contributions of great authors have been printed in books. Libraries are storehouses of literary treasures.

Music.   When primitive tribes beat out their first rhythm or used their voices to express feeling through pitch or tone quality, they were using music to communicate. When they invented instruments to express musical ideas, they were laying the foundation for today's orchestras and bands. When they expressed superstitions and beliefs through music, they were providing the beginnings of today's sacred music. When they used tone, pitch, and tempo, as well as rhythm to recreate concepts of emotional experiences, they were offering the beginnings of classical music. When they engaged in group experiences, they were starting the earliest forms of choral music. When they set traditional tales to simple music, they were starting the popular folk music of today. When people listen to or recreate musical forms, they are reliving the history of the human race and gaining an insight into the emotional experiences expressed through this medium. The learning of history, theory, notation, and composition will lead to the understanding of these experiences. Music has long been an important part of daily life.

Philosophy.   An area in which actuality exists only in the realm of the mind is known as philosophy. It deals with intangibles in the form of beliefs or theories. It cannot be experienced through the senses, but it does influence beliefs and actions in human relations based on accepted values. Philosophy is concerned with ideas, beliefs, theories, logic, and values.

How We Use the Humanities Today

The study of humanities is not relegated to museums and ancient history. Human relations are a vital living part of every day existence. The person who learns to understand and appreciate the expressions of others and to use the various media to express feelings and ideas is an effective individual. Kelley, writing for an ASCD yearbook (1:9–20) refers to this phase of development as "the fully functioning self," and Rogers (1:21–33) identifies the process as "becoming a fully functioning person." Combs (1:50–64) adds to this by describing a perceptual view of the adequate personality as one with a positive view of self. The person with such a viewpoint can identify with others and is open to experience and acceptance. In order to be this kind of person the child must learn to express ideas through the various media offered by the humanities, and to communicate feelings and ideas to others.

Expressing ideas. The expression of ideas calls for insight and independent thought. Skinner (21:173) says technology can only produce the material with which to think. He adds:

> A man who can execute behavior adequately is still not free if he must be told what to do and when to do it.

If children are to express ideas through the media of art, drama, dance, language, music, or philosophy, they must be led farther than the mere rote learning of the expressions of others. They must be led to think about experiences, to compare and contrast the thoughts of others, and to formulate their own ideas. They must be helped to see the humanities as tools they can use to create their own ways of expressing themselves as human beings.

Communicating with Others. A light under a bushel does little to brighten the environment. If the study of the humanities is to contribute to humanistic targets in curriculum development the learners must be able to communicate their thoughts, experiences, ideas, and feelings to others. They must learn to share enjoyment of rhythm and tone, appreciation of line, color, and form, understanding of feelings and emotions as presented in literary selections, and understanding of ideas through expression of personal beliefs and ideals. This is learned first through a study of what others have expressed, next through a repetition of what has been learned, and eventually through one's own creative self expression. When children become independent thinkers, doers as well as imitators, then they have learned to use the humanities as a part of self expression.

THE HUMANITIES IN THE ELEMENTARY CURRICULUM

If something is worth learning it is worth teaching. It is just as sensible to assume that children will assimilate their appreciation of the humanities through osmosis as to assume that they will learn arithmetic or reading without any direct instruction. True, they might "just pick it up," but too often incidental learning becomes accidental learning. There is a real need for planned curriculum targets in the areas of the humanities. Eisner, writing for the *NSSE Yearbook on Art Education*, (13:Chap. XIII), discusses trends and concludes that:

> We are now living in an age of science. Perhaps with vision in education it may also become an age of the arts.

And Neagley (14:300) points out that:

> The increased support of the Federal Government for elementary and secondary education and the creation of the National Foundation for the Arts and Humanities will.contribute greatly to the improvement of art and music offerings in the curriculum.
> By the 1980's all elementary schools will have specialists in art and music. Instead of being relegated to one or two periods per week, these important areas of the curriculum will be available to children on a daily basis.

Content to Be Included

A study of Fig. 10–1 will lend perspective to the reasons for including the humanities in the elementary curriculum. We have already identified five basic areas for curriculum planning. The chart develops each of these areas by first identifying the content to be taught. Then it presents the pupil first in the receptive role then in the expressive role.

Each area makes its contribution. Art and architecture appeal to the senses of sight and touch producing tangibles that can be preserved for repeated experiencing. Drama and dance make use of the body and the voice, appealing to the senses of sight and hearing. They may be preserved on tape or film for future enjoyment. Language and literature make use of the spoken or printed word. They may be preserved through rhythm, and tempo. The target of music teaching has changed from time to time. Ragan

(15:442) suggests it is the function of the elementary school to develop enjoyment in every child rather than to train a few professionals; and Shuster (20:359) contends that art and music do not provide legitimate areas of competition for children of elementary-school age. Philosophy may not be pursued as a formal course, but children will be influenced by the ideas they encounter, the theories and beliefs they consider, and the values they accept. As children generalize about what is good, what is polite, what is kind, what is important, what is right, and what is worthy, they are

AREA OF EMPHASIS	CONTENT	ACTIVITIES	
		THE LEARNER IN THE RECEPTIVE ROLE WILL BE	THE LEARNER IN THE EXPRESSIVE ROLE WILL BE
Art and Architecture	Pictures Sculpture Line Shape Form Color Texture	Observing Feeling Comparing Appreciating Knowing Understanding	Drawing Painting Sculptoring Modeling Designing Creating
Drama and Dance	Emotions Movement Rhythm Form Expression Dialogue	Watching Listening Empathizing Interpreting	Role playing Impersonating Dramatizing Dancing Creating
Language and Literature	Prose Poetry Speech Foreign Language Tradition	Listening Reading Enjoying Appreciating	Speaking Writing Composing Orating Interpreting Creating
Music	Vocal music Instrumentation Rhythm Tone Tempo History	Listening Watching Feeling Appreciating Emoting Understanding	Singing Playing Performing Moving Composing Creating
Philosophy	Ideas Beliefs Theories Logic Values	Recognizing Thinking Believing Valuing Accepting	Theorizing Reasoning Acting Expressing Creating

Figure 10-1.   *Perspective on the humanities in the elementary curriculum.*

learning to evaluate and accept what will become a philosophy of life. This will determine social relationships and moral values. It will influence political and religious beliefs, professional choices, family relationships, and use of leisure time.

The Roles of the Learners

Figure 10–2 brings into focus the values of the humanities in the curriculum. In all the areas listed the pupil needs to serve alternately in the receptive and the expressive roles to complete the cycle. These, then, are the justifications for including the humanities in the targets for the elementary curriculum. In pursuing these areas children learn to do, to know, and to become. They assume alternate roles of receiving and expressing. In order to move them into both roles you must plan definitely for classroom activities that will realize the goals.

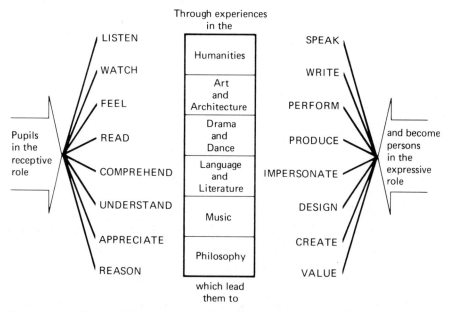

Figure 10-2. *The role of the humanities in the development of the individual.*

HOW TO TEACH THE HUMANITIES

Figure 10–3 differentiates among skills, knowledge, and attitudes to be developed in the areas of the humanities. In order to balance the program and provide needed experiences, you must know how to teach the various areas and how to organize the classroom and the curriculum targets for effective learning. We will be seeking answers to such questions

AREA	TO DO	TO KNOW	TO BE
Art and Architecture	The child will be able to: Draw Paint Weave Cut Paste Model Measure Cartoon Mix colors	The child will know about: Line Form Color Balance Proportion Perspective Materials Tools History	The child will develop: an appreciation of art forms an enjoyment in the ob- servation of art satisfaction in the use of art as a leisure time activity respect for contributions of others
Drama and Dance	The child will be able to: Role play Express emotions Dramatize Interpret characters Imitate objects Memorize Use body movement Use facial expression Balance React spontaneously	The child will know about: Voice control Gestures Expressions Use of stage settings Use of "props" History of dance Forms of expression	The child will develop: an appreciation for body movement as a form of expression enjoyment in participating through the use of own body responsibility as a member of an audience concern for the interests of others
Language and Literature	The child will be able to: read literature use language write ideas speak effectively use native tongue use a second language as needed	The child will know about: folk tales traditional stories legends myths lyric poetry narrative poetry Biblical literature	The child will develop: an appreciation for the contributions of authors love of good literature enjoyment in sharing wider interests worthy uses for leisure time

Music

The child will be able to:
- sing in tune
- play an instrument
- perform in a group
- perform before an audience
- read music

The child will know about:
- notation
- rhythm and time
- folk music
- sacred music
- classical music
- music history
- kinds of instruments
- great composers

The child will develop:
- a wide variety of interests in music in various forms
- enjoyment in listening
- enjoyment in performing
- respect for talent
- desire to improve

Philosophy

The child will be able to:
- think
- reason
- decide
- make choices
- act
- abide by own decisions
- evaluate
- judge

The child will know:
- good and bad
- right and wrong
- cause and effect
- logic
- theory
- values

The child will develop:
- logical thinking
- judgment
- willingness to abide by own decisions
- beliefs
- values
- satisfactions

Figure 10–3. *The place of the humanities in the elementary curriculum.*

as: What? When? How? and Who? What will be included? What time during the daily schedule? What portion of the school day? When in the year-by-year sequence? How to teach? What kinds of experiences? Who will do the teaching? What is the role of the specialist? What is the responsibility of the classroom teacher? How will the learnings be made functional in life both in and out of the classroom?

How to Develop the Concepts

Developing the concepts in the various curricular areas identified as the humanities calls for the ability to differentiate among doing, knowing, and being. A set of curriculum targets based on skills only makes the assumption that skills will automatically result in knowledge and attitudes, and furthermore that everyone needs the skills of the specialist in the area. Curriculum targets based on knowledge only assume that knowing will result in the needed practice that brings skill and in appreciating. Curriculum targets based on appreciation only begin on the assumption that the humanities are for spectators only and that to appreciate the contributions of others is sufficient for a full life. This misses the point that understandings and appreciations are deepened and enriched through increased knowledge, and through at least enough skill to understand what the specialist is doing. The curriculum in the elementary classroom needs to be balanced to provide some elements of all three approaches. Since we have already identified the areas of the curriculum and have established purposes, let us vary our approach in this section by looking at them as a group under the headings of skills, knowledge, and attitudes.

Developing Skills.   Skill implies how-to-do-it. It goes even farther and suggests doing it well, or with enough competency to make use of the learning in an accomplished manner.

One learns skill in *art* by practicing repeatedly the principles of perspective, by mixing colors, by modeling, and by trying the effects of various shapes and textures. This calls for a supply of all kinds of tools and materials, many of which are readily available without cost. Thus the learner will discover such principles as proportions of the human body, the horizon line, relative sizes, plasticity of materials, and the importance of arrangement and balance.

One learns skill in *drama and dance* by taking part in play acting, role playing, body movement, vocal expression, and informal appearances before a peer audience, where interpretation is more important than finished performance. Such opportunities present themselves in telling or pantomiming how a character might speak, how a fallen tree might feel, and how the wind moves.

Taking a turn at the easel is part of good citizenship in the classroom. This young painter is putting the finishing strokes on his "masterpiece." (Courtesy, Skiff School, Phoenix, Arizona)

One learns skill in *language and literature* through reading and listening, speaking and writing. Mastery of the native language or a second language depends on constant use. Literary selections become familiar through repeated experiences in reading, dramatizing, and discussing.

One learns skill in *music* through active participation. Knowing how is one thing, performing well requires enough repetition to insure automatic response, which comes only with purposeful practice.

Even skill in the field of *philosophy* depends on practice in thinking and reasoning. Children need opportunities to think their way through, decide what to do, and give reasons for actions. Opportunities for developing these skills present themselves in such situations as creating representations of reality, expressing ideas through body movement and speech, and making decisions about materials and actions. There are many opportunities for facing problems and for thinking and making decisions. It is your responsibility to see that they are used.

These skills are itemized in the "To Do" column of Fig. 10–3.

Accumulating Knowledge. Accurate information is necessary before skills can be mastered and attitudes formed. Practice based on inaccurate information or lack of information may result in useless or even harmful skills. Formulation of opinions, feelings, or attitudes without sufficient information results in prejudices, gullibility to propaganda, and emotional reactions. It is part of your responsibility to make sure knowledge is correct and relevant.

In *art* some knowledge can be discovered and some can be relayed through direct instruction. Knowledge thus gleaned can be applied to practice and understanding.

In *drama and dance* knowledge comes through experimentation and observation. Thus children learn to react to an audience, speak clearly, use gestures, make-up, and costumes, and recognize story settings.

In *language and literature* knowledge comes through repeated experiences in both the receptive and expressive roles. Children need to hear stories and poems from the time they are old enough to sit on the lap of a parent or other significant adult and help hold the book. The person who has experienced literary selections as a child will grow up to be the reader or listener who will understand such references as "opening Pandora's Box," "skating on thin ice," "turning into a pillar of salt," "building a house on the sand," "sleeping twenty years," "speaking for yourself, John," and "crossing the River Styx."

In *music* knowledge is essential to correct practice. Approaches to the teaching of music have changed from one of skill and drill to one of participating and enjoying, but with either approach knowledge will improve skill and deepen appreciation. Knowledge of principles, instruments, and history expands application.

Even logic and theory in *philosophy* can be planned and taught. Such understanding grows out of questions based on why, what if, and how. Seeing cause and effect, making choices, and justifying actions are basic.

These evidences of knowledge are listed in the "To Know" column of Fig. 10-3.

Developing Attitudes. Learning facts for a test is not enough. Mastering skills for performance is not enough. Unless pupils reach the point where they appreciate, understand, and desire the material, learning will go no farther than the daily lesson, the end of the course, or graduation. The goal of the humanities is the development of individuals who see human relations as important and themselves as both observers and participators as well as creators. It is through the humanities that one develops values that will influence use of leisure time, creative efforts, decisions, relations with others, and satisfactions from life itself. Goertzel and Goertzel (7:1962), in *Cradles of Eminence*, report on backgrounds of creative people and conclude that almost every conceivable handicap has been successfully overcome by some eminent person. This may imply that meeting problems and overcoming obstacles could be more significant than a rich background and plentiful materials in a sheltered environment. Torrance (25:28) says correlation tends to be low between measures of creativity and measure of intelligence, and Frost (4:184-5) indicates that the creative person is more likely to engage in divergent thinking. Getzels and Jackson (6:52) concluded that creative adolescents seem to enjoy risk and uncertainty in contrast to the high IQ adolescent who seems to be more concerned about the security of the "right" answer. These attitudes and understandings are itemized in the "To Be" column of Fig. 10–3.

How to Organize for Teaching

You still have to see the total program in perspective in order to establish the targets that will result in presenting the arts and the humanities effectively and in helping the pupil to appreciate humanity's cultural background. That means seeing this portion of the curriculum in relation to the other areas and even beyond. It means this part of the life of the child will lead beyond the school environment during school years and on into adult life. Getting organized for teaching is important. The following suggestions are designed to help you do just that.

The work bench and the tools were utilized in stringing up the puppets so they would work. The project combines practical and creative skills. (Courtesy, Lowell School, Mesa, Arizona)

Relation of Humanities to the Rest of the Curriculum.   Perhaps more so in this area than in any other there is an on-going all-day relationship between the targets of the curriculum and the rest of the program. You may need a period set aside for music or art. You may have a special teacher who comes to your room on a definite schedule. You may see literature or dramatization as a part of the reading program or as mere entertainment for opening exercise. You may think philosophy is beyond these children at this level. Whatever your program, you must have a definite plan to make sure the targets are reached. They must not be isolated; they must relate definitely to all the other areas in the curriculum. This must show in your planning and in the place they occupy in the daily schedule. You must have a vision of the future in order that you may go out and meet it.

The relation to the other school subjects is vital as a factor in establishing the appreciations and understandings in cultural areas. The children may illustrate their learnings in the *social studies* by drawing a picture, developing a large wall mural, building a model, decorating backs for a book, reproducing a scene, experimenting with ceramics, making costumes, cartooning historical events, preparing posters or programs for class presentations, and designing stage settings. They may reproduce the music or the dance of other countries or other times. They may read the literature connected with a period in history or a geographical setting. They may think about why the people live as they do and what they themselves might do under similar circumstances. These learnings all go beyond reading the information, collecting the facts, and reproducing the answers. They lead children to use knowledge to make decisions, to empathize with the people, and to become creative in their own way.

When the children study *science*, they can be led to see the repetition of design in nature, the rhythm of movement in life, the exactness of language in expressing factual information, the scientific basis for much of literary production, the tone quality in music, and even the logic on which scientific theories are based. As they read about the lives of scientists who have made contributions to the advancement of civilization, they will begin to see them as persons who have a humanistic concern for the improvement of life for human beings. Thus their knowledge will in turn deepen their appreciation for humanity.

In such routine learnings as *spelling, penmanship, grammar,* and *punctuation* the children will delve into the history of the language. They will learn how words have acquired their meanings. They will continue to see that all language has pattern and structure and that it develops through use. They will come to see grammar, not as the rules for the use of language, but as the description of how language functions, whether it be English or another language. They will come to see spelling, penmanship, and punctuation as tools for communication, and correct form as a courtesy to the potential reader rather than imposed school learnings. Human relationships will become the goal. Knowledge of form will become the means. And skill will become the by-product through repeated use. This places the entire curriculum in perspective based on human relations.

The rhythm of bodily movement, artistic form, and self expression are related to *physical education*. The human body will become an object of respect with a scientific basis and a heredity from one's own ancestors. Such respect will add to the feelings of self worth and the dignity of the individual. Once children have developed such respect for themselves, they are ready to transfer similar feelings to others and accord these others the same respect. Human relations are a vital part of the physical-education program.

All the humanities are in some way related to *mathematics*. The language of number is used to express ratio and proportion, and to identify the time element in music. It influences tempo and rhythm patterns. Even the pages of a book are numbered and the calendar records the sequences in time. Historical events are placed in perspective when one understands the time sequences of the centuries.

The place of the humanities in the school day becomes a vital issue when you see all these interrelationships. Shall we have a special period for music and art? Will drama or dance or logic appear on the daily schedule? If you have special teachers coming to your room for some of these areas, you may have to include them in the schedule. But if not, you may be left to your own devices. Whether you designate them on your program or not is your choice. Part of that depends on how self-disciplined you are. But Frost (4:417) insists that:

> Music instruction should yield more than off-key singing during opening exercises; art instruction should be more than providing paper and paint. The view that any direct help from the teacher might thwart the creative desires of children is as indefensible as the assumption that children need no assistance in reading and mathematics.

And Eisner writing on art education in the *NSSE Yearbook* (13:310) recommends more formal planning for the inclusion of art in the daily schedule. He says:

> Even if the number of trained teachers of art could be increased ten-fold, the art curriculum would still need to be developed far more systematically than it now is. Sequential courses of study, for example are provided in less than 40 percent of the elementary schools.

And Shuster (20:345) comments on the importance of the classroom teacher thus:

> Although the children's experiences in music do not require the teacher to be an outstanding performer, it is necessary that the teacher enjoy music, know the subject matter of music, and understand the relation of music to the school experiences of children.

The teacher who is able to sketch an idea on the chalkboard or on a large sheet of newsprint is bringing art into other activities. The one who is able to spring into song or rhyme to fit the occasion is moving learnings in the humanities into the rest of the curriculum. This happens when Mr. Davis looks out the window on a windy day and says, "I saw you toss the kites on high and blow the birds about the sky," or when he comes forth in the midst of a science lesson with, "I think that I shall never see a poem lovely as a tree," or when he intersperses into the history lesson the description of Barbara Fritchie in the poem by Whittier. The teacher who can calm a classroom with a softly hummed lullaby, challenge a lagging activity with a stimulating tune, or set the tone for a physical activity with a well chosen rhythm record is using music to serve other learnings. Calling attention to kinds of architecture, costumes of the people, physical features of the land, all these are ways of including the cultural background in other learnings. Even though you have the "subjects" on your daily schedule and the topics in your curriculum outline, don't forget to point out the applications all day every day in every situation where they fit.

A *prediction for the future* is significant because most of your teaching is ahead of you and you must be prepared for whatever is coming. The humanities have made for themselves a place in the curriculum. It is your responsibility to recognize this place and plan for it. How and when calls for planning and executing. The approaches may vary. The need continues to exist. New approaches may be ahead. Some predictions have been made. Wilson (27:248) suggests that:

> One of the considerations for opening the access to the arts is short term exploratory courses made available to help a student determine what areas are of greatest interest to him.

And Thompson (22:517–521) points out that:

> The fields of literature, music, and the graphic and plastic arts must have a place in the elementary school curriculum even in these days of pressure to teach more and more of the measurable content.

One area of the humanities that has experienced changing policy in regard to inclusion in the curriculum at the elementary-school level is the second language. Do you speak a second language? Are you teaching the children to speak a second language other than English? Or is English actually a second language to the children you are teaching? Are you prepared to meet these children on their own ground? Will the children under your instruction have use for another language in communicating with the rest of the world either now or in the years to come? What should we do about it? What can you do about it? Trends in the teaching of a foreign language in the elementary school have waxed and waned. Proximity to communities where other languages are used influences the decision. International relations often cause spurts of interest in certain languages. After the passage of the National Defense Education Act in 1957 a renewed interest was awakened and FLES (Foreign Language in the Elementary School) flourished for awhile. In a recent article entitled, "Now That FLES is Dead, What Next?", Kunkle (10:417–419) comments:

> There seems to be no question that FLES (Foreign Language in the Elementary School) spawned in most communities by the Sputnik-NDEA events, is an almost completely defunct creature.

He cites reasons for these failures as little influence on secondary-school language success, not enough results for time expended, and lack of qualified teachers to carry out the program. And Ragan (15:422) concludes that:

> The three areas of general education to which the fine arts make unique contributions are aesthetic growth, productive use of leisure time, and emotional development.

Without doubt the humanism of the curriculum is having its day. Your responsibility in the classroom will be to help the children become the kinds of people who can live in the rapidly changing world with peers as well as with predecessors and successors, and to help them see themselves as worthy and responsible. These goals imply that each learning is continuous and that teaching and learning do not stop when the bell rings.

Humanities Beyond the Classroom.   If learnings in the humanities are to extend into life, they must have an influence on how children use what they learn. They will learn to do and to know. They will learn to appreciate and create.

Tooting a horn is serious business for a child who hopes to be in the band some day.
(Courtesy, Skiff School, Phoenix, Arizona)

Performance is one goal of the arts. Some children will perform merely for their own pleasure. Some will become accomplished enough to perform for the pleasure of others. And some may even become skilled enough to earn a livelihood by devoting their lives to a career in one of the performing arts.

Knowledge is another goal of the arts. Some will read or hear about the arts as a passing interest to enrich their general understanding of life. Some may be well enough informed to pass their information along to others. They may become teachers in these areas. And some may go into the background deeply enough to do research and perhaps even add to the store of knowledge available.

Appreciation is a major goal of the arts and humanities. Not all of us can be completely knowledgeable or skillful, but all of us can know enough about the subjects to observe and absorb with some degree of appreciation. It takes some background to enjoy a theatrical production or a concert. It takes some knowledge to visit a museum or art gallery intelligently. Even the reading of literature depends on more than skill in reproducing the sounds of language in response to the printed word. Background in literature, folklore, and history adds to the insight and appreciation of each literary selection. One builds on the other through style and reference.

Creativity is the culmination of the targets in the humanities. Humanistic behaviors make of the individual a contributor as well as a consumer. Children who learn to experiment with their creative abilities and to use them to express ideas and feelings are leading a fuller life than the ones who wait to be told what to do. Torrance (24:2) says:

> The learning by authority occurs when the learner is told what he should learn and when he accepts something as true because an authority says that it is.

And he helps us identify the creative child when he tells us that:

> The child's "wanting to know" is reflected in the number and kinds of questions he asks. By the time the child enters school for the first time, he is on his way to learning the skills of finding out by asking questions. When he enters school, however, the teacher usually begins asking all the questions, and the child has little or no chance to ask any. Furthermore, the teacher's questions rarely are asked to gain information. The teacher almost always knows the answer. Questions for information are rare in the classroom.

If you want to be a teacher who uses the humanities to extend learning beyond the four walls of the classroom, you will see to it that the children have an opportunity to perform, each within the bounds of personal abilities. You will see to it that they are exposed to enough information to serve as a background for their own use. You will help them appreciate the contributions of others. And you will encourage them to be as creative as they individually are capable in whatever areas appeal to them.

SUMMARY

The humanities provide a basis for helping the child appreciate the cultural heritage. They include the areas of art and architecture, drama and dance, language and literature, music, and philosophy. They are the means people have used through the ages to express ideas and to communicate with others. They are included in the curriculum in order that the pupil may use the various disciplines in daily life. Some pupils will be in the receptive role, learning what others have done, and some will be in the expressive role, practicing the skills and sometimes moving on into the realm of creativity.

If you are going to make the best use of the children's time in their human relations, you will need to help them practice for skill in some areas, gain knowledge in other areas, and use both skills and knowledge to develop attitudes of understanding and appreciation in all areas. In doing this you will need to see the humanitarian fields in relation to the other subjects in the curriculum and to place them in their relative positions in the school day. Knowing what to do is not enough. You must also look into the future and be prepared to meet new trends when they come. And all this means carrying the learnings beyond the classroom and into life so that the child will be able to do, to know, to appreciate, and even to create.

SUGGESTED ACTIVITIES

Select one or more of the following activities for a special project to be carried out independently or with a committee and reported to the class.

1. Select one of the areas of the curriculum such as social studies, science, mathematics, or language, and list ways in which the humanities can be taught through this area. Develop in a chart form.
2. Plan a pair of lessons in a specific area, in each case a lesson that can be taught in one class period. (See Chap. 3 for lesson plan format.)

    In one lesson, plan the teaching of a fact in the humanities.

    In another lesson show how the same fact can be incorporated in a lesson in another area through integration.
3. Plan a unit of work in the social studies (See Chap. 3 for unit plan format.)

    Show specific examples of correlation through the use of the humanities.
4. Prepare a special report on one or more of the following topics:
    a. Primitive art
    b. Primitive peoples and their music
    c. Traditional stories and folk tales
    d. Architecture as a reflection of culture
    e. Interpretive dance
5. Write a concise statement of your philosophy of life, what you really believe is of value.

    Show how this will affect your teaching.
6. Debate the topic:

    Resolved: The arts in the classroom should be taught from the point of view of the receptive role with emphasis on appreciation only.
7. Justify the use of school time for such activities as orchestra or band practice and choir rehearsal.
8. Make a collection of materials showing creativity on the part of children from a local classroom or school.

    Classify them.

    Share them with the class through an exhibit.

SELECTED READINGS

1. Association for Supervision and Curriculum Development, NEA, Yearbook, *Perceiving Behaving Becoming, A New Focus for Education*, Washington, D.C.: ASCD, 1962. A yearbook of the society emphasizing self-concept, personality development, and creativity.

2. "Columbus Arts Impact," in *Today's Education*, Vol. 60, No. 8, Nov. 1971, pp. 20–24. The editor visited and described the arts program in Columbus, Ohio. A narrative account and a description of an actual program in operation.

3. EPSTEIN, EDWARD B., "Where the Fine Arts Can Flourish," in *Today's Education*, Vol. 59, No. 7, Oct. 1970. pp. 52–54. A series of questions to help determine the artistic climate of the school system as one in which the creative arts curriculum can flourish.

4. FROST, JOE L. and G. THOMAS ROWLAND, *Curricula for the Seventies*, Boston: Houghton Mifflin, 1969. Chapter 12 identifies the arts in the curriculum.

5. GAITSKELL, CHARLES D. and AL HURWITZ, *Children and Their Art*, (2nd edition) New York: Harcourt, Brace, Jovanovitch, 1970. Theory of art. Pragmatic methodology of teaching art.

6. GETZELS, JACOB W. and PHILIP W. JACKSON, *Creativity and Intelligence, Explorations with Gifted Students*, New York: John Wiley & Sons, 1962. Identifies varieties of giftedness and correlates with intelligence.

7. GOERTZEL, VICTOR and MILDRED G. GOERTZEL, *Cradles of Eminence*, Boston: Little, Brown, 1962. A study of the childhoods of over 400 famous twentieth century men and women.

8. JACKSON, MARY, "Let's Make Foreign Language Study More Relevant," in *Today's Education*, Vol. 60, No. 3, March 1971, pp. 18–20. Why foreign language? The teacher, the methods, the curriculum.

9. JARVIS, OSCAR T. and MARION J. RICE, *An Introduction to Teaching in the Elementary School*, Dubuque, Iowa: Wm. C. Brown, 1972. See Part V, Chaps. 16, 17, and 18. "Teaching the Fine Arts and Recreation."

10. KUNKLE, JOHN F., "Now that FLES Is Dead, What Next?" in *Educational Leadership*, Vol. 29, No. 5, 1972, pp. 417–19. Points out the deficiencies in foreign language teaching in the elementary school. Gives Canadian model as an alternative.

11. LINDERMAN, EARL W. and DONALD HERBERHOLZ, *Developing Artistic and Perceptual Awareness* (2nd edition), Dubuque, Iowa: Wm. C. Brown, 1960. Illustrated. Classroom practices described.

12. MODUGNO, ANNE D. "Electronic Creativity," in *Today's Education*, Vol. 60, No. 3, Mar. 1971, pp. 62–64. Music programs. How to create with electronic equipment.

13. National Society for the Study of Education, *Art Education*, Sixty-Fourth Yearbook, Part II, Chicago: University of Chicago Press, 1965. A collection of essays on art in the elementary-school program with guidelines for future development.

14. NEAGLEY, ROSS L. and N. DEAN EVANS, *Handbook for Effective Curriculum Development*, Englewood Cliffs, N.J.: Prentice-Hall, 1967. Puts curriculum decisions into every day practice. The practical approach gives impetus to the arts.

15. RAGAN, WILLIAM B. and CELIA BURNS STENDLER, *Modern Elementary Curriculum*, New York: Holt, Rinehart and Winston, 1966. Chapter 14 on enriching and beautifying life through the fine arts is appropriate to a study of the humanities.

16. REIMER, BENNETT, *A Philosophy of Music Education*, Englewood Cliffs, N.J.: Prentice-Hall, 1970. Develops the aesthetic viewpoint. Contains chapters on music program, performance, and relation to other arts. Practical applications to school music programs.

17. RUESCHOFF, PHIL H. and M. EVELYN SWARTZ, *Teaching Art in the Elementary School*, New York: The Ronald Press Co, 1969. Stresses content and continuity in school art programs. Illustrates teaching strategies.

18. SAWYER, JOHN R. and ITALO L. DEFRANCESCO, *Elementary School Art for Classroom Teachers*, New York: Harper & Row, 1971. Contemporary application to the teaching of art in the classroom.

19. SHANNON, JOSEPH, "Premises for Appreciation," in *Educational Forum*, Vol. XXXV, No. 4, May 1971, pp. 457–60. Points out that premises of appreciation are in the expectation of the viewer. Recommends inquiry and examination.

20. SHUSTER, ALBERT H. and MILTON E. PLOGHOFT, *The Emerging Elementary Curriculum*, Columbus, Ohio: Charles E. Merrill, 1963. Chapter 11 points out the role of the teacher is providing music and art experiences for all children.

21. SKINNER, B. F., *The Technology of Teaching*, New York: Appleton-Century-Crofts, 1968. A series of chapters some of which have been given as lectures. Chapter 8 on the creative student is appropriate to the arts.

22. THOMPSON, RALPH, "The Humanities in the Elementary School," in *Elementary English*, Vol. XLIX, No. 4, Apr. 1972, pp. 517–21. Points out that the fields of literature, music, and the graphic arts must have a place in the elementary-school curriculum even in these days of pressure to teach more of the measurable content.

23. TORRANCE, E. PAUL, "Creative Kids," in *Today's Education*, Vol. 61, No. 1, Jan. 1972, pp. 25–28. Children who present special challenges. Offers suggestions for interventions teachers may use to assist creative children at all levels of education.

24. TORRANCE, E. PAUL, *Encouraging Creativity in the Classroom*, Dubuque, Iowa: Wm. C. Brown, 1970. Points out specific techniques for encouraging children to be creative.

25. TORRANCE, E. PAUL, *Rewarding Creative Behavior, Experiments in Classroom Creativity*, Englewood Cliffs, N.J.: Prentice-Hall, 1965. An account of studies made to find out what can be done about creative behavior in the classroom. Emphasizes role of the teacher.

26. WACHOWIAK, FRANK and THEODORE RAMSAY, *Emphasis Art* (2nd edition), Scranton: Intext, 1971. Motivation as an aspect of art learning experiences. A comprehensive treatment.

27. WILSON, L. CRAIG, *The Open Access Curriculum*, Boston: Allyn and Bacon, 1971. Chapter 13 deals with music, drama, art, and technical education.

part three

Judging the Results of Teaching in Terms of Curriculum Goals.

AN INTRODUCTION

Eventually the time comes when you must ask yourself, "What have I accomplished?" School and teaching are more than meeting the children, putting in time, and keeping things running smoothly. If you are raising cotton you can weigh the product. If you are manufacturing automobiles you can count the number coming off the assembly line. But when you are educating children the evaluation is different. Weighing them or counting them gives no evidence of accomplishment. But you can measure some of the things they have learned, observe daily performance, give a test, and measure growth in certain skills and knowledge. This section will help you know what measuring devices are available and how they will help you.

Don't depend on memory. You need some records not only for the administration and the parents but also for yourself and the children. The records will provide a basis for communicating results to those who want to know what is happening.

We will attempt to help you with kinds of records and forms in which to keep them, and we will offer some help in the use of the records as a basis for planning next steps. Perhaps one of the practical uses for records is as a help in deciding how to classify children and when to move them on to another level for instructional purposes.

Records you keep will provide evidence of wide differences among the children, and will reveal variations in size, ability, and backgrounds. A thoughtful appraisal of these differences will equip you to meet the old and the young, the large and the small, the bright and the dull, the deprived and the affluent, and the minority cultures as well as the children from the main stream of American life. A look at what has happened in the past will enable you to appraise programs and materials which are available and to use them constructively.

Such an appraisal reveals the trend toward accountability. Society supports the schools and has great expectations from them. Educators spend their lives working in the schools and hope for results. Children spend their growing years in school and need evidence of accomplishment in return for energy expended. Tradition and need dictate some of the content of the curriculum. We must justify public trust and help children grow. The results we expected have changed over the years. The current emphasis is on measurable achievement in terms of behavioral objectives. This trend has led to a move toward national assessment and performance contracting. These trends have tended to influence not only *what* to teach, and *how* to teach, but also *who* shall teach. The law of supply and demand in the teacher market has fluctuated with the birth rate. As teachers become more plentiful, the competition for jobs becomes keener. Can you fit your professional training and curriculum knowledge into the needs of society for your services?

Our original goals were indicated as developing children who can do, who know, and who are. We return full circle to the questions:

What can they do?

What do they know?

What kinds of persons are they becoming?

11

MEASURING RESULTS OF TEACHING AND LEARNING

How Are We Doing?

Courtesy, Skiff School, Phoenix, Arizona

CHECKING UP

How do you feel about tests? How did you feel about them when you were a child in the elementary school? These are different viewpoints. Now you are ready to look at tests from still another angle. How will you feel about testing when you are the teacher planning and administering the tests? Why will you test the children? What will you expect to find out? How will you go about it? How will you construct the tests? Or if you are not going to make your own tests, where will you get them? How will you select a test that will tell you what you want to know? Then how will you administer and score it? How will you use the findings?

There are many different kinds of tests designed for different purposes. You may want to find out where you are starting, what the children are doing, what they are capable of doing, what their problems are, how much they have learned, or how they compare with others. You may be satisfied with an opinion or you may want an objective measure. Tests can be useful. Tests can be abused. If you know what they are for and how to use them, they can become invaluable tools. And where do the children fit into this? Are you going to frighten them or threaten them with tests? Or will you be able to take them along in the planning and help them see for themselves that tests really do answer, for both the teacher and the pupil, such questions as, "What do I still need to do?" and "How am I doing now?"

You need to have a reason for measuring results of teaching. You need to know more than one way of measuring or evaluating your efforts and the children's accomplishments. You need to know how to select suitable tests to accomplish your purposes. You need to know other ways of evaluating. If you are acquainted with the means and are aware of the trends, you will be equipped to meet the situation.

WHY MEASURE OR EVALUATE

There are many reasons for checking up on ourselves. We do it all the time when we glance at the speedometer, proofread a letter, or try again a piano exercise. Sometimes we are satisfied with an estimate and sometimes we want to know exactly. Evaluation is a logical and natural process and should be approached with an open and receptive mind. Self-evaluation is the ultimate goal in order to answer the question, "How am I doing?" Let us identify some of the reasons for evaluating in the classroom.

To Determine Attainment of Objectives

We have discussed goals, organization, and planning. We have surveyed the curriculum areas in terms of skills, knowledge, and attitudes. Now we are ready to ask, "What have I accomplished?"

Mastery of Skills.   In each of the curriculum areas we indicated that there are some things pupils learn how to do. These are itemized on the charts in Part Two. Evaluation comes when we ask, "Can they do it?" rather than how well or with what degree of accuracy. In most situations "about right" is not good enough. This applies to such situations as balancing a checkbook, performing on a musical instrument, following directions, and writing a letter. Employers who hire people to drive trucks, keep books, or repair plumbing are not interested in whether they ranked in the upper third of the class or made A's, but rather can they do the job. Children need to learn to ask themselves, not "What did I get?" but instead, "Can I do it?" and "What do I still need to do?"

Attainment of Knowledge.   The charts in Part Two listed types of knowledge to be acquired. There are tests designed to answer the question, "Do the children know?" Some of them are commercial and some teacher prepared. Many of them asked children to recall facts, supply information, fill in blanks, and repeat what they have learned. A test which stops there has not fulfilled its purpose. Merely repeating information on a test has little value unless children can use it in solutions to problems. That doesn't mean we shouldn't test for coverage of content and mastery of facts, but this is one step on the road to learning.

Development of Understandings and Attitudes.   If we see the ultimate goal as personal development, then we must go much farther than mere measurement of skills and facts. Objective testing yields scores but this is only the means to the end. We really want to know if the person is ambitious, sympathetic, philanthropic, charitable, diplomatic, conscientious, loyal, appreciative, patriotic, and moral. Measuring these achievements is difficult. They are judged in terms of acts rather than scores. They fluctuate from time to time and from one situation to another. Such evaluation is highly subjective and the results are not readily reducible to scores. For this reason it is frequently neglected. It needs more attention.

To Evaluate the Effectiveness of Teaching and Learning

In actuality the evaluation of learning is also an evaluation of the effectiveness of teaching. Children may show evidence of having learned things outside the curriculum goals; for example, positive or negative attitudes, careful or careless habits, and high or low self-appraisal. Managing the teaching-learning situation so each child is pursuing worth-while activities and producing evidence of accomplishment calls for careful planning. Being able to show through scores, anecdotal records, or types of responses that children have attained accepted goals is one way of checking on your own ability to organize material, manage the situation, and plan the work effectively.

To Identify Accomplishments

Being specific about accomplishments provides satisfying records. This applies to the individual as well as the class group, and average performance. It applies to curriculum coverage as well as teaching techniques. Some things may need reemphasis. Some techniques may need revising or abandoning. The findings of evaluation serve as a basis for planning next steps and future goals. You and your children need to be able to say this is done, this we still need to do.

HOW TO MEASURE OR EVALUATE

Effective measurement will help determine the extent to which objectives have been attained, and what you need to plan for the future. There are three basic techniques for evaluating which you use almost daily. Specifically identifying them so you know what they are and how you are using them will make them more effective. You watch to see what happens and make judgments. And on occasion you will test for specific answers to specific questions. Tests may take many forms. You need to know how to use all of them. And after making your observations and measuring the results with tests you will need to keep a record on which you can base further judgments.

Observation

When you live in the classroom with the children daily, you are constantly evaluating. Your observations when Johnny forgets his lunch money day after day, when Carol never has a pencil, when Billy always comes up with his home work, when Erma consistently volunteers for extra assignments, when Sam always seems to have stimulating ideas but is never able to put them into practice, or when Frank competes for the limelight and is not quite accepted by his peers are all ways of collecting evidence and providing data for evaluation. When you observe Sharon as she struggles with arithmetic and note her progress as a result of daily effort, you are collecting evidence to show growth. When you listen to Carl read and make the same mistakes over and over again, you are providing a basis for future teaching. Perhaps observation would be sufficient as a technique for evaluation if we did not have to account to others for our accomplishments. But the parents want to know how Mary is getting along. The school officials want to know whether our goals are being met. The curriculum planners want to know how effective the materials are. The children want to know what progress they are making. And you often feel the need for more tangible evidence than just "I think," or "I noticed," or "I like." Therefore, valuable as it is, observation is not enough. Your judgments demand something more tangible as a basis for next steps. For that reason we often turn to tests.

Testing

Where do you get the tests you use? What kinds of tests do you like to use with your class? Why? Giving a test because we always have one on Friday is not necessarily beneficial. Sometimes you know whether the goals have been reached without the support of a test score. Sometimes you need evidence provided by test results. Before you test, ask yourself why you are testing, what you expect to find out, and what kind of test will be most effective. Then you are ready to decide where you will get the test and the kind you will use. The children should know why they are taking a test and what it is supposed to measure.

Sources of Tests.   Tests need to be as carefully planned as any other lesson. Both you and the children should know why a test is being used and what it is supposed to tell. Some tests will be made by the teacher and some may be purchased from a publishing firm that specializes in the development of general testing materials. Which you will use will depend on your purposes for testing.

Teacher-made tests are usually informal and are constructed for the specific situation. Such tests may be made by the classroom teacher or by a team of teachers working on a common topic. Sometimes children may even participate in test construction by helping identify topics and perhaps even contributing questions. The purposes of the test will be to find out whether or not the children have mastered the areas covered, where the gaps are, and what still needs to be reviewed before leaving the topic.

Consider a test as another kind of lesson. A good test should be a learning situation for both teacher and pupil. The results should reveal what has been learned as well as what has not been learned, or what still needs further attention. When you plan a testing lesson, take the same steps recommended in Chap. 3 for lesson planning. Decide why you are going to test. List the areas or topics to be covered. Then plan specifically how you will go about it. A simple end-of-the-week test in spelling may be to determine the extent of mastery of the week's wordlist. The content, if you are using a textbook, may be determined by the printed list; or it may be supplemented if you are challenging the children with additional spelling words from other curriculum areas. The procedure merely may be to distribute papers or spelling tablets, dictate the word list, and score the results. A test in other skill areas such as mathematics, physical activities, music notation, or map reading may call for a more selective listing of content. A test in content areas will call for identification of information worthy of recall.

When you have decided on the purpose for the test and the content to be covered, you are ready to compose the test. Oral tests are used informally almost daily, but written tests come at spaced intervals after the completion of a given segment of the curriculum. If you decide to use an essay test in which the children must compose their own answers, the first step is to think carefully how you will word the questions. One of the best ways to judge the appropriateness of a question is to attempt to write the answer yourself. If you decide on a test composed of questions to which the children can react by filling blanks or by indicating choices from suggested answers, then composing the questions is a step that needs careful consideration. For examples of types of test questions that can be used in teacher-made tests sees the samples under "Forms of Tests" in this chapter on pp. 258–263. These include both subjective and objective questions. Some types lend themselves better to some areas than others. In mathematics you will probably want to include sample problems to be solved. In social studies you will probably want to include multiple-choice examples that will cause the children to think about the content and make selections in terms of possible answers. In an area such as literature you may see the need for more subjective test items that will draw the pupils out to express ideas or reactions. This type of response is more difficult to evaluate in terms of a score but is valuable nevertheless. Teacher-made tests are usually temporary in nature and are seldom preserved for repeated use. They are valuable but they serve a different purpose than the commercial tests that come in printed form with keys. manuals, and interpretations in terms of standards.

Commercial tests with established norms may vary depending on the purposes for which the publishers have prepared them. One possible type is the test especially prepared to go with a printed textbook or workbook. These tests will tend to cover the material that has just been taught. Other commercial tests are more general and are not designed to go with any particular curriculum material. Such tests may supply information about how well children read, what general skills in mathematics they possess, what general knowledge they have acquired in a content subject, and how they compare with other children of the same age or grade level.

General commercial tests usually cover a broad area on the assumption that some learnings are of enough value that all children probably will need them, regardless of geographical location, use of text materials, or plans for the future. When tests are thus constructed, they are usually subjected to careful preliminary screening before they are listed in catalogues for sale. After they have been administered to large numbers of children at given age or grade levels, the test makers are able to identify the scores that most children attain. The medians of such scores are established and published as what are called *norms*. A norm does not necessarily mean that this is the score the child "should" make, but rather it is the median score other children of the same age or grade have made on the test during the experimental stage before publication. Norms may be of several varieties. If the same test is administered to children at several different grade levels and medians are computed for all the children at each level regardless of age or ability, then the resulting figure is what is called a *grade norm*. If the test is given to all children at a given age regardless of grade placement, for example to all eight-year-olds whether they are in grade two, three, or four, then the median thus established is referred to as an *age norm*. Because admission policies and promotion standards differ from one school system to another, grade norms have certain weaknesses. They may compare nine-year-olds in grade four in one school system with ten-year-olds or eight-year-olds in grade four in another school system. On the other hand, comparing all eight-year-olds with one another may have similar disadvantages because some eight-year-olds may have started at a younger age and may have had more school-related experiences than their counterparts in another school system. Some test makers try to counteract these weaknesses by establishing what they call *modal age norms*. In order to do this they include only the children who are the usually accepted age for the grade. This practice excludes from the testing the young, immature child who has been accelerated and the older, duller child who has been retained, and it includes only those children who are of the usual, or modal, age for the grade. Before you can make a meaningful comparison of scores for either an individual or a group you must first identify the kind of norm with which you are dealing.

Whether you decide to make your own tests or use a printed test purchased from a publishing company will depend on what you want to find out. Both you and the children should be aware of the differences and should know what you are testing for. Then there should be definite plans for using the results for next steps in teaching.

Forms of Tests.   Whether the tests are teacher-made or commercial affects the content of the test itself. Both kinds can take different forms; however, most commercial tests do tend to be objective. Subjective tests depend on teacher judgment in the evaluation. Objective tests are supposed to have only one right answer for each part and can be scored from a key without the scorer having to decide whether or not the child's answer is acceptable. The subjective test has the advantage of stimulating thinking and leading pupils to compose their own thoughts in producing the responses. The objective test has the advantage of being more or less indisputable in the scoring. For these reasons the latter are sometimes preferred when comparisons and decisions about grading and promotion are factors. Each has its place. You need to know how to construct a test and how to choose a test to suit your special needs.

Subjective tests produce answers which are a matter of interpretation. They include the *essay test*, which poses a question for the child to think about and write an answer. Examples such as the following are illustrative:

Why do you think Tom won the race?
Describe the scene of the landing of the Pilgrims at Plymouth.
Write a character sketch about the hero in the story.
How is rural life different from urban life?

All these questions cause children to recall the information at their command, organize it into sequential ideas, and express themselves with language. In order to answer the questions, they must be able to write legibly and compose ideas in the form of sentences. When answers are completed, the teacher must read what has been written and form a judgment about the completeness and the quality of the responses. Such tests are interpreted in vastly different ways by different teachers. The same answer might be rated high by one teacher and low by another. Some teachers might be very critical of spelling, handwriting, punctuation, and sentence structure, while others might feel that these points are irrelevant if children show in their responses that they have command of the information. Subjective tests have value but they do not yield undisputed scores. They should be used with clear knowledge of their advantages and their limitations.

Other subjective tests may appear to be more objective because of their form but may still be highly subjective in interpretation. These include the ones where there are blanks to fill in or multiple-choice tests where there may be more than one acceptable response.

Examples of *completion exercises* with write-in responses which may vary are:

The three most important characters were_____

Some crops raised in this region are_____ _____

The election was a victory for the Pirates because_____

In these cases pupils are left to compose their own endings to the sentences. Different children may have different ideas about how the sentences should be completed. In a discussion period the children may be given the opportunity to defend their answers. One answer may be as good as another. The teacher may be in a position of having to decide which answers are acceptable, and if a score is desired, may even have to decide which one is "best" or "how much it is worth." This makes the scoring of the test less objective.

Examples of *multiple choice* questions which are subjective are:

The best material with which to build houses is

wood   concrete   brick

Paul, in the story, is best described by

honest   sincere   foolish   cowardly

In order to maintain good health one needs plenty of

food   rest   exercise   clothing

Here we find questions with a variety of answers from which the pupils may choose. They might choose only the best answer, or they might choose more than one answer. Once they have chosen they might find that the choice differs from that of their classmates. And, moreover, they might be able to produce convincing arguments to support their choices. Even though these questions appear to be objective in form, they lend themselves to interpretation and discussion. They are good questions for class discussion because they cause the pupils to think and to use oral language to express their ideas. They do not yield scores which can be counted objectively. Their values lie in the child's experience in forming judgments and in supporting thinking.

Objective tests leave little doubt as to the "right" answer. They have their place but also their limitations. Some are based on alternatives, some are multiple choice, and some call for simple recall. Here are some examples:

Questions which are based on *alternatives* tend to be one of three kinds. There is the yes-no question, the true-false statement, and the either-or test. Here are examples of each:

Mary was at the party.	True	False
Mary won first prize at the party.	True	False
Washington was our first president.	True	False

Is an atom an element?	Yes	No
Did the British troops land at Plymouth?	Yes	No
Can you subtract 8 from 4?	Yes	No

The pull of the earth on bodies is called
    rotation   gravity
Animals which produce living young are classified as
    reptiles   mammals
If you mix red and blue in equal proportions you get
    pink   purple

The examples show three different forms, but they have certain characteristics in common. The response in each case is based on a pair of alternatives from which the child must choose. One of the alternatives is right and the other is wrong. If Tom has no idea and merely guesses, he still has a fifty-fifty chance of being right. He does not have to construct an answer, but must only mark one of the answers which has been supplied. This means that he could be able to answer the question without knowing how to write, spell, or even read, if he got the idea of marking one of the answers in each case. Such questions are often used on tests. The teacher and the child should both know how the scoring is to be done and what will be the result of random guessing.

Sometimes guessing is compensated for by scoring rights minus wrongs. This penalizes the child for guessing wrong. For example, if there were ten questions and Bob was sure about six of them and unsure about the other four, he might answer only the six questions and get a score of 6. If there were no penalty for guessing, and he guessed wrong on the four he did not know, he would still come out with a score of 6. But if there were a penalty for guessing, the results would vary. If he guessed on the four and guessed right on all of them he would make a score of 6 plus 4 or 10. If he guessed and took a fifty-fifty chance, he might come out with two right guesses and two wrong guesses which would give him a score of 8 minus 2 or 6, the same as if he hadn't attempted the ones about which he was unsure. This procedure leaves much to be desired. And unless such a test is followed up with a discussion in which children can have an opportunity to tell why they selected the answers they did, it can yield little more than a score for the record.

Questions which are based on *multiple choice* call for recognition of a right answer. They may be highly objective but they can also be debatable. These differ from the either-or examples given above in that there are usually more than two possible responses, usually three and sometimes four or more. They differ from the subjective multiple-choice examples given earlier in that one answer is obviously right and all the others are obviously wrong thus making the scoring objective. Examples follow:

The sum of 3 and 5 and 7 is
     12   15   18
Mixing two parts hydrogen and one part oxygen yields
          water   salt   chlorophyl   air
The capital of New York is
          Buffalo   New York   Albany

In answering these questions children first have to be able to read the questions and the possible answers. They may select what they know to be the right answer. If they are uncertain, they may eliminate the answers they are sure are wrong, thus limiting the choices and increasing the chances of guessing correctly. When there are three possible answers, a guess has a 1 to 2 chance of being right. To compensate for this possibility, scoring is sometimes indicated as rights minus half the number of wrongs. If there are four possible answers, a guess has a 1 to 3 chance of being right. The correction, if applied, is rights minus one third the number of wrongs. Beyond this point it is not usually considered necessary to make such corrections.

Sometimes, in order to make the test more objective, the writer of the question makes the alternatives so obviously incorrect that there can be no argument about the acceptability of the rejected answers on the scoring key. Even then circumstances do make a difference. Consider the story of the preadolescent in a deprived area who was confronted with this question:

Carpenters   build houses,   sweep streets,   sell newspapers.

The lad marked the middle answer. It was marked wrong on his test, and when it was discussed his response was, "My dad is a carpenter and he ain't built no houses for three years." Perhaps he was right after all and the question was not as objective as the test maker intended for it to be. It depends on your point of view.

Perhaps the most difficult of the objective-type tests to construct and to take is the *simple recall* question. Here pupils are confronted with a blank to fill in. They must supply the word or phrase that completes the sentence. For example:

The capital of Brazil is _____
The Welland Canal joins _____ and _____.
The candidates in the current presidential election were _____ and _____.
The parts of a flower are _____, _____,
_____, and _____.

These questions are intended to produce answers that can be counted either right or wrong. There are times when one might be able to select the right answer from a list of given answers but would not be able to recall the answer from memory. There might even be reason to debate some of the answers. One might contend that there were more than two candidates in the current presidential election, or "I thought you meant the candidates for president and vice-president on the losing ticket." One might be able to identify more than four parts of a flower. The question is then one of deciding whether or not to put in the extras. And in scoring, if Marcia has supplied six parts, one of which is wrong, when only four parts were asked for should she be given credit for the extras, penalized for the one wrong, or given only the four possible points. And if her one wrong part was in one of the blanks instead of as an extra, should it be counted, or should one of the others be substituted. It is obvious that she knows something about the parts of flowers and that she has at least one misconception. The problem is not what she knows or doesn't know about flowers, but how to score the test. If objective means "indisputable," then this may not be as objective as the test writer thought.

Standardized tests have the advantage of providing an accepted standard against which to judge. Commercial tests may or may not be standardized. The standardization process implies that the examples have been used with large numbers of children in random groups and the results studied to see what scores these children attained. Then norms are established, not on the basis of what children of a given age "ought to do," but on the basis of the median achievement of children who have taken the test. In other words, if the test containing fifty examples has been administered to 100,000 children at a given level and the tabulations show that the median achievement for children at the beginning of the fifth grade is 38 correct answers out of the 50 possible, then the test makers can establish a norm of 38 for beginning fifth grade level. Even then consideration must be given to the selection of the form of the test to be used because floors and ceilings indicate the levels below or above which the tests measure. With such information the individual teacher is able to use the results to draw conclusions about the extent to which the entire class, or each individual in the class, measures up to the standard achieved by other children of that age and grade on these same test items. This still does not tell the entire story. Much depends on the curriculum content and the abilities of the children. If abilities are limited perhaps it is unreasonable to expect the children to measure up. If the curriculum has not exposed them to the content included in the test, then their inadequate responses might be due to something other than their abilities or the quality of the teaching. These matters all need to be considered carefully when analyzing test results. We will come back to this topic when we discuss the use of test results in Chap. 13.

It is possible, although perhaps not very practical, for teachers to standardize their own tests by repeating them year after year and keeping a record of results against which to judge future performances. However, as goals change the needs for testing change and accumulating enough scores on which to establish a norm may be unlikely.

Tests have their place. When you plan to administer one you must first know why you are testing and what you hope to find out. Some teacher-made tests are more appropriate for some situations than the most scientifically prepared of commercial tests. Sometimes a subjective test tells exactly what you want to know in a way that an objective test could never do. Objective tests serve the purpose of being time-savers for the teacher and furnishing a basis for comparison and evidence sans emotions or personalities.

Record Keeping

When you "jot it down," you have something tangible to which to refer in making decisions. There are all kinds of records which are helpful in evaluation. Some of them are informal and subjective. Some of them are formal and objective. Some are based on individual performance. Some relate to the class as a group. Examples will help you judge their values.

Anecdotal Records. Jotting down a brief account of a specific incident will help substantiate a judgment. Some such notes are highly subjective and of questionable value. Consider these:

Sara is a cooperative child.
Tommy frequently disrupts the classroom.
Mary is careless with her supplies.

These comments are all indefinite and judgmental without concrete evidence. A more helpful kind of anecdotal record would include such information as:

Sara saw to it that everyone in the room had a part in the play she was writing. She stayed after class to put away the books her committee had used. She remembered to bring the pan we needed for the science experiment.

Tommy left the group to get his supplies after we had started the discussion. He slammed them down on the table and let part of them fall on the floor. He grabbed the volume of the encyclopedia out of Marie's hands.

Mary spilled her paint today. She broke her pencil twice during the test. She lost two of her crayons and the janitor swept them up with the trash. She forgot her coat when she went home.

These examples indicate the kind of anecdotal records that will be helpful when it comes time for evaluation. They serve as evidence when talking with the child about his needs and/or accomplishments. They contain factual information to share with parents in a conference. They are helpful to the next teacher. They justify conclusions.

Individual Scores.   When you keep a record of actual accomplishments, you have objective evidence to support your judgments. When you record the facts that Mary missed one word in spelling the first week, no words the next three weeks, and one the fifth week, six the next week, and seven the next, you have tangible evidence to indicate that something has gone wrong with Mary's spelling and it has happened in the last couple of weeks.

While authorities differ as to the validity of individual scores on standardized group tests, a record from year to year does yield interesting information if viewed with the possible limitations in mind. It is helpful to record the scores on a standardized reading test each year and accumulate a record as shown in Fig. 11-1. Such a record provides a basis for saying, "Tommy seemed to get off to a slow start in reading, but when he gained some independence in word analysis he picked up momentum and is now making better than average progress." or "Sara got off to a slow start, seemed to have difficulty in generalizing on reading skills, and is moving at a slow pace. She gets farther and farther below the norm." and "Carla started slowly and has made steady progress. She is consistently gaining slightly less than a year's growth each school year."

GRADE LEVEL	INDIVIDUAL SCORES		
	Tommy	*Sara*	*Carla*
1st Grade	1.4	1.4	1.4
2nd Grade	2.3	2.0	2.3
3rd Grade	4.1	2.7	3.2
4th Grade	5.5	3.1	4.1
Growth	4.1	1.7	2.7

Figure 11-1.   *Reading Achievement Test Scores for three representative children in four successive years showing annual scores and growth in the three year interval.*

Group Scores.   If you discount the validity of individual scores on group standardized tests, then a study of class medians or even system-wide medians will reveal a different kind of comparison. This study can lead to comparisons of one group with another within the school or the school system, or it can be used to compare a given group with national norms.

Recording the median class scores on a standardized test each year for a period of years will result in an accumulation of data that not only will show annual levels of achievement but will offer comparison of levels from year to year and indicate resulting overall growth. Figure 11-2 gives a record that provides a basis for saying, "In 1973 this group of children, d.ring the second month in the third grade, attained a median score of 3.0, which was two months below the national norm.

SCHOOL YEAR	GRADE LEVEL	ACHIEVEMENT SCORES		
		National Norm	*School A*	*Deviation*
1974	4	4.2	3.9	− 0.3
1973	3	3.2	3.0	− 0.2
Growth	1 yr	1.0	0.9	− 0.1

Figure 11-2. *Comparison of Reading Achievement Scores for School A with national norms showing deviations at each checkpoint and growth in the year's interval.*

One year later when they were in the second month of the fourth grade they attained a median score of 3.9." Using the decimal system of recording grade scores as a basis for comparison leads to the conclusion that at that point they were 3 months below the national norm and had grown nine months in the year's interval, which is less than the expected growth by one month. Before the value of such growth or achievement can be assessed, one needs to know the native abilities of the individuals who make up the group. Another factor that should be taken into consideration is the changing personnel of the group. To compare this year's median with last year's median is unrealistic unless the selection of cases excludes all individuals except those who appear in both groups.

Records of Accomplishment.   When you keep a record of what has been done, you have a basis for drawing conclusions. A list of books each child has read provides such a reference. Samples of handwriting over a period of time, perhaps one a month, will provide evidence of improvement, or lack of it, and a basis for emphasis in future teaching. A tape recording of a child's speech at a given time can be used as a basis for comparison at a future date. A list of things to do can be posted, and the items can be checked off as they are finished. This can be individualized by letting each child make a personal list. This kind of record keeping can be shared with parents as evidence of accomplishment. It is convincing and satisfying. It is helpful to you in discussing with your supervisor or principal what has been accomplished.

Teacher records are those kept by the teacher for a variety of purposes. They help answer such questions as: Have we covered the curriculum prescribed? Have we attained the objectives indicated at the outset? Has there been growth? How much? Is it commensurate with the abilities of these children? What learnings need to be reemphasized? What comes next? What evidence do I have to report to the parents? To the administration? To the next teacher? Teachers need an abundance of information to serve as support for the program. Some such records are temporary and should be discarded when their purpose has been served. Some are permanent and need to be filed for future use.

Pupil records are those kept by the pupils themselves. Children are personally interested in comparing achievement from one point to another to see growth. They are concerned about completion of a given task. They need to be able to say, "Yes, I can do that," or "I have finished this," or "I need more practice on these skills," or "I have three more to do." These records help answer the question, "How am I doing?" Children don't always need a score to tell that progress is being made and they certainly don't need a teacher to "grade" their work to let them know whether or not they are learning. The highest type of evaluation is self-evaluation. It is when Alice wants to learn, and keeps tab on herself that she has reached that independent stage toward which all education is directed.

SELECTING SUITABLE TESTS

Now that you know why you are going to evaluate and something of the varieties of tests available for measurement, you are ready to select the kinds of tests you will use to answer such questions as: Where are we starting? How much can the child do now? What is each one capable of doing? What is the problem? How much has been achieved? How much growth has taken place? How does the individual compare with national norms? With others in the group? With previous performance? How does this group compare with other groups? Let's examine these questions and identify the types of tests that will be suitable.

Where Are We Starting?

It is the beginning of the year. You have a new group of children. You have access to their cumulative cards but the information recorded there tends to be subjective and influenced by the opinions of previous teachers. What you really want to know is where to start with your teaching. You have decided to test the children. You want to find out how much they already know about the material you are planning to teach. You want to find out the approximate level of difficulty they can cope with in using their skills. A *survey test* may serve your purpose. You may make it yourself or you may use a printed test published by a commercial firm. You want it to contain a sampling of the content to be taught. In this case you do not expect high scores. If the children, or some of them, do score high, perhaps that tells you the curriculum is inappropriate for them. There is no need to spend the semester teaching things they obviously already know. The pretest given in spelling on Monday is an example. If there are twenty-eight words in the list and Allen already knows how to spell twenty of them, it would be a useless waste of time for him to study the whole list.

Another type of test similar in nature to the survey test is an *inventory test*. It is designed to take inventory of accomplishments and needs. For example, you might construct an inventory test in arithmetic by going through the textbook, selecting two examples from each section that presents a new topic, and put them together as a test. When the children take this test, you will find out which types of examples they know how to do and which ones they do not know. For example, Donald might work successfully all the addition examples that do not involve "carrying" and all the subtraction examples that do not involve "borrowing." The inventory has told you what he can do and what he needs to be taught. A reading test, whether it is an informal classroom inventory or a standardized test, will tell you the approximate level at which the child can succeed. This helps you know where to start.

Another type of test useful at the beginning of a year or semester is a *scale test*, sometimes called a *power test*. It is constructed so that the beginning items are easy enough that the child will be sure to get them right. The items get progressively more difficult so that at the end no child is likely to answer them. Such a test serves as a scale indicating the level to which the child can climb at this point.

What Is the Child Capable of Doing?

This question needs to be answered along with the preceding one because knowing Danny cannot do a certain thing may or may not indicate the feasibility of teaching it to him now. Some learnings are graduated in difficulty. No matter how intelligent the children are, they may not be ready for the advanced learning without background. Finding out what Danny is capable of doing, then, is a matter of answering two questions: What background does he have? What ability does he possess?

Background.   Freda may be dealing with a subject in which sequence of skills makes a difference. In this case, you may decide that even though she is not able to multiply fractions, you cannot teach that next because she still does not know how to multiply whole numbers. You may find that she does not know the geographical features of the world but she is not even familiar enough with such information as the formations in the local environment to make adequate comparisons. You may decide that tumbling is worth teaching in physical education but that certain other physical feats must be mastered first. All these factors may persuade you to build some background before moving forward with the needed learnings indicated by the tests.

Ability.   This is a difficult question to answer. Does Johnny lack experience because he does not have the ability? Or does he lack ability because he has had limited experience? In physical development differences tend to be accepted without too much emotionalism, but when it comes to mental abilities the measurements are more difficult to obtain and the results are less likely to be accepted. Whether the child's mentality is limited or not depends in part on the perspective of the viewer. Most parents tend to believe, or want to believe, that their children are just as capable as others if they are given a chance. Teachers accustomed to working with groups of children tend to see some of them as more capable than others and to look on the lesser ones as limited in ability. Because of these observations, tests have been developed that attempt to measure native capacity. Whether they really measure "what the child was born with" or what the child has acquired through the environment is debatable. This discussion is not presented to settle that problem. It is only presented to help you view the differing abilities of the children you are trying to teach.

Tests designed to measure intellectual capacity are called *intelligence tests*. They are made up of exercises representing levels of development. Norms have been established based on the mean responses from large random groups. Some mental ability tests are designed for administration to groups. Others are planned for individual testing. Some of them are based on manipulative responses and others involve pencil-and-paper responses. Some of the responses call for following oral directions and others depend on the child's ability to read the directions. All these variations influence the results. The child who lacks experience, reading skill, or even emotional stability may do poorly on the test, not necessarily because of lack of intelligence, but because of lack of ability or self-assurance to produce the kind of response expected. The creative child may score low on the test, not because he does not know, but because he gives unusual responses not acceptable according to the answer key provided by the test makers.

Regardless of the situation influencing the response, such tests do tell us something. Scoring the child's test yields a raw score, usually nothing more than the number of acceptable responses. From a chart in the manual the raw score is translated into a mental age. This means that the child has performed on the test as well as the average child of that mental age. By comparing the child's interpreted mental age with the actual or chronological age, the tester can compute a ratio and arrive at a figure known as an *Intelligence Quotient* or IQ. If the mental age interpreted from the test is greater than the actual chronological age, that suggests ability to perform at a higher level than the average child of that age, a higher level of intelligence than expected, and therefore an IQ above 100. If Gene's mental age is lower than his chronological age, then he is not performing at as high a level as the average child his age and therefore his IQ is less than 100. The formula is to divide the mental age by the chronological age to determine the ratio. The quotient attained from such a division is a decimal fraction which can be simplified by multiplying by 100, thus eliminating the decimal point. Since mental age (MA) and chronological age (CA) are both expressed in years and months, the arithmetic involves the use of denominate numbers. To simplify the computation, the years and months are usually expressed in months. For example: Mary is 8 years and 10 months old. She has taken a mental test yielding a raw score which has been translated from the manual into a mental age of 7 years and 4 months. In order to compute her IQ take the following steps:

8 years and 10 months = 8 × 12 = 96 + 10 = 106 months CA
7 years and 4 months = 7 × 12 = 84 + 4 = 88 months MA

Since her mental age is less than her chronological age we will expect her IQ to be less than 100.

Dividing 88 by 106 we get a quotient of .83.

To eliminate the decimal point the next step is:

Multiplying .83 × 100 = 83 IQ

Freda is also 8 years and 10 months old. She has taken a mental test yielding a raw score which has been translated from the manual into a mental age of 9 years and 9 months. In order to compute her IQ, take the following steps:

8 years and 10 months = 8 × 12 = 96 + 10 = 106 months CA
9 years and 9 months = 9 × 12 = 108 + 9 = 117 months MA

Since her mental age is greater than her chronological age, we will expect her IQ to be greater than 100.

Divide 117 by 106 to get a quotient of 1.10.
Multiply 1.10 by 100 to get an I.Q. of 110.

Any child whose mental age exactly equals the chronological age obviously will have an IQ of 100.

Understanding the numerical relationships and knowing how the computation is done gives you insight into the meaning of the ratio commonly referred to as an I.Q. It is probably not necessary for you to practice and become skillful in such computation because charts, tables, or calculator wheels can be purchased for a small sum.

Now that you have a measure of intelligence, the question is what does it mean? This measurement should not be used to predetermine what you expect the child to do. It should be considered only as a substantiation for the teacher's observations. Jerry may have more potential than is indicated by the particular test, but the results do tell you the level at which he was functioning at the time he took the test and how he compares with other children nationwide who have taken the same test. If you consider that a child has a *functional IQ* which you have obtained and that this child may have a *potential IQ* somewhat higher if it were possible to get the individual to function closer to the peak of ability, then you have an estimate of ability that may be helpful. If used with caution and judgment such measures can be helpful to the teacher trying to find out what the child is capable of doing.

Other types of tests which yield answers to the question of capability are *aptitude test*, *special talent tests*, and *personality tests*. These are all just what their names imply. Music aptitude tests, art talent tests, physical capacity tests, writing tests, tests of creativity, interest inventories, vocational aptitude tests, and personality tests are designed to serve specific purposes. You will use them only if you need the information they will provide. Such use might better be left in the hands of specialists in the field.

What Is the Problem?

Sometimes you already know that Barbara is having difficulty in a particular area, for example mathematics. You may already know at what level she is functioning. You may have information to lead you to believe that she has native ability to function at a higher level. The question then is: What is the problem and why does it exist? To answer this, you may feel the need for a survey test or a diagnostic test.

The Survey Test.   A test designed to cover a number of areas in order to identify specific accomplishments as well as needs is referred to as a survey test. Its name is self-explanatory. It may tell you that the child can do multiplication but has difficulty with division, but doesn't tell you why. It may tell you the child lacks ability to gain meaning from what is read, but it doesn't tell you whether the lack is caused by inadequate word recognition skills or faulty concept formation. Such tests provide a general survey of the situation.

The Diagnostic Test. Some tests are designated as diagnostic tests, but that may well be a misnomer. The test cannot do the diagnosing. All it can do is yield the information that will enable you to make a diagnosis. A true diagnosis approaches a problem with two questions: What are the symptoms? and Why does the situation exist? The test results enable you to break down the specific learnings into smaller segments and to isolate the problem areas. The test cannot tell you why the problems exist or what has caused them. That is the problem of the diagnostician. After you have found out all the test can tell you, then you still must associate symptoms with probable causes and determine to the best of your ability what has caused this particular problem. One child may have difficulty in reading as evidenced by miscalling words because he cannot see well enough to distinguish the letters one from another. Another may be having similar difficulty with the same symptoms of miscalling words, but a careful study reveals a hearing loss indicating that she has never heard the words accurately in the first place. Still another child may have similar symptoms and a diagnosis may reveal that his vocabulary is so limited that the words have no meaning for him. Your next step is to determine "how the child got that way." Once you have identified the symptoms and determined the cause, or causes, you are ready to prescribe remedial treatment.

How Much Has Been Achieved?

This question is a very practical one. It usually comes at the end of a unit, the end of a semester, or the end of a school year. Both teacher and children get satisfaction from checking up to see if goals have been attained. If you have just finished a unit in social studies on the age of discovery, you may want to summarize the information about explorers, dates, places, and events and put this into a test to see if the children have assimilated it. You are either constructing a test or looking for a commercial test that will include the content of the curriculum just covered or the behavioral objectives stated at the outset.

Curriculum Tests. A test which examines the learners' mastery of the content of the curriculum just covered is often referred to as a curriculum test. Such tests are often provided by the publishing company to go with textbooks or workbooks on the assumption that after a certain area has been covered, a test to determine the extent of mastery is the basis for moving on to the next unit or the next level. It is quite possible and often customary for a teacher to construct a curriculum test to be used with a given group of pupils as a result of a study of a given topic or unit. The pursuit of the unit in the classroom may have led the group along tangents, special interests, local applications, and unexpected digressions to the point where no previously prepared test is adequate for the purpose. In this case you may elect to construct your own test to meet the specific needs of the group. You have been the decision maker in curriculum content and therefore are the one to determine the content of the test and the effectiveness of the teaching and learning.

Criterion-Referenced Tests. A similar type of test is sometimes referred to as a criterion-referenced test. Its name implies both its purpose and its content. You start out with definite behavioral objectives in mind. These may be stated in the planning stage together with the level of proficiency expected. You know the criteria to which the test refers.. You use the criteria to construct the test items. Sometimes such tests are available or are constructed before the actual teaching takes place. Obviously, a commercial test would not serve this purpose unless you are using a prestructured curriculum which has its own test to follow the teaching. In that case the textbook authors and the test makers have predetermined the curriculum and the only part you have had in curriculum decision making is whether or not to follow the prescriptions and at what rate to progress through the material. If you have identified the objectives in terms of the needs and abilities of your children with the help of the curriculum guides, then you will need to have a part in constructing the test measuring the extent to which the criteria have been met. Such a test will not provide grade scores or objective results as a basis for comparison with other groups. It will answer the questions: Have the criteria been met? To what extent? For example: The behavioral objective stated at the outset may be:

> Given: From a list of literary selections, the child will be able to identify each one in terms of literary form to at least 80% accuracy.

The objectively stated test item then may be constructed thus:

> At the left is a list of literary selections (studied in class). Match each one with the correct literary type by writing the appropriate number on the blank space at the right:

1. Shakespeare's "Hamlet"	_____ Novel
2. Emerson's "Compensation"	_____ Poetry
3. Aesop's "Fox and Grapes"	_____ Satire
4. DeFoe's "Robinson Crusoe"	_____ Fable
5. Longfellow's "Village Blacksmith"	_____ Essay
	_____ Drama
	_____ Short Story

Even then this type of test item has its limitations. If Marie is sure of all answers but one, she has arrived at a correct answer for the item she doesn't know by the process of elimination. If Sally guesses incorrectly on one answer, she limits her choice and may end up with two incorrect answers. Even if Betty can't read the questions, let alone the literary selections, by the law of averages she stands a good chance of getting one or two answers right merely by putting numbers in the blanks.

How Do the Results Compare?

Finally, you may want to know how your children compare with other children who have similar backgrounds. This could apply to the class as a group or to individuals in the class. To answer this question you may want to use objective tests. These tests will yield scores that will enable you to compare achievement of the class group or of an individual with national norms. You can also use them to compare the individual with others in the class group. This use should be applied with great caution, however. Perhaps an even more fruitful comparison is one made with the child's own past record. An objective test may be teacher-made or standardized. Your choice of test will depend on your purpose for testing.

Before you select any test or construct one yourself, you will find it advantageous to subject your planning to the same format we suggested in Chap. 3 on lesson planning:

    I. Why am I going to give this test?
    II. What materials will I need?
    III. How will I use the test and its results?
        A. Introduction—Preparing the class for the test.
        B. Administering the test.
        C. Conclusion—Scoring and interpreting the results as a basis for next steps.

TRENDS IN THE USE OF TESTS

Early introduction of testing is evident. Some form of testing has always accompanied attempts to help others learn. Tests are designed as a means of checking up on ourselves to find out whether or not we are accomplishing our goals or are making progress. The standardized-test movement came into the schools in the early part of the present century along with workbooks and studies of child development.

Self-appraisal is an important part of testing. If Kenneth is truly concerned about learning he will be more interested in what he is accomplishing, what his difficulties are, and how much progress he is making than in the score. If he is the best in the class but is making no progress, there is no achievement. If he is the poorest or in the lowest quarter of the class but is making significant progress, there is achievement. This point of view needs to be established if tests are to result in increased learning.

Sampling techniques enable us to get a measurement without having to cover all the points. The principle is used in surveys and polls as well as in tests. The basic principle is that beyond a certain point more evidence would not alter the trend. If Allen can solve ten examples of a given kind, he probably could solve another ten, or perhaps a hundred. Commercial tests are based on this principle, which you can use in the tests you construct.

Accountability is a national concern and its emphasis is reflected in the use of tests in our schools. The public is asking what is being accomplished. For want of a better device for answering this question, many professionals and laypeople alike have turned to tests as instruments of measurement. The program of National Assessment has already been launched. Feelings have run high. Some oppose it because they lack confidence in the program or feel threatened by the possible misuse of the results. Others sanction it because they believe it is possible to use sampling techniques and arrive at some specific answers about content, expectations, regional differences, and levels of achievement without undermining the individual or the schools. Overemphasis on accountability may influence teachers to become score conscious and median oriented in interpretation of results and thus lead them to teach to the test rather than teach to the students. Similarly, overemphasis on tests and scores may lead children to see the score on the test as the goal and miss the significance of growth, utility, or satisfaction in what has been learned.

Performance contracting has emerged out of this emphasis on accountability. This type of program is based on the principle of contracting for certain goals and agreeing to pay only for those who achieve. This approach to teaching and learning is based on the assumption that, given the right materials and the right instruction, any child will learn, and the curriculum writers and test makers can set up the objectives in behavioral terms that can be measured. Such use of tests makes the children the subject of the teaching rather than the active agents in their own learning. It poses a threat and encourages pressures from those who feel accountable for the child's learning. Reports from school systems that have signed performance contracts with commercial concerns vary. Some claim great results. Some are skeptical, and some are quite critical. We suspect much of the interpretation depends on the point of view and the prejudices of the interpreter. It is quite possible to gather evidence to support almost any premise you want to believe.

The publishing company which offers a contract saying, "This material used with your children at a given grade level will result in performance at 90% accuracy with 80% of the pupils," is entering into a business arrangement. Statistical results indicated by terminal testing may show accomplishments that yield a satisfactory profit for the company. But that still does not improve the learnings for those at the lower end of the scale. They represent that other 20% excluded by the contract. Likewise, the highly capable children who may be performing below their potential still contribute to the measure of successful performance guaranteed in the contract even though they are capable of doing much more and are not being challenged by the program.

Uses and *values* as well as *abuses* and *limitations* of tests must be noted. No test can be judged good or bad in and of itself. It all depends on the use that is made of it. If tests are abused by using them to threaten the learner, to destroy sense of self-worth, to punish for lack of ability, to provide evidence for failure, they are doing more harm than good. But if they are used as a means of self-appraisal, a basis for determining level of achievement at a given point, a source of information on which to base future teaching, an answer to questions about curriculum content, they can be useful and valuable. In the same way, if tests are used to threaten the teacher and evaluate teaching effectiveness in terms of pupil scores, they are encouraging teaching to the test and coercing the learners to conform. But if they are used as a means of appraisal at certain checkpoints in order to determine next steps, they can be both helpful and valuable.

SUMMARY

If we are to be accountable for what we are doing, we must have some means of checking up on ourselves and measuring the product. We measure to determine the extent to which our objectives have been met, to evaluate the effectiveness of both teaching and learning, to identify our accomplishments, and to provide a basis for next steps and future goals.

There are many ways of measuring accomplishment. Observation from day to day is one of the most common means of appraising results. In order to make the observations meaningful, record keeping in the form of anecdotal accounts of activities and scores on tests are helpful. Perhaps one of the more common means of measurement is the test. Tests may be teacher-made or purchased from a commercial publisher. They may be subjective, that is, based on opinion, or objective, which implies capable of being interpreted without the element of personal opinion. Standardized tests are those for which norms have been established. They provide a basis for comparison.

Selecting a suitable measuring device depends on identifying the question. What do you want to know? If you want to know where to start, a survey or inventory test will help. If you want to know what the child is capable of doing, use an aptitude test, a special talent test, a capacity test, or an intelligence test. If you want to know how much has been accomplished, perhaps you need a curriculum test or a criterion-referenced test designed to measure what has been taught. If you want to know how results compare with established norms you need a standardized achievement test.

Trends in testing show an early introduction of the testing movement into the schools. Sampling techniques have proven effective. Self-appraisal is personal. These have led to a movement toward accountability reflected in National Assessment and performance contracting. These have their uses but they can be abused. They have both values and limitations. It is your responsibility to determine purposes and select suitable measuring devices for the best interests of the pupils in your classroom. And once the tests have been administered it is your further responsibility to use the results to find out all you can about your pupils so you can plan future goals more effectively.

Now that you have measured the results of teaching, you are ready to make use of the information. That calls for keeping records of accomplishments. In the next chapter, we will take up the matter of record keeping in terms of kinds of information worth recording and forms in which records will be useful. Not the least of these will be the test results which will serve as a basis for reporting to children, parents, administrators, and other teachers what has been accomplished and what the present status is.

SUGGESTED ACTIVITIES

1. Collect samples of tests for a class exhibit.
   Identify them as:
   > Subjective or objective
   > Teacher-made or commercial
   > Informal or standardized
   > Achievement or ability
   > General or criterion

   Note: These categories will not be mutually exclusive; for example, one test can be objective, commercial, standardized, and a measure of general ability all at the same time. Another may be informal, teacher-made, subjective, and criterion-referenced in terms of achievement.
2. Construct examples of test questions to illustrate each of the following categories:
   > Essay form
   > Alternate answer form
   >> (a) Yes–No
   >> (b) True–False
   >> (c) Either–Or
   >
   > Multiple choice
   > Simple recall (filling blanks)
   > Completion

3. Administer a test to a group of children, or to your classmates. Score the test.

   Analyze the results:

   (a) In terms of what the test tells about accomplishment.
   (b) In terms of what the results tell about the effectiveness of the test itself.

4. Give a test and diagnose the results by determining:

   (a) Areas of accomplishment
   (b) Areas of need
   (c) Probable causes of difficulty

   Prescribe remedial teaching to correct the problems.

SELECTED READINGS

1. BLOCK, JAMES H. and ROBERT L. EBEL, "Criterion Referenced Measurements: Limitations," in *School Review*, Vol. 79, No. 2, Feb. 1971, pp. 282–88. Title suggests content.

2. BLUM, STUART H., "Group Test Administration: Promises and Problems," in *Educational Forum*, Vol. XXXIII, No. 2, Jan. 1969, pp. 213–18. Presents both sides of the question of the use of group tests.

3. BRAIN, GEORGE B., "National Assessment Moves Ahead," in *Today's Education*, Vol. 60, No. 2, Feb. 1971, p. 45. Public concern, results now available in three areas, current reports in the first series.

4. BRAZZIEL, WILLIAM F., "Criterion-Referenced Tests—Some Trends and Prospects," in *Today's Education*, Vol. 61, No. 8, Nov. 1972, pp. 52–53. Identifies criterion-referenced tests and points out both advantages and disadvantages. Names publishers and tests.

5. COSTA, ARTHUR L., "Who's Accountable to Whom?" in *Educational Leadership*, Vol. 28, No. 1, Oct. 1970, pp. 15–19. Autonomy or immunity? The autonomous teacher, instant autonomy. Accountability to whom? For what? Negative attitude toward accountability.

6. DZIUBAN, CHARLES D. and KENNETH V. VICKERY, "Criterion-Referenced Measurement: Some Recent Developments," in *Educational Leadership*, Vol. 30, No. 5, Feb. 1973, pp. 483–86. Points out a score may indicate level of achievement but does not tell which items were missed or what the pupil can do. Emphasizes need for identifying criteria before designing tests.

7. GREEN, JOHN A., *An Introduction to Measurement and Evaluation*, New York: Dodd, Mead & Co., 1970. Real and practical problems in test construction and interpretation. Nontechnical. Part III is on evaluating and reporting to parents.

8. GUMM, GEORGE H., "National Assessment: A Point of View," in *Educational Forum*, Vol. XXXIV, No. 3, Mar. 1970, pp. 407–08. Defends the program on the theory that proper use of results can become the means by which the public will rally to the aid of the educational program.

9. HOLEMEN, MILTON G., and RICHARD F. DOCTOR, "Criticisms of Standardized Testing," in *Today's Education*, Vol. 63, No. 1, Jan.–Feb. 1974, pp. 50–54 and 58–60. Points out basic criticisms of use of standardized tests. Recognizes constructive contributions to human assessment as beneficial.

10. HOLT, JOHN, "I Oppose Testing, Marking, and Grading," in *Today's Education*, Vol. 60, No. 3, Mar. 1971, pp. 28–31. Points out difficulties. Recommends that teachers refuse to give them.

11. HOOVER, KENNETH H. and PAUL M. HOLLINGSWORTH, *Learning and Teaching in the Elementary School*, Boston: Allyn and Bacon, 1970. Part IV on coping with persistent instructional problems contains a chapter on assessing learning.

12. JARVIS, OSCAR T. and MARION, J. RICE, *An Introduction to Teaching in the Elementary School*, Dubuque, Iowa: Wm. C. Brown, 1972. Chapter 20 is on measuring the results of instruction, and evaluating and reporting pupil growth.

13. JOHNSON, GEORGE H., "National Assessment: Where Is It Now?" in *Educational Leadership*, Vol. 29, No. 4, Jan. 1972, pp. 327–28. Brings the history up to date and indicates what results are currently available.

14. KARMEL, LOUIS J., *Measurement and Evaluation in the Schools*, New York: Macmillan, 1970. Part Four discusses group standardized testing and Part Five discusses teacher-made tests and grades.

15. LESSINGER, LEON M., *Every Kid a Winner: Accountability in Education*, New York: Simon and Schuster, 1970. Places emphasis on skill acquisition and the use of standardized tests. Influenced by funding. Will affect organization and management in education.

16. LONDON, HERBERT I., "The Futility of Testing: Simulations as a 'Test' Case," in *Educational Leadership*, Vol. 28, No. 1, Oct. 1970, pp. 93–95. Feels educators have been obsessed with scientific testing and that the results tell us very little.

17. MAGER, ROBERT F., *Developing Attitude Toward Learning*, Palo Alto, Calif.: Fearon, 1968. Seeks to answer such questions as Where Am I Going? How Shall I Get There? and How Will I Know I've Arrived?

18. MAGINNIS, GEORGE H., "Measuring Underachievement in Reading," in *The Reading Teacher*, Vol. 25, No. 8, May 1972, pp. 750–53. Points out the use of measures of intelligence as a means of indicating achievement expectations in reading and some of the faulty assumptions and confusing comparisons that result from this practice.

19. MARSHALL, JON C. and LOYDE W. HALES, *Classroom Test Construction*, Menlo Park, Calif.: Addison-Wesley, 1971. Devoted to the construction and analysis of classroom tests. Types of tests, scoring, evaluation.

20. MECKLENBURGER, JAMES A., "Performance Contracts? One View," in *Educational Leadership*, Vol. 29, No. 4, Jan. 1972, pp. 297–300. Points out claims of advocates. Presents the case against as caused by overemphasis on stereotypes and business greed.

21. NUNNALLY, JUM C., *Educational Measurement and Evaluation* (2nd edition), Principles of testing. Using, scoring, and interpreting. Testing Programs. Prediction. Standardized tests.

22. Reading Teacher, "Testing and the Classroom Teacher," in *The Reading Teacher*, Vol. 26, No. 3, Dec. 1972. pp. 260–310. A series of seven articles dealing with testing in reading. Discusses informal testing, inventories, criterion-referenced tests, national assessment, and standardized tests. Evaluates use of test results in terms of both process and product. Contributions by eleven different authors.

23. SCHOER, LOWELL A., *Test Construction: A Programmed Guide*, Boston: Allyn and Bacon, 1970. A programmed text giving an overall view of testing. Provides examples.

24. STAKE, ROBERT E., "Testing Hazards in Performance Contracting," in *Phi Delta Kappan*, Vol. 52, No. 10, pp. 583–89, June 1971. Points out dangers.

25. TYLER, RALPH W., "First Reports from the National Assessment," in *Educational Leadership*, Vol. 28, No. 6, Mar. 1971, pp. 577–80. What children are learning. Facts, skills, and attitudes. Effects of gain in experience.

26. TYLER, RALPH W., "Testing for Accountability," in *Nation's Schools*, Vol. 86, No. 6, Dec. 1970, pp. 37–39. Differentiates between testing for achievement and testing for accountability.

27. WILES, JON WHITNEY, "The Hidden Cost of Performance Contracting: Viewpoint," in *Educational Leadership*, Vol. 28, No. 5, Feb. 1971, pp. 533–35. He believes that the current promotion of the performance contract as a panacea for better schools is nothing short of a sham.

28. WILLIAMS, LOIS, "Governance Is Integral to Accountability," in *Today's Education*, Vol. 60, No. 4, Apr. 1971, pp. 59–60. Teacher standards and licensure act. NEA stand. State legislation. Need for professional autonomy.

12

KEEPING RECORDS AND REPORTING RESULTS

What Information to Record and How to Tell What Happened

Courtesy, Skiff School, Phoenix, Arizona

RECORD KEEPING

How good are you at keeping things? Records for instance? Do you come to the end of the month wondering what you did with your money? Do you come to the end of the week wondering where your time went? Are you going to let yourself come to the end of the semester or the year wondering what your children have accomplished? This will happen if you don't keep some systematic records.

Do you know what kind of information is worth recording? What do you know or what can you find out about the children's personal backgrounds? Does this information have any bearing on your teaching? How can you find out what the children accomplished last year? The year before? What kind of information will you pass along to the teacher who will meet them next year? Who's going to keep all those records? And when? Can the children help?

Do you know in what form to keep the records so they will be most useful? Can records be detrimental? Can you keep too many records? What will you do with them after you have kept them? Merely filling up the file case is not the objective, you know.

With whom will you share the records? With the principal? With the parents? With the children? With the other teachers? For what reasons? You will have in your possession much professional information which must be used with discretion and communicated judicially. Just as doctors and lawyers do not divulge professional information about their patients and clients, neither must you be indiscriminate in discussing facts or opinions about your students.

Keeping the score doesn't necessarily mean finding out who is the winner. It may mean knowing the answers to such questions as: "How much progress are we making?" "How are we doing?" "What of the future?" Every worker likes to know what the goal is and what steps will lead to its accomplishments. To stand at midpoint and look back enables you to see what has been accomplished to date. To turn and look in the opposite direction helps to keep your eyes on the goal. To compare today's work with yesterday's achievements gives a measuring stick by which to gauge progress. This is true for both you and the pupil.

One of the surest ways to provide concrete evidence for such measurement is to keep a record. What one did long ago often looks inadequate and immature in comparison with what has been done in the interim or is being done now. Samples of work performed over a period of time and a record of activities or scores provide a baseline from which to measure progress. Information thus accumulated is good for sharing with others—the children, the parents, the administration, the other teachers. If you know how to keep useful records, you will provide yourself with a needed basis for planning next steps as well as for communicating with others. If you know how to transmit the information effectively, you are on your way to success. You will be checking up daily as well as intermittently. You will have subjective information and objective data. Part of your responsibility as a teacher will be preserving and organizing this information so that it will be available when needed.

KEEPING RECORDS OF PROGRESS
TOWARD CURRICULUM TARGETS

Although record keeping may be viewed as a routine and uncreative task, it is a very necessary part of your work. The more complex society becomes the more essential carefully kept records become. This fact is obvious in our governmental, hospital, and personal records. In order to make your records your servant and not your master, you need to know what kind of information is worth recording and in what form it will be most useful.

What Kinds Of Information Are Worth Recording?

It is possible to keep too many records and to provide too much detail. Such a practice ends in an avalanche of paper that is too confusing to be useful. Voluminous records carefully filed and never used are a waste of paper, time, and energy. There are, however, some personal and scholastic records that can be very useful.

Personal Records. Knowing the child as a unique human being is basic to effective teacher-pupil relationships. Children come in all ages, sizes, shapes, and colors. They come from all kinds of backgrounds. You will find your understanding of each child deepened if you know something of family background, health history, personality, and general ability. How much of that information is relevant to the targets of the curriculum is a matter of opinion. How much of it is so personal that the schools could be accused of "invasion of privacy" may be debatable.

Family background information is customarily recorded for each child. This includes date and place of birth, facts concerning current residence, and type of household. Other information might include occupation of the father, and perhaps of the mother. There are those who would question the right of the school to record race, marital status of parents, family income, and court records. You will probably be furnished with standard forms indicating types of information you should record. It is your responsibility to conform to the requirements of the school system in securing as much of this information as possible. Collecting and recording any additional information is your own decision. All such information should be considered just as confidential as that held by a doctor or lawyer.

Health history is usually recorded for each child. Any disabling conditions certainly should be known in order that you may adjust school expectations to existing limitations. Knowing what diseases Sam has had, what immunizations he has had, something about his vision and hearing, and perhaps even his height and weight will be helpful not only in understanding Sam, but also in carrying out the health program of the school. Such records serve an additional function of service to the family since some parents do not keep an accurate record or do not have a regular family physician who keeps such records for them.

Personality and general ability records are subjective and more likely to be questioned. Tests of personality and of general intelligence exist that yield scores or other kinds of information. Such information may give insight into a child's attitudes and potential. Great care should be exercised to see that this kind of information is not misinterpreted and is properly used. There is the danger that such information recorded on permanent forms may influence teacher attitudes and even "brand" the child, thus actually deterring adjustment to school and learning.

Scholastic Records.   What takes place in the school in the pursuit of the targets of the curriculum is for the record. It is not only the right of the school, but also its duty to keep such records in order to keep both child and parents informed of achievements and progress, and to provide information for the administrators and other teachers who will be responsible for next steps. How much is enough? How much is too much? What information should be provided for temporary use and then be discarded? What facts should be recorded in permanent form to follow the child during an entire school career? You may save samples of each child's work, write narrative accounts of events to support conclusions and record such objective information as test scores.

Samples of work serve as a record of accomplishment and growth. One teacher who followed a group of children through first and second grade kept a dated sample of writing papers collected at the end of each six weeks period. By the end of the second grade there were twelve papers for each child. When the papers were arranged in sequence and bound together into a booklet, they provided the parent as well as the child with tangible evidence of growth. Similar examples can be accumulated in any area. They may be illustrations, snap shots, tape recordings, or informal notes written by the children themselves. They serve as evidence of learning or lack of growth. A file folder for each pupil has merit. Children can contribute to the file and inspect it from time to time. It should be "weeded out" at intervals.

Narrative accounts of what is occurring are helpful. You think you will remember, but you won't. A week later you won't remember for sure whether it was Anne or Karen who brought in the specimen so useful in the science class, or whether it was a story or an arithmetic problem that left Inez in tears. It is a good idea to establish a large looseleaf notebook with a page inserted for each child. Then form the habit of spending a few minutes at the end of each day writing up your diary. Turn the pages and as you come to the page for a child with whom something noteworthy has happened that day, jot it down. And don't forget to date your notes. What you record may be positive or negative, trivial or consequential, but the fact that you noticed it and bothered to record it will help to make that child stand out as an individual. You may make such brief notes as:

11–13	Forgot her lunch money again.
11–21	Insisted she had the money for her pictures and someone took it.
12–1	Didn't finish arithmetic paper because she couldn't find her pencil.

You won't need to write the child's name each time because it is at the top of the page. As these records accumulate, they may tend to form a pattern. A comment such as "careless" is judgmental. A fact is a basis for a judgment. You won't write about every child every day, but if a month goes by and you have made no notes on Gene's page, it will become obvious that you are not completely aware of him and need to take notice.

Such records may or may not be shared with the child or the parents. As soon as children gain some skill in writing, they can start keeping their own records. When Charles makes a daily entry under "What I have done today" he has an answer to his father's question, "What did you learn at school today?" Sometimes he says, "Nothing," not because nothing happened but because he was not aware of the significant happenings.

Objective records such as test scores furnish evidence of accomplishment. These may be kept in the child's file folder, recorded in your class register, or entered on the cumulative card. Caution needs to be exercised here lest you become merely a tester accumulating evidence to support marks and promotions. Measurement from time to time is a good basis for evaluation and further planning, but make sure you spend much more time in teaching the children how to do something than in checking up on them to see that they did, or counting mistakes for the record.

In What Forms Are Records Useful?

Some records may be informal and subjective. Others may be formal and objective. You need to know the difference and what purposes each kind serves.

Informal Records: Subjective Information.   Some of the records you keep may pertain to the entire class and others may relate only to small groups or individuals. We have already mentioned the diary accounts of individuals. More extensive records might include classroom accounts of activities planned or completed, case histories, or sociometric studies of interpersonal relationships.

Anecdotal records may pertain to an individual or a group. The important thing to remember in keeping such a record is to make sure it is factual rather than evaluative. Avoid such notations as:

> Mary is usually pleasant and happy.
> Tommy is bothersome in the group.
> Billy accumulates junk and is messy.
> Carol loses things.
> Frances is a joy to have in the room.

If you are pressed to justify any of these conclusions, you may find it difficult to recall specific incidents; or you may find that one tantrum at the beginning of the year conditioned you to see Sally as an emotionally disturbed child, and you may have formed a judgment that cannot be substantiated by accumulated evidence. The record is more helpful if it contains hard facts in the form of such notations as:

> Billy left his sweater on the playground.
> Tommy forgot to return his report card.
> Sally has been late three mornings this week.
> Grace has finished her workbook.
> Mildred finished reading her fourth library book.

Records of activities either planned or completed serve as a good basis for checking the use of time, balance in the curriculum, or interrelationships among the areas of study. You might find it expedient from time to time to list such items as "Things to do," "Topics to be included in this unit," or "Books and supplies to get ready." Making lists and crossing off items makes sure things get done and helps you keep organized. You might want to share this kind of record keeping with the children by discussing with them "What we need to do today." Make a list and check off the items completed, or hold an evaluation session at the end of the day. With older children these planning sessions may cover a longer period of time such as a week, a grading period, or the duration of a unit. Older children can keep their personal lists.

Case histories have value especially when a pupil becomes a problem. It is doubtful if you will want to write case histories for a large number of your children. Most of them, even though they are unique as individuals, do manage to survive the rigorous environment of the home, the school, and the community and make a reasonably satisfactory adjustment. Occasionally you will find a child who needs more than the usual amount of attention. If Carl's problems are so great that he needs to be referred to the doctor, the psychologist, or a psychiatrist, you may find it helpful to record some of the pertinent details in the form of a case history. This will include notes from your anecdotal records as well as factual information about family, health, performance in school, and even test scores. Such a record will aid specialists trying to add their insights to the understanding of the problem. Case histories should always be considered confidential information and should be destroyed when problems have been resolved.

Sociometric studies help you see the child as a member of a group. There are various ways of gleaning the information for making a sociogram, but, in any case, the techniques should be obscured from the child. You might observe and make notes on which children play together or choose each other. You might ask the children to tell you who are their best friends. You could give each one a first, second, and third choice of seat partners or committee workers. Once you have the information you can organize it into a chart and a diagram that will help you identify the children who are popular, the ones who are "loners," and the rejected children. Such information can be recorded on a chart showing choices each one makes. See Fig. 12–1.

From this chart the following conclusions can be drawn:

Each child made one choice.
Alice and Patty are popular. Each was chosen by three others.
Carol, Lynn, and Gaye are acceptable to at least one or two others.
Five children did not get chosen at all. They are Mary, Erma, Betty, Barbara, and Nancy.
Carol and Alice are mutual choices.
Patty and Lynn are mutual choices.
The other six made choices that were not reciprocated.

From this information you can identify not only the leaders but the children who need support. Fig. 12–2 puts this information into a sociogram showing the class divided into two distinct groups with Patty the focus of one group and Alice the focus of the other. There is no cross over from one group to the other. Barbara is on the fringe of one group and Erma on the fringe of the other group. They are the isolates, if not the rejected ones.

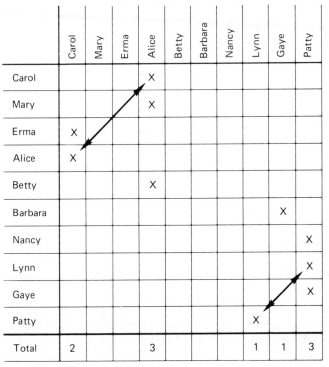

	Carol	Mary	Erma	Alice	Betty	Barbara	Nancy	Lynn	Gaye	Patty
Carol				X						
Mary				X						
Erma	X									
Alice	X									
Betty				X						
Barbara									X	
Nancy										X
Lynn										X
Gaye										X
Patty								X		
Total	2			3				1	1	3

Figure 12-1. *Record of children's choices of partners for a class project.*

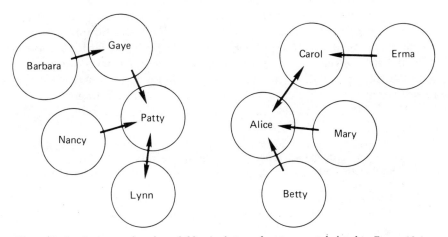

Figure 12-2. *Sociogram based on children's choices of partners as tabulated in Figure 12-1.*

Formal Records: Objective Data. Other records may be more formal and objective. Some of them will include individual data and others will be group records with studies of central tendencies. They may include attendance data, health records, and test scores. All these will be useful in studying the progress of the individual and in evaluating the results of teaching.

Attendance and progress records on the cumulative card tell a story. The child who is always present and on time, who progresses through the school at a normal rate year after year, and who remains in the same school throughout the elementary years is building up a record of stability which will affect the kind of person he or she is becoming as well as the quality of learning. Irregular attendance, frequent illnesses, moving from school to school, and repetitions of grade-level assignments may result from poor school adjustment, or may cause poor adjustment. Such cumulative records are worth keeping and worth noting.

Factual data recorded by previous teachers on cumulative cards may give you clues to some of the problems you face with your children. There may be events during the year that will seem significant enough to record, such as a major accident, a prolonged absence, the loss of a parent, the birth of a sibling, the winning of a contest, a special honor bestowed, or a drastic change in scholastic attainment. Such information should be entered in the record as a statement of fact without subjective interpretation.

Scores on tests objectively tell what has transpired. Even though external factors sometimes do influence test scores, they are still worth recording for the sequential story they tell. A record of standardized tests given each year indicates the approximate level of achievement at a given point and implies the amount of growth from year to year. These records may be expressed in raw scores, percentiles, or grade scores. *Raw scores* tell only the number right and are not comparable from one area to another or from one year to the next. *Percentiles* tell the child's position in the total population. An individual might remain in the sixtieth percentile year after year and still be making good progress. *Grade scores* compare the child with the total population at a given level. Figure 12–3 shows a child's record on the cumulative card. It can be viewed in terms of progress.

From this record one can make the following observations:

The battery mean indicates near normal growth from year to year and satisfactory growth (+ 4.3) over the four-year interval.

Arithmetic computation shows more growth (+ 4.9) than problem solving (+ 3.0).

Growth is greater in vocabulary (+ 4.4) than in comprehension (+ 3.6).

Spelling skills show satisfactory growth (+ 4.6).

GRADE LEVEL	READING VOCAB.	READING COMPRE.	ARITH. COMPUT.	PROBLEM SOLVING	SPELLING	BATTERY MEDIAN
2	2.8	2.7	3.0	2.4	2.9	2.6
3	3.9	3.6	4.2	3.2	4.0	3.8
4	5.0	4.5	5.5	4.0	5.3	4.9
5	6.1	5.4	6.9	4.8	6.7	6.0
6	7.2	6.3	7.9	5.4	7.5	6.9
Growth	4.4	3.6	4.9	3.0	4.6	4.3

Figure 12-3. *Record of an individual's test scores year by year on an achievement battery showing growth over the four-year interval.*

Skills tend to be better than reasoning and thinking as evidenced by growth:

Skills		*Thinking*	
Vocabulary	+ 4.4	Reading Compre.	+ 3.6
Arith. Comp.	+ 4.9	Prob. Solving	+ 3.0
Spelling	+ 4.6		

The needs for teaching will be revealed by similar data for the class as a whole with a record of spread from high to low as well as a measure of central tendency. See Fig. 12-4. Suppose a test indicates that the class median is 5.4. This may seem satisfactory for a fifth grade at the middle of the year, but if the scores distribute themselves so that there is a wide range, the teaching problem may be far from normal. The records indicate:

2 children working at eighth grade level
3 children working at seventh grade level
5 children working at sixth grade level
10 children working at fifth grade level
4 children working at fourth grade level
4 children working at third grade level
3 children working at second grade level

This shows a class of thirty-one children with a median achievement near the middle of fifth grade level, but this does not mean you can teach them all at the same level. Such a record will help you in identifying strengths and weaknesses. It will be beneficial for planning teaching in terms of needs.

GRADE SCORES	NUMBER OF CASES	
8.0–8.9	2	
7.0–7.9	3	
6.0–6.9	5	
5.0–5.9	10	Mode
4.0–4.9	4	
3.0–3.9	4	
2.0–2.9	3	
Total	31 cases	
Median	5.4	
Norm	5.4	

Figure 12-4. *Distribution of achievement scores in reading for a fifth grade class during the fourth month of the school year.*

REPORTING RESULTS

If you keep the records and then file them away, they serve no useful purpose. You should use them to help you understand the children and their needs. They can also serve as a medium of communication. Some of the records are of value in judging the overall program of the school. Some of them contain information of personal interest to parents and children. Some of them will be helpful to others working with these same children in the ensuing years. Knowing to whom the information should be reported is a professional responsibility. Knowing in what form to report such information is a skill you need to acquire.

To Whom Should Reports Be Made?

Unused information is of no value. Information incorrectly used can be harmful. As a teacher, you will have in your possession much information that should be considered confidential. Of course, you will never discuss one child with another in any way that might be detrimental or embarrassing to either. For the same reason, you will not discuss with a parent the problems of other people's children. Such matters are not their concern and should not be used for comparison purposes either to blame or to exalt a child. Any tendency to "gossip" about the children should be studiously avoided even among your fellow teachers. Even if you may meet your coworkers or the parents of your pupils socially you should remember that this is definitely not the place to exchange confidences. Not only should information not be divulged, but the subject should be carefully avoided.

Reporting To The Child.   The child is the most important person in the whole situation. David has every right to know what his scores are, how he is doing, and what is in his file. He may have direct access to some of these records and you will certainly want to discuss some of them with him from time to time. He has some responsibility for contributing to the records.

Reporting To The Parents.   Parents have more involvement in the development of the child than anyone else. They also have much to contribute to the records and are entitled to as much information as they are able to handle effectively. Some educators consider results of intelligence tests outside this domain, but even this information is subject to the criteria of handling it effectively. Parents who understand the principle of intelligence testing and the variability of such results may be entitled to know something of the potential of their own children. On the other hand, perhaps such information should be withheld from the parent who thinks the child is perfect if 100 is obtained on the I.Q. test, the one who administers physical punishment because the child made a low score, or even the one who uses a high score to brag at the bridge party. Test scores may reveal helpful information but must be correctly handled. Certainly health records should be open to parents. You will often have to make personal judgments about anecdotal records you have kept. The first criterion in keeping any record and in reporting it to anyone is, "What is in the best interest of the child?" Making such judgments is your personal responsibility, and even then you cannot always be sure.

Reporting To The Administration.   Administrators may require certain records such as enrollments, attendance, withdrawals, grade placement, and birth dates. These should be kept accurately. And the sooner you learn that a certain amount of conformity is essential to the smooth functioning of the whole school, the sooner you will form the habit of dispensing with such routine promptly and accurately. If you are late with your attendance report, you cause the principal to hold up the report for the entire school. Such seemingly minor frustrations are often the cause of unnecessary friction.

Reporting To Other Teachers.   Other teachers will be able to work more effectively with the children if they have access to background information. If you are a member of a teaching team, or special teachers work with some or all of your children, they too, should have access to the records. This also applies to special service personnel such as remedial teachers, school nurses, counselors, and supervisors or administrators. Care must be exercised in opening personal records to noncertified personnel such as paid teachers' aides, volunteer help, custodial staff, or cafeteria workers. Any records passed along to the next teacher should be carefully selected to be helpful in planning for the best interests of the child. Preparing your reports for sharing calls for great care. Make sure they are accurate, concise, fair, and always designed to be advantageous to the child. Remember you are not here to pass judgment or throw stumbling blocks in the way, but rather to help each one learn and grow.

In What Forms Should Reports Be Made?

Probably more committees have spent more time in designing forms for keeping records and reporting results than on any other school problem. No doubt that item even outranks the planning of curriculum content in the demands it makes on the professional worker. Cumulative record forms are revised frequently to meet new demands. Report cards are a perennial source of concern both in designing the forms to be used and in collecting and recording the information to put on them. A modern trend is to supplant at least a part of the work of the report card with planned parent conferences. And these call for carefully kept records if they are to be fruit-ful.

Cumulative Records.   Records may be kept on forms purchased from some commercial publisher, or forms may be developed to fit an individual school system. You, as a teacher, probably will not have much to say about the design of such a record unless you remain in the same position long enough to be asked to work on a committee revising the forms. It is your responsibility to handle the forms for the children assigned to you. Children new to the school need new cards started. This applies to kindergarteners or first graders, and to any new enrollees entering the system. Any information recorded on that card is entrusted to you as a professional. Handle it with integrity. Any information you add to the card will follow the child. Be sure that you add only what is accurate and helpful. Critical comments and biased judgments have no place here. Any negative implications should be in the form of facts, not judgments. One can't emphasize too often that these records are solely for the benefit of the child.

Formal Report Cards.   As soon as pioneer schools reached an organized basis where children were passed from one teacher to another, a formal method of communicating the needs and achievements of the students had to be devised. And so report cards came into being. A collec-tion of reporting forms representing a one-hundred-year span reveals much about the history and philosophy of education. A composite list assembled from a collection of report cards from various school systems over a period of years is summarized in Fig. 12–5. This alphabetical listing merely shows the extent and range of such reporting. There is duplication, but the list shows what different people thought was worth reporting in different schools at different times.

Arithmetic	Declamation	Language	Penmanship
Art	Deportment	Language Arts	Phonics
Art Appreciation	Dramatization	Literature	Physical Education
Behavior	Drawing	Manners	Physical Exercise
Bible Study	Elocution	Manual Training	Physiology
Bookkeeping	English	Mathematics	Play
Catechism	General Science	Morals	Reading
Chorus	Geography	Music	Science
Ciphering	Government	Music appreciation	Sewing
Citizenship	Grammar	Music Memory	Sex Education
Civics	Gymnasium	Nature Study	Singing
Composition	Handwork	Needlework	Social Studies
Computation	Handwriting	Numbers	Speech
Conduct	Health	Nutrition	Spelling
Constitution	History	Oral Language	U.S. History
Cooking	Hygiene	Oral Reading	World History
Cooperation	Industrial Arts	Orthography	Writing
Crafts	Knitting	Participation	Zoology

Figure 12–5. *Composite list of items appearing on a collection of elementary school report cards.*

Forms for reporting have varied from a simple one-page card with a listing of subjects and a column for recording marks at the end of each grading period to complex booklets with major headings and subheadings, keys for interpretation, and sometimes full-color illustrations. The significant factor is the code or key used for transmitting the message. These are varied and have included percentages, scales, symbols, descriptive terms, and personal notes. Some of them bear further consideration and evaluation.

Percentage marks are based on the assumption that all the children are working at a common level and have been given the same assignment. Some children did all the work while others did lesser amounts which can be measured on a percentage scale. Or all the children did the same work with varying degrees of perfection which can be measured in terms of percent correct. Such a score becomes the basis for identifying a point which can be considered "satisfactory" or "passing."

A, B, C, D, E Scale is a five-point scale which is supposed to be a simplification of the percentage scale. This form differs from the percentage scale however, in that it is based on the principle of a normal curve. Such a curve has been found to apply to certain characteristics in large unselected groups, with the largest number of cases falling in the middle and decreasing numbers falling at the extremes. This assumes that a large portion of the class will be "average" no matter what the standard.

Numbers such as 1, 2, 3, 4, 5 constitute a scale which serves essentially the same purpose as the A, B, C, scale. The numbers provide a five-point scale for comparison. The 3 becomes the "average" and the high point can be either the 5 or the 1. This distribution is an arbitrary decision.

Symbols such as a plus mark (+), a check mark (✔), and a minus sign (−) are devices representing a further attempt to simplify the system. Interpretation of these symbols varies. They can stand for:

> above average, average, and below average
> above grade level, at grade level, and below grade level
> achieving a high level, satisfactory, and could do better

In addition, they could have any other interpretation the designers or users wish to apply to the system. They are still based on the concept of a scale that measures the child against a standard or in comparison with others in the group.

Descriptive terms such as satisfactory and unsatisfactory are sometimes used and are represented by the letters S and U. This reduces reporting to a two-point scale. The application is based on the teacher's judgment as to what is satisfactory. And what is satisfactory for one child, that is, representing the child's best efforts, could be quite unsatisfactory for another child who has more ability. Attempts at comparison are difficult to explain.

Personal notes sometimes accompany or are used in lieu of formal report cards. These are as varied as the users. Some of them may lack meaningful communication and some deteriorate into stereotyped cliches. They can be helpful if well planned and carefully written. Extreme care must be exercised both in the content of the note and the grammatical structure of the message.

Report cards are customarily issued at spaced intervals ranging all the way from once a month or once each six weeks, to twice a semester, or even twice a year. Some schools try to individualize this communication by presenting the cards at different times for different children. Sometimes the report card is issued at the time of the planned conference. Whenever it is issued, it is meant to serve two purposes, to report on achievement and progress, and to record for future reference.

Planned Parent Conferences.   It is becoming increasingly common to hold face-to-face conferences between parents and teachers in order to open channels of communication. Each has a contribution to make. The parent sees the child subjectively. The teacher should see pupils more objectively.

Both points of view have value. Through effective communication they can work toward a common goal. Some contacts may be quite informal and incidental; others may be prearranged. Some communications may be in group meetings with parents who have common concerns. Others will be private and individual.

The business like procedure of the formal communication will be easier if there is mutual understanding and trust and if there is careful preliminary preparation. The parent may feel more comfortable when receiving a friendly invitation such as:

Dear _____,

    I hope you can find a neighbor or friend to help you out for a half hour or so by letting your children play in her yard while you come to school for a discussion of Billy's work. Can you come next Wednesday at 3:30?

                        Sincerely,

_____

Some teachers find it more convenient to make such appointments by telephone, and some even plan home visits. Much of the way you manage the conferences will depend on the policies of the school. There may be a definite schedule or mimeographed forms for you to use. If so, use them, but remember, the parent is interested and concerned. It is your task to make the parent welcome and to see that the communication is helpful in producing mutual understanding of the child. Approach the conference in a friendly manner. Have samples of the child's work ready. Give the parent an opportunity to contribute to the discussion and to ask questions. You might start by asking such questions as:

    What kind of papers does Tommy bring home?
    What kind of school work does he do at home?
    What does he seem to do best?
    What kind of help does he seem to need?

Then you might want to contribute such information as:

    Here are his arithmetic papers for this week.
    Here are samples of his handwriting, one a week.
    He made a report on butterflies. He told us he got the information from an encyclopedia he has at home.
    He has finished the basic reader and is now working in the individualized reading group using library books.
    He needs encouragement in spelling. He often hurries over the assignment to get back to his reading which he seems to enjoy more.

You may want to conduct the conference with a checklist in hand. Such a list made up ahead of time and duplicated can save time; ensure that all the points are covered; and furnish a record of what transpired in the conference. A suggested example is shown in Fig. 12-6. You can follow this format or make up your own for other areas. Insert a sheet of carbon paper between two copies of the list. Fill out the blanks as you discuss each item with the parent. At the end of the conference hand the parent the original and slip the carbon copy in the child's folder. When it comes time for the next conference you will have a record of what was communicated previously. And furthermore, the parent cannot say, "Nobody told me." Also, you will be able to report objectively what has happened to your supervisory officials.

Informal Communication.   Incidental contacts often build bridges for better relations. Do more than just say, "Come to visit." Send home a note saying, "If you will let us know when you can come, we will be glad to rearrange our schedule so your child will be participating while you are here." Plan with the children once a week to list, "What we have done," and share it with the parents. While the children are dictating, perhaps you can type on a ditto carbon such items as the following:

> This week:
>> We finished reading Unit III.
>> We wrote letters to Mr. Sanders, the principal.
>> We learned two new songs.
>> We played a new game in gym.
>> We have started a collection of old books.
>> Our guppies had babies.

Then run it off on the ditto machine at once and let each child take home a copy to share with the family.

Try to see to it that some communications are kept in a positive vein. Too often parents hear from the school only when something is wrong. Send home an occasional note saying something like the following:

> Dear Mrs. _____
>> Just thought you'd like to know how much we enjoyed Linda's book. Thanks for letting her bring it.
>
> _____

or make a brief telephone call to say something like this, "Thank you for letting Debbie bring the pictures of your trip to the zoo. The children learned much about animals from her report."

Date: _____

Name of Child _____

Record of Progress:

    Reading:

        Approximate level of reading _____

        Reads with comprehension (yes or no) _____

        Uses good expression _____

        Attacks new vocabulary independently _____

        Reads library books _____

        Is showing growth _____

        Applies reading skills in other areas _____

        Comments: _____

    Arithmetic

        Does accurate work _____

        Produces neat papers _____

        Can solve story problems _____

        Knows basic facts _____

        Uses mathematical skills in other areas of the curriculum _____

Figure 12-6. *Sample form for planned parent conference.*

And if communication must call attention to a problem, keep channels of communication open by avoiding making a judgment beforehand. Consider these two notes:

Dear Mrs. _____

    Johnny's work has not been up to standard and his promotion is doubtful. I would like to talk with you about it. When can you come to school?

Dear Mrs. _____

    I am very much interested in the progress Johnny is making. Before we get any farther into the year's work, may we arrange a time when we can discuss together how we both can help him and what would be best for him for next semester or next year?

The parent who received the first note felt threatened and came to school ready to defend Johnny and find someone else to blame. The one who received the second note appreciated the teacher's concern and came to school to find out what she could do to help.

Before you record any information, either subjective or objective, ask yourself these questions:

Will it be helpful or harmful to the child?
Should it stay in the permanent record for years to come?
Will it have value to the school system, or to the next teacher?
It is true and accurate?

Before you report either orally or in writing any information to anyone ask yourself these questions:

Does the person receiving the information have any need for it?
Does he or she have a right to know?
Will it help the child?

After you have answered these questions to your satisfaction, make notes and records with discretion. Examine them at intervals and eliminate any that are no longer useful. Keep the welfare of the child uppermost in your mind at all times.

HISTORY, TRENDS, AND RECOMMENDATIONS

Perhaps only the child who works with a private tutor can truly progress at an individual pace without regard for the accomplishments of other children. Since the private tutor is in daily contact with the parents, there may be little need for formal records and written reports. But in a society that attempts to educate the masses at public expense and to teach children in groups, there is a need for some system of records and reports. When the itinerant teacher early in our nation's history "boarded around" in the homes of the pupils, the contacts were direct. When pioneer communities were isolated and the teacher in the one room school taught the child for the entire school year, there was enough carry-over to reduce reporting needs to a minimum. But times have changed in many ways.

Increasing Complexity

As society becomes more complex, as people become more transient, as teacher-pupil contacts become briefer in duration, and as children contact more different teachers, the needs for records become imperative. In these days of large schools, increased distances between home and school, and fewer direct contacts between home and school, the need for still more records and reports grows. The itinerant family needs a record to go with the child from school to school. The teacher on the move needs to find records to help in orientation to a new assignment. The administrator in a large complex organization needs more records in order to keep a finger on the pulse of the situation.

Evolution of Grading Systems and Report Cards

We have already described the changes which have taken place in the content and the form of records and reports. What to report to the parents is a constantly recurring problem. Most reporting forms are based on comparison of the child with a predetermined standard or with the rest of the group. These kinds of reports tend to answer such questions as:

> How do they measure up?
> What is it worth?
> How do they compare?

Such comparisons or evaluations tend to assume "what they ought to do." They suggest that what is normal for the majority should also be normal for the individual. They tend to classify each pupil as succeeding or failing, as above or below average. Such comparisons tell little about what the child is learning and even less about how much growth is taking place.

Curriculum Needs and Current Trends

Even though Robert is actually growing and making progress, he may still remain "at the bottom of the class." Should he be given a low mark because he compares unfavorably with the rest? Or should he be given a high mark because he is making progress? This is the dilemma which every teacher faces when the time comes to fill out a report card using a coded marking system. You may not be able to change the system but you can go "the extra mile" by supplementing mandatory reports with additional information.

Recommendations for Additions and Changes

Additional information should be planned to replace the what-is-it-worth or the what-did-you-get concept with an answer to such questions as:

> What has been accomplished?
> What can Johnny do?
> How much growth has taken place?

If you ask Dick, "What did you get?" he can answer with, "An A," "A plus," or "A–2," whatever that means. This only tells how he rates, not what he has learned. But if you ask him, "Can you do it?" or "What have you done?" he can't respond to these questions with the same answers. If you must use a formal report card that doesn't quite seem to tell the story, try supplementing it. This will enable you to report much more than mere marks or scores. Sometimes the supplement will be informative enough that it will take the pressure off the marks and perhaps even help in arriving at the marks. The supplement may go with the report card, or it may be timed at spaced intervals to increase the home-school communication. Below are some concrete ideas to try.

1. Duplicate a list of all the readers that are available in the room. Give each child a copy of the list with his or her name on it. Let Betty check the ones she has read and take it home. That will tell the parents how many and at what level. Probably no child in the room will have read them all because the list will include books below, at, and above grade level. If a child is in the third grade and she has read one second reader, six third readers, and one fourth reader, something definite is communicated not only about the level of reading but also about the extent. If another third grade child has read three second readers and is just starting a third reader, something different is communicated. If the total list contains thirty or more books and a child has read few or many, a basis for comparison and evaluation is provided which is better than A or a *plus* sign, or *Average*.

2. When a child finishes a basic reader either individually or in a group, send home a report in duplicated form something like the one sketched in Fig. 12–7. Again this tells what has been accomplished rather than how much it is worth.

READING RECORD

Name _____

has satisfactorily completed the reading of _____

_____

(title of book)

which is a reader at the _____ grade level.

    Signed: _____

                                (teacher)

    Date: _____

Figure 12–7. *Suggested form for reporting reading achievement.*

READING REPORT

Did you know that _____
(name of child)

1. Has read _____ readers this semester.
2. Has read _____ library books.
3. Can read _____ words per minute.
4. Reads independently at _____ grade level.
5. Can attack new words independently _____.

Figure 12-8. *Suggested form for reporting extent and level of reading achievement at the end of a semester.*

3. Make up a form to report what is going on. Duplicate it to save your time. See sample in Fig. 12-8. Fill it in for each child to take home. You might want to hold an individual conference and let the child help fill it out. Then the child will be able to explain it to his or her parents.

4. Prepare a supplement to go with the report cards. This may give added information not included in a check mark or a letter grade. Figure 12-9 is suggestive. This may be supplemented by a personal note or you may decide to save time by listing all the learnings and then check off the ones Harry has accomplished. The list can be secured from the curriculum guide, or in a subject like arithmetic, from the chapter headings and subheadings. You may want to prepare a different checklist for each subject, or you may want to condense them all into one report.

PROGRESS REPORT

_____ can:
(name of child)

read and write fractions
reduce fractions to lowest terms
change common fractions to decimal fractions
change decimal fractions to common fractions
add fractions with unlike denominators
subtract fractions with unlike denominators
multiply fractions by whole numbers
divide fractions by whole numbers

Signed: _____
(teacher)

Date: _____

Figure 12-9. *Suggested report card supplement.*

5. Make up some certificates and run them off on the duplicator. When a child has mastered a certain goal, provide the evidence to take home. Figure 12–10 suggests putting such a record in the form of an award or a "diploma" suitable for framing, or at least for displaying on the family bulletin board until another higher accomplishment takes its place.

DIPLOMA

This is to certify that

_____
(name of child)

has satisfactorily mastered the 100 basic facts in multiplication and has written them all correctly in _____ minutes.

Signed: _____

Date: _____

Figure 12-10.   *Suggested form recognizing specific achievement.*

6. If you report achievement records in an objective form, try making them meaningful. Help the children keep a running record of their daily assignments with the number of correct responses in terms of points. Compute the totals at the end of the grading period. Provide each child with a copy of the points earned by the whole class, and let each one circle personal scores on the composite sheet. Figure 12–11 provides a sample. From such a summary the parent and the child can tell:

a. That there were 168 spelling words in the lists for the period and Johnny got 141 of them right.

b. That Johnny did better in mathematics than in other areas.

c. That he probably should have a higher mark in mathematics than in spelling.

Children can help keep their own records. They can watch scores accumulate from day to day. They know what it means and can explain it to their parents. They can see how they rank in comparison with the rest of the class in terms of actual accomplishments rather than in terms of teacher judgment.

7. Do you share standardized test results with the parents? If you do, use them to show growth rather than status or comparison with others. If the grade scores are recorded on the cumulative cards, you have the necessary data to send home a report similar to the one illustrated in Fig. 12–12. This takes the emphasis off the score or rank and puts it on growth. A child who shows little or no growth has evidence to substantiate a low mark. A child with good growth has proof of accomplishment. And sometimes it is the high achiever who is showing less growth. Even though some authorities

discourage the use of individual scores on group standardized achievement tests, the records tell a story that is worth noting if they are used with discretion and with full knowledge of their limitations.

REPORT OF ACHIEVEMENT

Name _____

for the period ending _____

Cumulative Record of Points

Points	Spelling	English	Soc. St.	Mathematics
Possible total	168	557	130	972
High	168	482	120	809
	168	481	99	753
Points	168	464	97	752
earned	168	463	94	730
by	167	447	87	668
class	164	442	79	653
	152	391	64	641
	141	351	54	548
	101	347	47	419
Low	28	227	32	191

Figure 12-11. *Summary sheet showing scores and class distribution for the current grading period. Status of each individual is indicated by circle.*

SEE HOW I HAVE GROWN

Name _____

Date: _____

We have just finished our tests.

Here are my scores for this year and last year.

Time	Reading	Spelling	Arithmetic
This year	5.3	6.1	5.9
Last year	4.1	4.9	4.9
Growth	+ 1.2	+ 1.2	+ 1.0

Figure 12-12. *Comparison of standardized test scores at one-year interval showing growth.*

8. Parents can help with the record keeping and the reporting. Send home a note saying, "I have difficulty finding time to hear all the book reports. If you will listen to _____ 's report on the book he or she has finished and return the enclosed statement signed and dated, he or she will be given credit on our reading record." Duplicating such a note will save your time. And duplicating the form for the parent report will provide authenticity and uniformity to the records. See Fig. 12–13.

BOOK REPORT

This is to certify that _____
                                                      (child's name)

has read the book _____
                                            (title of book)

I have listened to her report and am satisfied that she has read the book successfully.

Signed _____
                                      (Parent)

Date: _____

Figure 12–13. *Suggested parent report on outside reading.*

The above suggestions are only a sampling of the ideas for changing reporting from "What did you get?" to "What have you accomplished?" They are meant to be personal and to act as a supplement to formalized reporting required by the school system. Try creating some of your own. Then share your ideas with your fellow teachers.

SUMMARY

It's in the records. They will provide you with evidence when you need to render a jugment, make a decision, or plan next steps. You will have in your possession personal information about the children that will help you understand their family backgrounds, health histories, and personalities. You will know much about their abilities through records of tests, samples of work, and narrative accounts of happenings. Much of this information is confidential and should be handled with professional integrity.

Informal records are subjective. Anecdotes, case histories, sociometric studies, and narrative accounts are temporary and perhaps should be eliminated from the files after they have served their purposes. Formal records based on objective data are more permanent. Records of attendance, mobility, promotion, and room assignments are historical and factual. Test scores tell what was being accomplished at a given time. Some of this information may be useful in the future. It should be handled judicially, always remembering that it is the child who should be served.

Reports become increasingly important as the organization becomes larger and more complex. Certainly, the child and the parents have a right to know what is being accomplished and how much progress is being made. The administration is responsible for the overall program of the school and therefore needs information which will answer questions about the effectiveness of the program. Such information should be available to other teachers who are working concurrently with the children or will be working with them in the future.

Cumulative records and report cards furnish tangible evidence of accomplishments. They have their values but planned parent conferences and informal communications should not be overlooked as a means of building bridges between home and school. As society becomes more complex, there is more need for written records. The grading system and report cards have gone through stages of change, many of which have failed to serve the child.

There is need for moving away from the success-failure syndrome, the how-much-is-it-worth concept, and toward an evaluation that answers the questions:

What can they do?
Can they do it?
How much progress is being made?

Now that you have kept all these records, they must serve a useful purpose to justify the effort. In the next chapter, we will identify their uses. With a new group they can serve as a means of taking inventory to find out where the children are and what problems exist. This involves both appraisal and diagnosis. But don't stop there! That is only the basis for planning for the future which means setting attainable goals and planning an instructional program. Another use for records is the classification and promotion of pupils. These are ever-present problems and ones for which carefully kept records will prove invaluable.

SUGGESTED ACTIVITIES

1. Make a collection of report cards from as many school systems as you can find. This may include old cards as well as ones currently in use. List all the items included for evaluation. Identify the marking systems used.

2. Examine cumulative record forms from several school systems. List all the types of information recorded.

3. Visit a classroom and observe an individual child over a period of time, for example for one day a week for six weeks.

   Write an anecdotal record which will substantiate judgments about the child and his or her school work.

4. Assume you have just administered a test which has a possible score of 89 points. The same test has also been administered in three other classrooms at the same grade level. Here are the scores:

SCORE	CLASS A	CLASS B	CLASS C	CLASS D	TOTAL
80—89	1		6		7
70—79	3		8	3	14
60—69	5	1	10	9	25
50—59	12	8	6	8	34
40—49	5	10		7	22
30—39	3	7		3	13
20—29	1	3			4
Below 20		1			1
Totals	30	30	30	30	120

You are to grade the pupils with A, B, C, D, and E.

How would you grade the pupils in each class?

Justify your grades to a dissatisfied parent.

Justify your grades to an administer or a statistician who insists on adherence to a normal curve.

5. Assume you are teaching a class. You have constructed an objective test which covers 180 points to be emphasized in the course. You administer the test the first day of the term, collect the papers, and file them without comment. Then on the last day of the term you administer the same test again. The scores on the two tests for ten of the pupils are given below:

	TEST SCORES		
	First Test	Final Test	Growth
John	174	175	1
Alice	160	175	15
Mary	150	169	19
Sam	82	171	89
Fred	155	170	15
Sara	80	160	80
Tom	150	152	2
Bill	121	153	32
Helen	98	150	52
Freda	102	148	46

Who knew the most at the beginning?
Who knew the most at the end?
Who learned the most?

Assume that you must assign a mark of A, B, C, D, or E to each member of the class.

To whom will you give the A's? Justify it.

To whom will you give an E? Justify it.

Evaluate your own teaching in terms of the above record.

6. Working with a committee in your class, design a report card form which you will feel will be adequate in terms of reporting to parents what the child has accomplished.

SELECTED READINGS

1. BEARG, ESTHER M., "Individualized Reporting," in *Today's Education*, Vol. 60, No. 2, Feb. 1971, p. 50. A two column record indicating what "I said," and "They said," contrasting teacher's statement with child's statement. Clever.

2. CRAWFORD, RONALD E., "In Defense of Cumulative Records," in *Educational Forum*, Vol. XXXIV, No. 1, Nov. 1969, pp. 127–29. Response to a 1968 Forum article by David E. Denton.

3. DENTON, DAVID E., "Cumulative Records: Invalid and Unethical," in *Educational Forum*, Vol. XXXIII, No. 1, Nov. 1968, pp. 55–58. Criticizes records and the way they are used.

4. HINES, N. RAY, "Grading As A Cultural Function," in *Clearing House*, Vol. XLVII, Feb. 1973, pp. 356–61. Identifies types of grading systems in use and evaluates them in terms of society rather than in terms of learning.

5. HOOVER, KENNETH H. and PAUL M. HOLLINGSWORTH, *Learning and Teaching in the Elementary School*, Boston: Allyn and Bacon, 1970. Chapter 12 is on assessing learning.

6. JARVIS, OSCAR T. and MARION J. RICE, *An Introduction to Teaching in the Elementary School*, Dubuque, Iowa: Wm. C. Brown, 1972. See Chapter 20 on record keeping.

7. NEA, Editor, "Marking and Reporting Pupil Progress," in *Today's Education*, Vol. 59, No. 8, Nov. 1970, pp. 55–56. Current ideas on marking and reporting and descriptions of various plans proposed. Research Summary, 1970–71, NEA Publications.

8. NEFF, WARREN C., "The Case for Cumulative Records," in *Educational Forum*, Vol. XXXV, No. 1, Nov. 1970, pp. 105–07. Illustrates kinds of facts and forms of statements useful on records.

9. NUNNALLY, JUM C., *Educational Measurement and Evaluation* (2nd edition), New York: McGraw-Hill, 1972. Principles of testing. Using, scoring, and interpreting tests. Testing Programs.

10. TEITELBAUM, VIVIEN STEWART, "School Records Can Be An Invasion of Privacy," in *Today's Education*, Vol. 60, No. 5, May 1971, pp. 43–45. Computer technology, ethical and legal questions, rights, interpretations.

11. YELON, STEPHEN L., "An Alternative to Letter Grades," in *Educational Forum*, Vol. XXXV, No. 1, Nov. 1970, pp. 65–70. Treats letter grades critically and lightly. Recommends use of multiple statements implemented in an organized fashion. Performance statements tell what has happened.

12. ZACH, LILLIAN, "The IQ Debate," in *Today's Education*, Vol. 61, No. 6, Sept. 1972, pp. 40–43, 65–68. Traces beginnings of IQ testing and reasons for debate. Identifies the controversies and points out advantages and limitations.

13

USING THE RECORDS AS A BASIS FOR APPRAISAL

Classification and Promotion

Courtesy, Lowell School, Mesa, Arizona

APPRAISAL:
CLASSIFICATION AND PROMOTION

Now that you have kept such careful records, what will you do with them? Of what use are they to you? To the children? There are at least two good reasons for records: to allow for appraisal of present status and to provide a basis for planning for the future. These uses involve groups as well as individuals.

When you appraise the present status, you answer such questions as: Where are we now? What is the general level of achievement of the class as a group? How much spread of ability in the group? What has each individual accomplished to date? What are the special needs of individuals? What problems exist? What are the specific difficulties? What are some of the probable causes?

When you plan for the future you ask such questions as: What goals are reasonable and attainable for these children? How can I estimate their potential and predict future attainments? What remedial measures are needed? How can I assure continuous growth for each child?

Then there is the problem of classification and promotion. When the end of the year comes, you cannot evade these questions: What shall I do with them? How should they be classified for the coming year? What will I do about promotions? How can I decide? And once I have decided, how shall I communicate the decision to the children? To their parents? What is my responsibility to the administration? To the rest of the staff?

Planning for further teaching involves estimating, predicting, remedying, growing, and moving along. This last step eventually leads to classification and promotion. Your records will serve as a means of taking inventory. They can also serve as a basis for further planning and give you a basis for setting up goals, calling for estimating potential and predicting the future. They will help you plan an instructional program which may mean remediation for some and continuous growth commensurate with ability for others.

TAKING INVENTORY: APPRAISAL AND DIAGNOSIS

Any well run business is based on awareness of the stock on hand and the potential for the future. Every business executive takes inventory at regular intervals. Similarly, you as a teacher need to take inventory to find out where you are now and what the problems are. This provides the basis for reporting progress to date, and what is even more important, setting goals for the future. Before goals can be set, the problems and their causes have to be identified so the planning can be based on a realistic view of the situation.

Where Are We Now?

Time spent in taking inventory of present status is time well spent. Teaching day after day by moving on to the next page, the next book, or the next topic may result in repetition for some and lack of understanding for others. Neither the textbook nor the curriculum guide is meant to be your master. Each is there to help you in identifying the goals. A careful appraisal of the class as a group, and of individuals in the class, will reveal what they already know, so you can direct your teaching to those items which have been recommended for the level at which you are teaching, and which the children do not already know. Such an inventory calls first for an appraisal of accomplishments and then for an analysis of problems.

Appraising the Class Group. You will probably be faced with a roomful of children either identified as at a given grade level or within a year or two of the same chronological age. But this does not mean that they are all alike or that you can treat them as a homogeneous group with identical needs and abilities. Whether they have been selected with some thought to homogeneity or not, they will vary from one area to another and the spread will be greater than you might first think. In Chap. 5 we identified that spread and suggested that a class analysis chart would help you see the overall picture. You still need to know approximate levels and spread of ability, as well as achievement in subject matter areas.

Level of achievement tells you approximately where to begin. It suggests that the goals won't be the same for each child.

Level of ability tells you approximately what to expect. Is this group well advanced? Are they considered a "slow group"? Have they completed the work prescribed for the preceding level?

Spread of achievement may show a median score approximately at grade level and still indicate a range of from four to six or eight years. Even though these children are classified as fourth graders, some may be performing at approximately second-grade level and others at sixth or eighth grade level. This spread may vary from one subject area to another.

Spread of ability is still another factor. Some may be quick and alert. Some may be slow and inattentive. Some may be deliberate but thorough. Some may be hasty and capable, but flighty and ineffective in their work habits.

Appraisal of Individuals.   It isn't enough to appraise the class as a total group. You must also appraise each individual. Such an appraisal may show you what Tony can do in each area of the curriculum and identify something of his special needs.

Accomplishments to date can be determined by means of an inventory which may range from informal observations to a complete battery of tests. You will be wise to take some time with a new group to find out what they can do. Listen to them read. Sample their performance on written work. Talk with them about their interests. Give some teacher-made tests to identify the level at which they can work independently. Study available standardized test results to see what they tell you about abilities and level of attainment.

Special needs will show up as you study accomplishments. Make note not only of what the children can and cannot do but also why. Observe Carol's letter formations in penmanship. Note Carl's inaccuracies in computation. List Freda's reversals and substitutions in reading. Observe the thoroughness with which Paul collects information for a report. All these evidences will serve as a basis for planning for individuals.

What Are The Problems?

It isn't enough to know what they have done, or what they can do. You also need to know what the problems are and exactly where the points of difficulty are. Tests may tell you what the children can or can't do, and they may help you identify the specific items causing the difficulty, but they can't tell you why. You must make your own diagnosis. That is where your professional training comes in. Use it wisely.

Determining the Difficulties.   As you observe the children at work, make note of special difficulties. Notice that Susan makes "o's" and "a's" so much alike that her spelling is difficult to assess. Notice that Frank works so rapidly he is inaccurate in his computation. When he is brought to task he really does know. He doesn't need more drill. Notice that Sally reads in a cursory fashion and often misses the point. When she reads orally you detect that she confuses "then" and "when," "left" and "felt," and "palace" and "place." Inaccuracies seem to be the cause of her lack of comprehension. But Tommy is a different matter. He pronounces the words accurately but is so slow that he is unable to synchronize the total meaning of a sentence. The difficulties are so many and so varied that buying a workbook and drilling the whole class on the same exercises won't solve the problems. You need a list for each child. Then you may find a few of the children with common difficulties that can be taught as a group for a time, but even then they will grow at different rates and won't remain as a permanent group.

Diagnosing the Situation. Observation and testing will help you collect the evidence. Diagnosis is based on determining the causes of the difficulties. You may need to study the child's background, previous learning experiences, behavior patterns, and attitudes to arrive at a reasonable conjecture about causes. Identifying causes is at best an educated "hunch." Of course, the more expert and experienced you are, the more likely you will be to identify causal factors early in the diagnostic process. Perhaps Mary reads poorly because she is hungry, Tom because he has a hearing loss, Sharon because she has a limited background of experience, and Alan because he lacks the keen mind we had expected. Each case will be diagnosed differently.

Specific problems show up in the analysis. List them for each child in a special record folder. Some of them will be personal and some of them will be educational.

Probable causes will come to light as you learn more about each child. And be sure you see the word "causes" as plural because seldom does a single cause stand out as basic to a child's lack of successful school performance. Bert may be boisterous because he is unsuccessful in school. He may be unsuccessful because he lacks experiential background. He may lack experience because he comes from a deprived environment. The boisterousness which causes you to identify inattention as a cause of poor school work may be only a symptom of much deeper problems. Harold may be inaccurate because he is confused. He may be confused because he was not there when the explanation was given. He may have been absent because he was ill. He may have been ill because he lives in a home with such an irregular schedule that he exhausts himself staying up too late and eating irregularly. And yet he may come from what seems like an affluent home where poverty cannot be identified as a causal factor. A true diagnosis collects *all* the evidence and considers the interrelatedness of *all* the factors before making a determination of the difficulty and its causes. And bandaging the wound won't help much if there is a deep infection. A true diagnosis considers all the possible causes and explores every avenue to help the child.

PLANNING FOR THE FUTURE

Now you are ready to plan for the future. The inventory has told you where the children are as a group and as individuals. It has told you what the problems are. You have used the knowledge revealed by the inventory and your findings about the children as a basis for diagnosing the situation. You have pinpointed some specific problems and have formulated some theories about their probable causes. Whether or not your theories are right remains to be proved or disproved. Based on what you know and what you believe, you are ready to set some goals and plan an instructional program designed to alleviate the problems and keep the children moving forward. If your theories are right, the plans will yield results. If your theories are faulty, they will have to be revised as new information comes to light while you work with the children on their problems. As the theories are revised and the plans are altered and you begin to make progress, you are moving the children along toward new goals.

Setting Attainable Goals

Unless you have goals toward which to work, there is the possibility that you will put in time, run in place, and go around in circles getting nowhere. You may provide interesting experiences, keep the children happy and satisfied, enjoy teaching, and the children may do some quite nice things. But all this may result in little or no educational advancement from where they were when they started. On the other hand, you may have high ideals and set goals that sound challenging, but if the children find the objectives beyond their reach, they may resist and drop out. Then how do you know what goals are attainable? In order to determine realistic goals you must estimate the potential of the children and predict future attainments in terms of reality.

Estimating Potential.   Not all children have the same potential. This fact makes uniform planning for an entire group impractical. Shuster (28:450) says:

> If the all-inclusive goal of education is the fullest self-realization of every child, then teachers must recognize and accept the fact that there must be differences in standards for various children.

Then how can potential be determined? In the preceding chapter we identified record keeping and testing as means of amassing data to help evaluate the learner in terms of potential as well as progress. We discussed intelligence tests in terms of potential and function. The intelligence test may not tell you the highest possible level at which Billy is capable of functioning, but it will tell you the level on which he was functioning on that particular test at the time it was given. Ragan (25:458) suggests that:

> An intelligence test cannot measure capacity but only intellectual functioning.

Then how can we use our subjective observations and the findings of intelligence tests to help us estimate the potential of the children with whom we are working? Let us begin on the assumption that intelligence tests are not infallible and that the results may vary from one test to another. At best they are only indicators of the level at which the child was functioning on that particular test. If Eva scores consistently low on successive intelligence tests, we may not know for sure what her IQ is or even that it is actually low, but we do know that she functions at a low level on whatever it is that intelligence tests measure, and therefore, unless we can help her to function at a higher level on such tests, we are not likely to find her functioning on a much higher level in the academic learnings for which we are trying to set attainable goals. By the same token, if she functions at a high level on several intelligence tests, we have some basis for establishing goals in keeping with that finding.

What of the general intelligence level of the group? One of the first things that intelligence tests reveal is that there is a wide spread of ability in large unselected groups and that the scores tend to follow a normal curve. Figure 13–1 indicates an approximate distribution of intelligence levels you might expect to find in a large unselected group. Interpreting these figures in terms of a random classroom group of 30 children, one might expect to find one very superior child some year but not every year. There might be three or four children classed as superior. There might be ten or eleven high average and another ten or eleven low average, making the bulk of the class fall between an IQ of 85 and 115. But there is a lot of difference between these two extremes. There might be three or four inferior learners. If there is no special provision for the mentally retarded, you might expect to have one of the very inferior learners in your room some years.

LEVEL OF INTELLIGENCE	IQ RANGE	PERCENT OF NATION'S POPULATION
Very superior	Above 130	3%
Superior	115–130	12%
High average	100–114	35%
Low average	85–99	35%
Inferior	70–84	12%
Very inferior	Below 70	3%

Figure 13–1. *Classification and distribution of levels of intelligence in large unselected groups.*

Predicting Future Attainments. Deciding what to expect or setting curriculum targets must be done in terms of individuals rather than groups. It is unrealistic to set a goal of a grade score of 5.9 in all areas for all the fifth graders by the end of the year. Let us take three typical examples to illustrate this point. Figure 13–2 shows the projection for Larry with a measured IQ of 75, George with an IQ of about 100, and Fred with an IQ of about 125. Chronological age (CA) is a record of actual age in years and months. Mental age (MA) is computed using the IQ as a ratio. Anticipated achievement (AA) is derived by translating MA into an equivalent grade score or level of expectancy. From Fig. 13-2 we can conclude that Larry will move at less than the "normal" rate, George will move along at about the average rate, and Fred will progress somewhat more rapidly. How much difference can we expect to find in their progress as they go through school year by year? Note that the chronological age increases one year for each calendar year of life—the same for each of the three. Since George is considered "average," his mental age and the estimated level of achievement progress at the same rate as his chronological age. While Larry grows chronologically at the same rate as the other two, his rate of mental growth is somewhat slower, and while Fred grows chronologically at the same rate as the other two, his mental growth moves ahead at a more rapid pace.

From this projection, then, it can be seen that to expect beginning first grade work of Larry when he is six years old is setting goals beyond the probability of attainment. And to set such a goal for Fred is to pitch the work beneath his ability and probably beneath his present level of performance. Larry may be approximately eight years old before you can reasonably expect him to succeed at beginning reading. Whether his entrance should be delayed or he should be "held back" is debatable. Fred could possibly complete the academic requirements of the elementary school by the time he is nine years old. Whether he should have been permitted to enter at a younger age, or should be moved along at a faster pace to work with older children is another matter, which we will discuss later in connection with classification and promotion policies.

By the time Larry is twelve years old, he will probably have spent one year in kindergarten and six years in the elementary grades. Whether he is moved along to seventh grade may depend on the policies of the school and the convictions of the teachers who have worked with him. Whether he is in fourth grade or seventh grade or some place in between, it is likely that he will be performing at about the level of a nine-year-old in many of the curriculum areas.

By the time Fred is twelve years old he also will probably have spent one year in kindergarten and six years in the elementary school. In many respects, he might compete favorably with other pupils in the ninth or tenth grade, read such literature as "Treasure Island," or "The Tale of Two Cities," handle mathematical computations using algebra and geometry or even trigonometry, and do research in science or social studies that would reflect the mature skills of a high school student. But physically, he is just twelve years old. He would not make the football team, or be accepted socially at the high school party. Whether he should be classified with his chronological age group or with his mental age group is debatable. But if he is in your room, you need to recognize his potential and plan work that will keep him challenged and growing.

LARRY (IQ = 75)			GEORGE (IQ = 100)			FRED (IQ = 125)		
C.A.	M.A.	A.A.	C.A.	M.A.	A.A.	C.A.	M.A.	A.A.
5–0	3–9	0.0	5–0	5–0	0.0	5–0	6–3	1.3
6–0	4–6	0.0	6–0	6–0	1.0	6–0	7–6	2.6
7–0	5–3	0.3	7–0	7–0	2.0	7–0	8–9	3.9
8–0	6–0	1.0	8–0	8–0	3.0	8–0	10–0	5.0
9–0	6–9	1.9	9–0	9–0	4.0	9–0	11–3	6.3
10–0	7–6	2.6	10–0	10–0	5.0	10–0	12–6	7.6
11–0	8–3	3.3	11–0	11–0	6.0	11–0	13–9	8.9·
12–0	9–0	4.0	12–0	12–0	7.0	12–0	15–0	10.9

Figure 13-2. *Progression chart showing rate of growth in Chronological Age (CA), Mental Age (MA), and Anticipated Achievement (AA) over a seven-year span for three pupils representing IQ levels of 75, 100, and 125 respectively.*

This kind of information about children's potential and their growth patterns helps give you a preview of what to expect in a typical classroom. Figure 13–3 indicates not only the levels of ability to expect but also the spread within a group at any given grade level. One significant item to note is that the higher the grade level the wider the spread. This says something for the importance of varying goals and individualizing the instructional program to incorporate goals that are both possible and challenging for the pupils. This suggests that each year you may expect a chronological-age span of about two years, sometimes expanding to three or more years depending on the school's policies about retentions and/or double promotions.

If you have pupils at this grade level	You can expect a chronological age span of	And you can expect a mental age span of
K	4–5–6	3–4–5–6–7
1	5–6–7	3–4–5–6–7–8
2	6–7–8	4–5–6–7–8–9–10
3	7–8–9	5–6–7–8–9–10–11
4	8–9–10	6–7–8–9–10–11–12–13
5	9–10–11	6–7–8–9–10–11–12–13–14
6	10–11–12	7–8–9–10–11–12–13–14–15

Figure 13-3. *Span of chronological ages and mental ages in typical classes in grades K through 6.*

At the same time, you will have children in all these age groups who vary in ability as indicated by the three typical examples shown in Fig. 13-2. With these variations you will find mental ages spreading over a wider span than chronological ages and over an increasingly wider span as the years progress. For example, a kindergarten teacher might expect to find mental ages spreading over a four-year span from a low of three to a high of seven. By the time the group reaches third grade, the mental age span may extend from a low of five to a high of eleven, or a six-year span. And by sixth grade it is not at all uncommon to find some children with mental ages as low as seven and others as high as fifteen, representing an eight-year span. These differences make impractical if not impossible the setting of common goals for all. What is attainable for the "average" is beyond the expectations of the lowest, and a waste of time for the highest.

In order to visualize the spread of ability in an ordinary classroom, you can divide your groups chronologically and intellectually and place them on a grid as shown in Fig. 13-4. This tells you that Mary, Pamela, and Sharon are among the older children in the class but their abilities range from low through average to high. Edith, Betty, and Paul are among the younger children in the room and their abilities also vary. Claude, Fred, and Anne are about the normal age for their grade with varying abilities. Even though Mary, Claude, and Edith have limited ability, the extra year or so of age that Mary has over Edith will make a difference in the level of work she can do. Similarly, Sharon, Anne, and Paul are all capable children, but Paul is young and may not be able to compete successfully with Sharon who is a year or more older. Knowing these facts about your class will enable you to predict with more preciseness what they are capable of doing and thus set reasonable and attainable goals.

C.A.	LEVEL OF ABILITY		
	LOW	AVERAGE	HIGH
Old for Grade	Mary	Pamela	Sharon
Average for Grade	Claude	Fred	Anne
Young for Grade	Edith	Betty	Paul

Figure 13-4. *Chronological age and mental age distribution of children in a typical elementary classroom.*

Figure 13–5 shows another study you can make of your class using the nine-square grid and comparing measured ability with evidences of achievement. Not all children will be working at a level in keeping with ability as indicated by measures of intelligence. From the intelligence tests, you can determine estimated level of ability. Della-Piana (4:41–42) recommends estimating potential by computing current mental age and subtracting 5 to arrive at an anticipated achievement expressed in grade score. His reasoning is thus: Most six-year-olds are in first grade, most seven-year-olds are in second grade, most eight-year-olds are in third grade, and so on. The difference in each case is five years. Therefore, he concludes that a child with the mental ability of a nine-year-old might reasonably be expected to do work at approximately the fourth grade level, a ten-year-old at fifth grade level, and so on. This represents only a quick mental estimate, not a statistical criterion however, and note that it is based not on chronological age but on computed mental age dependent on a variable score from an intelligence test.

ESTIMATED ACHIEVEMENT LEVEL	ESTIMATED LEVEL OF ABILITY (AA)		
	LOW	AVERAGE	HIGH
Above grade level			Sharon Anne
At grade level	Mary	Pamela Fred	Paul
Below grade level	Claude Edith	Betty	

Figure 13–5. *Comparison of achievement level with ability level for nine typical cases.*

Using what information you have about the level of work each child is currently doing either as revealed by a standardized test or as observed as you work with the class you can place each child on the nine-square grid. From the scattergram in Fig. 13–5 you can conclude:

1. Sharon and Anne have considerable ability and are achieving at a level above their grade placement. This is to be expected. They need to be recognized and challenged.
2. Paul has considerable ability but from Fig. 13–4 we noted he is quite young. Perhaps working at grade level is enough for him.

3. Pamela and Fred have average ability and are working near grade level. This is probably satisfactory. Too often we teach as if all children fell in this category.

4. Betty may be working below grade level but this may be due to immaturity since Fig. 13–4 shows her to be young for her grade and only average in ability.

5. Mary seems to have limited ability but is managing to work up to grade level. Remember she is one of the older children in the group.

6. Claude and Edith may not be working up to grade placement, but they have limited ability and are young for their grade. They may be doing all they can.

All these observations will help you in estimating what the children may be able to do and in seeing them in relation to their abilities. Setting goals then becomes a matter of recognizing where each child is and the capability of each so that success will be possible as well as probable.

Planning The Instructional Program

Now you are ready to do something about it. Obviously, you can't expect all the children in the class to do the same work at the same rate. Some will have problems that must be remedied before they can be expected to make progress. Some will need the work pitched at a level with which they can cope. And all will need to set goals in terms of growth rather than in terms of an established norm.

Remediation.   In your diagnosis you were looking not only for types of difficulties but for possible causes. If you have determined that Betty's reading problems stem from frustration caused by an early start that left her with a sense of failure, you may decide to begin at a low level where she can have the satisfaction of succeeding. But to let her stay there forever would be fruitless. Once you have convinced her that she can, keep moving the sights and keep her stretching for growth. If you have decided that Arthur's reading problem really is a vision problem, you may decide to see if you can persuade his parents to have his eyes examined. If not, then perhaps you can get their cooperation, or at least their permission to refer him to a service agency in the community. If you have decided that Carl's poor handwriting is really a muscular coordination problem, you may find just the help you need from the physical education teacher. The types of difficulties are many and varied and the possible causes are legion. Each one must be studied individually. When you have made a decision, it is your responsibility to prescribe a remedy. If you try a certain workbook and it helps, you have made a good diagnosis. If it does not yield results, try something else. When you have gained enough experience to prescribe successfully most of the time, you have become a true diagnostician and a successful teacher.

Continuous Growth.   If you pitch the work at a low enough level that the children can do it with ease, you have provided success and encouragement but no opportunity for growth. If you pitch it at such a high level that they struggle and fail, they may become discouraged and quit trying. You need to find that fine point between too little and too much—the point at which each child can succeed but still be challenged. The level will differ with each child and the rate will vary from one child to another. The child must see success as possible and must accept the goal before benefiting from the effort. Full (8:165) differentiates between self-accepted goals and teacher-imposed goals and quotes Carl Weinberg as saying:

> External criteria for performance is oppressive, internal criteria realistic. If one sets his own goals and works in his own style . , . he does not set up or have set up for him the myriad threats to his ego that are associated with failure. If he is not in the race, he does not worry about losing.

And in discussing the problems involved in basing goals on competition he says further that: (8:160)

> As long as competition is the mode, someone has to decide the winners. If competition should disappear, and with it the judging teacher, it is likely that students will react more positively to attempts to help them discover their capacities for enjoying the worlds that education can open for them.

Too often unrealistic goals result in pressures to meet superimposed standards. Pressures create frustrations and fears. Frustrations and fears induce withdrawal and resistance. And that kind of reaction actually impedes learning. Doll and Fleming (5:21–34) point out some of the pressures to which children are exposed:

Pressure for academic achievement
Pressure for scholastic attainment
Pressure to push advanced curriculum into lower grades
Pressure for excessive homework
Pressure of questionable school practices

They review the cycle of events leading educators to place children in groups where such pressures exist and to create competition which builds up resistance. They say that (5:30–31):

So, again, in the 1960's we see an upsurge of the practice of grouping pupils even in the first grade as "high potential," "middle potential," and "low potential" students and assigning them to classes and teachers on this specious basis. This vicious practice has evil effects on both children and teachers. The clouds of "low expectancy" permanently settle over the lowest third of the pupil population; once assigned to the lowest third, a child may have received a life sentence to failure.

And finally, take heed as to what will happen if you pitch the work at a level suitable for each child and plan for growth commensurate with individual abilities.

Point of departure is a first consideration. The ones who start at a lower level and have a slower pace will move along at a rate somewhat less than "average." The ones who start at a higher level and move along at a pace somewhat greater than average will make more progress. In actuality, if you are a good teacher, you will create ever wider and wider differences in the group.

Rate of progress accentuates these differences. Recall Fred, George, and Larry, whom we first met in Fig. 13-2. They are all making progress year by year but at different levels and at different rates. Notice that the gap gets wider as they progress through the grades. Good teaching makes this so. It is poor teaching which "puts the lid on" Fred and "stretches the rubber band to the snapping point" for Larry. Whether each makes gains in keeping with ability will depend on the extent to which the work and the goals have been adjusted to individual abilities.

CLASSIFICATION AND PROMOTION

No matter how much you like a group of children or how well the year goes, you can't keep them forever. Some teachers do keep the same children more than one year and some manage to work with the same groups in the succeeding years by participating in a team teaching situation or a semidepartmentalized plan whereby they teach a given subject area to the same children the following year. But even then time passes and eventually they go on to another room, another teacher, or another school. How and when to move them along is a perennial problem. This involves the matter of, "What shall we call them?" and "On what basis shall they be moved on?" These are not instructional problems. They are administrative problems. Most good teachers are quite capable of determining what the children need to be taught and how to teach them. But when the teaching is done, the matter of passing judgment is another problem. To say that they have learned, or that they have grown is one thing, but to satisfy an administrative requirement or to answer the public for accountability demands that you say to what extent they have measured up. The question is, "Measured up to what?" *Classification* involves putting children into teachable groups and getting them organized within the building and within the classroom for purposes of accounting. *Promotion* involves a final decision as to whether or not to move the child along to the next group. Those problems bother teachers perhaps more than any others they face. And no matter what the decision, you can always think of reasons why it might have been better otherwise. But eventually you have to recognize the problem and face the issue.

Recognizing The Nature Of The Problem

Part of your task as a teacher is pupil accounting. Attendance reports must be kept. The tax support base requires that we know who is in school, where they are, and what they are called. This calls for grading in the sense of fitting the structure of the graded school which has been with us ever since Horace Mann conceived the idea for the schools in Quincey, Massachusetts in 1847. We have made some changes, but the outlook for the future is for even more drastic changes. We might even do a bit of forecasting and think about what might be.

Purposes For Classifying And Promoting Pupils.   When the children come to school, they have to be put somewhere. The principal usually assumes the responsibility for receiving the new pupils and introducing them to a teacher who will make them welcome as members of a group. Immediately Ralph becomes a statistic on the class roll. He is entered in the register for purposes of pupil accounting and a label is attached to him indicating that he is in third grade or whatever the group may be called. And if any type of homogeneous grouping is attempted, he may be further classified as grade four, group one, indicating that he is in the "best" section of the fourth grade. Now he gets counted for attendance records. He gets reported for financial reimbursement. Administratively he is a part of the school system. That may, or may not have anything to do with what he is taught or how he is taught. And he may stay in that room or with that group for the rest of the year. At the end of the term, traditionally, our schools count up the score, complete the records, and close the books. Children are dismissed for a long summer vacation and groups tend to dissolve. In the fall the children come back or perhaps move to another locale, and we start all over again. When we start over, we again face the problem of classification. The teacher the year before, and that may very well be you, has made that decision when checking on the report card in the space that says:

Promoted to _____ grade
or
Retained in _____ grade

Trends.   Over the years we have oscillated as to what is the best means of classifying children and what is the best thing to do about moving them along. And the decisions aren't easy. Back in 1943, Elsbree (6:12–13) reported that as long ago as 1921, studies of the effects of nonpromotion have concluded that repeating a grade level assignment has not resulted in improved learning.

In the early days of the graded school, it was thought by some that homogeneous, teachable groups could be established by providing the same curriculum for all, taking them through the year's assignments at a predetermined pace, and retaining or failing the ones who did not "keep up." As a result of such a policy, the schools were populated with overage pupils and misfits. Then came the studies discouraging such a practice. These emphasized personal adjustment rather than academic attainment. In the heyday of the progressive movement, the personal development of the child was thought to be of more consequence than the maintaining of academic standards based on subject matter. Some mistaken conceptions crept into school philosophy. Some educators were quoted as saying, "It doesn't matter whether Betty meets the standards or not, you should still move her along with her social and age-level group." By placing the period too soon, they were *mis*quoted as saying, "It doesn't matter whether she meets the standards or not." This led to a laissez faire attitude on the part of some misinformed, partially informed, or uninformed teachers, children, and parents. Many children were moved along with their social or age-level groups with the result that they found themselves in a higher grade classification unable to cope with the curriculum and exposed to a teacher who expected them all to conform.

This led to a dilemma that emphasized spread of ability within a group and need for adapting instruction to individual differences. The more the efforts were directed toward this end the wider the spread became. As a consequence, the grade level classification became more a matter of accounting for children than of planning the curriculum content. A classification of fifth grade came to mean little more than that children had been in school for four years and this was their fifth year of attendance. The test results revealed the wide spread. As long as problem cases remained within one school, they could be discussed among the staff and moved along. But eventually some one had to teach the children the last year they were in the school, that is, in the sixth grade if they were in a six-year elementary school, or in the eighth grade if it were an eight-year school. Then the children were sent to the junior high school or the senior high school. On arrival at the next level, the problem of standards reared its head and questions were asked as to why the children did not measure up, or else why they were sent on without meeting standards.

There are all kinds of pro and con arguments about moving children along rather than retaining them. Some contrasts might help us view the problem with perspective. Those who advocated social promotions pointed out that such a plan:

(1) kept the children with their age groups,
(2) saved face for the slow learner,
(3) resulted in better educational growth in the long run,
(4) prevented overcrowding in the lower grades,
(5) reduced pressures on slow learners, and
(6) eliminated the stigma of failure.

Those who opposed social promotions claimed that such practices:

(1) encouraged the child to get by,
(2) increased the spread of achievement in the upper grades,
(3) broke down standards,
(4) permitted acceptance of poor quality of work,
(5) reduced teacher responsibility and accountability, and
(6) lowered the value of promotion.

Both have their points. Neither one solves the problem of what is best for each child.

Some Alternate Proposals.   Consider the possibilities of an administrative organization in which the children can enter, move on, and exit at any time. This is the way children enter and leave family life. This is the way employees enter and leave business concerns. It is the way families move into and out of neighborhoods. Why is it so necessary that we start school the first of September and close up shop the first of June? We don't operate that way in any other system. The eight- or nine-month school year was developed to fit the needs of an agrarian society so the children would be available to help with the crops during the harvest season. This need has long since ceased to be pertinent but the tradition still governs our school calendar. There is no reason that all children must be six years old by a given date in order to enter school on the first of September. We have already shown that such a plan results in a full year's spread in chronological ages and an even wider spread in mental ages in any given grade group. It results in admission of children unready for school because of lower mental age, lesser experience, and slower learning rate. It also results in unfairness to the more mature child who is capable and who could benefit from formal schooling sooner. No matter what entrance date is established the situation still exists. Since we have moved into the open classroom, team teaching set-ups, multilevel groupings, and adaptation of instruction to individual differences, we are now ready for a new look at admissions, classifications, and promotions.

Consider the feasibility of a plan that would admit a child to the kindergarten or first grade on the fifth or sixth birthday, whenever that is. That would mean that we would never have the entire group all new at one time as on the first of September. It would be fair to all because it would be the same for all. It would open up the sequences so that a child could move along when ready rather than having to wait till the end of the school term in June. Such a plan would lessen many of the now existing problems. It is not as revolutionary as might seem on the surface. Jones (15:195-202) presents a feasible plan for continuous admission and contrasts such a plan with the traditional once-a-year plan. It is summarized in Fig. 13-6.

No doubt Shuster (28:485) was predicting some such innovation when he said:

> When teachers have freedom in designing the curriculum for the individual student, perhaps the day is not too far distant when problems of promotion will be matters of pure academic curiosity, since children will be facing those learning experiences that are designed for them, and progress at a rate suitable for them—there is literally no failure according to the traditional use of the term.

Facing The Issue

Is there a better way? This question has puzzled both teachers and administrators for over a century. Shall we retain those who don't measure up? Or shall we pass them along whether they are keeping up or not? Some would go to one extreme, some to another. Perhaps there is no one answer that will guarantee success in all cases. One suggestion would be to look at each questionable case individually and try to determine what placement would be best for that child. Eventually you will have to decide what you are going to do about the recommendations you will make for the classification of your pupils for the following year. True, the matter may come up from time to time during the year. You may need to discuss with a parent the lagging learning of an individual pupil or make a recommendation for a pupil who is moving to another school. You may have to face some readjustments if there are fluctuating enrollments and some children must be moved to another room during the year. You may participate in a staff meeting where test results are being discussed or new policies are being established. But in each case you can talk about the problem without actually facing it. You can make a tentative decision and postpone your commitment till later. But "later" will eventually come. At the end of the year the record forms have to be filled out. Too often the child will take home a report card that says either, "Promoted," or "Retained." You can't say, "Maybe." Some teachers have worked out a scheme for avoiding the

AREA	ONCE-A-YEAR ADMISSIONS	CONTINUOUS ADMISSIONS
Entrance	All pupils will enter as new enrollees on the first day of school.	Only those with summer birthdays will be new in the fall. The rest will be carried over from the previous year. New ones will enter during the year on their birthdays.
Enrollment	All will be there to be enrolled on the first day	Only new ones will be enrolled on the first day. The rest will be enrolled one at a time as they come on their birthdays.
Induction	All children will be new and strange at once. There will be little time for individual attention. The confusion may overwhelm the timid child.	A small group will be inducted in the fall. Each new child entering during the year will be given personal attention. The rest of the group may help with orientation. Later this child may help orient others.
Grouping	Typically children either work or play as a total group or else each one works independently while the teacher supervises.	As children mature they will form small groups and assume some responsibility for their own work while the teacher works with newcomers. Pupil leadership will emerge.
Promotion	At the end of the year all the pupils are either promoted to the next grade or retained in the present assignment another year.	Groups of from 5 to 10 children will be moved on to another room at any time during the year. Decisions will be based on pupil maturity and availability of space.
Personnel of the group	The group remains constant for the duration of the academic year except for family mobility.	There would seldom be a totally new group all at one time. There would be a gradual turnover during the year as individuals moved in and groups moved on.
Advantages	It is easier to keep on with a familiar pattern than to change. Record keeping practices fit this system. It is traditional.	Admission age will be the same for all. Less emphasis will be placed on competition. Time spent in one level of assignment will vary and stigma of failure will be reduced. Promotion can be any time.
Limitations	Establishing a best date for admissions is impossible. Pressing all children into a common mold is indicated. Competition and pressures are emphasized.	Orientation and preplanning would be needed to communicate the idea to teachers as well as parents. Record keeping patterns now in use would not fit the plan.

Figure 13-6. *Contrast in plans for once-a-year and continuous admissions.*

decision, or putting it on the next teacher, by "passing on condition." But somebody has to decide where the child will be when fall comes. And the likelihood of Donald's being "put back" once he has been "passed on condition" is not very great.

How To Decide.   Are you going to be a stalwart educationist and uphold the standards of the school at any cost? Or are you going to be a humanitarian and decide what is best for the child? Then how will you justify making one decision for one child and what seems like a contradictory decision for another? How will you face the day of decision? Did Mary pass? Or didn't she? No matter what you say—that she is being retained, or reclassified, or needs to adjust to a younger group, or needs to take a little more time for the work—there is still the parent who will look you squarely in the eye and say, "Yes, I understand, but what will her daddy say?" or "Yes, but what will the neighbors think when they find out she has failed?"

Learning is evident. Sequential growth is obvious. And differences are accepted. But when it comes to the mechanics of pupil classification, in most schools the child has to be placed somewhere and called something. And the question of promotion, or nonpromotion is so mixed up with emotions and personal pride that a sense of perspective is often lost. How to solicit cooperation from the parents, prepare them for making a wise decision, and help the child at the same time is the problem. No one method works for all and no rule guarantees right answers.

How will you make the decision? What are the factors? How can you decide what is really best for Mary, or Tommy, or Eva, or Freddie, or Alan? What is best for one may not necessarily be best for another. Some are more mature socially, physically, and emotionally, yet are struggling with their academic work due to intellectual limitation. Others are intellectually capable, yet so immature in other ways that they are misfits in the group where they are. A score won't answer the question. An administrator can't lay down a rule which relieves you of facing the issue. Each teacher must analyze carefully each child and decide, under existing circumstances, what action will be best. Using a check list similar to the one in Fig. 13–7 might help. It divides the decisions into four categories and looks at the child as a member of a social group, an emotionally maturing person, a physically developing organism, and an educational entity. It is not a formula or an objective scale. It is only a device for calling attention to related factors. It does not yield a score or make a decision for you, but it does help you look at all sides of the question before you decide. If most of the answers are "No," perhaps the child might better adjust to a younger group. If most of the answers are "Yes" in the first three categories but "No" in the educational category, perhaps that child is a suitable subject for a social promotion. In the end the teacher, that's you, will have to make

Name _____   Present CA _____

Date _____   Present MA _____

Present Grade Assignment _____   Recorded IQ _____

AREA OF EVALUATION	NO	YES

Social Traits

Is the child accepted by the group in games, committees, etc?   _____ _____
Does the child assume responsibility for group work?   _____ _____
Does the child ever assume positions of leadership?   _____ _____
Are the other children willing to accept the child's leadership?   _____ _____
Is the child willing to be a follower part of the time?   _____ _____
Does the child play with other children of the same age?   _____ _____

Emotional Traits

Does the child seem to enjoy school?   _____ _____
Does the child have an "I can" or an "I'll try" attitude?   _____ _____
Does the child welcome new experiences?   _____ _____
Is the child able to make decisions independently?   _____ _____
Is the child willing to abide by own decisions?   _____ _____
Does the child accept consequences of own acts?   _____ _____
Is the child willing to adjust to a younger group?   _____ _____
Are the child's parents willing to help him or her make the
   adjustment?   _____ _____

Physical Traits

Is the child as big, or bigger than most of the classmates?   _____ _____
Does the child have muscular coordination equal to that of the
   majority of the children in the group?   _____ _____
Is the child successful in group competition?   _____ _____
Does the child possess physical stamina?   _____ _____
Is the child's attendance unhindered by illnesses?   _____ _____
Are the child's health habits conducive to effective work?   _____ _____

Educational Traits

Is the child's achievement on standardized tests within one
   grade level of present grade placement?   _____ _____
Does the child have good study habits?   _____ _____
Is the child consistent in day-to-day work?   _____ _____
Is the child persistent in performing assigned tasks?   _____ _____
Does the child assume any self-assigned tasks?   _____ _____
Does the child experience some successes each day?   _____ _____
Is the child able to identify own problems?   _____ _____
Is the child able and willing to seek help when needed?   _____ _____
Is achievement equal to capacity?   _____ _____
Can you predict success at the next level?   _____ _____

Recommended assignment for next year _____

Figure 13-7.   *Tentative guide for evaluating success and deciding on placement (promotion or retention) for questionable cases.*

the decision. And even then you will have trouble with your conscience. If you decide to retain Harry, and he cries or his parents object, you will find yourself torn with indecision. If you decide to promote him and the next teacher challenges your standards, you will find yourself professionally on the defensive. The decision isn't easy. Perhaps I would lean more toward the humanitarian point of view along with Manning (18:286–287) who says:

> There are still many schools, however, that fail children who do their very best because their best is not good enough.
> To fail a child, however, for not achieving a task which is impossible for him to achieve is senseless and cruel.

At this point it seems reasonable to conclude that the system that demands that you meet a situation and make a decision about retention or promotion is antiquated. Be that as it may, however, we are still living with it and much as you might like to change it, you may find yourself living within it. Being realistic demands that you recognize the problem, face the issue, and do something about it. You may lend your energies to changing the point of view for the future and hope for improvement, but if you are working in a school which still classifies pupils and moves them along at the end of the year, we would not advocate that you be a complete rebel and refuse to cooperate. There are ways of working within the system while you are seeking to improve it. That often calls for going the "extra mile" by doing a little more than is required. The above suggestions may help you decide what to do, but the hardest part is still to come, that is, how to tell the children and their parents what you have decided, especially if the verdict is one they will not like.

How To Communicate The Decisions.   Juan and his parents want to know the verdict. Communicating to the administrator and the next teacher may be a more professional matter, but even that has its problems. What will you say? What will you do? Here are some ideas worth considering.

The child looks forward to promotion. Certainly no child should receive a report card on the last day of school and have to hide it under the desk while peeping apprehensively to find out whether it says "promoted" or "retained." Such an approach suggests that the pupil has been kept "in hot water" till the "day of judgment." Paul dreads to look, yet wants to know. If the news is good, he shows his card to his peers and brags. If the news is bad, he is humiliated beyond endurance and avoids his peers and their prying questions. And furthermore, he dreads to go home because of what the family will think or say. Children should never face that situation. They should be taken into your confidence with opportunities from time to time to discuss the level of work they are doing and the problems they are facing. They can even discuss the level of work they will be ready for next year, and with what group they might expect to work most effectively. If they are going to be asked to work with a younger group they can help make the decision, and be brought to accept the idea before facing the issue. They might even be placed in mixed groups where they have an opportunity to make friends with younger peers working at comparable levels. Now when they receive report cards it will be no shock. They have already had an opportunity to "save face" by making adjustments and facing peers and family with their own decisions.

The parents are equally concerned. Certainly no parent should ever be put in the position of being surprised on the last day of school when the child brings home a report card that says, "Retained." The parent's immediate reaction is, "Why didn't they tell me Gene wasn't getting along all right?" Such a parent will be moved to call the school and protest. This puts the principal and you both on the defensive and creates a conflict between home and school. If the decision seems wise, you should be in contact with the parents long before the last day and let them participate in making it. It is hoped you will win their support and have them help make the decision with the child. Even if you do not win them, at least they will not be shocked on the last day of school when the decision becomes final.

Professionals work with you and take up the task where you leave it. Facing your coworkers is an important part of decision making and communication. A wise principal makes an opportunity for teachers to discuss the best arrangements for the children for the following year. In the spring a meeting of all kindergarten and first-grade teachers can be devoted to discussion of placement for next year's first graders. Here the kindergarten teachers have an opportunity to present their children as individuals with needed adjustments, to indicate their decisions and perhaps to justify them, and to communicate their philosophies. The first-grade teachers get a preview of what is to come and are alerted to some of the problems that they may meet the next year. At least when fall comes they won't say to the kindergarten teacher, "Why didn't you keep that child another year?"

Then the next step is a meeting of all first- and second-grade teachers. Here the process is repeated. The first-grade teachers present their children, justify their decisions, and make recommendations in the best interests of individuals. The second-grade teachers are made aware that not all children will "measure up" to their standards and are prepared to meet them where they are. They may not agree with all the decisions of the first-grade teachers, but at least they will be informed and will know why they are receiving the children at the level they are. The same process can be repeated through the grades with meetings of teachers at adjoining levels each time passing along helpful information basic to a smooth organization at the opening of the new term.

Now that you have made the decisions and have communicated them to all the persons who are involved, you can look back and think, "Did I do the right thing?" "If I had it to do over again would I still make the same decision?" "What if I had done it differently?" And no matter what decisions you make, you will always wonder, "What if . . .?" But one thing is sure, you can't go back and do it the other way to find out. Perhaps next year you will handle a similar decision differently, but you still will have the same qualms. Knowing what the problem is and being forewarned about its complexity may not make it any easier but it will make it more tolerable to face.

SUMMARY

Yes, you need to take inventory to know where you are and what the problems are. You need to face the problems and set goals that are possible to attain. This means estimating capacities, determining expectancies, and planning for growth on the part of all the pupils. These measures help you meet the instructional problems with some assurance that you are helping the children learn and grow. As long as you are working in a school system that classifies the children for purposes of accounting and reorganizes groups each year, you will have to face the issue of promotion and communicate your decisions to the children, the parents, and your professional coworkers. You may not make all "right" decisions, but if you know what is expected of you and why you made the decisions you did, you will be more comfortable when you have to discuss them with those concerned.

SUGGESTED ACTIVITIES

Choose one or more of the following suggested activities and develop it as a project to share with the rest of the class. Work independently or with a committee.

1. Ask a classroom teacher to share a set of standardized test results with you. Remove the names of the children in order to prevent inappropriate dissemination of personal information. Tabulate the results showing:
   a. Level of achievement of individuals
   b. Spread of achievement in the group.
   Recommend grouping patterns and teaching procedures to meet the evident needs of the group.
2. Work with a pupil who is having difficulty in a particular area.
   Identify the specific problems being experienced.
   Note level of attainment and evidences of improvement.

3. Ask ten teachers to tell you some of the causes of poor school work among the children they are teaching.

   Tabulate your findings indicating the types of difficulties and the number of times each is mentioned.

4. Ask ten parents to tell you some of the causes of difficulty their children have experienced in school.

   Tabulate your findings indicating the sources of "blame" and the number of times each is mentioned.

5. Interview at least five administrators. Ask them:

   When new pupils enter your school, how do you decide where to place them?

   Tabulate and share your findings with the class.

6. Interview five teachers. Ask them:

   When new pupils enter your room, how do you find out about their backgrounds and decide where to fit them into the existing organization in your room?

   Tabulate and share your findings with the class.

7. Interview five children who have changed schools. Ask them:

   When you went to the new school how did they decide where to place you?

   Report your findings to the class.

8. Find out the promotion policies in at least one school district. Explain it to the class.

9. Debate the issue:

   Resolved: Children should be kept with their chronological age group for purposes of classification.

SELECTED READINGS

1. Association of Classroom Teachers, NEA, "Performance Based Instruction," in *Today's Education*, Vol. 61, No. 4, Apr. 1972. pp. 33–40. Identifies performance based education and performance based Teacher Education. Summarizes a speech by Robert B. Howsam. Identifies expectations of teachers and of teacher education programs. Suggests necessary steps to make it work.

2. ATKIN, J. MYRON, "On Looking Gift Horses in the Mouth," in *The Educational Forum*, Vol. XXXIV, No. 1, Nov. 1969, pp. 9–20. Reviews the program of federally financed education since 1958. Points out trends, influences, and effects.

3. BUTLER, JACQUELINE S., "Student Council, Elementary Style," in *Today's Education*, Vol. 59, No. 6, Dec. 1970, pp. 58–59. Presents an account of an actual program.

4. DELLA-PIANA, GABRIEL M., *Reading Diagnosis and Prescription*, New York: Holt, Rinehart and Winston, 1968. Presents formula for estimating potential. (See page 41.)

5. DOLL, RONALD C. and ROBERT S. FLEMING, *Children Under Pressure*, Columbus, Ohio: Charles E. Merrill Books, 1966. Points out ways schools and parents apply pressures. Identifies symptoms, causes, and remedies.

6. ELSBREE, WILLARD S., *Pupil Progress in the Elementary School*, New York: Teachers College, Columbia University, 1943. Reports of research on promotion, classification, grouping, marking, and reporting.

7. FISHER, ROBERT J., "Too Many Textbooks, Say the English," in *Educational Forum*, Vol. XXXIII, No. 4, May 1969, pp. 527–32. Quotes English exchange students as suggesting that American schools have too many textbooks at the elementary, secondary, and college levels. Criticizes the "textbook teacher" for believing that she cannot be creative because she has "too many books to cover."

8. FULL, HAROLD, *Controversy in American Education*, New York: Macmillan, 1967. An anthology of crucial issues based on society, the school, the students, and the profession. Points out challenges and conflicts, pressures and responses, demands, issues, and innovations. Numerous authorities.

9. GLASSER, WILLIAM, "Roles, Goals, and Failure," in *Today's Education*, Vol. 60, No. 7, Oct. 1971. Roles versus goals demonstrate that learning can be joyful and exciting for both teachers and pupils.

10. GLASSER, WILLIAM, *Schools Without Failure*, New York: Harper & Row, 1969. Identifies causes of failure in the public schools and describes techniques of reality therapy as a means of changing pupil self-concept and redirecting their sights toward success.

11. GLASSER, WILLIAM, "A Talk with William Glasser," in *Learning*, Vol. 1, No. 2, Dec. 1972, pp. 28–29, 58–60. Editor Louis Dolinar interviews Dr. Glasser about the philosophy of "Schools without Failure." He concludes that schools are only going to get better when teachers get involved with one another, and with their children, and begin to face the problems of today's world.

12. HICKS, BRUCE L., "Will the Computer Kill Education?" in *Educational Forum*, Vol. XXXIV, No. 3, Mar. 1970, pp. 307–12. Suggests that computer-assisted instruction can serve education either badly or well. Depends on the use that is made of it. Avoid passivity, impatience, bigotry, and irrationality. Apply creativity, patience, tolerance, and objectivity.

13. HOLT, JOHN, *How Children Fail*, New York: Dell, 1964. A criticism of present day practices in the public schools which teach children how to fail instead of how to succeed.

14. HOLT, JOHN, *How Children Learn*, New York: Pitman, 1967. A sequel to *How Children Fail*. Attempts to explain how children learn with a look into the minds of children through games, experiments, talk, and sports.

15. JONES, DAISY M., "A Feasible Plan for Continuous Admission," in *Education*, Vol. 89, No. 3, Mar. 1969, pp. 195–202. A description of a proposed plan for admitting children to school throughout the year. Chart compares proposed plan with traditional plan.

16. JONES, DAISY MARVEL, *Teaching Children to Read*, New York: Harper & Row, 1971. A practical approach to reading written from the viewpoint of the classroom teacher. Presents a plan for estimating pupil potential (pp. 312–17).

17. KOWITZ, GERALD T., "The Tiger in the Curriculum," in *Educational Forum*, Vol. XXXV, No. 1, Nov. 1970, pp. 55–63. The computer in education. Identifies data that are not information, information that is not intelligence, and intelligence that is not value. Shows kinds of information that can be derived from computer. Values and limitations.

18. MANNING, DUANE, *Toward a Humanistic Curriculum*, New York: Harper & Row, 1971. Makes a plea for a more humanistic approach to evaluation, classification, and promotion of children.

19. MARION, DAVID J. and BERNARD J. SHAPIRO, "Uses and Abuses of 'Intelligence'," in *Educational Forum*, Vol. XXXV No. 1, Nov. 1970. pp. 100–102. Criticizes use of IQ's as a basis for judgments. Says it can lead to a dead end.

20. MARTIN, JOHN HENRY, and CHARLES H. HARRISON, *Free to Learn-Unlocking and Ungrading American Education*, Englewood Cliffs, N.J.: Prentice-Hall, 1972. An attack on contemporary schools. Seeks to identify causes of failures and offers stimulus to reform.

21. MERRILL, M. DAVID, "Teacher or Teachers," in *Educational Forum*, Vol. XXXVI, No. 3, March 1972, pp. 351–57. Differentiated staffing, issues and distinctions. Suggests kinds of teaching skills as a basis for differentiation as opposed to subject matter areas of competence or seniority.

22. MOSMANN, CHARLES J., "Computers and the Liberal Education," in *Educational Forum*, Vol. XXXVI, No. 1, Nov. 1971, pp. 85–91. Suggests content for introductory courses in computers—appreciation, technology, and methodology. Sees the subject as a rich source of learning that has not been explored.

23. NAGLE, NUHN M., "The Tenth Amendment and Uncle Sam," in *Educational Forum*, Vol. XXXIV, No. 1, Nov. 1969, pp. 21–30. Discusses the effects of Sputnik on American education since 1957, Federal aid to education acts, and their impact on curriculum. Identifies the various acts and Titles and their place in curriculum planning.

24. NEA Editorial Board, "Instructional Technology: Special Feature," in *Today's Education*, Vol. 59, No. 8, Nov. 1970, pp. 33–40. A series of signed reports on the following topics: Programmed Learning Systems, Dial Access Systems, Tape Cassettes, Satellite TV, Cable TV, Videotape, Computers. Some implications for teachers.

25. RAGAN, WILLIAM B. and CELIA BURNS STENDLER, *Modern Elementary Curriculum*, New York: Holt, Rinehart and Winston, 1966. Chapter 15 discusses evaluating pupil progress, cumulative records and reporting practices.

26. ROSENTHAL, ROBERT and LENORE JACOBSON, *Pygmalion in the Classroom*, New York: Holt, Rinehart and Winston, 1968. An account of experimental studies showing the effects of teacher expectancies on pupil achievement.

27. ROWLAND, THOMAS, "The Americanization of Jean Piaget," in *Educational Forum*, Vol. XXXII, No. 4, May 1968, pp. 481–86. Translates the theories of Piaget in terms of present day practices in the classroom.

28. SHUSTER, ALBERT H. and MILTON E. PLOGHOFT, *The Emerging Elementary Curriculum*, Columbus, Ohio: Charles E. Merrill, 1963. Chapter 14 is on evaluation in the elementary school.

29. TORKELSON, GERALD M., "Technology: New Goals for Individualization," in *Educational Leadership*, Vol. 29, No. 4, Jan. 1972, pp. 315–18. Points out the potentials of technology and the teacher's place in the program. Evaluates the program.

MEETING VARYING NEEDS

Each One is Different

Courtesy, Lowell School, Mesa, Arizona

INDIVIDUAL DIFFERENCES

Line up a group of eight-year-olds and look at them. No two are alike. They have different sizes, different colors, different body builds. They have different color eyes, hair, and skin. They have different expressions on their faces. Each is a unique personality. And what works on one probably won't turn out the same if you try to repeat it on another.

The graded system was established on the assumption that all the children of a given age are alike and have the same needs. Failure of the "system" has caused increasing concern for the uniqueness of the individual in society as well as in the classroom. The recognition of this problem has led to the need for readjustments of programs and the development of some new approaches to education.

What kinds of differences can you expect to meet in your classroom? How extensive will they be? How will you identify them? What has caused them? How will one community differ from another? How much variety will you find in your community? These are questions you will face and must answer for yourself.

What have we been doing about the problems created by these differences? What happens when we try to get them all to conform? How can programs be adjusted? How can we help each child? What effect has the influx of Federal moneys had on our programs, our materials, and our staff?

And what of the outlook for the future? What is demanded of us? How can we prove that we are accountable for our own goals?

There are all kinds of differences among the children who appear in our schools. The differences are probably greater than you think and are increasing. There have been many different approaches to the problems created by these differences and the areas of emphasis have changed from time to time. The outlook for the future is for still greater attempts to develop a society that seeks not to eliminate the differences but to recognize them and capitalize on them. The strength of our society lies in its diversity.

KINDS AND EXTENT OF DIFFERENCES

Differences among individuals are physical, intellectual, social, and cultural. They exist in varying degrees in different communities and the more you learn about the children and the better acquainted you become with them, the more obvious these differences will be.

337

Physical Differences

The facts of physical differences are more obvious and more readily accepted than other kinds of differences. Height and weight are evident, and except for extremes, seem to create little concern. The child who has a physical problem that interferes with normal activities can be accepted and helped through glasses, hearing aids, wheel chairs, crutches, special rooms, ramps, large print, adapted furnishings, and extra rest periods. If you have a physically handicapped child under your instruction, you must be prepared to meet the needs and make success possible within the limits of capabilities. You may even find yourself teaching a special group for the physically handicapped.

Intellectual Differences

We have already discussed measures of intelligence. The *range* within a given classroom may extend from slow learners to highly intelligent learners, but no matter what the range, there will always be that slowest one. The range may depend partly on how the children are grouped in the school and on the type of community. We have already explored types of groupings and the advantages and limitations of each. Be careful not to let a "slow" group discourage you from working for growth, or a superior group cause you to relax and enjoy accomplishment without challenge. Don't ignore the evidence suggested by intelligence tests, but, on the other hand, don't accept it fatalistically. For some the measure of intelligence might be only the level at which they were functioning at the time the test was administered, and if you can provide enriching experiences you might stimulate some of them to use more of their potential. That doesn't necessarily mean the results of the intelligence test were wrong; it only means that the test didn't challenge the child to use of fullest potential. Don't expect the impossible, and don't be satisfied with less than each child's best efforts.

Mental retardation may be caused by brain damage, mental dysfunction, or injury. The causes may be congenital or functional. Opinions differ on what is the best arrangement for children with this learning difficulty. Some would remove them from intense competition while others would keep them in a stimulating environment. However, if such a child is in your room or under your instruction you are obligated to help him or her work and learn to capacity.

Language problems are related to intellectual differences in that learning is dependent on adequate communication. The problem may be a language other than standard English, or it may be unintelligible speech influenced by colloquialisms or speech defects. The child who comes from a barren background may have had little opportunity to learn. If children have picked up profanity and vulgarity, they may soon learn that it is better to keep still than to risk censure. Helping each child communicate is the necessary first step.

Social and Cultural Differences

The problems of cultural differences because of minority group membership, inner-city slum dwelling, migrant family life, and broken homes have received increased attention recently. *Culturally different children* may lack experiences or may have had different experiences. They may *feel* unwanted. The may even *be* unwanted. *Migrant children* come from people on the move. That does not always mean the poor and the unattached. Frequent changes in living arrangements and school experiences create either problems or challenges for children depending on how they are handled. *Minority cultures* are represented by children of *different racial* or *national origins*. Much has been done to recognize their needs and much more needs to be done to help them adjust to the society in which they are living. It is your challenge to meet all children on their levels when they come and to find out all you can about their needs. The most important thing you can do for them is to give them a feeling of self-worth and help them learn. Whether they learn what is prescribed in the curriculum for your grade level is beside the point. Treat their differences with respect. Accept them as they are and teach them what they can learn and need to know.

APPROACHES TO THE PROBLEMS

The problems of varying needs of different children have been with us for a long time. The first step was recognizing it. Many attempts have been made to solve it. It is still not solved but progress is evident. The outlook for the future is varied and you will be on the firing line doing something about it in the 1980's and 1990's. Over the years we have attempted first to make the child conform to the system and more recently to adapt the program to the child. We have worked at the local level and at the national level. We have worked with limited funds, and more recently with considerable financial support. We have been left to our own devices with little or no public interest except trust. And we have moved into a vast expenditure of funds and widespread public interest which has resulted in a demand for measurable results. Public schools are in the spotlight and you, as the teacher, are very much in the line of action. Before we can predict the future we must look at the past.

Attempts at Conformity

Before the advent of the child study movement it was generally believed that children were miniature adults and that they were all alike. It was accepted that children who deviated should be brought into line and made average. The American schools were based on a White-Anglo-Saxon-Protestant society. Any children who were nonwhite, of national origin other than Anglo-Saxon, and of a religion other than Protestant, were considered different and nonconforming and were to be brought into the majority culture by making them like the rest. This pressure for conformity extended into social patterns, intellectual abilities, and school achievement. The curriculum was set up on the assumption that all children should learn the same things at the same age and with the same degree of perfection. Children who did not conform were penalized through being ostracized or punished. The schools exercised such penalties through humiliation, low grades, and nonpromotion. Children who did not conform were branded as failures. They were often assigned to groups set aside for slow learners, retained and kept in a class with younger children who could exceed them in academic performance, and often subjected to repetition of the same curriculum through which they had already passed without succeeding.

The principle of the graded school is based on this structure. It assumes that all children "ought to do" the same things. The comparative grading system designates which ones do and which ones don't and assigns them marks based on the degree to which they conform. It uses these marks to assign them to groups indicating the quality of work and sometimes the quality of the person.

Attempts at forcing all children into a common mold have proven ineffective, yet there are many schools that are still working within this framework. In your own teaching experience, you may find yourself torn between the conflict of your convictions about how children learn and the administrative practices followed by the school system. You may have to face the issue and fill out report cards with A's, B's, and C's on them and decide on promotion or retention at the end of the year, but you will never be able to make all the children white, middle class, average Americans. No plan of grouping, grading, and promotion will affect this so long as individuals come from widely different backgrounds.

Attempts to Adjust the Program

Once it was recognized that no grading plan and no curriculum could make the children all alike, there were attempts to adjust the program to the children. Early efforts along this line still tended toward a uniform curriculum and made the variations in terms of rate of progress through the program rather than a different curriculum for different children. This was reflected in attempts to make all children speak English, pursue the same reading program at age six, use the same textbooks in content areas, and follow the same curriculum outlines. Early attempts at individualized instruction tended to accept prestructured material and varied the rate at which the children pursued it. This called for programmed material, individual records of progress, and series of tests to indicate level. This created new problems with grading and classification. If Thelma was working at a lower level but performing satisfactorily, should she be given a good mark? If the level at which she was performing was not in keeping with her grade classification based on age, should she be marked down or reclassified? Moving at a slower pace might result in sequential learning, but what of the grade standards, the honor rolls, and the college admission requirements?

Teachers found their allegiances divided between concern for the individual and standards of performance. Publishing companies made an honest attempt to help with the problem through the kinds of materials they provided for the use of the schools. Textbooks were written with careful controls over vocabulary. At one time a so-called sixth-grade social studies text which could claim a fifth-, or even a fourth-grade reading level of difficulty was a good selling item. Then came our concern for challenging the intellectually elite and such books were considered not a suitable diet for capable children. Publishing companies also tried to meet the expressed needs of the schools by sequencing their materials and providing record keeping devices which enabled the child to become self-propelled. Camouflaging the levels by means of color keys or symbols did not deceive the children. They knew who was ahead and who was lagging behind the "norm." They soon detected the system and used their own devices to compete. As long as succeeding meant winning they figured out a way.

Attempts To Meet The Child's Diversity

More recent adaptations to individual differences have been based on recognizing diversity. Instead of measuring children to see if they were either keeping up or conforming, we redirected our thinking in terms of special talents or abilities, individual background, and culture. We need to determine the level at which each child is capable of performing. We need to study cultural background to see what experiences and beliefs are influential. We need to find out what Howard, and his people, think is important for him. We need to work to attain *his* standards, as well as ours. Much has been done along this line as illustrated by renewed interest in bilingual education, study of local history, preservation of minority cultures, and recognition of special contributions of minority groups to the culture of society.

Effects Of Federal Moneys

There was a time when federal aid to education was a debatable issue. States rights were proclaimed and proudly preserved. Local control of schools was considered a "right." With the increasing mobility of our population and the industrialization of certain communities, the distribution of the nation's wealth no longer conformed to the distribution of the children who needed educating. Our agrarian society began changing. No longer did the independent family farm constitute the basis for our society, let alone our tax structure. Large numbers of children tended to cluster where limited resources for taxation were available, and taxable wealth tended to concentrate in areas where families with children did not reside. This was true not only within states but across state lines. Certain regions became known as poverty areas while others abounded in taxable wealth. The principle of equal opportunity made it necessary to change the perspective.

The experience of seeing our nation surpassed by another in the space race caused the public to turn to the schools and say, "What's wrong? Aren't we turning out as capable scientists as our rivals?" Along with this emphasis came a concerted effort on the part of educational organizations to raise the status of the profession through increased financial support in the form of better supplies, better buildings, and better financial remuneration for the people who were devoting their lives to educating the nation's children. The loudly voiced cry for more financial support for the schools was answered by increased taxation. Since World War II salaries have gone up. New buildings have been built. Technology has entered the classroom. And all this has been the result of increased money. In order to make the distribution equitable, the federal government entered the picture. The cry was to collect the taxes where the wealth is and spend the money where the children are. Because of the professional agitation, and the emotional stress of having our national pride disturbed, the public responded. This response took the form of changed programs, improved materials, and additional help in the classroom.

Programs. This response has resulted in increased support for subsidiary programs. *Medical attention* has been supplied in the form of health examinations, dental care, immunizations, and free health services to those in need. *Nutrition programs* have supplied supplementary feeding where needed and instruction for parents where helpful. Free lunches, breakfast programs, and family supplements have been provided. Special programs to provide educational help in the home as well as in the school have been developed to meet the needs of those who could not, or would not, provide for themselves. *Educational programs* have been stimulated through additional help, additional materials, and increased financial support.

Materials. Many items have been purchased with federal funds. In most cases these have had to be accounted for in terms of specific progress connected with national defense or with specific needs connected with deprived children. The NDEA (National Defense Education Act) of 1957 allotted federal funds for science, mathematics, and foreign language on the theory that those were the areas in which education needed strengthening in order to increase our defenses in the world. Other areas were temporarily neglected. The ESEA (Elementary Secondary Act) of 1968 brought funds into the schools at both the elementary and secondary levels to increase the educational opportunities for children who lived in deprived areas, were culturally different, or had special needs. Out of this has grown the use of federal funds for special learning disabilities, programs for migrants, bilingual programs, and problems of minority groups in local communities.

Additional Help. Reducing teacher-pupil ratio and adding special teachers to meet the needs in special areas has resulted in expanded personnel. Special teachers in science, mathematics, and foreign language have been added. Consultants in areas calling for special talents have been employed. Special teachers to meet the problems of deficiency in areas such as reading have been included in school planning. Counselors and psychologists have been employed to study the needs of the children and to recommend special help. The advent of the paraprofessional has lent a new dimension to the staffing of the schools. Teacher's aides have been added. They represent both paid and volunteer services. They are usually people who are not professionally trained but have some contribution to make to the team effort at providing better education for the children. Some of them are given short-term training to fit them for local assignments. Sometimes the purpose for employing them has a two-pronged objective—that of providing help in the classroom and that of providing employment for the needy person in the local community.

The services of aides offer just what the name implies, aid to the teachers who are professionally trained so they can spend their time at actual teaching instead of at clerical tasks and housekeeping duties. There have been many variations of this principle in actual practice. Some aides have been assigned actual teaching duties. There are cases where they have been assigned to "rejected" children for care or instruction. At times they have been placed in teaching duties without proper professional qualifications. Some federal programs have limited the types of assignments that can be given to individuals who are paid for specific programs such as working with bilingual children. Reaction has been varied. If you find yourself with the services of an aide, it is to be hoped that you will see such assistance not as help for you, a means of making your task easier or lighter, but as an opportunity for you to render more educational services to more children.

OUTLOOK FOR THE FUTURE

The likelihood that you will meet different kinds of children in your classroom in the future is increasing. No longer can you expect to be securely established in a comfortable middle-class neighborhood where you will see children whose backgrounds are similar to your own. No longer can you expect to be protected from the realities of children who are culturally different, economically deprived, or aggressively rebellious. Teaching has become a profession of working with children whose needs are legion. The extent to which you can meet these needs will determine the extent to which your services will be essential.

The need for specialized services probably will increase. You may want to go into special education meeting the needs of the physically handicapped, the mentally deficient, or the culturally deprived. You may want to become a counselor and a specialist in the field of learning disabilities. You may become a diagnostician and a team leader working with special kinds of problems. You may find your professional training useful as a manager of a learning situation staffed by interns, aides, volunteer help, and tutors. You may find yourself on the appraisal end of the teaching-learning act studying the results of instruction, developing new techniques for measurement, and indicating needs. You may find yourself as a member of a research team studying the effects of different programs and different materials as a basis for determining next steps. You may find your professional talents leading you into work for a commercial company developing curriculum materials, printed matter, or technological equipment designed to improve educational facilities. You may find yourself a member of a team rather than an authority in your own classroom. The days of the one-room school with the security and isolation of one teacher and a flock of charges for whom that teacher is solely responsible for a contractual year are fast receding. If you are new to the profession you cannot teach as you were taught. If you have been in the profession for ten or more years, you may find that what you did last year may not suffice for next year. Change is inevitable. The question is not "Will you change?" but rather, "How will you change?"

You will no longer accept a uniform curriculum and common targets and standards for all and attempt to fit the children to the program. You will no longer find adjustments of rate of progress sufficient adaptation to individual differences. You will no longer find a prestructured program based on organization of subject matter suitable for today's children. You will have to study each child as to ability, culture, and standards and accept all of them as they are and attempt to help them with their own growth patterns. You will be caught up in a program that goes far beyond intellectual development and academic learning. Schools will take increasing responsibility for medical and nutritional needs. They will add to that the social and cultural needs peculiar to different communities. They will extend their services downward to include younger children and upward to include adults. They will extend the school day and the school year in order to make more effective use of tax supported public school facilities and at the same time provide for more of the needs of more of the people. You are entering a complex profession. You need a broad perspective in order to find your own niche in the total program.

SUMMARY

Children are different but some are more different than others. And some differences are accepted while others create resistances. It is your job to help all children become the best they can be rather than to attempt to change them.

Physical and intellectual differences can be measured and noted. In some cases remedial attention may be given. Other cases demand adjustment to the nature of the child. Social and cultural differences have been given increased attention in the current decade. Efforts have been made to provide compensatory education for deprived children. Programs have been established especially for migrant children. Minority cultures have been recognized partly out of concern for their needs and partly in response to their demands. Minority may be based on color or race, on geographical origin, or on social sects. In any case, the child who feels different, and that the difference is unacceptable to the majority, is developing a low self-concept that will interfere not only with education but with adjustment to the world of work.

Many attempts have been made to meet the problems created by these diversities. Sometimes we have attempted to make the learner conform. Sometimes we have attempted to adjust the rate of progress through the program to an individual pace. Sometimes we have attempted to meet the child and adjust the content of the program in terms of unique characteristics. Federal moneys have greatly accelerated these adjustments through the addition of new programs, the purchase of materials and equipment, and the employment of additional help. The outlook for the future is for even more adaptation in terms of individual needs.

SUGGESTED ACTIVITIES

Choose from among the following one or more activities to carry out as a basis for a class report. Work alone or with a team.

1. Go into any classroom and look at the children. Pick out the ones representing these differences:
   a. The tallest one
   b. The shortest one
   c. The heaviest one
   d. The lightest one
   e. The darkest one
   f. The fairest one
   (These represent physical differences.)
   Take their pictures and look at them. Consider the implications.

2. Study the surnames of the children in a given classroom.
   Attempt to classify them according to cultural and geographical backgrounds. Discuss the significance in terms of pupil needs and curriculum patterns.

3. Ask ten people, perhaps classmates, to help you make a geneological study of origins.
   Have each one list the surnames of four grandparents.
   For each surname listed identify the cultural, national, and/or geographical origin.
   Build a family tree for each showing the "stem" and the "roots."

4. Find out from a teacher the extent of mobility in a classroom by determining:
   a. The total enrollment for the year.
   b. The number of pupils who entered on the first day.
   c. The number of pupils who entered after the first day of school.
   d. The number who were there the first day but withdrew before the end of the year.
   e. The number who entered and withdrew both during the year.
   Indicate the implications for curriculum coverage.

5. Investigate the amount of federal money being spent in a local school system with which you are familiar.
   Find out what the money is being used for and what the restrictions are on its use.
   Find out what means are used to account for the money and for the results achieved as a consequence of the increased expenditures.

SELECTED READINGS

1. ABRAHAMS, ROGER D., "Cultural Differences and the Melting Pot of Ideology," in *Educational Leadership*, Vol. 29, No. 2, Nov. 1971, pp. 118–21. The melting pot is no more. Need for investigating other cultures without totally rejecting one's own.

2. BLACK, HUGH C., "Pestalozzi and the Education of the Disadvantaged," in *Educational Forum*, Vol. XXXIII, No. 4, May 1969, pp. 511–21. Identifies present-day practices with the theories of Pestalozzi.

3. BLOOM, JOHN H., "The Potential of Teacher Aides in Instruction," in *Educational Forum*, Vol. XXXVII, No. 1, Jan. 1973, pp. 195–99. Recommends expansion of the role of teacher aide as an improvement in learning opportunities for the pupil.

4. BLUME, ROBERT, "Camping with Inner-City Kids," in *Today's Education*, Vol. 60, No. 3, Mar. 1971, pp. 32–33. Experience, outcomes, ways.

5. BOURGEOIS, A. DONALD, "Honor My Diversity," in *Educational Leadership*, Vol. 28, No. 6, March 1971, pp. 595–600. Topics: Accepting the Unwanted Truth, We Didn't Dig Our Blackness, We Quit Hiding Our Nigger, and Whites Have Dishonored My Diversity.

6. BRICKMAN, MOLLY, and MOLLIE HALPRIN, "Intensive Care for the Academically Disabled," in *Today's Education*, Vol. 61, No. 1, Jan. 1972, pp. 24–25. Lists ingredients for the program.

7. BRODBELT, SAMUEL, "Disguised Racism in Public Schools," in *Educational Leadership*, Vol. 29, No. 8, May 1972, pp. 699–702. Points out school practices that imply racism.

8. CARTER, THOMAS P., *Mexican Americans in School: A History of Educational Neglect*, New York: College Entrance Examination Board, 1970. A history and a criticism.

9. CASE, C. C., "Navajo Education: Is There Hope?" in *Educational Leadership*, Vol. 29, No. 2, Nov. 1971, pp. 129–32. Cultural contrasts. Characteristics of the Navajo.

10. CLIFT, VIRGIL A., "Further Considerations in the Education of the Disadvantaged," in *Educational Forum*, Vol. XXXIV, No. 2, Jan. 1970, pp. 223–37. Previews programs. Discusses segregation, mental testing, use of standard English, equality, and justice. Points out responsibility of the schools.

11. CLINE, BETTY SMITH and BERT ISHEE, "Specific Learning Disabilities," in *Today's Education*, Vol. 61, No. 1, Jan. 1972, pp. 19–22. Lists symptoms and suggests treatments.

12. COHEN, SOL, "Minority Stereotypes in Children's Literature: The Bobbsey Twins, 1904–1968," in *Educational Forum*, Vol. XXXIV, No. 1, Nov. 1969. pp. 119–125. Concrete examples of stereotypes.

13. COLEMAN, ALWIN, B., "The Disadvantaged Child Who Is Successful in School," in *Educational Forum*, Vol. XXXIV, No. 1, Nov. 1969, pp. 95–97. Identifies specific behaviors of disadvantaged children who succeed.

14. COSTANZO, FRANCES S., "Language of the Six-Year-Old Child," in *Elementary English*, Vol. XLIX, No. 3, Mar. 1972, pp. 382–86. Research in phonology, grammar, and vocabulary. Growth from 2–8. Differentiates between white middle class and disadvantaged.

15. D'ARRIGO, PETER, "Variables and Instructional Arrangements for the Non-English Speaking child in the School Program," in *Elementary English*, Vol. XLIX, No. 3, Mar. 1972, pp. 405–09. Identifies four variables, ability, age-grade, attitude of school, and teacher.

16. DELLA-DORA, DELMO, "The Schools Can Overcome Racism," in *Educational Leadership*, Vol. 29, No. 5, Feb. 1972, pp. 443–49. Points out organizational and instructional practices that lead to grouping and discrimination.

17. DIVOKY, DIANE, "Education's Hardnosed Rebel: Ziggy Engleman," in *Learning*, Vol. 1, No. 3, Jan. 1973, pp. 29–31, 68. Interview with Engleman, author of reading-language program. Ideas on teaching difficult children.

18. FAIRMAN, MARVIN, "Individualizing Instruction Through IPI," in *Educational Leadership*, Vol. 28, No. 2, Nov. 1970, pp. 133–36. Discusses value of individually prescribed instruction.

19. FRAMPTON, MERLE E., REGINA SCHATTNER, and ELLEN KERNEY, *Forgotten Children: A Program for the Multihandicapped*, Boston: Porter Sargent, 1969. Points out problems of treating difficult cases.

20. FRIEDLANDER, BERNARD Z., "The Bereiter-Engleman Approach," in *Educational Forum*, Vol. XXXII, No. 3, Mar. 1968, pp. 359–62. Questions the approach until it is proved through research.

21. GATES, JUDITH RAE, "The Bilingually Advantaged," in *Today's Education*, Vol. 59, No. 9, Dec. 1970, pp. 38–40, 56. Sees bilingualism as an advantage.

22. GAY, GENEVA, "Needed: Ethnic Studies in Schools," in *Educational Leadership*, Vol. 28, No. 3, Dec. 1970, pp. 292–95. Minority studies, authentic programs, new perspective, promising medium.

23. GOMEZ, SEVERO, "Bilingualism Education in Texas," in *Educational Leadership*, Vol. 28, No. 7, Apr. 1971, pp. 757–61. Positive self-image a number one priority in Mexican American communities.

24. HENRIKSON, HAROLD A., "Role of Teacher Attitude in Educating the Disadvantaged Child," in *Educational Leadership*, Vol. 28, No. 4, Jan. 1971, pp. 425–29. Self-fulfilling prophecy.

25. HOWARD, HARRIET K., "The Face of a Child," in *Today's Education*, Vol. 59, No. 7, Oct. 1970, pp. 81–82. Exceptional children and special education.

26. JARVIS, OSCAR T. and MARION J. RICE, *An Introduction to Teaching in the Elementary School*, Dubuque, Iowa: Wm. C. Brown, 1972. See Chaps. 22 and 23 on integration and the culturally disadvantaged.

27. KURITZ, HYMAN, "Education and the Poor in the 18th Century America," in *Educational Forum*, Vol. XXXV, No. 3, Mar. 1971, pp. 367–74. History of education of the poor 200 years ago. Influence of Calvinism, the Dissenters, and the Puritans.

28. LUND, ARLINE, "Reading: Teaching Migrant Children," in *Today's Education*, Vol. 60, No. 7, Oct. 1971, pp. 49–51. Special problems and what has worked.

29. MORGAN, ARGIRO L., "I . . . Couldn't Be a Mouse: Some Semantic Variations in Words Spoken by Lower Middle Class Children," in *Elementary English*, Vol. XLIX, No. 3, Mar. 1972, pp. 395–400. Semantics.

30. NEA Center for Human Relations, "Ideas for Teaching about Black Americans," in *Today's Education*, Vol. 60, No. 1, Jan. 1971, pp. 57–58. Suggestions that can be adapted to other minority cultures and the observance of Human Relations Day.

31. NEA Committee on Professional Ethics, "Discrimination and Professional Ethics," in *Today's Education*, Vol. 60, No. 3, pp. 34–35. Points out court decisions, identifies principles, makes recommendations.

32. O'BRIEN, CARMEN A., *Teaching the Language-Different Child to Read*, Columbus, Ohio: Charles E. Merrill, 1973. Identifies problems caused by differences in speech sounds, cultural backgrounds, and unfamiliarity with both language and concepts.

33. O'REILLY, ROBERT P., *Racial and Social Class Isolation in the Schools: Implications for Educational Policy and Programs*, New York: Praeger, 1970. Just what title indicates.

34. ORNSTEIN, ALLAN C., "Who Are the Disadvantaged?" in *Educational Forum*, Vol. XXXVI, No. 1, Nov. 1971, pp. 81–84. Identifies areas of deprivation as economic, racial, geographical, social, cultural, cognitive, and emotional. Sees the average suburban elementary pupil as bigoted and hypocritical and achievement tests as biased.

35. PRATTE, RICHARD, "The Racial Problem: Four Analogies," in *Educational Forum*, Vol. XXXVI, No. 1, Nov. 1971, pp. 93–98. Compares problems to herds, jungles, marketplaces, and organisms.

36. SCHNEIDER, MARY, "Black Dialect: The Basis for an Approach to Reading Instruction," in *Educational Leadership*, Vol. 28, No. 5, Feb. 1971, pp. 543–49. Linguistically different rather than linguistically deficient. Well ordered but different system. Obstacles to learning to read.

37. SCHREIBER, ELLIOTT H., "The Educable Mentally Retarded Child—A Rejected Individual," in *Educational Forum*, Vol. XXXVI, No. 1, Nov. 1971, pp. 109–110. Rejection, its cause and what to do.

38. SCHULTE, EMERITA SCHROER, "Today's Literature for Today's Children," in *Elementary English*, Vol. XLIX, No. 3, Mar. 1972, pp. 355–63. Need for literature on ethnic differences, poverty, religious differences, war, violence, boy-girl relationships, and drugs.

39. SCUDDER, JOHN R. JR., "Educational Uncle Tomism," in *Educational Forum*, Vol. XXXIV, No. 4, May 1970, pp. 463–69. Recommends maximum enculturation for all students.

40. STEINBERG, STEPHEN, "The Language of Prejudice," in *Today's Education*, Vol. 60, No. 2, Feb. 1971, pp. 14–17. Minorities, racial conflict, humanitarianism, opinion polls.

41. TANNER, DANIEL and LAUREL N. TANNER, *Curriculum Development: Theory into Practice*, New York: Macmillan 1975. Gives special treatment to the education of minority groups.

42. TILLMAN, RODNEY, "Do Schools Need IPI? No!" in *Educational Leadership*, Vol. 29, No. 6, Mar. 1972, pp. 495–98. The case against individually prescribed instruction. Identifies variable pacing arrangement.

43. Today's Education, "Sexism in the Elementary School,"—A Special Feature on the Schools and Sex-Role Stereotyping, in *Today's Education*, Vol. 61, No. 9, Dec. 1972, pp. 20–31. A collection of five articles on the theme.

44. WASSON, WILFRED C., "Hindrances to Indian Education," in *Educational Leadership*, Vol. 28, No. 3, Dec. 1970, pp. 278–80. Characteristics lead to built-in failure.

45. WEST, CAROLE TEPLITZ, "Middle-Class Children: North and South," in *Educational Forum*, Vol. XXXV, No. 2, Jan. 1971, pp. 219–26. Paints a portrait of middle class children.

46. WIGGINS, PHYLLIS, "Redirecting the Focus on the Black Student, Viewpoint," in *Educational Leadership*, Vol. 29, No. 6, Mar. 1972, pp. 539–41. A personal opinion of the problem.

47. WILLIAMS, PERCY V., "Education of Disadvantaged Youth: Teachers vs. Administrators," in *Educational Forum*, Vol. XXXIV, No. 2, Jan. 1970, pp. 229–34. Identifies needs, blocks to learning, beneficial activities for teachers, and responsibilities of the schools.

48. YETTER, CLYDE C., "Do Schools Need IPI? Yes!" in *Educational Leadership*, Vol. 29, No. 6, Mar. 1972, pp. 491–94. The case for individually prescribed instruction as an approach to individualization for children. A rebuttal for Tillman's article in the same issue.

15

RELATING OUTCOMES TO GOALS

Did We Hit the Targets and What of the Future?

Courtesy, Jim Clark, Prentice-Hall

BEING ACCOUNTABLE FOR THE FUTURE

Like the last day of school and graduation, there always comes a last chapter. It means that you must check up on yourself. In the final accounting you either pass or fail. What did you start out to do? Did you get it done? How do you know? What have you accomplished? Can you prove it?

Did you set up suitable conditions for learning? Did you know what you were doing and why? Were you organized? Did you have your schedule made and your plans ready to meet the children? And the parents? And the rest of the staff?

Were you familiar with all the areas in the curriculum? Did you know what the targets were in the communication skills? In the social studies? In the sciences? In mathematics? And in the areas of the arts and humanities?

Did you know how to measure what had been learned? And did you know how to keep the records and make good use of them in planning next steps for all the children, including the ones who are different?

Then you are ready to check up on yourself. Are you accountable? To whom? For what? And why?

And what is the outlook for the future? Where will you put your emphasis? How will you demonstrate your responsibility for results? Have you hit the targets? What can your children do? What do they know? What kinds of persons are they becoming?

If you have read this far, you are ready to look back and see the road you have traveled and check up on what you have done. That is accountability, but don't stop there. Look into the future to see how you will use your professional education, what demands will be made on you, what place there is for you in the new outlook, and decide whether you will be a follower, an innovator, or a leader.

ACCOUNTABILITY

If you are going to be accountable you need to have some idea where you are going. You need to know to whom you are accountable, what you are accountable for, and why it is necessary. You need to be able to predict the future and be a realist as well as an idealist. You need to be able and willing to meet new situations, accept new ideas, and change your ways to meet new concepts. Learning to live with change is perhaps the most important single learning either you or your pupils will experience.

Accountability To Whom

In Chap. 1 we raised the question, "Who influences the curriculum?" In answering our own question, we identified members of society outside the school, professionals outside the classroom, and educators and paraprofessionals within the school. Those same persons are the ones to whom you are accountable for results. What do they expect?

Society outside the school expects evidences of accomplishment. Parents want the best for their children but they are not always sure what is best. They look at honor rolls, grades, report cards, and test scores for evidence. Lay persons look at costs, physical plants, and news stories. Employers look at proficiency in skills, behavior, and appearance.

Professionals outside the schools are looking for educational goals. Publishers of instructional materials view the successes of the learners as a measure of the effectiveness of their products. Designers of buildings and furnishings measure their products in terms of the use made of them and eventually in terms of sales.

Educators within the schools include both nonteaching and teaching personnel as well as the pupils themselves. Leaders have a long range view and help coordinate the materials, activities, and curriculum content. Teachers see the day-by-day results and individual pupil growth. Pupils themselves are the ultimate reason for education. Unless the pupils accept the targets, master the skills, accumulate the knowledge, and become the kinds of people society needs, nothing has been accomplished.

Accountability For What and Why

In Chap. 1 we suggested that curriculum content is influenced by tradition, need, and content. Whether we approve or not, tradition often exerts a real influence on curriculum. The fact that "we have always done it that way" may be reason enough for some people for keeping it in the curriculum. If traditional content is to be uprooted, we must have something to offer in its place. If needs of society are to be met through the curriculum, thought must be given to what must be uprooted as well as what should be added. The ability of the learner is the ultimate guide in selecting content to be taught. This applies to what to teach, when to teach, and how to teach. If you have used effective measures of ability and skillful observation to know your pupils, you are ready to prescribe their program.

Concerns for accomplishment in today's schools are genuine. The public has trusted us with their children and has depended on us to guide growth, set sights, and influence attitudes. We must justify that trust. Society demands that we help children explore the past and present to determine what is worth preserving, and look to the future to consider what might be. Only as we teach children how to learn and to set their sights in terms of discovery can we reach those goals. The ultimate goals are better people in a better world.

OUTLOOK FOR THE FUTURE

The public schools of the twentieth century are different from those of the eighteenth and nineteenth centuries when our country was an agrarian society with emphasis on land ownership, family solidarity, and individual initiative. The schools of the twenty-first century will meet new problems and new challenges which will call for new techniques. The schools of the 1970s are different from those of the 1940s, 1950s, and 1960s. Increased financial support, increased mobility, increased population, and increased technology have changed the perspective of what the schools are and what they ought to do. The schools of the 1980s and 1990s will be still different. You may read the history to find out what happened in previous centuries. You may remember from your own school experiences what happened ten or twenty years ago. But you are living in the here and the now. You will probably be teaching for the next ten or twenty years, or longer. And some of you may teach beyond the year 2000. What will be the demands of society then and how will they be met?

Emphasis on Results

No sooner had we received support from the public than there was a demand for evidence of results. The tax payers began to ask such questions as: What are we getting for our money? Is education any better than in the olden days? Do children learn more when more money is spent? What is included in the modern curriculum? Why? What good is it doing? How do the children measure up? How do they compare with others their own age? With children in other communities? Or in other parts of the country? Or in other countries? How does education in the United States compare with that in foreign countries? Answering these demands has led to accountability, behavioral objectives, and performance contracting. You may find yourself teaching in a situation where your ideals and your practices are caught up in conflicting theories. You need perspective to recognize the problems and resolve your personal philosophy in terms of the situation.

Points of Emphasis. Such questions have brought about renewed emphasis on objective testing and curriculum content. The targets of the curriculum have tended to emphasize measurable skills and quantitative learnings. The affective domain has sometimes been looked upon as nonproductive, a frill, an extra. Humanism in the curriculum has been neglected at times, but it is currently reentering the picture through public interest in the British primary schools, emphasis on the "open classroom" concept, and team teaching. Even progressive education, which thrived in the 1930s, waned in the 1940s, and died in the 1950s, is being given another look. These emphases have left many educators torn between serving two masters—one the objective evidence of results and the other the welfare of the individual child.

Influence On The Curriculum. Measurable skills have received emphasis through teaching techniques, technology, programmed materials, and objective testing. Factual information has been emphasized partly because it can be measured and verified. Performance in terms of modified behaviors has been stressed. Reading tests tend to measure vocabulary mastery and comprehension of factual information rather than appreciation, insight, inference, understanding, and enjoyment. Mathematics tests tend to measure factual information and performance skills in spite of the fact that the "new math" claims to be based on insight into the structure of the discipline. Objective measures in the content fields tend to emphasize facts because they can be counted and proved. There is a need for other kinds of measurement before we can effectively direct our efforts toward different goals. That is what Ragan (17:477) was talking about when he said:

> We need to develop tests which place more emphasis on creativity, discovery, and independence in learning.

Demand for Accountability

The public demands that teachers be accountable for their acts. This is a natural outgrowth of the expenditure of funds, the support of the educational program, the expansion of services, and the questions raised. They want to know. They have a right to ask. In attempting to answer their questions the profession has been put on the defensive. Behavioral objectives are an attempt to state clearly what are the goals. Performance contracting is an attempt to guarantee that they will get "their money's worth." National Assessment is a search for some answers. And teacher supply and demand is a consequence of fluctuating needs of society. These are all tied in with the trend toward accountability. We must ask, "Accountable for what? And to whom?" You are obviously accountable for your own acts, but are you accountable for the acts of others? The children who come under your instruction, for instance? And if so, how can you guarantee that they will perform according to expectations? You might bribe them; or coerce them; or challenge them; or lead them. If your own self-preservation and your personal livelihood depend on *their* performance, you may use questionable means of getting the desired results. Let's take a look at the problems.

Behavioral Objectives.   For many years teachers have been stating objectives in terms of desired results. Sometimes these goals were indefinite and elusive; for example:

> To develop appreciation of literature.
> To increase understanding of the implications of certain events in history.
> To provide practice on needed skills.

Such statements of objectives sound important, but proving that they have been attained is a bit difficult. How do you know whether a child appreciates literature or not, and if so, to what degree? How do you know whether a child understands the implications of such a historical event as the revolt of the colonies? How do you know that the practice on skills is going to result in improved performance? These types of objectives have given way to more specific statements which identify the behaviors resulting from the instruction. Behavioral objectives attempt to state specifically what the learner will be able to do as a result of the planned instruction. For example:

> Given a literary selection the child will be able to identify the two main characters and state specifically how each one contributed to the plot of the story.
> Given an account of a historical event the child will be able to recall the date, the leaders, and the outcome.
> Given a set of examples involving subtraction with two digit numbers with the subtrahend number in the one's place greater than the corresponding minuend number the child will be able to make the necessary changes from ten's place and to perform the operation correctly.

With these objectives the learnings can be directed toward specific performances, and the test can be constructed to prove that the children are performing as expected. Sometimes the objective even includes a statement of the percent of accuracy with which the skill will be performed or the facts will be stated. Education has been described as changed behavior. If you know what behavior you want to change and in what direction you want the change to take place, you will be able to direct the teaching toward that end and to prove the results through objective measurements.

National Assessment.   Measuring the results in terms of objective scores has moved beyond the classroom to the school-wide level, the district level, the state level, and the national level. In the days when the parent paid the tutor, the teacher was accountable to the individual parent for the learnings of the pupil. When funds came from local taxation, accountability was limited to giving local satisfaction. State funds and state control over education have long been considered a part of the states rights portion of our constitution. Differences from one state to another were accepted along with differences in financial ability to pay and local concern for quality education. The trend toward federal support of education has led logically toward a national concern for quality education. If the children throughout the nation are to be given equal opportunity, then the next logical question is, "Are we getting equal results?" This has led to the controversial question of National Assessment. Tests have been developed in an attempt to measure abilities and general levels of performance rather than mere coverage of specific curriculum content. These tests have been used to establish "norms" or general levels of performance achieved by children at given grade or age levels. These norms have come to mean "expectancies." Comparison with a national norm then becomes a goal. The extent to which children in a given locality measure up to these goals has come to be used as a measure of the effectiveness of the school program.

The whole program of National Assessment has become a controversial issue. Much of its original intent has been misunderstood or misinterpreted. In the *Sixty-Eighth Yearbook*, Part II of the National Society for the Study of Education, Chap. XIII Jack C. Merwin and Frank B. Womer (13:309), who worked with a committee under the chairmanship of Ralph W. Tyler to consider development of an assessment program that could provide landmarks of educational progress as a basis for meeting changing educational needs of our society over the years, point out the following guidelines:

1. Reports should be on the basis of age-level groups.
2. For each group included in a National Assessment, there should be an attempt to describe:
   a. things that almost all persons of that age level have accomplished,
   b. things that average persons have achieved, and
   c. things that the most advanced persons of that age level have accomplished.

In discussing the program of National Assessment Neagley and Evans (14:289-90) list the following implications for curriculum development:

1. Local districts will examine objectives.
2. Teachers will examine techniques.
3. Materials and resources will be modified.

4. Evaluation instruments will be improved.
5. Learning differences will be authenticated or disproved.
6. There will be renewed interest in curriculum development.

The question is no longer do we want federal support but rather how will we use federal funds. And we can no longer ask the question, "Are we accountable on a broader scale?" The real question is, "With what and how shall we measure results and on what will we base our comparisons?" The proponents of National Assessment insist that there is to be no attempt to publish scores for a specific region, state, or local community. There is to be no attempt to identify weaknesses or fix blame. The intent of the National Assessment program is to find out what is being accomplished at given age levels rather than at designated grade levels. The results are to be used as a standard against which local schools can evaluate their own effectiveness. In calculating scores and accumulating the evidence, a sampling technique is being used. Representative individuals at designated age levels will participate in selected samplings of the tests. No individual will take the entire test. No school will be tested in its entirety. No individual will be tested a second time. The results are not to be considered judgmental. the purpose is fact finding.

Performance Contracting. The logical questions following the revealing of lack of achievement are, "Why?" and "What can we do about it?" There are those persons with methods, techniques, materials, and technology who believe they can produce results. They consider education a business and are willing to stake their procedures on a contract just as the business executive sells a product with "satisfaction guaranteed or your money back." This is what is implied in performance contracting. A commercial concern provides materials and a program with a guarantee that certain results will be obtained or the school system does not have to pay. Such an approach to education means that the learner is being manipulated and must produce in order for the company to collect and for the school to justify the expenditure of funds. Now the objective becomes performance in terms of behavioral objectives rather than development of the individual. A number of such programs that have been set up about the country have received wide publicity. Whether they have been a success or a failure depends on whose account you read. Some have claimed startling results in terms of test scores. Critics have pointed out the fallacies in their claims and have cited evidences of unethical practices and faulty interpretations. You may become involved in an educational program where such procedures are in operation. If so, you need to be aware of what the contract stipulates, what you are expected to do with the materials, and with your children, and how the results are to be measured. You, too, may find yourself torn between your allegiances to standards and to the children.

Teacher Supply and Demand.   All this emphasis on accomplishment and accountability directly reflects on you and your plans for a teaching career. And the law of supply and demand is currently affecting the probability of the young teacher getting suitable employment. We have lived through teacher scarcity and teacher surplus. The conditions are readily predictable. The United States Department of Health Education and Welfare has published figures on numbers of live births. These were printed in *Saturday Review* in an article by Paul Woodring (25:54–55) predicting that "There'll be Fewer Little Noses to Count." His predictions were:

> In 1972 the number of children in the first grade in all U.S. schools will be 15 percent smaller than it is today. (1967) This not a guess but a fact, or a projection of a fact, for all the babies have been born and counted. Only a dramatic change in our immigration policy or a catastrophic rise in the infant death rate could change it materially.
>
> The decline in numbers will mean that if the present (1967) pupil-teacher ratio is maintained the demand for primary teachers will fall off sharply.

That prediction has already come to pass. School systems are noting the effects in their enrollments and in their budgets. The resulting surplus of teachers can result in teachers without jobs, lowered teacher-pupil ratios, or more auxiliary services. It can also result in trained teachers turning to other fields for employment; for example development of materials, research, or private schools.

In order to understand the impact of the lowered birth rate in the United States one needs to look at the facts as graphically represented in Fig. 15–1. The solid line shows the estimated number of beginners in the nation's schools based on the actual number of live births at five-year intervals from 1910 to 1970. The dotted line estimates the population from which beginning teachers will be recruited on the assumption that they will enter the employment market in their early twenties. Assuming then that a beginning teacher will be approximately 15 years older than a first grade child we can superimpose one graph upon the other. This indicates that in 1935, 1940, and 1945 there were more twenty-one-year-olds than six-year-olds thus creating the surplus from which beginning teachers were drawn during the depression years of the 1930s. By 1950 the low birth rate of the 30's was beginning to produce young adults who were the source of beginning teachers. The birthrate meanwhile had gone up shortly after 1945 and the limited supply of beginning teachers was felt, hence the teacher shortage which extended through the 1950s and began to taper off after 1965. By 1970 the ratio had changed and was reflected in a teacher surplus as predicted by Paul Woodring. The surplus was not caused by more teachers or fewer pupils so much as by a change in the ratio of six-year-olds to young adults. This is of immediate concern to you in seeking suitable employment.

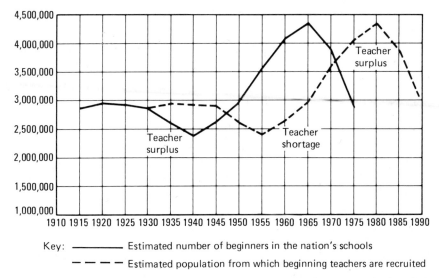

Key: ———————— Estimated number of beginners in the nation's schools

— — — — Estimated population from which beginning teachers are recruited

Figure 15-1. *Comparison of number of beginning pupils in the elementary schools with the population from which beginning teachers are recruited 1930 to 1990.*

The supply of teachers for the 1980s and 1990s is already determined. The children who will enter the schools as beginners by then are yet be born. One can only conjecture what the trends will be. All this may affect the manner in which you will be using your professional training as a teacher.

Curriculum Targets

In Chap. 1 we indicated that the targets of the curriculum in the elementary school were to develop skills, to impart knowledge, and to influence attitudes. In other words to do, to know, and to be. It is predictable that these targets will remain much the same in the years to come. The differences will be in what the children learn to do, what they are expected to know, and what they will become.

Skills needed today may no longer be needed in the year 2000. Technology and employment are changing so rapidly that many of the skills taught in school today may not be needed. Will children still need to know how to read? Will they need the same word mastery skills and reading patterns as they are now learning? Will they need to know how to spell? Will a machine take voice dictation and do our spelling for us? Will they need penmanship skills or will everyone have his own personal typewriter which will produce more legible transcriptions than the human hand can hope to master? Will computation with numbers be a necessary skill? Will one even need to be able to drive a car, operate a machine, compute the cost of groceries, or perhaps read the ads? Will marketing all be computerized? Will mass media of the audio-visual type completely replace the printed word and the daily newspaper? Will transportation make permanent living arrangements obsolete? These are all conjectures that may materially affect the skills taught in the schools.

Knowledge may no longer be the same. Facts accepted today may be totally untrue twenty-five or thirty years from now. What is the capital of Norway? Will that fact remain the same? What is the largest city in the world? Will that be the same in the year 2000? And are you talking about the geographical boundaries of a political unit or the metropolitan area adjacent to the complex? How long does it take to go to India? To the South Pole? To the moon? Will those facts be altered? Is the polar cap habitable? Is there life on other planets? Will these answers remain unchanged? How many elements are there? Will science find new ways of doing things? Will history even remain the same? The work of historians, anthropologists, and archeologists could very well reveal new knowledge that makes the facts we learned yesterday untrue tomorrow.

Attitudes may seem more everlasting, but even they may be open to question. One may still appreciate the arts, but the music, the art forms, the interpretive dance one appreciates may be different. People may respect their contemporaries but neighbors may no longer be limited to those who live next door. They just might live on the other side of the world, in a space capsule, or even on another planet. What the world will be like beyond tomorrow is a matter for conjecture.

We cannot hope to educate today's children for tomorrow's problems. The best we can hope to do is to teach them sources of knowledge, respect for accuracy of information, and skills that will make them lifetime learners. Then they will be more able to make the adjustments demanded by their changing world. The only thing that is certain is the inevitability of change. First of all you need to learn to live with change yourself, and then you need to teach your pupils how to anticipate change, how to accept change, how to adjust to change, and how to keep on learning so that change will not bypass them. Alvin Toffler (24:23–24) brings the stupendousness of change vividly to attention when he says:

> Let us look at a few—change in the process by which man forms cities, for example. We are now undergoing the most extensive and rapid urbanization the world has ever seen. In 1850 only four cities on the face of the earth had a population of 1,000,000 or more. By 1900 the number had increased to nineteen. By 1960 there were 141, and today world urban population is rocketing upward at a rate of 6.5 percent per year, according to Edgar deVries and J. P. Thysse of the Institute of Social Science in the Hague. This single stark statistic means a doubling of the earth's urban population within eleven years.

One way to grasp the meaning of change on so phenomenal a scale is to imagine what would happen if all existing cities, instead of expanding, retained their present size. If this were so, in order to accommodate the new urban millions we would have to build a duplicate city for each of the hundreds that already dot the globe. A new Tokyo, a new Hamburg, a new Rome and Rangoon—and all within eleven years. (This explains why French urban planners are sketching subterranean cities—stores, museums, warehouses and factories to be built under the earth, and why a Japanese architect has bluprinted a city to be built on stilts over the ocean.)

Children meet many situations requiring them to change their living habits and daily routines, their personal relationships, and even their beliefs. When a new sibling is added to the family, there is a need for change in status. When parents separate, the stability of life is changed. When work causes the family to move from one part of the country to another, there is need for adjustment to change in living arrangements. Starting to school is a change in personal adjustments. Each new school year creates a new situation calling for more adjustments. Sometimes there are even changes in teachers, classmates, and other school personnel in the midst of a school year. Textbooks change and new ones look unfamiliar. Old buildings are remodeled or discarded and new ones take their place creating a change in the setting in which learning takes place. School policies change and the child needs to learn to meet new requirements. Reporting forms change and new interpretations become necessary. Even a street repair project which causes the children to find a different route to school on a temporary basis calls for change in habits. New equipment is added to the classroom. Technology takes over. Children learn different ways of doing things. If you can help the children recognize these changes, pave the way through anticipation, and give a helping hand where needed until the children can let loose of the old, feel comfortable with the new, and make the adjustments, you will have helped them learn to live with change. Talk with them about forthcoming changes. Help them plan what to do. Give them support as long as they need it.

AND FINALLY

The ultimate goal of education is to be found in the kinds of persons we are developing. Since the business of education is learning, let us think of the learner first as a pupil, then as a student, and eventually as a scholar.

A *pupil* is one who waits to be taught.

A *student* is one who studies and seeks help in learning, thus taking the initiative.

A *scholar* is one who not only takes the initiative but is creative and original in identifying the problems and charting the course, thus making a contribution.

Most young children are pupils. Once people assume some responsibility for their own learning, they may move from the category of pupils to that of students. This might even happen with a young child. It should be true of any person beyond the age of compulsory school attendance. However, the college student who says, "Is this the way you want me to do it?" or "What must I read?" is not a student. This person is still a pupil waiting for the teacher to make the decision and tell him or her what to learn.

Once the learners go beyond the absorbing stage and see themselves as contributors to the welfare of humanity through their own initiative and creative efforts, then they may become scholars. That is true of the scientist who discovers new relationships, the literary critic who interprets work in terms of a particular point of view, the genius who creates in any media such as art, drama, dance, literature, music, science, and other fields of self expression.

The objective of all education should be to move every learner beyond the pupil stage and into the student stage to become self-propelled and continue to learn beyond the school setting and beyond the years of formal education.

These sixth graders are leaving school. This is the same door they entered as kindergarteners six years before. What has been accomplished? (Courtesy, Skiff School, Phoenix, Arizona)

An even higher objective is that of stimulating the most capable students to move even beyond the realm of student and into that of scholar. It is through the scholars that the next generation will go on from where we are now.

Are you a pupil, a student, or a scholar?

Are you teaching the children in your classroom to be pupils, or students, or scholars?

How can you tell?

Once you have identified the targets, have implemented them in terms of content and activities, and have surveyed the end result, you have gone full circle and are ready to start over again. Each assignment, each school year, each new group of pupils, each day offers you a new beginning. And each time you come to meet a new group of pupils or a new school year, in fact each day, you are given one more chance at a new beginning. I hope the ideas and suggestions in this book will help you reflect on these things and make the most of your opportunities as a teacher.

SUGGESTED ACTIVITIES

1. Consult a number of persons with the question, "What do you expect of the schools?"

   Include in your list:

   parents, laypeople, employers
   critics, publishers, architects
   administrators, teachers, pupils

   Summarize your findings and report to the class your conclusions.

2. Identify content still residual in the curriculum due to tradition.

3. Identify needs which suggests additions to a modern curriculum.

4. List different occupations or lines of work for which you might use your professional training in education.

5. Make a study of the population growth in your home community over a period of twenty years. From these figures predict:

   a. the number of beginners in school each year
   b. the potential number of beginning teachers each year.

6. Examine textbooks in a subject of your choosing—reading, spelling, arithmetic, science. Select at least four with copyright dates at approximately five year intervals.

   Note the eliminations, additions, and alterations in content.

   Justify changes in terms of skills, knowledge, and attitudes.

7. Write a letter dated twenty years from the present date. Tell what you have done in the teaching profession in the interval. Let your imagination run rampant here.

SELECTED READINGS

1. BOWERS, C. A., "Accountability From A Humanist Point of View," in *Educational Forum*, Vol. XXXV, No. 4, May 1971, pp. 479–86. Sees holding teachers accountable as incompatible with academic freedom. Quotes Raymond Callahan's "Education and the Cult of Efficiency" as dating accountability from 1915.

2. CALLAHAN, RAYMOND E., *Education and the Cult of Efficiency*, Chicago: The University of Chicago Press, 1962. A study of the social forces that have shaped the administration of the public schools.

3. COLLINS, BENNIE MAE, EVANGELINE MORSE, and GERALD KNOWLES, "Beyond 'Sesame Street': TV and Preschoolers," in *Educational Leadership*, Vol. 28, No. 2, Nov. 1970, pp. 143–46. A look at the future for education of the very young.

4. DIBLE, ISABEL W., "The Teacher in a Multi-Mediated Setting," in *Educational Leadership*, Vol. 28, No. 2, Nov. 1970, pp. 123–28. Media then and now. Hardware and humanism. What next? Sees the teacher as a director of learning.

5. FISCHER, JOHN H., "Public Education Reconsidered," in *Today's Education*, Vol. 61, No. 5, May 1972, pp. 22–31. A fresh look at public education. Redirection, evaluation, criticisms, and prospects for future.

6. GANTT, WALTER N., "Occupational Preparation in the Elementary School," in *Educational Leadership*, Vol. 28, No. 4, Jan. 1971, pp. 359–63. Man and work and some recommendations.

7. GOODLAD, JOHN I., "The Child and His School in Transition," in *The National Elementary Principal*, Vol. LII, Jan. 1973, pp. 28–34. Hypothesizes on the kind of schools we need in the future. Recommends phases, not grades, and individual fulfillment rather than conformity to established standards.

8. HERMAN, BARRY E., "Community School: New Thrust in Education," in *Educational Leadership*, Vol. 28, No. 4, Jan. 1971, pp. 419–23. Description of a community school in action.

9. HUNKINS, FRANCIS P., "New Identities for New Tasks," in *Educational Leadership*, Vol. 29, No. 6, March 1972. pp. 503–06. Identifies new tasks, recommends some crystal ball gazing, points out new identities for teachers.

10. KRAVETZ, NATHAN, "Education's New Crisis: Shortage of Jobs for Teachers," in *Kappa Delta Pi Record*, Vol. 8, No. 4, Apr. 1972, pp. 97–98. Indicates areas of shortages and predicts continuation for next ten years. Suggests openings and qualifications to provide jobs for those who are qualified, able, and willing.

11. MARTIN, JOHN HENRY, and CHARLES H. HARRISON, *Free to Learn—Unlocking and Ungrading American Education*, Englewood Cliffs, N.J.: Prentice-Hall, 1972, An attack on contemporary schools. Seeks to identify causes of educational failures and offers stimulus to reform.

12. MICKLER, WALTER A. JR., "New Roles Can Facilitate Change," in *Educational Leadership*, Vol. 29, No. 6, Mar. 1972, pp. 515–17. Points out needed changes and suggests ways to effect change.

13. National Society for the Study of Education, *Educational Evaluation: New Roles, New Means*, Chicago: University of Chicago Press, 1969. Sixty-Eighth Yearbook, Part II, Chap. XIII, "Evaluation in Assessing the Progress of Education to Provide Bases of Public Understanding and Public Policy," by Jack C. Merwin and Frank B. Womer, pp. 305–34.

14. NEAGLEY, ROSS L. and N. DEAN EVANS, *Handbook for Effective Curriculum Development*, Englewood Cliffs, N.J.: Prentice-Hall, 1967. Chapter 12 predicts the curriculum for the 1980's.

15. ORNSTEIN, ALLAN C. and HARRIET TALMAGE, "The Rhetoric and the Realities of Accountability," in *Today's Education*, Vol. 62, No. 6, Sept.–Oct. 1973, pp. 70–71. Discusses basis for accountability and basis of need, especially in teaching.

16. PRASCH, JOHN, "New Roles for Educators," in *Educational Leadership*, Vol. 29, No. 6, Mar. 1972, pp. 499–502. Predicts the teacher of the future will be a manager and an organizer of earning activities and environments.

17. RAGAN, WILLIAM B. and CELIA BURNS STENDLER, *Modern Elementary Curriculum*, New York: Holt, Rinehart and Winston, 1966. Part IV discusses evaluation and a look into the future.

18. ROBBINS, GLAYDON, D., "New Preparation for Teachers," in *Educational Forum*, Vol. XXXVI, No. 1, Nov. 1971, pp. 99–102. Lists as newcomers individualization, nongradedness, organization, flexibility in scheduling and grouping, continuous progress, team teaching, differentiated staffing, and media and technology. Sees student teaching replaced by internships prior to certified career teaching.

19. ROBINSON, DONALD W., "Alternative Schools: Is the Old Order Really Changing?" in *Educational Leadership*, Vol. 28, No. 6, March 1971, pp. 604–07. Predictions for kinds of changes to come.

20. SHANE, HAROLD G., "Reassessment of Educational Issues," in *Phi Delta Kappan*, Vol. LIV, Jan. 1973, pp. 326–37. Takes a look into the future and recommends that we weed out such doubtful practices as fixed admission age, ability grouping, school year of fixed length, conventional report cards, grade levels, annual promotions, and arbitrary divisions of education into elementary, secondary, and post secondary.

21. STENNER, JACK and MICHAEL H. KEAN, "Four Approaches to Educational Performance Contracting," in *Educational Leadership*, Vol. 28, No. 7, Apr. 1971, pp. 721–25. Competitive performance, sole performance, modified sole performance, comparative performance, advantages and disadvantages of each.

22. TANNER, DANIEL and LAUREL N. TANNER, *Curriculum Development: Theory into Practice*, New York: Macmillan, 1975. Treats the subjects of performance contracting and accountability on an up-to-date perspective. Describes characteristics of the open classroom.

23. TANNER, DANIEL, *Using Behavioral Objectives in the Classroom*, New York: Macmillan, 1972. Relates the objectives in the cognitive, affective, and psychomotor areas to actual goals in the classroom and shows how to utilize all three in planning instructional goals.

24. TOFLER, ALVIN, *Future Shock*, New York: Random House, 1970. Makes predictions about the speed and the suddenness of some of the changes the future holds. Applicable to education.

25. WOODRING, PAUL, "There'll Be Fewer Little Noses," in *Saturday Review*, Mar. 1967, pp. 54–55. Gives birth statistics and predicts decreasing enrollments and reduced demand for teachers in the near future.

INDEX